SAAB
95, 96, 99, & SONETT
1967-1979
SHOP MANUAL

By
RAY HOY

ERIC JORGENSEN
Editor

JEFF ROBINSON
Publisher

CLYMER PUBLICATIONS

World's largest publisher of books
devoted exclusively to automobiles and motorcycles

12860 MUSCATINE STREET · P.O. BOX 20 · ARLETA, CALIFORNIA 91331

Copyright © 1976, 1979 Clymer Publications

All rights reserved. No part of this publication may be reproduced, stored in a retrieval system, or transmitted, in any form or by any means, electronic, mechanical, photocopying, recording or otherwise, without the prior written permission of Clymer Publications.

FIRST EDITION
First Printing November, 1976
Second Printing October, 1977

SECOND EDITION
Revised by Ray Hoy to cover 1977-1979 models
First Printing June, 1979
Second Printing October, 1980

Printed in U.S.A.

ISBN: 0-89287-121-0

R01196 14867

Chapter One
General Information

Chapter Two
Lubrication, Maintenance, and Tune-up

Chapter Three
Troubleshooting

Chapter Four
Engine

Chapter Five
Fuel and Exhaust Systems

Chapter Six
Cooling and Heating Systems

Chapter Seven
Emission Control System

Chapter Eight
Electrical System

Chapter Nine
Clutch, Transmission, and Differential

Chapter Ten
Front Suspension, Wheel, and Steering

Chapter Eleven
Rear Suspension

Chapter Twelve
Brakes

Chapter Thirteen
Performance Improvement

Supplement
1977 and Later Service Information

Index

CONTENTS

QUICK REFERENCE DATA XI

CHAPTER ONE
GENERAL INFORMATION 1
    Manual organization   Recommended tools
    Vehicle identification   Service hints

CHAPTER TWO
LUBRICATION, MAINTENANCE, AND TUNE-UP 10
    Routine checks   Engine tune-up
    Preventive maintenance

CHAPTER THREE
TROUBLESHOOTING 30
    Starter   Clutch
    Charging system   Transmission
    Engine   Differential
    Ignition system   Brake
    Fuel system   Cooling system
    Exhaust emission control   Steering and suspension

CHAPTER FOUR
ENGINE 39
    Engine removal   Separating engine and
    Engine installation   automatic transmission
    Separating engine and   Engine disassembly/assembly
        manual transmission   Specifications

CHAPTER FIVE
FUEL AND EXHAUST SYSTEMS 77
    Carburetor   Electric fuel pump
    Fuel injection system   Fuel tank
    Mechanical fuel pump   Exhaust system

CHAPTER SIX
COOLING AND HEATING SYSTEMS 89

    Radiator
    Expansion tank
    Water distribution pipe and
      water hoses

    Water pump
    Thermostat
    Changing coolant
    Fan motor

CHAPTER SEVEN
EMISSION CONTROL SYSTEM 99

    Deceleration valve
    Carburetor
    Air cleaner
    Evaporative loss system

    Crankcase ventilation
    Exhaust emission control system
    Air injection system

CHAPTER EIGHT
ELECTRICAL SYSTEM 113

    Battery
    Alternator
    Voltage regulator

    Starter
    Starter solenoid
    Ignition system

CHAPTER NINE
CLUTCH, TRANSMISSION, AND DIFFERENTIAL 120

    Clutch
    Clutch control
    Clutch master cylinder
    Slave cylinder

    Manual transmission
    Automatic transmission
    Free wheel
    Differential

CHAPTER TEN
FRONT SUSPENSION, WHEEL, AND STEERING 129

    Ball-joint replacement
    Steering gear
    Front end alignment

    Shock absorbers
    Wheels

CHAPTER ELEVEN
REAR SUSPENSION 136

    Rear springs and rubber bumpers
    Rear axle
    Center bearing

    Side links
    Shock absorbers
    Hubs/wheel bearings

CHAPTER TWELVE
BRAKES 149

    Master cylinder
    Brake lines and hoses
    Rear wheel cylinders
    Front brake pistons and seals
    Wheel cylinders and
      disc brake housings
    Brake disc

    Brake pads
    Drum brakes
    Handbrake
    Bleeding
    Adjustment
    Brake pedal

CHAPTER THIRTEEN
PERFORMANCE IMPROVEMENT 182

    What do you want?
    The basics
    Chassis modification
    Engine modifications
    Stage I
    Stage II

    Stage III
    Turbocharging
    Drive train
    Body modification
    Accessory sources

SUPPLEMENT
1977 AND LATER SERVICE INFORMATION 201

    Preventive maintenance
    Engine tune-up
    Engine torque specifications

    Breakerless ignition
    Transmission torque specifications

INDEX 207

SAAB
95, 96, 99, & SONETT
1967-1979
SHOP MANUAL

QUICK REFERENCE DATA

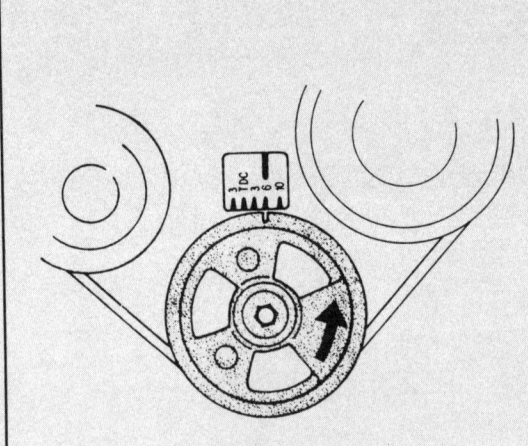

TIMING MARKS

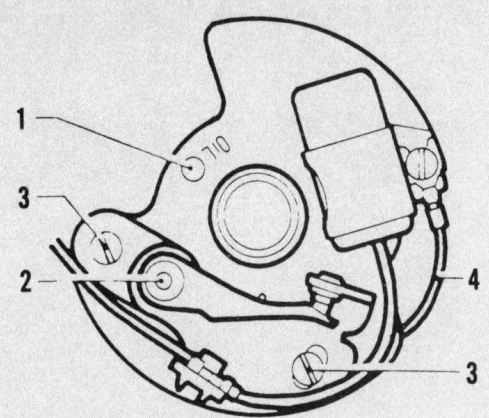

BREAKER POINTS

1. Oil hole for lubricating pad
2. Breaker arm
3. Breaker contact retaining screws
4. Ground lead

TUNE-UP SPECIFICATIONS

V4 Engine
    Firing order   1-3-4-2
    Spark plug gap   0.024-0.028 in. (0.6-0.7mm)
    Idle speed
        Saab 95/96   800 rpm
        Saab Sonett   900 rpm
    Contact breaker gap   0.016 in. (0.4mm)
    Dwell angle $50° \pm 2°$
    Valve clearance
        Inlet   0.014 in. (0.35mm)
        Exhaust   0.016 in. (0.40mm)
    Ignition timing
        Saab 95/96 (through 1970)   6° BTDC @ 800 rpm (vacuum hose disconnected)
        Saab Sonett   3° BTDC @ 900 rpm (vacuum hose disconnected)

Inline-4 Engine
    Firing order   1-3-4-2
    Spark plug gap
        1969-1972   0.025 in. (0.6mm)
        1973   0.025-0.030 in. (0.6-0.7mm)
        1974-1979   0.024-0.028 in. (0.6-0.7mm)
    Idle speed
        1969-1972   800-850 rpm
        1973-1974   850 rpm
        1973-1974 (automatic)   800 rpm
        1975-1979 (manual and automatic, 875 ± 50 rpm
            engine warm, fan off)

(continued)

TUNE-UP SPECIFICATIONS (continued)

Contact breaker gap
  1969-1974   0.012-0.016 in. (0.3-0.4mm)
  1975-1977   0.016 in. (0.4mm)
  1978-1979   Breakerless

Dwell angle
  1969-1974   40°±2°
  1975-1976   50°±2°
  1977   50°±3°
  1978-1979   Breakerless

Valve clearance
  Intake   0.006-0.012 in. (0.15-0.30mm)
  Exhaust   0.014-0.020 in. (0.35-0.50mm)

Ignition timing
  1972 (carburetor equipped)   9° BTDC
  1973 (carburetor equipped)   14° BTDC
  1974 (carburetor equipped)   4° BTDC
  1972 (injected)   5° BTDC
  1973 (injected)   8° BTDC
  1974 (injected)   4° BTDC @ 800 rpm (vacuum hose plugged)
  1975-1976 (injected, 49-state models) 14° BTDC @ 800 rpm (vacuum hose plugged)
  1975-1976 (injected, Calif. models)   12° BTDC @ 800 rpm (vacuum hose plugged)
  1977-1979 (injected)   20° BTDC @ 2,000 rpm (vacuum hose disconnected)

RECOMMENDED LUBRICANTS

Engine oil	SE 10W-30 or 10W-40
Automatic transmission	ATF Type A, Suffix A, or Dexron conforming to FLM specifications M2C 33F.
Automatic final drive	SAE 75 or 80 EP oil conforming to specifications API-GL-4 or API-GL-5
Manual transmission	SAE 75 or SAE 80 EP oil to specifications API-GL-4 or API-GL-5 (models through 1977); SE 10W-30 (1978-1979 models)
Power steering	ATF-FLM Specifications M2C 33F

TIRE PRESSURES

Model	Front	Rear
95/96	24 psi[1]	24 psi[1]
95/96	27 psi[2]	27 psi[2]
Sonett	25 psi	22 psi
99	27 psi[1]	27 psi[1]
99	30 psi[2]	30 psi[2]

1. Lightly loaded.
2. Fully loaded. (NOTE: On the Saab 95 station wagon, rear tires should carry 30 psi when fully loaded.)

CHAPTER ONE

GENERAL INFORMATION

This book provides general maintenance and repair information for Saab models 95, 96, Sonett, and 99 from 1967 through 1976. Both the V4 and inline 4-cylinder engines—carburetted and injected—are covered in 1.5, 1.7, 1.85, and 2.0 liter versions. Procedures common to different models are combined to avoid duplication.

Specific information on 1967-1976 models and general information on all models is contained in Chapters One through Thirteen. Specific information on 1977-1979 models is contained in a supplement at the rear of the book.

MANUAL ORGANIZATION

This chapter provides general information on the Saab line, plus valuable service hints and a brief description of recommended hand tools and test equipment useful for preventive maintenance, tune-up and troubleshooting.

Chapter Two explains all periodic lubrication and routine maintenance, and recommended tune-up procedures required to keep your car in top running condition.

Chapter Three provides methods and suggestions for finding and fixing troubles fast. Troubleshooting procedures discuss typical symptoms and logical methods to pinpoint the trouble.

Subsequent chapters describe specific systems such as the engine; fuel and exhaust systems: cooling and heating systems; emission control systems; electrical systems; clutch, transmission, and differential; front suspension, wheels, and steering; rear suspension; and brakes.

Each chapter provides disassembly, repair, and assembly procedures in easy-to-follow, step-by-step form. All procedures are given in the most practical sequence. Complex and lengthy operations are described in detail and are thoroughly illustrated.

Installation and assembly procedures are given where they differ from removal and disassembly procedures.

Italic notes of caution or operation emphasis appear throughout the text to ensure safety and working efficiency.

VEHICLE IDENTIFICATION

The location of the engine, gearbox, and chassis numbers for the 95/96, and Sonett are shown in **Figures 1 and 2**. The location of the engine, gearbox, and chassis number for the 99 are shown in **Figure 3**.

Saabs manufactured since 1972 utilize 11 digits in the chassis code number. The meaning of the digits is shown in the following example: Saab 99, 1973 car with a serial number reading

2 CHAPTER ONE

① **VEHICLE IDENTIFICATION NUMBERS**
(Models 95/96)

CHASSIS NUMBER (on body)

COLOR CODE AND CHASSIS NUMBER PLATES

GEARBOX NUMBER

ENGINE NUMBER

GENERAL INFORMATION

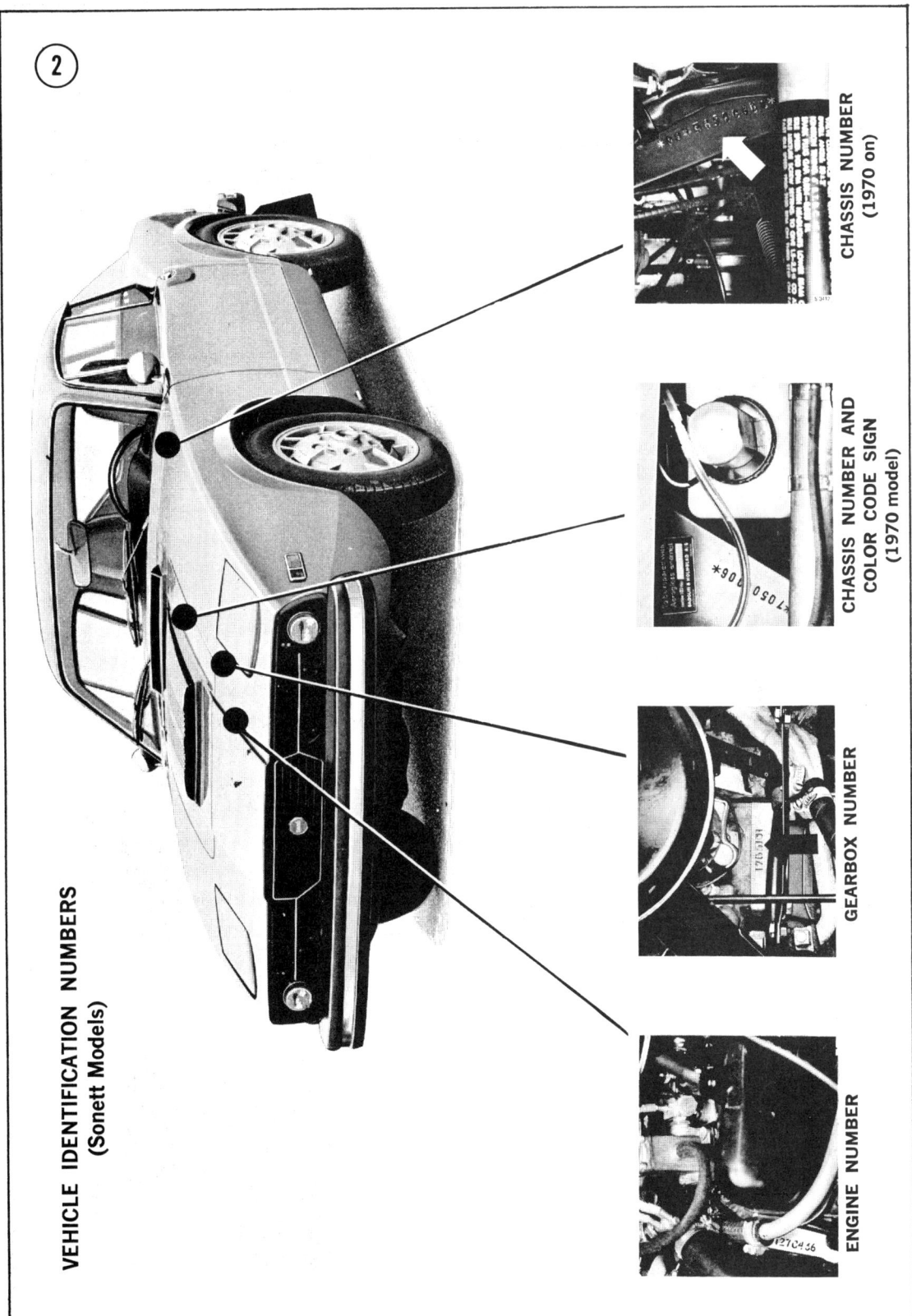

② VEHICLE IDENTIFICATION NUMBERS (Sonett Models)

CHASSIS NUMBER (1970 on)

CHASSIS NUMBER AND COLOR CODE SIGN (1970 model)

GEARBOX NUMBER

ENGINE NUMBER

CHAPTER ONE

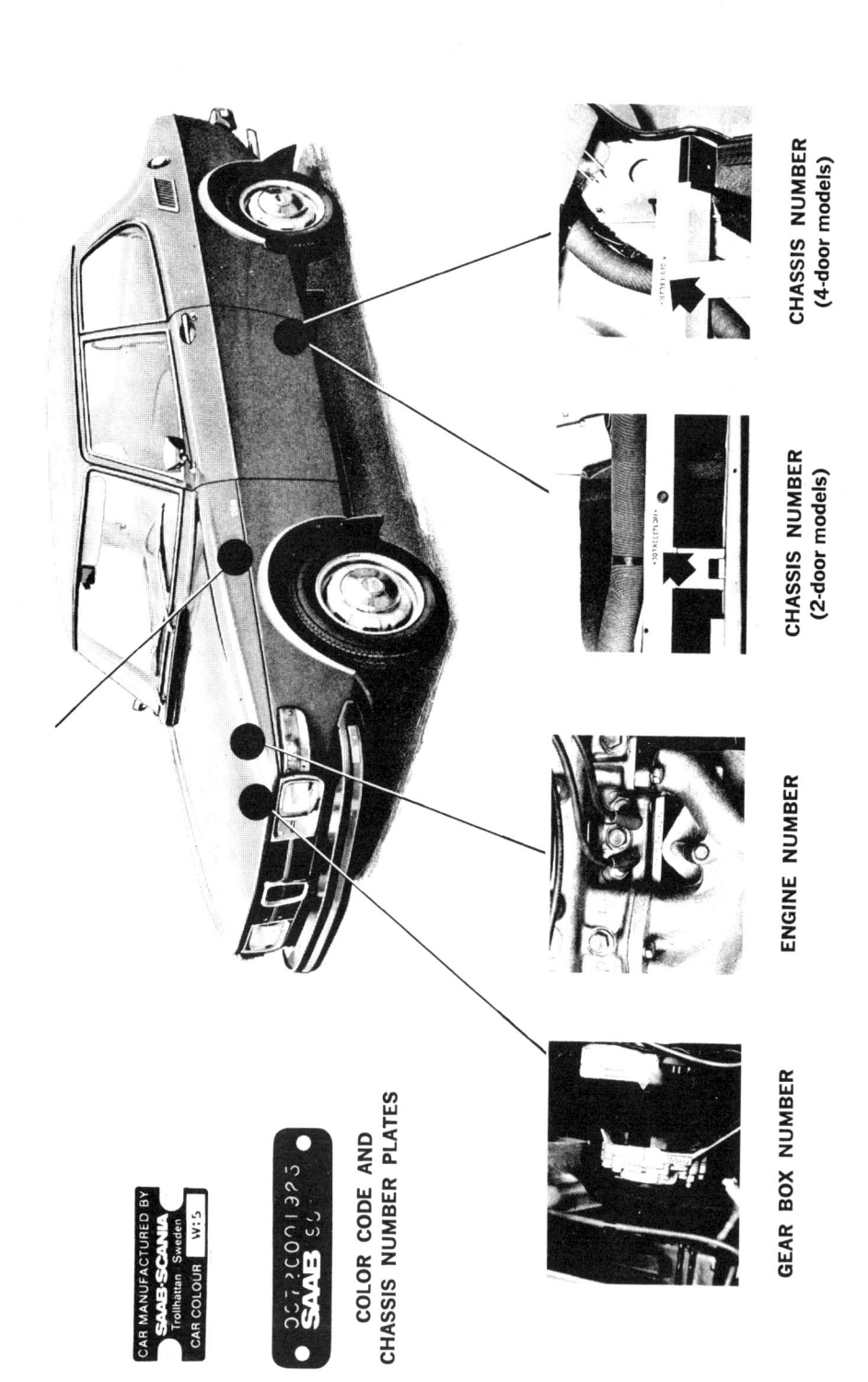

GENERAL INFORMATION

99736000001. The first 2 digits (99) is the car model; the second 2 digits (73) is the model year; the next digit (6) is the place of manufacture (2—Trollhattan, 6—Nystad (Finland), 7—Malines (Belgium); and the last 6 digits make up the serial number (each model year begins with 000001).

In front of the engine number are 2 letters punched. The first letter is J in all engines. The second letter varies as follow:

B—1.7 carburetted engine, Europe
C—1.7 carburetted engine, U.S.A.
D—1.7 fuel injection engine
E—1.85 carburetted engine, Europe
F—1.85 carburetted engine, U.S.A.
G—1.85 fuel injection engine

After the engine numbers the following letters are punched:

HE—Indicates high compression engine and are punched on all engine types.
A —Engines intended for installations with automatic transmissions.

The coding used on 2-liter engines is as follows: The first letter is the engine type (B—gasoline engine, carburetor; BE—gasoline engine, electronic fuel injection); the first 2 digits indicate cylinder volume in liters; the next 3 letters/digits indicate "PO1, PO3" for manual transmission, "PO2" for automatic transmission, and "PO3" for special U.S.A. design; and the last 6 figures make up the engine serial number.

RECOMMENDED TOOLS

For proper servicing, you will need an assortment of ordinary hand-tools. Recommended are:

a. Combination wrenches
b. Sockets, socket extension(s), and a socket wrench
c. Plastic mallet
d. Small hammer
e. Snap ring pliers
f. Pliers
g. Phillips and straight-blade screwdrivers
h. Feeler gauge
i. Tire pressure gauge

Any owner/mechanic intent on saving money and aggravation by doing his own repair and maintenance work should invest in the following test equipment:

1. *Hydrometer* (**Figure 4**). The hydrometer gives a useful indication of battery condition and charge by measuring the specific gravity of the electrolyte in each cell. Such an instrument is available at any auto parts store and through most large mail order outlets.

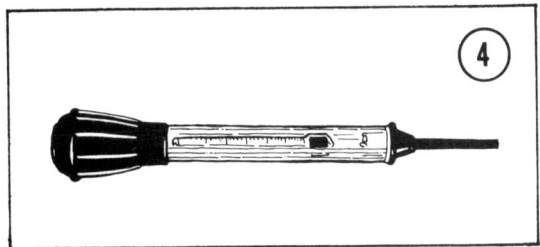

2. *Compression Gauge* (**Figure 5**). The compression gauge measures the compression pressure in each cylinder. Interpretation of compression test results can indicate general cylinder and valve condition. The gauge shown has a flexible stem, which enables it to reach cylinders where there is little clearance. Inexpensive ones are available at most auto accessory stores or by mail from large catalog order outlets. See Chapter Two for complete details on the correct use and interpretation of compression readings under the *Compression Test* heading in the *Tune-up* section.

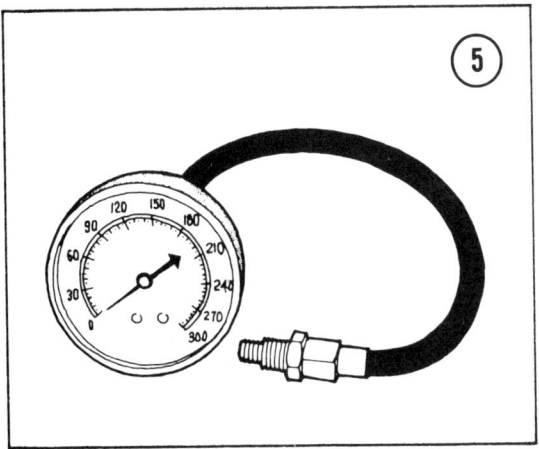

3. *Vacuum Gauge* (**Figure 6**). The vacuum gauge is one of the easiest instruments to use,

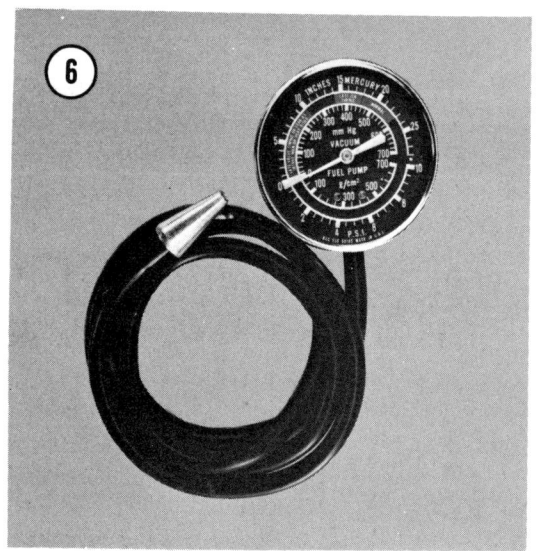

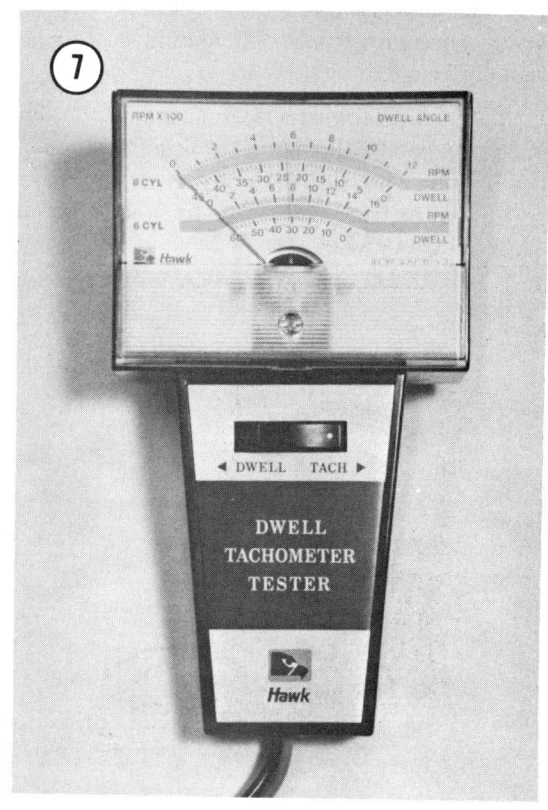

but one of the most difficult for the inexperienced mechanic to interpret. Used in conjunction with the compression gauge, the results can provide valuable information as to an engine's condition.

4. *Dwell Meter* (**Figure 7**). A dwell meter measures the distance in degrees of cam rotation that the breaker points remain closed while the engine is running. Since this angle is determined by the breaker point gap, the dwell angle is an accurate indication of point gap.

5. *Tachometer* (Figure 7). A tachometer measures engine speed and is necessary for setting ignition timing and adjusting carburetors. The best instrument for this purpose is one with a range of 0-2,000 rpm. Tachometers with an extended range (0-6,000 or 0-8,000 rpm) lack accuracy at lower speeds. The tachometer should be capable of detecting changes of 25 rpm.

Many tachometers intended for testing and tuning incorporate a dwell meter.

6. *Strobe Timing Light* (**Figure 8**). This instrument permits extremely accurate engine timing. The light flashes precisely at the same instant that the No. 1 cylinder fires, so the position of the crankshaft pulley relative to a fixed timing mark at that instant can be seen. The timing mark on the pulley must be in alignment with the stationary timing mark. This is accomplished by adjusting the distributor.

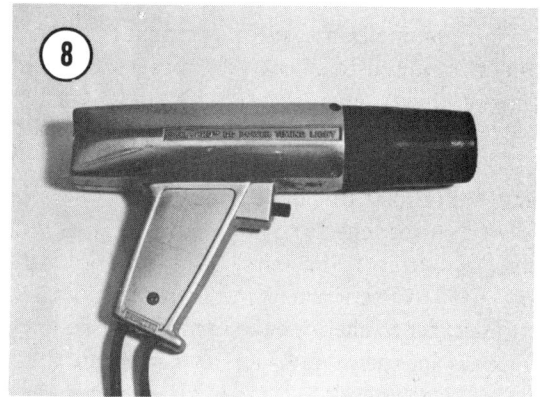

Suitable timing lights are neon bulb and xenon strobe types. Neon bulb timing lights are difficult to see and must be used in dimly lit areas. Xenon strobe timing lights can be used in bright sunlight. Use the light according to the manufacturer's instructions.

7. *Fuel Pressure Gauge.* This instrument is vital for evaluating fuel pump performance. It measures the force that the pump is exerting to

GENERAL INFORMATION

push the gasoline through the fuel lines. Often a fuel pressure gauge is combined with a vacuum gauge.

8. *Voltmeter, Ammeter, and Ohmmeter* (**Figure 9**). A good voltmeter is required for testing the ignition and electrical systems. The meter should range from 0 to 20 volts, and have an accuracy of ½ volt.

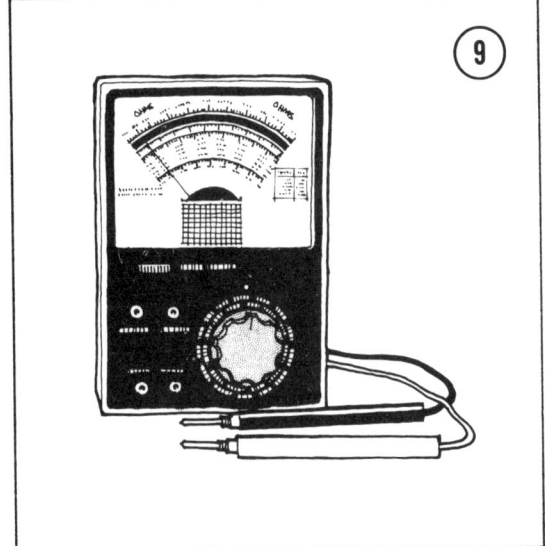

10. *Exhaust Analyzer*. This instrument is necessary to check emission control adjustments accurately. It samples the exhaust gases from the tailpipe and measures the thermal conductivity of the exhaust. Since different gases conduct heat at varying rates, thermal conductivity of the exhaust is a good indicator of the gases present.

Exhaust analyzers are relatively expensive to buy, but some large "rent-all" dealers have them available at a modest price.

SERVICE HINTS

Observing the following practices will save time, effort, and frustration, as well as prevent possible injury:

1. Throughout this manual "Front" refers to the front of the car. The front of any component such as the engine is that end which faces towards the front of the car. The left and right side of the car refer to a person sitting in the car facing forward. For example, the steering wheel is on the left side.

2. When working under a car, do not trust a hydraulic or mechanical jack alone to hold the car up. Always use jackstands. Saabs have a rigid self-supporting body which lacks the natural application points for a jack that a conventional frame offers. However there are special engagement recesses built into the chassis pan which are designed to take the jacks: both sides of the car, under the engine compartment floor, and at the back of the car behind the fuel tank. See **Figure 11**.

3. Disconnect the battery ground cables before working near electrical connections and before

The ohmmeter measures electrical resistance and is required to check continuity (open and short-circuits), and to test fuses and lights.

The ammeter measures electrical current. One for automotive use should cover 0 to 10 amperes and 0 to 100 amperes. An ammeter is useful for checking battery charging and starting current. The starter and generator (alternator) inspection and repair procedures use an ammeter to check for shorted windings.

Some inexpensive VOM's (volt-ohm-milliammeter) combine all 3 instruments into one. The ammeter ranges are usually too small for automotive work, however.

9. *Torque Wrench* (**Figure 10**). A torque wrench measures the exact amount of twisting force being applied to a nut or bolt and is one of the most essential tools for exacting mechanical work. While it does not exactly qualify as a piece of "test equipment," it is of a specialized nature and therefore included with this equipment.

CHAPTER ONE

FRONT END RAISED

REAR END RAISED

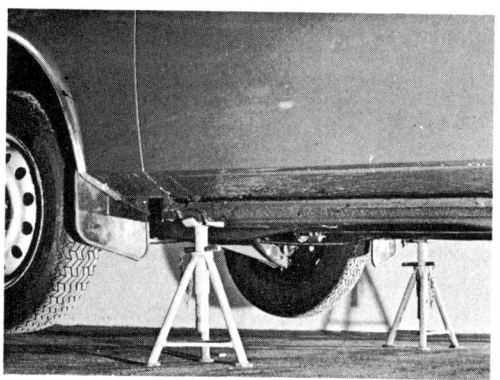
FRONT END BLOCKED UP ON JACKSTANDS

REAR END BLOCKED UP ON JACKSTANDS

ONE SIDE JACKED UP

⑪

GENERAL INFORMATION

disconnecting wires. Never run the engine with the battery disconnected; the alternator could be seriously damaged.

4. Tag all similar internal parts for location and mark all mating parts for position. Record number and thickness of any shims as they are removed. Small parts such as bolts can be identified by placing them in plastic sandwich bags and sealing and labeling bags with masking tape.

5. The thread system used in Saab cars is mainly Unified Coarse (UNC), with the inch as the unit of measurement. The width of UNC screw heads and nuts, measured across the flats in inches, corresponds to the designation of the wrench that fits in each instance. (In a few cases the Unified Fine (UNF) system is used. Exceptions to the standard thread system are found in some components supplied by subcontractors, and in models from 1972 on, where the metric thread system is used.

6. Protect finished surfaces from damage or corrosion. Keep gasoline and brake fluid off painted surfaces.

7. Frozen or very tight bolts and screws can often be loosened by soaking with penetrating oil, then sharply striking the bolt head a few times with a hammer and punch (or screwdriver for screws). Avoid heat, unless absolutely necessary, since it may melt, warp, or remove the temper from many parts.

8. Avoid flames or sparks when working near a charging battery or flammable liquids such as brake fluid or gasoline.

9. No parts, except those assembled with a press fit, require unusual force during assembly. If a part is hard to remove or install, find out *why* before proceeding.

10. Cover all openings after removing parts to keep dirt, small tools, etc., from falling in.

11. When assembling 2 parts, start all fasteners, then tighten evenly to avoid warping the part(s).

12. Read each procedure in its entirety while looking at the actual part before beginning. Many procedures are complicated and errors can be disastrous. When you thoroughly understand what is to be done, follow the procedure step-by-step.

13. In procedural steps, the term "replace" means to discard a defective part and replace it with a new or exchange unit. "Overhaul" means to remove, disassemble, inspect, measure, repair or replace defective parts, reassemble, and install major systems and parts.

Cleanliness is *essential* for proper servicing. Dirt or other foreign substances in a precisely machined part can quickly destroy that component. For example, before working on brake components, wheel bearings, etc., it is a good idea to clean the insides of fenders and the space around the work area to prevent dirt, etc. from dropping into the bearings and other vulnerable parts.

Lay protective coverings over the seats and upholstery to protect them from dirt. The fenders and other body components should also be protected with suitable coverings.

NOTE: If you own a 1977 or later model, first check the Supplement at the back of the book for any new service information.

CHAPTER TWO

LUBRICATION, MAINTENANCE, AND TUNE-UP

To ensure good performance, dependability, and safety, regular preventive maintenance and periodic lubrication is necessary. This plus a thorough tune-up at the recommended intervals will keep your Saab in top operating condition.

ROUTINE CHECKS

The following simple checks should be performed at each fuel stop.

1. Check engine oil. The engine should be warm and the car parked on level ground. Turn the engine off. Remove the dipstick, wipe it clean, and reinsert it for an accurate reading. The level should not be below the lower mark on the stick, or above the upper mark. Replenish as necessary with oil of the proper viscosity. See **Figure 1**.

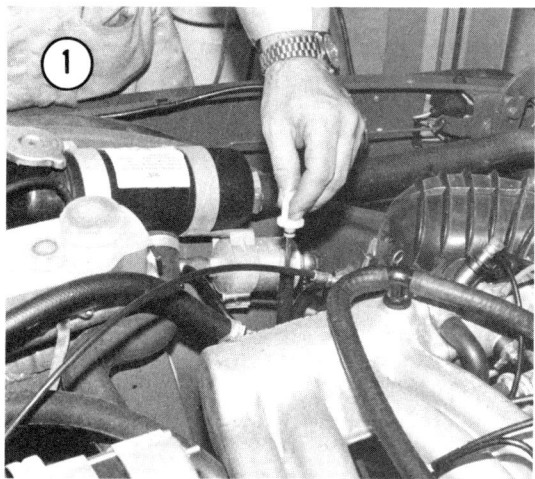

2. Check the battery electrolyte level. It should be ¼-⅓ in. (6-8mm) above the tops of the cell plates. Replenish with distilled water if low. See **Figure 2**.

3. Check tire air pressures, preferably when tires are cold. Models 95 and 96 should carry 24 psi front and rear when lightly loaded, 27 psi front and rear when fully loaded. (The rear tires on the 95 station wagon should carry 30 psi when fully loaded). Sonett models should

LUBRICATION, MAINTENANCE, AND TUNE-UP

carry 25 psi front, 22 psi rear. Saab 99 models require 27 psi front and rear (light load) and 30 psi front and rear (full load).

NOTE: *Add 1 psi to front tires on 99 models equipped with air conditioning.*

PREVENTIVE MAINTENANCE

Performed less frequently than the routine checks described preceding, scheduled checks and maintenance keep a car running smoothly. Adherence to the following recommendations will ensure top performance.

Engine Compartment

Check the entire engine compartment for leaking or deteriorated oil and fuel lines. Check electrical wiring for breaks in insulation caused by deterioration or chafing. See **Figure 3**. Check for loose or missing nuts, bolts, and screws.

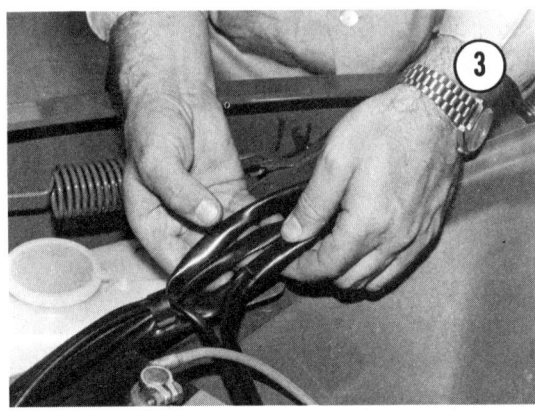

Radiator Coolant

Check the radiator level only at oil change intervals, unless there is evidence of leakage or overheating. Ethylene glycol is recommended as an anti-freeze fluid. For maximum protection against freezing and rusting the gylcol mixture should be 50/50 with clean water.

WARNING
Use care when removing radiator cap on a warm or hot engine. Hot water under pressure can boil out when pressure is released and cause severe scalding or burns. Loosen radiator cap to first notch and wait for pressure to escape before removing cap.

The cooling system should be drained, flushed with clear water, and refilled with anti-freeze at least every 24 months.

Replace any hoses that are cracked, deteriorated, or extremely soft. Make sure all hoses are correctly installed, and all clamps secure. See **Figure 4**.

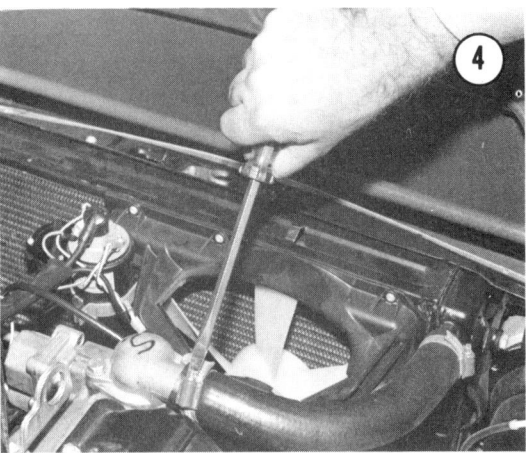

See Chapter Six for radiator removal and installation procedures.

Drive Belts

Inspect all drive belts every 15,000 miles for wear, fraying, cracking and improper tension. A belt should be retightened only when it deflects more than 0.4 in. (10mm) with moderate thumb pressure (approximately 3.3 lbs. force) when applied midway between pulleys. See **Figure 5 and 6** (Saab 99 illustrated).

A wise move is to replace belts every 24,000 miles.

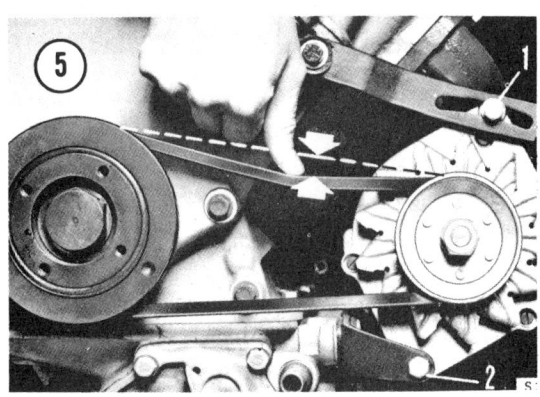

1. Adjusting bolt   2. Retaining bolt

CHAPTER TWO

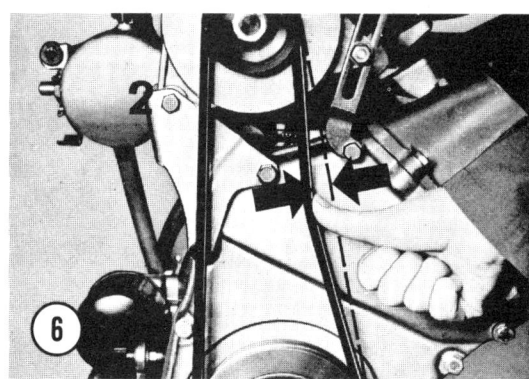

1. Adjusting bolt 2. Retaining bolt

Battery

Water is the only component of the battery which is lost as the result of charging and discharging. It must be replaced before the electrolyte level falls to the top of the battery plates.

> NOTE: *If the plates become exposed they may become permanently sulphated, which would impair the performance of the battery. Also, the plates cannot take part in the battery action unless they are completely covered by the electrolyte.*

Add distilled water as often as necessary to keep the electrolyte level at 0.4 in. (10mm) above the top of the battery plates. Do not overfill.

When working with batteries, use extreme care to avoid spilling or splashing the electrolyte. Electrolyte is sulfuric acid, and can destroy clothing and cause serious chemical burns. If any electrolyte is spilled or splashed on clothing or body, it should *immediately be neutralized* with a solution of baking soda and water, then flushed with plenty of clean water.

> **WARNING**
> *Electrolyte splashed into the eyes is extremely dangerous. Safety glasses should always be worn when working with batteries. If electrolyte is splashed into the eyes, call a physician immediately, force the eyes open, and flood with cool, clean water for about 5 minutes.*

If electrolyte is spilled or splashed onto painted or unpainted surfaces, it should be neutralized immediately with baking soda and water solution and then rinsed with clean water.

Keep the battery clean by brushing it with an ammonia or baking soda solution; flush off with clean water. Apply petroleum jelly to the battery terminals to retard corrosion. See **Figure 7**.

Refer to Chapter Eight for battery removal and installation, and battery charging information.

Engine Oil Change

Oil change intervals vary, depending on the type of driving you do. For normal driving, including some city traffic, change oil every 6 months or 6,000 miles (7,500 miles on 1976 models). If driving is primarily short distance with considerable stop-and-go city traffic, or if conditions are particularily dusty, change oil more often (possibly even twice as often). Change oil at least twice a year if the car is driven only a few hundred miles a month. To drain oil:

1. Warm the engine to operating temperature.
2. Remove drain plug from oil pan. See **Figure 8** (manual) and **Figure 9** (automatic).

1. Engine 2. Transmission

LUBRICATION, MAINTENANCE, AND TUNE-UP

1. Engine   2. Final drive

3. Let oil drain for at least 10 minutes.
4. Install oil drain plug.
5. Change oil filter (see procedure below).
6. Remove oil filler cap. Refill with engine oil which conforms to requirements of API Service SE or Ford specifications ESE-M2C-101C. Use SAE 10-W-30 or 10-W-40. In extremely cold conditions ($-4°$ F or below) use oil with a viscosity of SAE 5-W-20, but under no conditions use it at temperature above $+32°F$.

Engine Oil Filter

Replace oil filter every 6,000 miles (7,500 miles on 1976 models). Install new filter after oil has been drained and before new oil poured in.

To remove filter, unscrew it by hand or with a filter wrench. See **Figure 10 and 11**. When installing new filter, lubricate the new gasket with clean engine oil. Install filter by hand until the gasket just touches the base, then tighten ½ turn by hand. Snug down with a filter wrench,

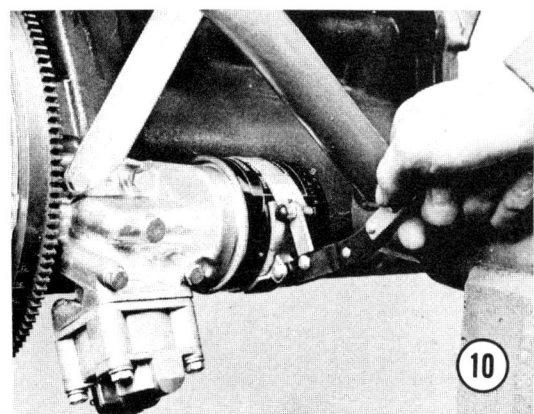

but do not overtighten as the rubber seal may be twisted, which will cause leaking.

Power Steering

Check the oil level in the power steering fluid container every 6,000 miles. The oil should be level with the strainer in the container. If low top up with ATF Type F fluid.

Clutch

Check clutch pedal for proper adjustment every 6,000 miles. The clutch operation is hydraulic. Every 3 months check to be sure the fluid level is up to the mark on the outside of the reservoir. If necessary, fill with brake fluid conforming to SAE J1703 or SAE 70R3. Never use reclaimed fluid, mineral oil, or fluid inferior to that recommended above.

See Chapter Nine for clutch adjustment procedure.

Manual Transmission and Differential

The transmission and differential form an integral unit with the engine. Part of the transmission case serves as the engine oil sump; the forward portion of the transmission comprises a primary gear delivering power from the engine to the gearbox.

Check the oil level in the transmission every 6,000 miles and change it every 12,000 miles. Check the oil level by unscrewing the oil level plug. If oil level is below the plug opening, add oil until it runs out of the opening (Figure 8). Use SAE 75 or SAE 80 EP oil to specification API-GL-4 or API-GL-5. (In cold climates SAE 75 must be used).

When changing transmission oil drive the car for 15 to 20 minutes before draining oil. Clean the magnetic drain plug, then add fresh transmission oil through the transmission filler plug opening until it runs out of the level plug opening. Remember that it takes some time for the oil to run from the primary gear housing into the transmission case. See **Figure 12 and 13**.

> NOTE: *On some transmissions (up to number 36472) there are 2 drain plugs with specially shaped recesses requiring the use of special tool 839153. Both plugs must be removed to drain the transmission oil. The plug with the square recess is for draining engine oil.*

See Chapter Nine for transmission removal and installation procedures.

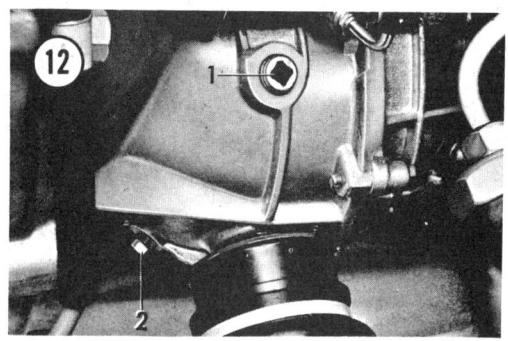

1. Filler plug   2. Level plug

Automatic Transmission

The oil in the automatic transmission does not need changing, but it should be checked every 6,000 miles. The filler tube with graduated dipstick is located where shown in **Figure 14**. The dipstick has different graduations for hot and cold oil. Check the oil with the car on level ground. Idle the engine for several minutes with the gear selector lever at "P." Shut the engine off and check the dipstick. The oil level should be between the minimum and maximum markings.

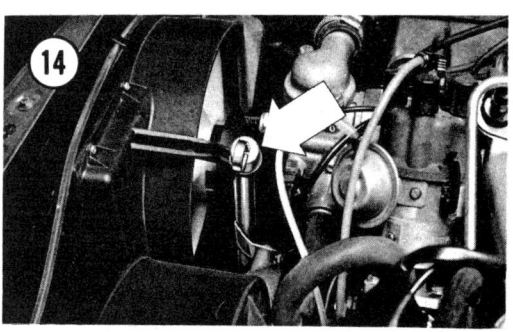

If transmission is low, add transmission oil conforming to Ford specification M2C-33F or automatic transmisison oil Type A, Suffix A, or Dexron. Do not overfill or seals may be damaged.

Final Drive (Automatic Transmission)

Check final drive lubricant level every 6,000 miles (**Figure 15**); change it every 12,000 miles. Use SAE 75 or 80 EP oil to specification API-GL-4 or API-GL-5.

See Chapter Nine for removal and installation procedures.

Exhaust System

Examine exhaust pipes, mufflers, and hangers for rust, holes, and other damage. Replace any

LUBRICATION, MAINTENANCE, AND TUNE-UP

worn parts. See Chapter Five for removal and installation procedures.

Brakes

Check fluid level in master cylinder. See **Figure 16**. Maintain level between minimum and maximum reservoir marks. Use fluid in accordance with DOT 3 or DOT 4.

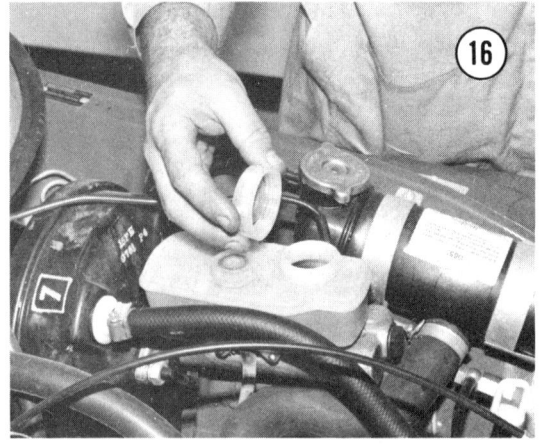

Check brake lines and hoses for leaks and wear. Replace defective part after determining and correcting cause.

On disc brakes, check condition of pads and discs while wheels are removed during tire rotation. (Front brakes are self adjusting so wear cannot easily be detected by "feel" through the brake pedal). See **Figure 17**. Have scored or corroded discs turned down. Replace pads that are contaminated with oil, grease, or brake fluid, or worn to a thickness of less than 0.08 in. (2mm).

Check wheel cylinders and calipers for brake fluid leaks. Rebuild or replace defective calipers or cylinders.

Rear brakes on the 95, 96, and Sonett models are drum type, mechanically adjustable. Inspect linings for contamination (oil, grease, or brake fluid) and wear. Replace linings worn to less than 0.1 in. (2.5mm). The linings can be inspected by looking through the inspection holes in the rear brake drums. See **Figure 18**.

1. Inspection hole

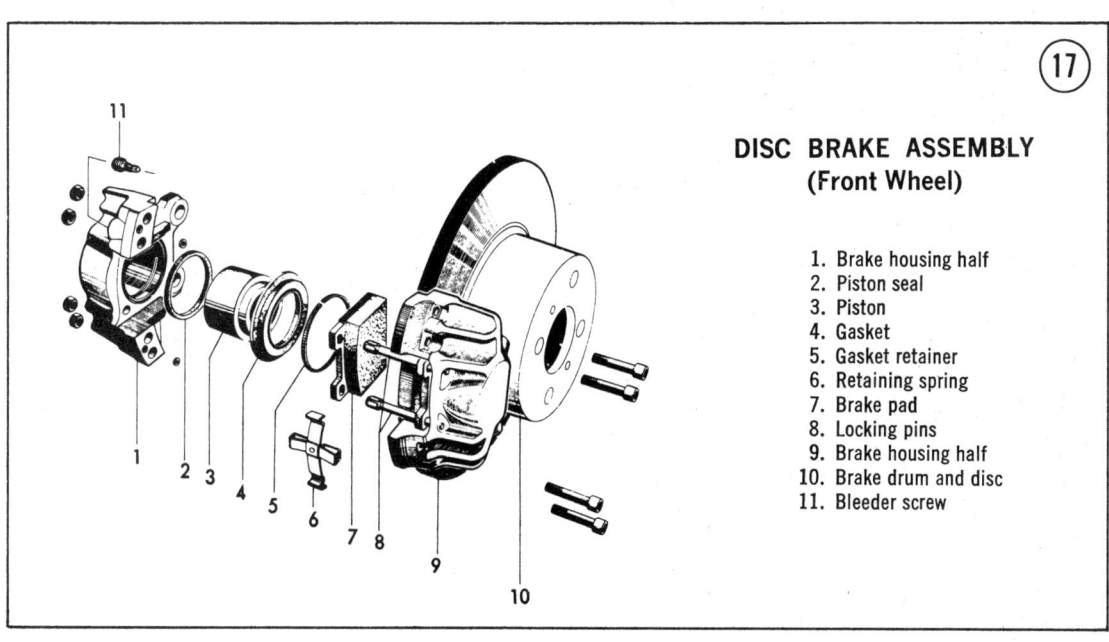

DISC BRAKE ASSEMBLY (Front Wheel)

1. Brake housing half
2. Piston seal
3. Piston
4. Gasket
5. Gasket retainer
6. Retaining spring
7. Brake pad
8. Locking pins
9. Brake housing half
10. Brake drum and disc
11. Bleeder screw

The parking brake on 99 models is mechanical and acts on the front wheels through drums in the disc brake hubs. The handbrake is located between the front seats. Operation of the lever transmits the movement to the parking brake via cables which are permanently lubricated. See **Figure 19**. Replace the parking brake shoes when thickness of the lining becomes less than 0.2 in. (0.5mm).

The parking brake on 95, 96, and Sonett models is also mechanical, but movement of the handbrake lever (also mounted between the front seats) is transmitted to the rear brake drums via permanently lubricated cables. The handbrake is adjustable.

See Chapter Twelve for procedures pertaining to the brake system.

Tire and Wheel Inspection

Check condition of all tires, including spare. Check local traffic regulations concerning minimum tread depth. Most recommend replacing tires when tread depth is less than 1/32 in. The tires should be rotated every 8,000 miles.

Be sure to adjust tire pressures after rotation.

Check wheel lug nuts for tightness. Tighten in the sequence shown in **Figure 20**.

Steering and Suspension

All Models: Check condition of the rubber boots on the steering gear and inner and outer universal joints, and the rubber seals for the ball-joints and tie rod ends.

Saab 95, 96, and Sonett: The front suspension and steering should be lubricated every 6,000 miles. When lubricating the ball-joints the front of the car should be jacked up until the front wheels are off the floor. Turn each wheel outward to provide easy access to ball-joints and outer drive shaft universal joints.

Tie rod grease nipples are more easily reached if the front of the car is jacked up and the wheels turned fully toward the opposite side.

Avoid excessive lubrication of the steering gear. Check that rubber boots are not swollen after lubrication and that they are free of defects likely to cause loss of grease. While greasing, turn the steering wheel to full left lock so that the grease also penetrates to the right-hand part of the steering gear.

Saab 99 through 1972: Since the 99 series features permanently lubricated steering and suspension, the tie rod end assemblies, upper and lower ball-joints, and steering gear should only be repacked with grease in the event of an overhaul. All parts should be thoroughly cleaned before repacking to prevent the entry of dirt.

Saab 99, 1973: The steering gear should be checked every 30,000 miles, as follows:

1. Clean the tie rod and the clamp around the bellows on the left side. Loosen the clamp and remove it.

2. Insert a screwdriver between the bellows and tie rod along the underside of the tie rod.

3. Position the front wheels so they point straight ahead. Jack up the right side of the car so the wheels are 2 in. off the floor.

4. The oil will begin to drip out next to the screwdriver if the steering gear contains the proper amount of oil. If it is low, use an oil can

LUBRICATION, MAINTENANCE, AND TUNE-UP

filled with type EP 90 oil to bring the oil level to the top.

5. Replace the clamp, making certain that the threaded end of the clamp screw is fitted with a rubber cap.

6. Perform all of the above steps on the right side.

Saab 99, 1974-1976: Check every 30,000 miles as follows:

1. With the front wheels pointing straight ahead and the car on level ground, jack up the front end until the front bumper brackets are 17.7 in. from the floor (in order to place the tie rod at the proper angle).

2. Unfasten and remove the bellows clamp on the tie rod.

3. Insert a screwdriver into the bellows under the underside of the bellows (same procedure on both the left and right sides). If the steering gear contains the correct amount of oil the oil will begin to drip out. If it is low, refill it with an oil can filled with type EP 90 oil.

4. Replace the clamps.

Step-by-step procedures pertaining to the front suspension, wheels, and steering are in Chapter Ten.

Shock Absorbers

Inspect shock absorbers for damage or leaks. See **Figure 21**. Shock absorbers require no lubrication with the exception of the arm type used on the 95 (rear only). Every 12,000 miles these shocks should be inspected and filled, if necessary, with a high quality shock absorber fluid. See **Figure 22**.

Body

Every 6,000 miles lubricate the door hinges, door locks and striker plates, lock and lock support for the luggage compartment lid, and door stops. See **Figure 23**.

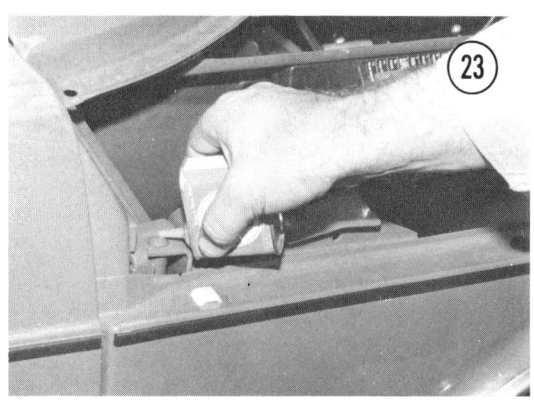

Additional Maintenance

Components which require periodic maintenance and lubrication such as the replacement of air and fuel filters, lubrication of the throttle control and distributor breaker cam, etc., are covered in *Engine Tune-up* section, following.

ENGINE TUNE-UP

The purpose of a tune-up is to restore power and performance lost over a gradual period of time due to normal wear.

Because of Federal laws limiting exhaust emissions, it is important that the engine tune-up is done accurately, using the specifications listed in **Table 1** at the end of the chapter.

Economical, trouble-free operation can be assured if a complete tune-up is performed at

CHAPTER TWO

12,000 mile intervals (Saab 95, 96, and Sonett) or 15,000 miles (Saab 99).

Tune-ups consists of 3 general categories: compression, ignition, and carburetion. Carburetion adjustments should not be attempted until the compression and ignition phases have been completed. Carry out the tune-up in the same sequence in this chapter for best results.

Tune-Up Equipment Hook-Up

A description of the various tools and specialized test instruments can be found in Chapter One. Always follow the manufacturer's recommendations for the use of test equipment. If such instructions are not available, the following can be used as a general guide.

a. *Voltmeter*—Connect the positive lead to the resistor side of the coil, and the negative lead to the ground.

b. *Timing Light*—Connect the positive lead to the positive battery terminal; connect the trigger lead to the No. 1 spark plug; connect the negative lead to ground.

c. *Tachometer*—Connect the positive lead to the distributor side of the coil, and the negative lead to ground.

d. *Dwell Meter*—Connect the positive lead to the distributor side of the coil, and the negative lead to ground.

Valve Clearance Adjustment (95, 96, and Sonett)

1. Remove the air cleaner, detach the ignition cables from the spark plugs and valve cover, and remove the screws from the valve cover. Lift off the valve cover being careful not to damage the gasket.

2. Set the mark on the pulley directly opposite the dead center mark on the transmission cover. The rocker arms on the first and fourth cylinder will "rock" if the crankshaft is turned slightly back and forth in this position.

3. If the rocker arms "rock" at cylinder 4, adjust valves 1, 2, 4, and 6 (**Figure 24**). If rocker arms rock at cylinder 1, adjust valves 3, 5, 7, and 8 (**Figure 25**). The correct valve adjustment is 0.014 in. (0.35mm) for intake valves; 0.016 in. (0.40mm) for exhaust valves.

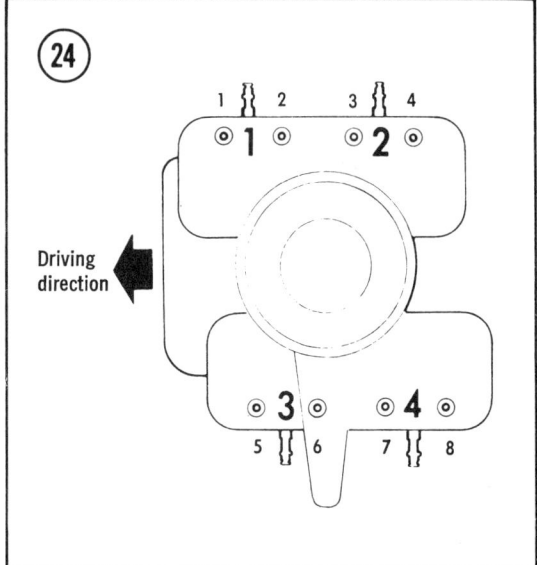

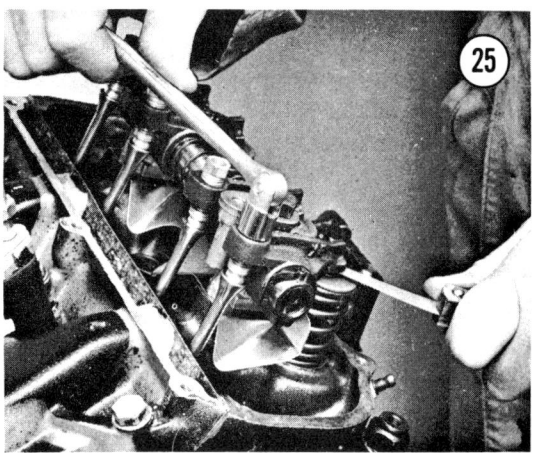

4. If a new gasket is to be installed on the valve cover, press the gasket tabs into the valve cover recesses (see **Figure 26**). Position the valve cover on cylinder head. Torque hold-down screws to 4 ft.-lb. evenly. Install ignition cables to the valve covers and spark plugs. Install air cleaner.

NOTE: *The valve cover with the oil filler cap must be installed on the right side of the engine.*

Valve Clearance Adjustment (Saab 99 Models)

1. Remove the preheater hose (1.7 and 1.85 engines only); disconnect the crankcase ventilation hose; detach the ignition cables from the

LUBRICATION, MAINTENANCE, AND TUNE-UP

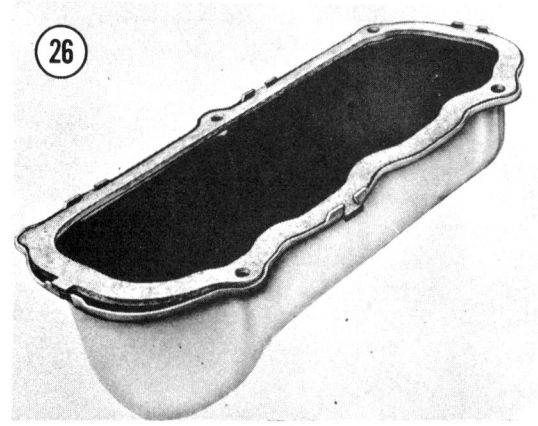

spark plugs and camshaft cover; remove the screws holding down the camshaft cover. Carefully remove the cover, so as to not damage the gasket.

2. The valve clearance should be checked with the engine cold. To accomplish this the free wheel drive must be locked and the transmission placed in third gear. Push the car forward and backward to bring the camshaft cams into the correct measuring positions (with the cam of the valve to be measured pointing 180 degrees away from the valve stem). Two cams will be in the measuring position at the same time.

3. Measure the valve clearance with a feeler gauge. See **Figure 27**. The tolerance limits are 0.006-0.012 in. (0.15-0.30mm) for inlet valves; 0.014-0.020 in. (0.035-0.050mm) for exhaust valves. If the clearance on any valve is outside the permissible limits all valves will have to be measured and adjusted.

NOTE: *The valve clearance is very stable and adjustment is seldom needed. However, if it is necessary the work should be done at your dealer, as special tools are required to adjust the valves on an overhead cam engine.*

4. Replace the original valve cover gasket in the valve cover if still in good condition. Carefully position the valve cover and insert all hold down screws. Torque them evenly to 4 ft.-lb. Connect the ignition cables and crankcase ventilation hose.

Compression Test

A compression test is performed to check for worn piston rings and/or valves. After adjusting the valves, check compression as follows:

1. Start engine and run it until normal operating temperature is reached. Shut engine off.

2. Remove spark plugs and washers from cylinder head (see *Spark Plug Inspection and Service,* following, for proper removal procedure).

3. Firmly insert a compression gauge into the spark plug hole (see **Figure 28**). Have an assistant crank the engine over several revolutions to obtain the highest possible reading on the compression gauge. Write it down on a piece of paper.

4. Check compression on each cylinder. Repeat the compression check once more on each cylinder. Select the highest compression reading for each cylinder. The compression is considered normal if the lowest reading cylinder is more than 75 percent of the highest reading cylinder. See **Table 2**. This table may be used as a quick reference when checking cylinder compression

CHAPTER TWO

Table 2 **COMPRESSION PRESSURE LIMITS**

Pressure (psi)		Pressure (psi)	
Maximum	Minimum	Maximum	Minimum
134	101	188	141
136	102	190	142
138	104	192	144
140	105	194	145
142	107	196	147
146	110	198	148
148	111	200	150
150	113	202	151
152	114	204	153
154	115	206	154
156	117	208	156
158	118	210	157
160	120	212	158
162	121	214	160
164	123	216	162
166	124	218	163
168	126	220	165
170	127	222	166
172	129	224	168
174	131	226	169
176	132	228	171
178	133	230	172
180	135	232	174
182	136	234	175
184	138	236	177
186	140	238	178

pressures. It has been calculated so that the lowest reading number is 75 percent of the highest reading number.

Example: After checking the compression pressures in all cylinders it was found that the highest pressure obtained was 182 psi. The lowest pressure reading was 145 psi. By locating 182 in the maximum column, it is seen that the minimum allowable pressure is 136 psi. Since the lowest reading obtained was 145 psi, the compression is within satisfactory limits.

5. If one or more cylinders read low, pour a tablespoon of engine oil through the spark plug hole in the low reading cylinders. Repeat the compression check on these cylinders. If the compression improves considerably, the rings are worn. If the compression does not improve, the valves are sticking or seating poorly. If two adjacent cylinders indicate low compression and injecting oil does not increase compression, the cause may be the head gasket leaking between the cylinders. Engine coolant and/or oil in the cylinders could result from this defect.

Spark Plug Inspection and Service

Spark plugs are available in various heat ranges hotter or colder than the plug originally installed at the factory.

Select plugs of a heat range designed for the loads and temperature conditions under which the engine will run. Use of incorrect heat ranges can cause seized pistons, scored cylinder walls, or damaged piston crowns.

In general, use a lower-numbered plug for low speeds, low loads, and low temperatures. Use a high-numbered plug for high speeds, high engine loads, and high temperatures.

> NOTE: *Use the highest numbered plug that will not foul. In areas where seasonal temperature variations are great, the factory recommends a high-numbered plug for slower winter operation.*

The reach (length) of a plug is also important. A longer than normal plug could interfere with the piston, causing permanent and severe damage. Refer to **Figures 29 and 30**.

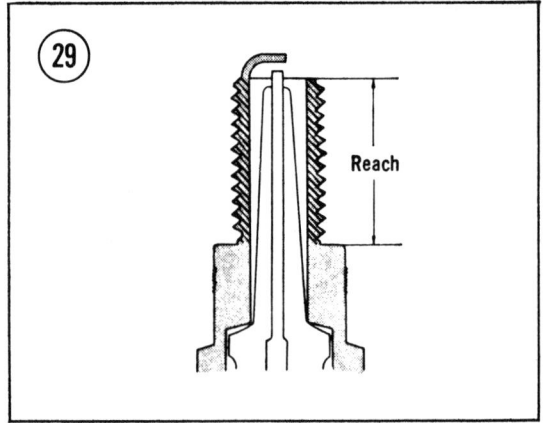

A quick test can be made to determine if the plug is correct for your usage. Accelerate hard and maintain a high, steady speed. Shut the throttle off and kill the engine at the same time, allowing the car to slow, out of gear. Don't allow the engine to slow the car. Remove the plug and check the condition of the electrode area. Spark plugs of the correct heat range, with the

LUBRICATION, MAINTENANCE, AND TUNE-UP

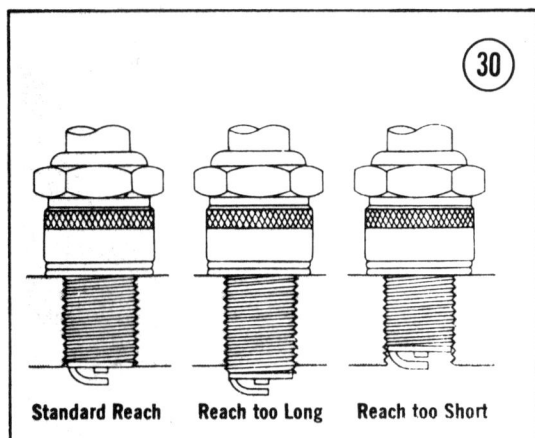

Standard Reach Reach too Long Reach too Short

engine in a proper state of tune, will appear light tan. See **Figure 31**.

If the insulator is white or burned, the plug is too hot and should be replaced with a colder one. Also check the setting of the carburetor, for it may be too lean.

A too-cold plug will have sooty deposits ranging in color from dark brown to black. Replace with a hotter plug and check for too-rich carburetion.

If any one plug is found unsatisfactory, discard the set.

Changing spark plugs is generally a simple operation. Occasionally heat and corrosion cause the plug to bind in the cylinder head, however, making removal difficult. Don't use force; the head is easily damaged. Here is the proper way to replace a plug:

1. Blow out any debris which has collected in the spark plug wells. It could fall into the hole and cause damage.

2. Gently remove the spark plug leads by pulling up and out on the cap. Don't jerk the wires or pull on the wire itself.

3. Apply penetrating oil to the base of the plug and allow it to work into the threads.

4. Back out the plugs with a socket that has a rubber insert designed to grip the insulator. Be careful not to drop the plugs where they could become lodged. See **Figure 32**.

5. Remove the spark plug gaskets from the spark plug holes. Clean the seating area after removal being careful that no dirt drops into the spark plug hole.

6. Remove grease and dirt from the insulator with a clean rag. Inspect the insulator and body of each spark plug for signs of cracks and chips. Replace if defective.

7. Clean the tips of the plugs with a sandblasting machine (some service stations have them) or with a wire brush and solvent.

8. File the center electrode flat. Clean and file all surfaces of the outer electrode. All surfaces should be clean, flat, and smooth.

9. Using a round feeler gauge, adjust clearance between the electrodes as specified in Table 1. See **Figure 33**. Do not bend the inner electrode or damage to the insulator may result.

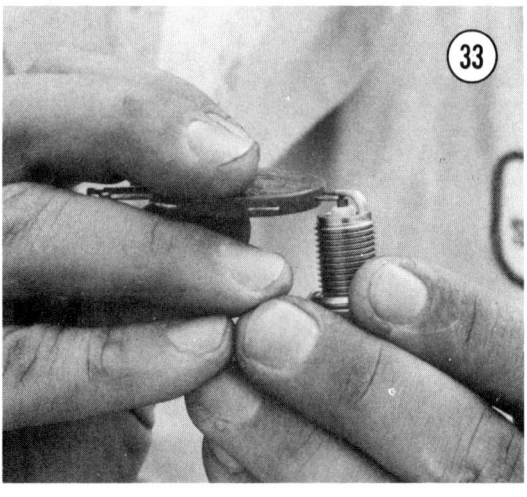

10. Use a new gasket if the old plugs are to be reused after cleaning. Apply a dab of graphite to spark plug threads to simplify future removal.

11. Thread the plug into the spark plug holes finger-tight, then tighten ¼ turn more with a

SPARK PLUG CONDITION

③

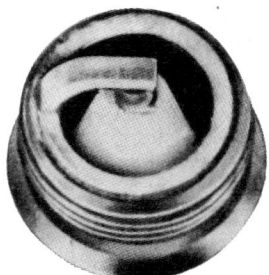

NORMAL
- Identified by light tan or gray deposits on the firing tip.
- Can be cleaned.

GAP BRIDGED
- Identified by deposit buildup closing gap between electrodes.
- Caused by oil or carbon fouling. If deposits are not excessive, the plug can be cleaned.

OIL FOULED
- Identified by wet black deposits on the insulator shell bore electrodes.
- Caused by excessive oil entering combustion chamber through worn rings and pistons, excessive clearance between valve guides and stems, or worn or loose bearings. Can be cleaned. If engine is not repaired, use a hotter plug.

CARBON FOULED
- Identified by black, dry fluffy carbon deposits on insulator tips, exposed shell surfaces and electrodes.
- Caused by too cold a plug, weak ignition, dirty air cleaner, defective fuel pump, too rich a fuel mixture, improperly operating heat riser, or excessive idling. Can be cleaned.

LEAD FOULED
- Identified by dark gray, black, yellow, or tan deposits or a fused glazed coating on the insulator tip.
- Caused by highly leaded gasoline. Can be cleaned.

WORN
- Identified by severely eroded or worn electrodes.
- Caused by normal wear. Should be replaced.

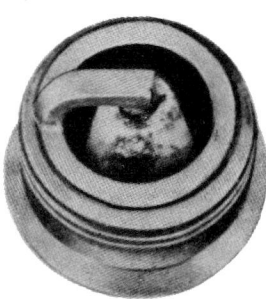

FUSED SPOT DEPOSIT
- Identified by melted or spotty deposits resembling bubbles or blisters.
- Caused by sudden acceleration. Can be cleaned.

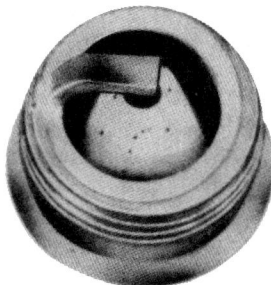

OVERHEATING
- Identified by a white or light gray insulator with small black or gray brown spots and with bluish-burnt appearance of electrodes.
- Caused by engine overheating, wrong type of fuel, loose spark plugs, too hot a plug, low fuel pump pressure, or incorrect ignition timing. Replace the plug.

PREIGNITION
- Identified by melted electrodes and possibly blistered insulator. Metallic deposits on insulator indicate engine damage.
- Caused by wrong type of fuel, incorrect ignition timing or advance, too hot a plug, burned valves, or engine overheating. Replace the plug.

LUBRICATION, MAINTENANCE, AND TUNE-UP

wrench. Further tightening will flatten the gasket and cause binding. If a torque wrench is available, torque the plugs to 20 ft.-lb.

12. Connect the spark plug wires to the spark plugs, making sure you do not get the wires crossed. Push plug wire connectors firmly onto the spark plug tips.

Distributor

The distributor is the heart of the ignition system, which consists of the distributor, contact breaker points, condenser, coil, and high and low tension circuit parts. The low tension (primary) circuit consists of the power source (battery), contact breaker points, condenser, and ignition coil primary winding. The high tension (secondary) circuit consists of ignition coil secondary winding, rotor arm, distributor cap electrical contacts, high tension cables, and spark plugs.

Most of the trouble encountered in the distributor will be in the cap, rotor, contact points, condenser, or wiring. The distributor should not make any noise while the engine is running. If noises are apparent, either the bearings or gears are worn and should be replaced. Refer to Chapter Eight for detailed procedures.

The contact points should be serviced and replaced periodically. Replace the rotor and condenser whenever the contact points are replaced. Replace the distributor cap if worn or damaged.

Saab 95, 96, and Sonett V4 models use a Bosch distributor mounted at the rear of the engine block. The distributor rotates clockwise and is driven by the camshaft via an angle drive. The firing order is 1-3-4-2. The distributor is equipped with a combination centrifugal/vacuum advance. The centrifugal advance regulates the ignition timing relative to the engine speed. The double-acting vacuum advance increases or decreases ignition timing depending on engine load. See **Figure 34**.

Saab 99 models use 2 types of distributors, the AC Delco unit used on carburetor engines (**Figure 35**); and the Bosch unit used on fuel injection engines (**Figure 36**).

The Delco distributor (carburetor engines) is mounted on the front of the engine block. It

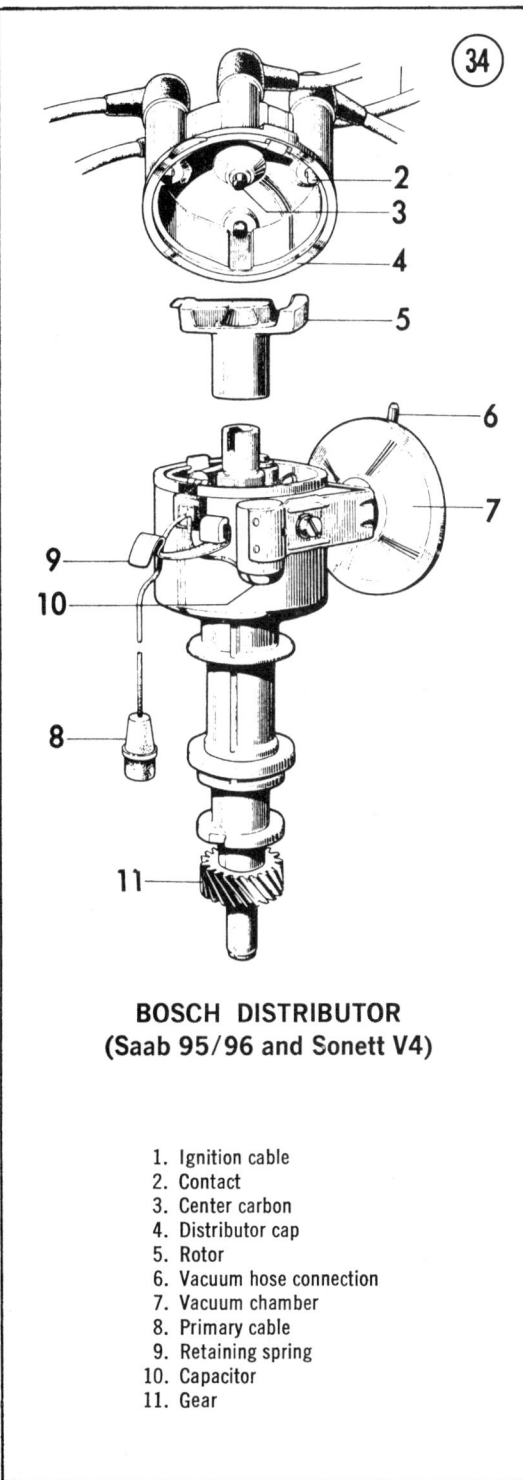

BOSCH DISTRIBUTOR
(Saab 95/96 and Sonett V4)

1. Ignition cable
2. Contact
3. Center carbon
4. Distributor cap
5. Rotor
6. Vacuum hose connection
7. Vacuum chamber
8. Primary cable
9. Retaining spring
10. Capacitor
11. Gear

rotates counterclockwise and is driven by a worm gear from the idler shaft. The distributor uses a combination centrifugal/vacuum ad-

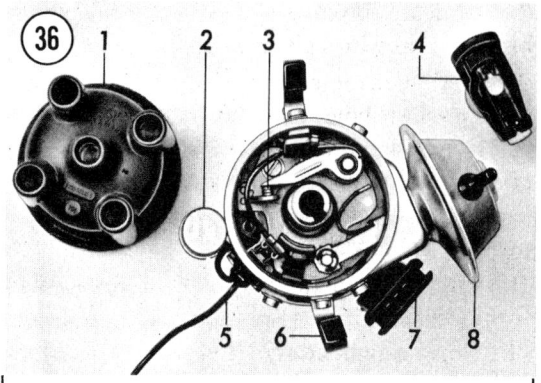

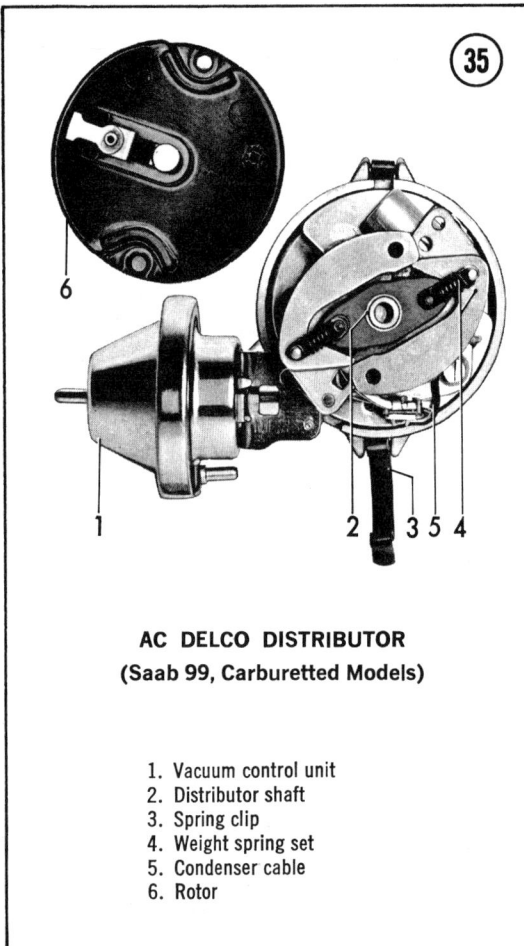

AC DELCO DISTRIBUTOR
(Saab 99, Carburetted Models)

1. Vacuum control unit
2. Distributor shaft
3. Spring clip
4. Weight spring set
5. Condenser cable
6. Rotor

BOSCH DISTRIBUTOR
(Saab 99, Fuel Injected Models)

1. Cover
2. Condenser
3. Breaker contacts
4. Rotor
5. Low voltage connection
6. Spring clip
7. Connection for trigger contacts
8. Vacuum control unit

vance. The centrifugal advance controls the ignition setting relative to engine speed; the double-acting vacuum system controls ignition setting relative to engine speed; the double-acting vacuum system controls ignition seting in relation to engine load. The order of engine firing is 1-3-4-2 (cylinders numbered from rear to front). No vacuum regulator is used on the 2.0 liter engine.

The Bosch distributor (fuel injection engines) also uses a combination centrifugal/vacuum advance system. It also has 2 sets of impulse contacts mounted on the bottom of the distributor housing. These contacts, which require no maintenance, supply the electronic injection system with information on engine speed, which regulates the amount of fuel injected into the combustion chamber. The vacuum regulating action is negative (ignition is retarded by increasing negative pressure).

Contact Point and Rotor Replacement (95, 96, and Sonett V4)

1. Release distributor cap retaining clips. Remove cap.

2. Remove rotor. Inspect for wear or damage.

3. Disconnect breaker arm lead. Remove washers and clip from breaker pivot on distributors designated 0231146044 and 0231146024.

4. Remove breaker arm after pressing leaf spring out of hole in contact support. Collect shims on distributors designated 0231146044 and 0231146024.

5. Remove retaining screw holding the fixed breaker point.

6. Remove breaker point on distributor designated 0231146033.

CAUTION
Do not get grease or oil on contact point surfaces.

7. Install fixed breaker point of breaker unit by inserting retaining screw (but do not tighten it firmly).

LUBRICATION, MAINTENANCE, AND TUNE-UP

8. Lubricate pivot and bearing bushing on breaker arm with light grease.

9. Insert breaker arm leaf spring in the contact support hole on distributors designated 0231146044 and 0231146024. The faces of the contact points must be parallel to each other. Correct misalignment with shims, or by aligning the fixed breaker point.

10. Fit shims and clip on the pivot on distributors designed 0231146044 and 0231146024.

11. Apply a light coat of grease to the breaker cam and fiber peg.

12. Connect breaker arm lead. Adjust contact point gap and dwell angle as follows under *Contact Point Adjustment* and *Dwell Angle Adjustment*.

Contact Point Adjustment
(95, 96, and Sonett V4)

1. Crank engine until widest contact point gap is obtained (the heel of the contact arm is lifted to the highest position on the distributor cam).

2. Insert a screwdriver between the 2 adjusting lugs and slot. Turn the screwdriver to set the gap to 0.016 in. (0.4mm). Tighten retaining screw and recheck contact point gap.

Dwell Angle Adjustment
(95, 96, and Sonett V4)

1. Connect dwell angle meter. With ignition in the ON position, crank engine over with the starter. Adjust dwell angle to 50±2 degrees by adjusting the fixed breaker point. Tighten retaining screw and recheck gap.

2. The relationship between gap A and dwell angle S is illustrated in **Figure 37**. The shaded point illustration shows the gap at the widest position. Set new breaker points for the narrower dwell angle illustrated, as the dwell angle will increase as the points wear.

3. Soak the lubricating felt in the distributor shaft with SAE 40 oil.

4. Push the rotor firmly in place and set the distributor cap in position. Secure cap with 2 retaining clips.

MEASURING DWELL ANGLE (37)

A = Breaker point gap
S = Dwell angle

Gap A too narrow
Angle S too wide

Gap A too wide
Angle S too narrow

Gap A correct
Angle S correct

Ignition Timing
(95, 96, and Sonett V4)

Refer to **Figure 38**.

1. Connect timing light, dwell angle meter, and tachometer.

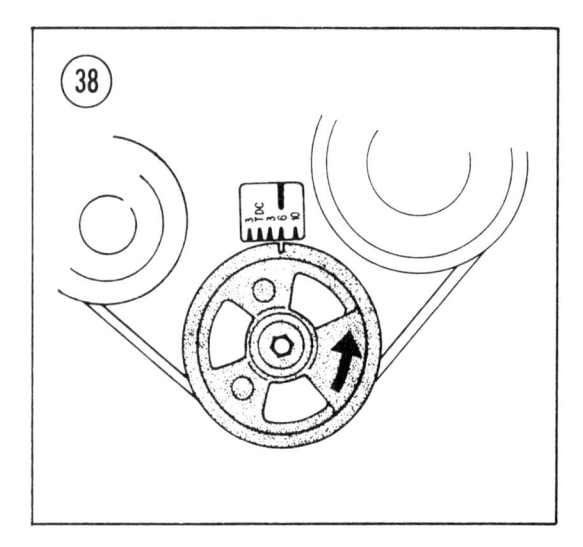

2. Disconnect vacuum hose(s).

3. With engine idling, check dwell angle. Adjust if necessary to 50±2 degrees.

4. With engine idling at approximately 500 rpm, check and adjust if necessary, the ignition timing (see Table 1). Adjust ignition timing by loosening retaining clamp and turning distributor housing to the left to advance the ignition, or to the right to retard it.

5. Reconnect vacuum hose(s). Adjust engine idling speed (see Table 1 for specifications).

Contact Point and Rotor
Replacement (Saab 99)

1. Release distributor cap retaining clips. Remove cap.

2. Remove the 2 rotor arm retaining screws. Remove the rotor. Inspect for wear or damage. See **Figure 39**.

3. Pull breaker arm leads away from contact plate. Loosen the retaining screws from fixed breaker contact and remove it, complete with attached breaker arm. See **Figure 40**.

4. Insert the new fixed breaker contact with attached breaker arm. Insert retaining screws but do not tighten fully.

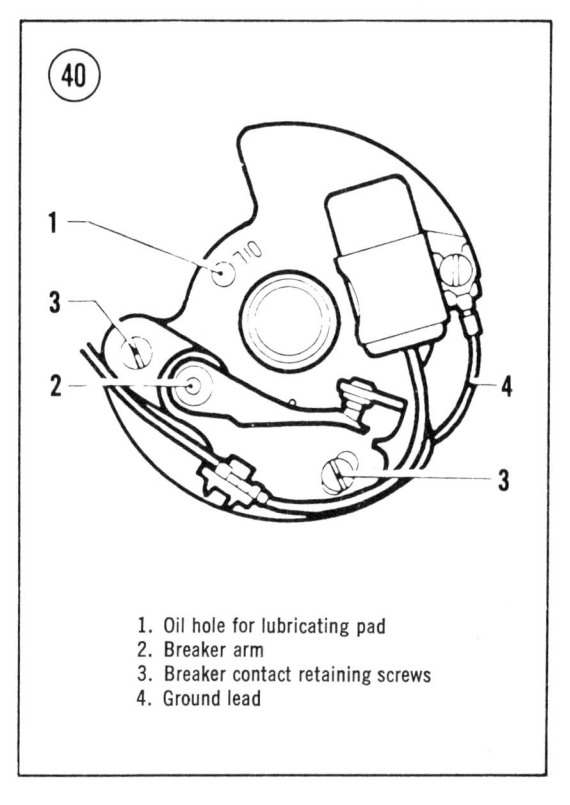

1. Oil hole for lubricating pad
2. Breaker arm
3. Breaker contact retaining screws
4. Ground lead

5. Connect wiring to contact plate on breaker arm. The pressure of the breaker arm leaf spring will hold cable shoes in position.

6. Apply light grease to breaker cam.

Contact Point Adjustment (Saab 99)

1. Crank engine until widest contact point gap is obtained (the heel of the contact arm is lifted to highest position on the distributor cam).

2. Insert screwdriver in the adjusting groove and slot on the fixed breaker contact. Adjust gap

LUBRICATION, MAINTENANCE, AND TUNE-UP

to 0.012-0.016 in. (0.30-0.40mm) on models through 1974; 0.016 in. (0.40mm) for 1975-1976 models.

3. Tighten retaining screws and check gap.

Dwell Angle Adjustment (Saab 99)

1. Connect dwell angle meter. With ignition in the ON position, crank engine over with starter. Adjust dwell angle to 40±2 degrees by adjusting the fixed breaker contact. Tighten retaining screw and recheck gap.

2. The relationship between gap A and dwell angle S is illustrated in Figure 37 (see page 25). The shaded point illustration shows the gap at the widest position. Set the new breaker points for the narrower dwell angle illustrated as the dwell angle will increase as the points wear.

3. Soak the lubricating felt in the distributor shaft with SAE 40 oil.

4. Set the rotor in place making sure that its square locating stud engages the distributor shaft. Set the distributor cap in place and secure it with the 2 retaining clips.

Ignition Timing (Saab 99)

1. Connect a timing light and disconnect the vacuum hoses.

2. With engine idling, check the ignition timing. Adjust if necessary by loosening the retaining clamp and turning the distributor housing to the left (to advance the ignition), or to the right (to retard it).

3. Disconnect the timing light and reconnect vacuum hoses. Adjust engine idling speed.

> NOTE: *Refer to Table 1 (see page 29) for ignition timing and engine idling specifications.*

Fuel System

Due to strict government regulations regarding exhaust emissions it is recommended that adjustments to the carburetor or fuel injector is left to your dealer. He has the specialized equipment and latest service data to keep your exhaust emissions within legal limits.

Throttle Control

All throttle control bearings are accessible from the engine compartment. Lubricate every 6,000 miles. (From 1972 models on, only the wire bearing should be oiled.)

Carburetor Oil Damper

The oil level should be high enough so that the damping piston dips into the oil before the thread of the plastic screw cap engages. Use same oil for the damper as for the engine.

Air Filters

The filter insert is made of a special grade of paper and must not be washed or wetted. The only form of cleaning between replacement intervals is that it is permitted to tap the filter lightly against a hard object to shake loose dust and other debris. Compressed air can be used to finish the cleaning operation. Replace filter at regular tune-up intervals.

The filter for 99 carburetor models is shown in **Figure 41**; for 99 fuel injection models in **Figure 42**. Replace filter every 15,000 miles (more often if car is driven under particularly dusty conditions). The filter for the Saab 95, 96, and Sonett V4 models is shown in **Figure 43**. Replace the air filter insert every 12,000 miles (more often if car is driven under particularly dusty conditions).

Fuel Filter

On carburetor models the fuel pump is located on the left-hand side of the engine and is

28 CHAPTER TWO

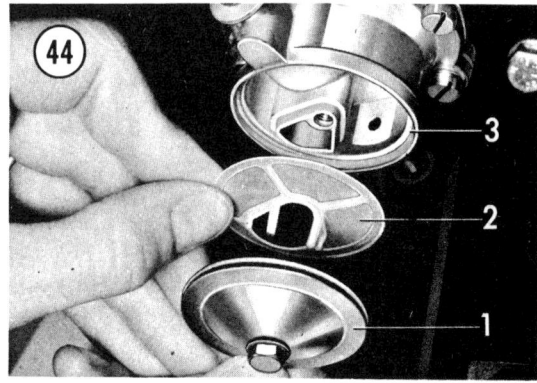

1. Cover with gasket   2. Filter   3. Pump body

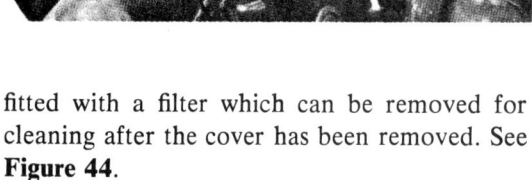

fitted with a filter which can be removed for cleaning after the cover has been removed. See **Figure 44**.

CAUTION
When reassembling the fuel filter be certain that the gasket between the filter and the cover is positioned correctly.

On fuel injection models the fuel pump is situated behind the fuel tank along with a separate fuel filter. (A lid in the trunk provides access to the filter.) See **Figures 45 and 46**.

Clean the filter every 7,500 miles; replace every 15,000 miles.

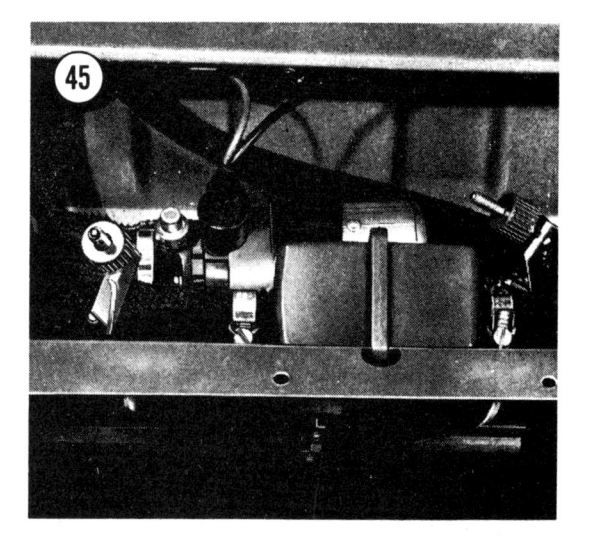

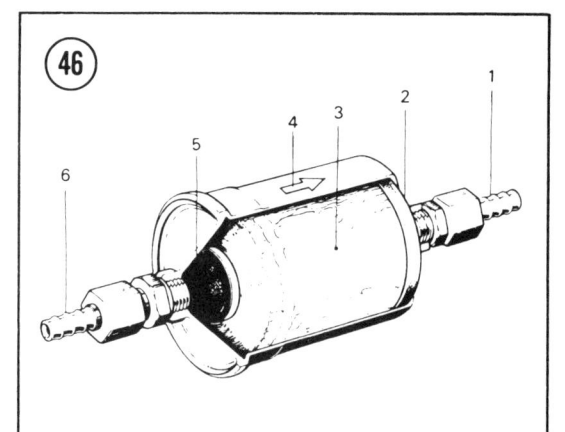

FUEL FILTER

1. Outlet
2. Nylon strainer
3. Paper element
4. Arrow marking cross flow direction
5. Rubber cone
6. Inlet

LUBRICATION, MAINTENANCE, AND TUNE-UP

Table 1 TUNE-UP SPECIFICATIONS

V4 Engine

Firing order	1-3-4-2
Spark plug gap	0.024-0.028 in. (0.6-0.7mm)
Idle speed	
Saab 95/96	800 rpm
Saab Sonett	900 rpm
Contact breaker gap	0.016 in. (0.4mm)
Dwell angle	50° ± 2°
Valve clearance	
Inlet	0.014 in. (0.35mm)
Exhaust	0.016 in. (0.40m)
Ignition timing	
Saab 95/96 (through 1970)	6° BTDC @ 800 rpm (vacuum hose disconnected)
Saab 95/96 (1971-1973)	3° BDTC @ 800 rpm (vacuum hose disconnected)
Saab Sonett	3° BTDC @ 900 rpm (vacuum hose disconnected)

Inline-4 Engine

Firing order	1-3-4-2
Spark plug gap	
1969-1972	0.025 in. (0.6mm)
1973	0.025-0.030 in. (0.6-0.7mm)
1974-1976	0.024-0.028 in. (0.6-0.7mm)
Idle speed	
1969-1972	800-850 rpm
1973-1974 (manual transmission)	850 rpm
1973-1974 (automatic transmission)	800 rpm
1975-1976 (manual and automatic)	875 ± 50 rpm
Contact breaker gap	
1969-1974	0.012-0.016 in. (0.3-0.4mm)
1975-1976	0.016 in. (0.4mm)
Dwell angle	
1969-1974	40° ± 2°
1975-1976	50° ± 2°
Valve clearance	
Intake	0.006-0.012 in. (0.15-0.30mm)
Exhaust	0.014-0.020 in. (0.35-0.50mm)
Ignition timing	
1972 carburetor engine	9° BTDC
1973 carburetor engine	14° BTDC
1974 carburetor engine	4° BTDC
1972 injected engine	5° BTDC
1973 injected engine	8° BTDC
1974 injected engine	4° BTDC @ 800 rpm (vacuum hose plugged)
1975-1976 injected California engines	12° BTDC @ 800 rpm (vacuum hose plugged)
1975-1976 injected cars for U.S., except California	14° BTDC @ 800 rpm (vacuum hose plugged)

CHAPTER THREE

TROUBLESHOOTING

Troubleshooting mechanical problems can be relatively simple if you use orderly procedures and keep a few basic principles in mind.

The troubleshooting procedures in this chapter analyze typical symptoms, and show logical methods of isolating causes. These are not the only methods. There may be several ways to solve a problem, but only a systematic, methodical approach can guarantee success.

Gather as many symptoms together as possible to aid in diagnosis. Note whether the engine lost power gradually or all at once, what color smoke (if any) came from the exhaust, and so on. After the symptoms are defined, areas which could cause the problems are tested and analyzed. Guessing at the cause of a problem may eventually provide the solution, but it can easily lead to frustration, wasted time, and a series of expensive, unnecessary parts replacements.

You don't need exotic, complicated test gear to determine whether repairs can be made at home. A few simple checks could save a large repair bill and time lost while the engine sits in a dealer's service department. On the other hand, be realistic and don't attempt repairs beyond your abilities. Service departments charge heavily to correct other people's mistakes.

The following are commonly encountered problems.

STARTER

Starter system troubles are relatively easy to isolate. The following are common symptoms.

Engine Cranks Very Slowly or Not at All

Turn on the headlights. If the lights are very dim, the battery or connecting wires most likely are at fault. Check battery condition with hydrometer. Check wiring for breaks, shorts, and dirty connections. If the battery and wires are all right, turn the headlights on and crank the engine. If the lights dim drastically, the starter is probably shorted to ground.

If the lights remain bright or dim slightly when cranking, the trouble may be in the starter, solenoid, or wiring. To isolate the trouble, short the 2 large solenoid terminals together (not to ground); if the starter cranks normally, check the solenoid and wiring to the ignition switch. If the starter still fails to crank properly, remove and test it and overhaul as required.

Starter Turns, but Does Not Engage With Flywheel

Usually caused by defective starter pinion gear in starter or solenoid shifting fork. The pinion gear teeth, flywheel ring gear teeth, or both may be worn or stripped, preventing proper meshing.

TROUBLESHOOTING

Starter Engages, but Will Not Disengage When Ignition Switch Is Released

Usually caused by defective solenoid, but occasionally the pinion may jam on the flywheel. The pinion can be temporarily freed by rocking the car in fourth gear.

Loud Grinding Noises When Starter Runs

The teeth on the pinion and flywheel ring gears are not meshing properly or the overrunning clutch mechanism is defective. Remove the starter and examine the gears for damage.

CHARGING SYSTEM

Charging system troubles may be in the alternator (generator), voltage regulator, or fan belt. The following symptoms are typical.

Dashboard Indicator Shows Continuous Discharge

This usually means battery charging is not taking place. Check fan belt tension. Check battery condition with hydrometer and electrical connections in the charging system. Finally, check the alternator (generator) and/or voltage regulator.

Dashboard Indicator Shows Intermittent Discharge

Check fan belt tension and electrical connections. Trouble may be traced to defective alternator or generator parts, as described in Chapter Eight.

Battery Requires Frequent Addition of Water or Lamps Require Frequent Replacement

Alternator or generator is overcharging the battery or the voltage regulator output is faulty.

Excessive Noise From Alternator (Generator)

Check for loose mountings and/or worn bearing. Check condition of belt.

ENGINE

These procedures assume the starter cranks the engine normally. If not, refer to the *Starter Troubleshooting* section of this chapter.

Engine Won't Start

Could be caused by the ignition or fuel system. First, check to make sure the car has fuel in the fuel tank. Secondly, determine if high voltage to the spark plug occurs. To do this, disconnect one of the spark plug wires. Hold the exposed wire terminal about ¼ to ½ inch from ground (any metal in the engine compartment) with an insulated screwdriver. Crank the engine. If sparks don't jump to ground or the sparks are very weak, the trouble is probably in the ignition system. If sparks occur properly, the trouble is probably in the fuel system. Check as follows:

1. Check the fuse for the electric fuel pump (when so equipped). Scrape any oxide deposits away by rotating the fuse several times in its holder. The electric pump can generally be heard for a second or two when the ignition is switched on before stopping automatically.

2. Check the fuel injection system (when so equipped) to see if the cable terminals are plugged into the pressure transmitter (located forward on the left wheel housing). Also check the terminals on the coolant temperature transmitter (under the intake manifold) and the starter motor.

NOTE: *These terminals fit one way only and must not be pushed in by force.*

3. Check the wiring connection to the electric fuel pump (when so equipped). The pump is accessible through an access plate in the floor of the trunk.

4. Check the fuel system for loose hoses.

5. Check the fuel injection system (when so equipped) by turning the ignition switch to K. Open the hood and work the throttle control up and down. You should be able to hear a clicking sound from two of the injection valves. (To cut the other two injector valves in, the engine must be cranked one revolution.)

Engine Misses Steadily

Using a heavily insulated tool, remove one spark plug wire at a time and ground the wire. If engine miss increases, that cylinder is working properly. Reconnect the wire and check the other spark plugs. When a wire is disconnected and engine miss remains the same, that cylinder is not firing. Check spark as described above. If no spark occurs for one cylinder only, check distributor cap, wire, and spark plug. If spark occurs properly, check compression and intake manifold vacuum.

Engine Misses Erratically at All Speeds

Intermittent trouble can be difficult to find. It could be in the ignition system, exhaust system, or fuel system. Follow troubleshooting procedures for these systems to isolate trouble.

Engine Misses at Idle Only

Trouble could be ignition or carburetor idle adjustment. Check idle mixture adjustment and check for restrictions in carburetor idle circuit.

Engine Misses at High Speed Only

Trouble is in the fuel or ignition system. Check accelerator pump operation, fuel pump delivery, fuel lines, etc. Check the spark plugs and wires.

Low Performance at All Speeds, Poor Acceleration

Trouble is usually in ignition or fuel system. Tune-up engine as described in Chapter Two.

Excessive Fuel Consumption

Could be caused by a number of seemingly unrelated factors. Check for clutch slippage, brake drag, defective wheel bearings, poor front end alignment, faulty ignition, leaks in gas tank or lines, and carburetor condition.

Low Oil Pressure Indicated by Oil Pressure Indicator

If the oil pressure indicator lights with the engine running, stop the engine immediately. Coast to a stop with the clutch disengaged. The trouble may be caused by low oil level, blockage in an oil line, defective oil pump, overheated engine, or defective pressure sending unit. Check the oil level and fan belt tension. Check for a shorted oil pressure sending unit with an ohmmeter or replace with a new unit. Remove and clean the oil pressure relief valve. Do not start the engine until you know why the low indication was given and are sure the problem has been corrected.

Engine Overheats

Usually caused by trouble in the cooling system. Check level of coolant in radiator, condition and tension of the fan belt, and water hoses for leaks and loose connections. Can also be caused by late ignition or valve timing.

Engine Stalls as It Warms Up

The choke may be stuck closed, the manifold heat control valve may be stuck, the engine idle speed may be set too low, or the emission control system valves may be defective. Low speed carburetor idle circuit may be faulty.

Engine Stalls After High-Speed Driving

Vapor lock within the fuel lines caused by an overheated engine is the usual cause. Inspect and service the cooling system. If the trouble persists, changing to a different fuel or shielding the fuel line from engine heat may be helpful.

Engine Backfires

Several causes are possible; ignition timing, overheating, excessive carbon buildup in combustion chambers, worn ignition points, wrong heat range spark plugs, hot or sticking valves, and/or defective distributor cap.

Smoky Exhaust

Blue smoke indicates excessive oil consumption usually caused by worn rings. Black smoke indicates an excessively rich fuel mixture.

Excessive Oil Consumption

Can be caused by external leaks through broken seals or gaskets, or by burning oil in the combustion chambers. Check the oil pan and the

TROUBLESHOOTING

front and rear of the engine for oil leaks. If oil is not leaking externally, valve stem clearance may be excessive, piston rings may be worn, cylinder walls may be scored, rod bearings may be worn, or carburetor vacuum pump diaphragm may be ruptured.

Noisy Engine

1. *Regular clicking sound*—valves out of adjustment or defective valve lifters.

2. *Ping or chatter on load or acceleration*—spark knock due to low octane fuel, carbon buildup, overly advanced ignition timing, and causes mentioned under engine backfire.

3. *Light knock or pound with engine not under load*—worn connecting rod bearings, misaligned piston pin, and/or lack of engine oil.

4. *Light metallic double knock, usually heard during idle*—worn or loose piston pin or bushing and/or lack of oil.

5. *Chattering or rattling during acceleration*—worn rings or cylinder walls, low ring tension, and/or broken rings.

6. *Hollow, bell-like muffled sound when engine is cold*—piston slap due to worn pistons or cylinder walls, collapsed piston skirts, excessive clearances, misaligned connecting rods, and/or lack of oil.

7. *Dull, heavy, metallic knock under load or acceleration, especially when cold*—regular noise indicates worn main bearings; irregular noise, worn thrust bearings.

IGNITION SYSTEM

The following procedures assume the battery is in good enough condition to crank the engine normally.

No Spark to One Plug

The only causes are defective distributor cap, rotor, or spark plug wire. Examine the distributor cap for moisture, dirt, carbon tracking caused by flashover, and cracks. Check condition of rotor and spark plug wire for breaks and loose connectors.

No Spark to Any Plug

This could indicate trouble in the primary or secondary ignition circuits. First, remove the coil wire from the center post of the distributor. Hold the wire end about ¼ inch from ground with an insulated screwdriver. Crank the engine. If sparks are produced, the trouble is in the rotor or distributor cap. Remove the cap and check for burns, moisture, dirt, carbon tracking, cracks, etc. Check rotor for excessive burning, pitting, and cracks.

If the coil does not produce any spark, check the secondary wire for a break. If the wire is good, turn the engine over so the breaker points are open. Check the points for excessive gap, burning, pitting, and loose connections. With the points open, check voltage from the coil to ground with a voltmeter or test lamp. If voltage is present, the coil is probably defective. Have it checked or substitute a coil known to be good.

If voltage is not present, check wire connections to the coil and distributor. Disconnect wire leading from the coil to the distributor and measure from the coil terminal to ground. If voltage is present, the distributor is shorted. Examine breaker points and connecting wires carefully. If voltage is still not present, measure the other coil terminal. Voltage on the other terminal indicates a defective coil. No voltage indicates a broken coil-to-battery wire.

Weak Spark

If the spark is so small it cannot jump from the wire to ground, check the battery. Other causes are defective breaker points, condenser, incorrect point gap, dirty or loose connection in the primary circuit, or dirty or burned rotor or distributor. Check for worn cam lobes on distributor shaft.

Missing

This is usually caused by fouled or damaged plugs, plugs of the wrong heat range, or incorrect plug gap.

FUEL SYSTEM

Fuel system troubles must be isolated to the carburetor, fuel pump, or fuel lines. The following procedures assume the ignition system has been checked and is in proper working order.

Engine Will Not Start

First, determine that fuel is being delivered to the carburetor or fuel injectors. If it is, check the carburetor or fuel injectors and choke system for dirt and/or defects. If fuel is not delivered, the trouble is either a defective fuel pump or blockage in fuel line.

Engine Runs at Fast Idle

Misadjustment of fast idle screw or defective carburetor.

EXHAUST EMISSION CONTROL

Failure of the exhaust emission control system to maintain exhaust emissions within acceptable limits is usually due to defective carburetor, general engine condition, or defective exhaust control valves. Generally, if defects are suspected in the emission control system, refer testing and service to your dealer.

CLUTCH

Several clutch troubles may be experienced. Usually the trouble is quite obvious and will fall into one of the following categories:
1. Slipping, chattering, or grabbing when engaging.
2. Spinning or dragging when disengaged.
3. Clutch noises, clutch pedal pulsations, and rapid clutch disc facing wear.

Clutch Slips While Engaged

Improper adjustment of clutch linkage, weak or broken pressure springs, worn friction disc facings, defective flywheel, and grease, dirt, or oil on clutch disc.

Clutch Chatters or Grabs When Engaging

Usually caused by misadjustment of clutch linkage, defective release bearing, dirt or grease on clutch/flywheel/pressure plate mating surfaces, or broken and/or worn clutch parts.

Clutch Spins or Drags When Disengaged

The clutch disc normally spins briefly after disengagement from the flywheel and pressure plate and takes a moment to come to rest. This sound should not be confused with drag. Drag is caused by the friction disc not being fully released from the flywheel or pressure plate as the clutch pedal is depressed. The trouble can be caused by clutch linkage misadjustments or defective or worn clutch parts.

Clutch Noises

Clutch noises are usually most noticeable when the engine is idling. First, note whether the noise is heard when the clutch is engaged or disengaged. Clutch noises when engaged could be due to a loose clutch disc hub, loose friction disc springs, and misalignment or looseness of engine or transmission mountings. When disengaged, noise can be due to a worn release bearing, defective pilot bearing, or misaligned release lever and clutch linkage.

Clutch Pedal Pulsates

Usually noticed when slight pressure is applied to the clutch pedal with the engine running. As pedal pressure is increased, the pulsation stops. Possible causes include misalignment of engine and transmission, bent crankshaft flange, distortion or shifting of clutch housing, release lever misalignment, warped friction disc facing, and/or damaged pressure plate and flywheel.

Rapid Friction Disc Facing Wear

This trouble is caused by any condition that permits slippage between facing and the flywheel or pressure plate. Probable causes are "riding" the clutch, slow releasing of the clutch after disengagement, weak or broken pressure springs, pedal linkage misadjustment, and warped clutch disc or pressure plate.

TRANSMISSION

Hard Starting Into Gear

Common causes are failure of clutch to release, misadjustment of linkage, linkage in need of lubrication, bent shifter forks, sliding gear

TROUBLESHOOTING

tightness on shaft splines, damaged sliding gear teeth, and damaged synchronizer.

Transmission Sticks in Gear

May be caused by clutch not releasing, gearshift linkage out of adjustment, linkage needing lubrication, detent ball stuck, or gears tight on shaft splines.

Transmission Slips Out of Gear

Gearshift linkage out of adjustment, misalignment between engine and transmission, excessive main shaft end play, worn gear teeth, insufficient shift-lever spring tension, worn bearings, or defective synchronizer. Gear may be loose on the main shaft.

No Power Through Transmission

May be caused by clutch slippage, stripped gear teeth, damaged shifter fork linkage, broken gear or shaft, and stripped drive key.

Transmission Noisy in Neutral

Transmission misaligned, bearings worn or dry, gears worn, countershaft worn or bent, and excessive countershaft end play.

Transmission Noisy in Gear

Defective clutch disc, worn bearings, loose gears, worn gear teeth, and faults listed above.

Gears Clash During Shifting

Caused by the clutch not releasing, defective synchronizer, or gears sticking on main shaft.

Oil Leaks

Most common causes are foaming due to wrong lubricant, lubricant level too high, broken gaskets, damaged oil seals, loose drain plug, and cracked transmission case.

DIFFERENTIAL

Usually, it is noise that draws attention to trouble in the differential. Some clue as to cause of trouble may be gained by noting whether the noise is a hum, growl, or knock; whether it is produced when the car is accelerating under load or coasting; and whether it is heard when the car is going straight or making a turn.

Noise During Acceleration: May be caused by shortage of lubricant, incorrect tooth contact between drive gears and drive pinion, damaged or misadjusted bearings in axles or side bearings, or damaged gears.

Noise During Coasting: May be caused by incorrect backlash between drive gear and drive pinion gear or incorrect adjustment of drive pinion bearing.

Noise During Turn: This noise is usually caused by loose or worn axle shaft bearing, pinion gears too tight on shaft, side gear jammed in differential case, or worn side gear thrust washer and pinion thrust washer.

Broken Differential Parts: Breaking of differential parts can be caused by insufficient lubricant, improper use of clutch, excessive loading, misadjusted bearings and gears, excessive backlash, damage to axle case, or loose bolts.

Humming Noise: A humming noise in the differential is often caused by improper drive pinion or ring gear adjustment that prevents normal tooth contact between gears. If ignored, rapid tooth wear will take place and the noise will become more like a growl. Repair as soon as the humming is heard so that new gears will not be required. Tire noise will vary considerably, depending on the type of road surface. Differential noises will be the same regardless of road surface. If noises are heard, listen carefully to the noise over different road surfaces to help isolate the problem.

BRAKE

Brake Pedal Goes to Floor

Worn linings or pads, air in the hydraulic system, leaky brake lines, leaky wheel cylinders, or leaky or worn master cylinder may be the cause. Check for leaks and worn brake linings or pads. Bleed and adjust brakes. Rebuild wheel cylinders, calipers, and/or master cylinder.

Spongy Pedal

Usually caused by air in the brake hydraulic system. Bleed and adjust brakes.

Brakes Pull

Check brake adjustment and wear on linings and disc pads. Check for contaminated linings, leaky wheel cylinders, loose calipers, lines, or hoses. Check front end alignment and look for suspension damage such as broken front or rear springs and shock absorbers. Tires also affect braking; check tire pressures and condition.

Brakes Squeal or Chatter

Check brake shoe and pad lining thickness and brake drum and rotor condition. Ensure that shoes are not loose. Clean away all dirt on shoes, drums, rotors, and pads.

Brakes Drag

Check brake adjustment, including handbrake. Check for broken or weak shoe return springs, swollen rubber parts due to improper brake fluid or contamination. Check for defective master cylinder or brake servo unit.

Hard Pedal

Check brake linings and pads for contamination. Check for brake line restrictions.

High Speed Fade

Check for distorted or out-of-round drums and rotors and contaminated linings or pads.

Pulsating Pedal

Check for distorted or out-of-round brake drums or rotors. Check for excessive rotor runout.

COOLING SYSTEM

Engine Overheats

May be caused by insufficient coolant, loose fan belt, defective fan belt, defective thermostat, defective water pump, clogged water lines and passages, incorrect ignition timing, and/or defective or loose hoses. Inspect radiator and all parts for leaks.

Engine Does Not Warm Up

Usually caused by defective thermostat or extremely cold weather.

Loss of Coolant

Radiator leaks, loose or defective hoses, defective water pump, leaks in cylinder head gasket, cracked cylinder head or engine block, or defective radiator cap may be the cause.

Noisy Cooling System

Usually caused by defective water pump bearings, loose or bent fan blades, or a defective fan belt.

STEERING AND SUSPENSION

Trouble in the suspension or steering is evident when any of the following occur:
   a. Hard steering
   b. Car pulls to one side
   c. Car wanders
   d. Front wheels wobble
   e. Excessive play in steering
   f. Abnormal tire wear

Unusual steering, pulling, or wandering is usually caused by bent or misaligned suspension parts. If the trouble seems to be excessive play, check the wheel bearing adjustment first. Next, check steering freeplay and king pins or balljoints. Finally, check tie rod ends for looseness by shaking each wheel.

Abnormal tire wear should always be analyzed to determine the cause. The most common are incorrect tire pressure, improper driving, overloading, and incorrect wheel alignment. **Figure 1** (next page) identifies wear patterns and their most probable causes.

Wheel Balancing

All 4 wheels and tires must be in balance along 2 axes. To be in static balance (**Figure 2**), weight must be evenly distributed around the

TROUBLESHOOTING

Underinflation—Worn more on sides than in center.

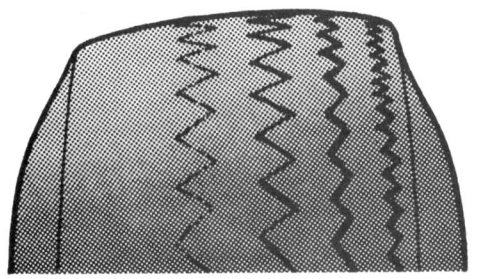

Wheel Alignment—Worn more on one side than the other. Edges of tread feathered.

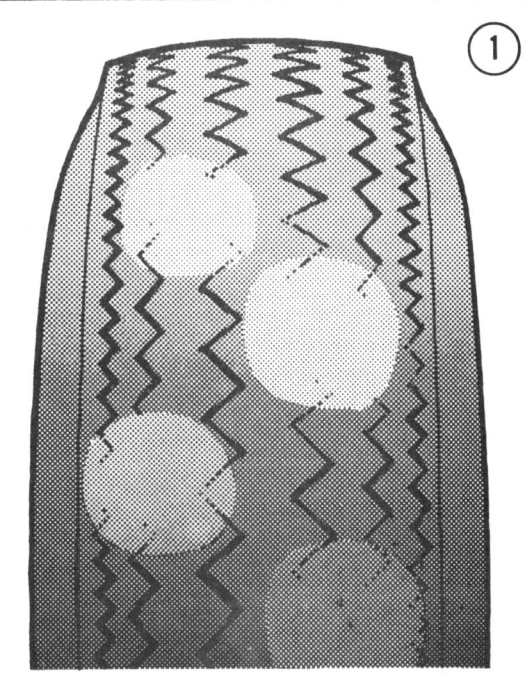

Road Abrasion—Rough wear on entire tire or in patches.

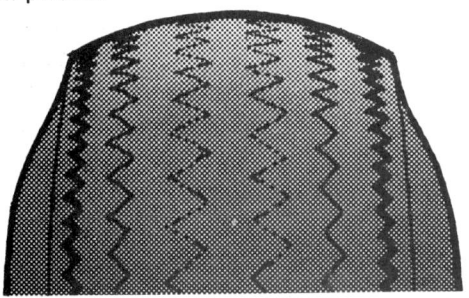

Overinflation—Worn more in center than on sides.

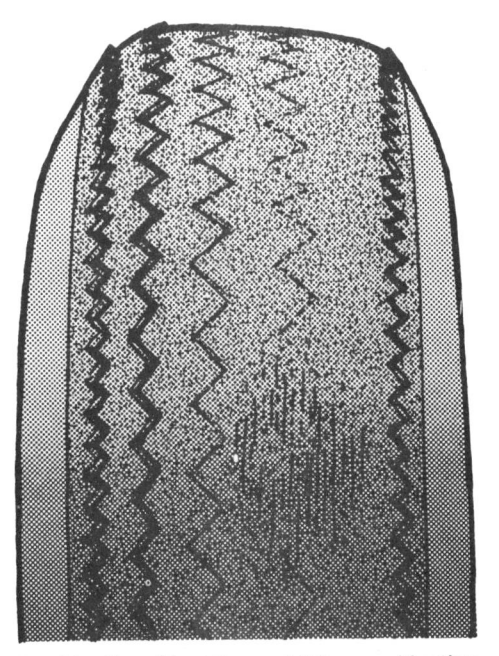

Wheel Balance — Scalloped edges indicate wheel wobble or tramp due to wheel unbalance.

Combination—Most tires exhibit a combination of the above. This tire was overinflated (center worn) and the toe-in was incorrect (feathering). The driver cornered hard at high speed (feathering, rounded shoulders) and braked rapidly (worn spots). The scaly roughness indicates a rough road surface.

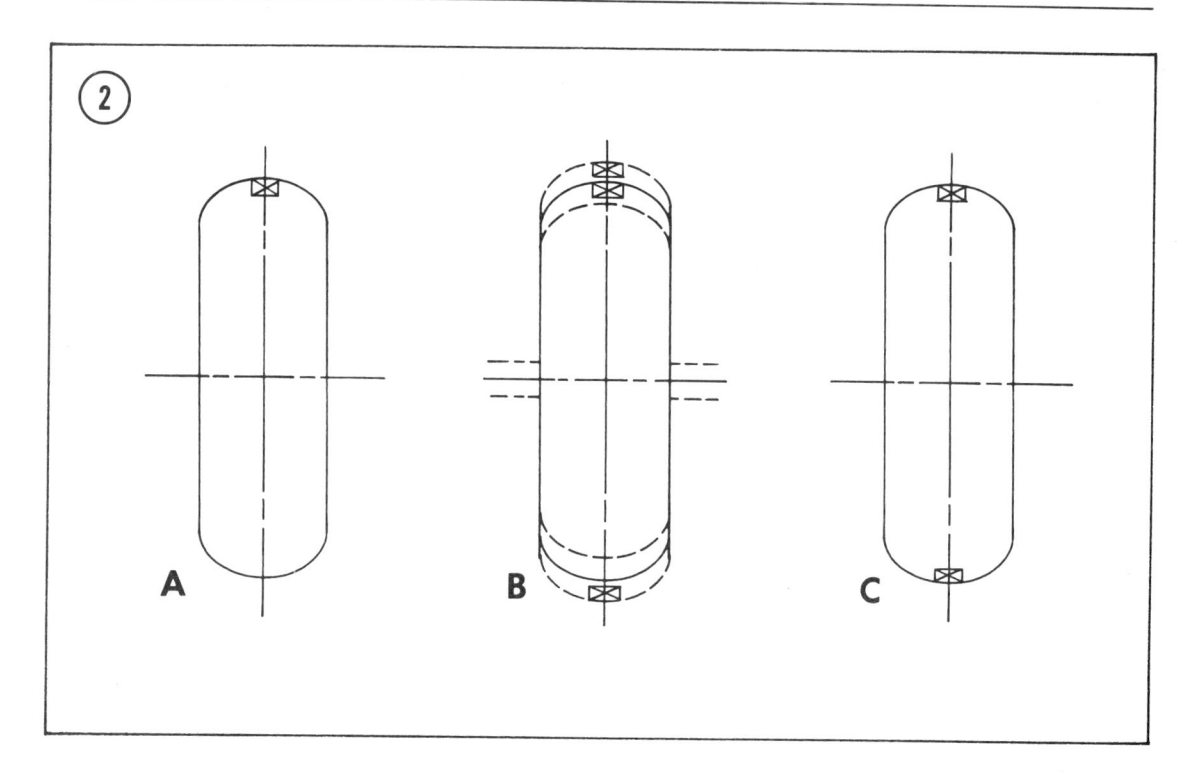

axis of rotation. (A) shows a statically unbalanced wheel. (B) shows the result — wheel tramp or hopping. (C) shows proper static balance.

To be in dynamic balance (**Figure 3**), the centerline of weight must coincide with the centerline of the wheel. (A) shows a dynamically unbalanced wheel. (B) shows the result — wheel wobble or shimmy. (C) shows proper dynamic balance.

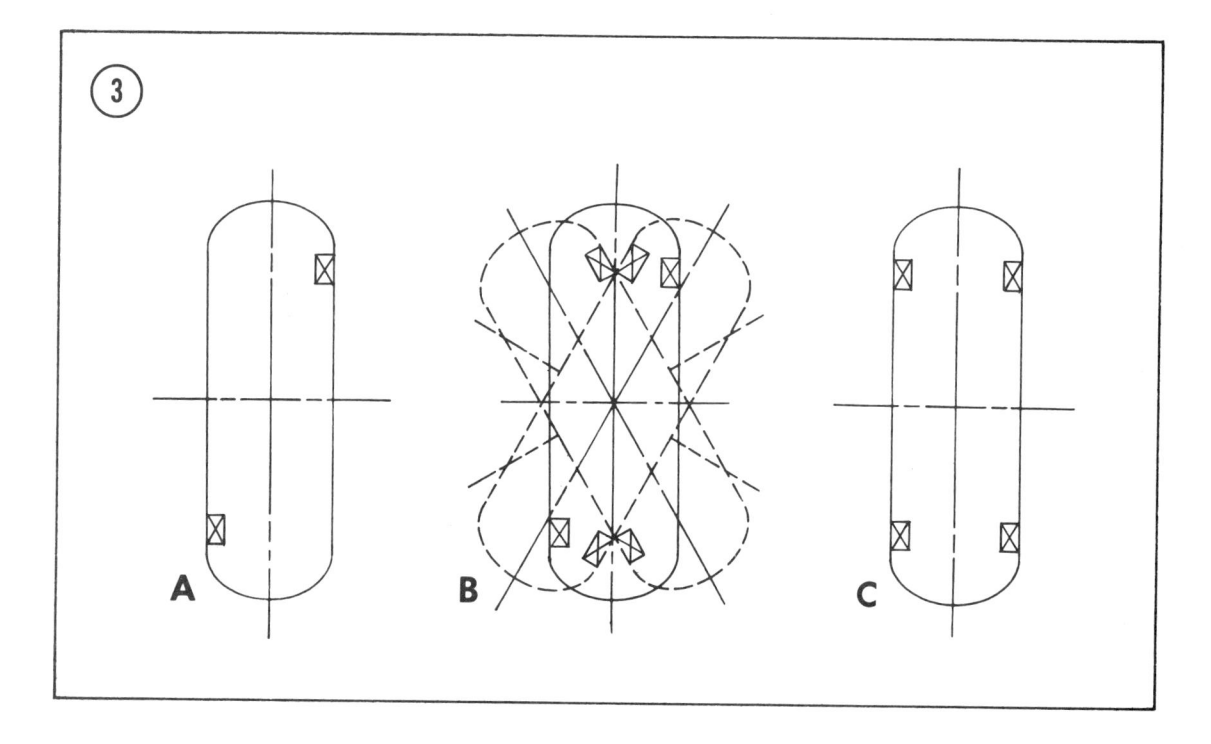

> NOTE: If you own a 1977 or later model, first check the Supplement at the back of the book for any new service information.

CHAPTER FOUR

ENGINE

The engine used in the 95/96 and Sonett is a 4-stroke, 4-cylinder, water-cooled overhead valve unit with the cylinders arranged in a vee configuration, fed by a single downdraft carburetor. See **Figures 1 and 2** for left- and right-hand views.

The 99 engine is a 4-stroke, 4-cylinder, water-cooled overhead camshaft unit with the cylinder arranged inline. Carburetors were used exclusively until 1970 when a Bosch electronic fuel injection system made its appearance. Both systems were used through 1974. The 1975-76 Saabs feature a mechanical fuel injection system (only) by Bosch. **Figures 3 and 4** show left- and right-hand views of the 1.7 and 1.85 fuel injection equipped engines; **Figures 5 and 6**, left- and right-hand views of the 1.7 and 1.85 engines with carburetion; **Figures 7 and 8**, left- and right-hand views of the 2.0 carburetted engine with automatic transmission as used through 1974; **Figures 9 and 10**, left- and right-hand views of the 2.0 fuel injection engine with manual transmission as used through 1974; and **Figures 11 and 12**, left- and right-hand views of the 1975-1976 2.0 engine equipped with fuel injection and automatic transmission.

Engine specifications and torques are given at the end of the chapter (**Tables 1 through 4**).

ENGINE REMOVAL

For major work on the engine and transmission, both must be removed as a unit. Removal of the engine itself is not recommended (and in some instances, not possible).

1. Remove the hood.

2. Disconnect all electrical, fuel, water, oil, vacuum, hydraulic, throttle linkage, exhaust pipes, and battery ground cable.

3. Remove battery.

4. Detach slave cylinder on manual transmission models and hang it up in a convenient, out-of-the-way place.

5. Move the free wheel lever (where applicable) forward to the locked position. Release wire clamp at transmission, and free cable from holder at right-hand differential bearing seat (manual transmission).

6. Drain radiator, engine block, and (where applicable) heater core. Remove all water hoses.

7. Remove any accessories that interfere with the engine removal.

8. Remove radiator.

9. Loosen engine mounts. Jack car up and support with jackstands.

CHAPTER FOUR

①

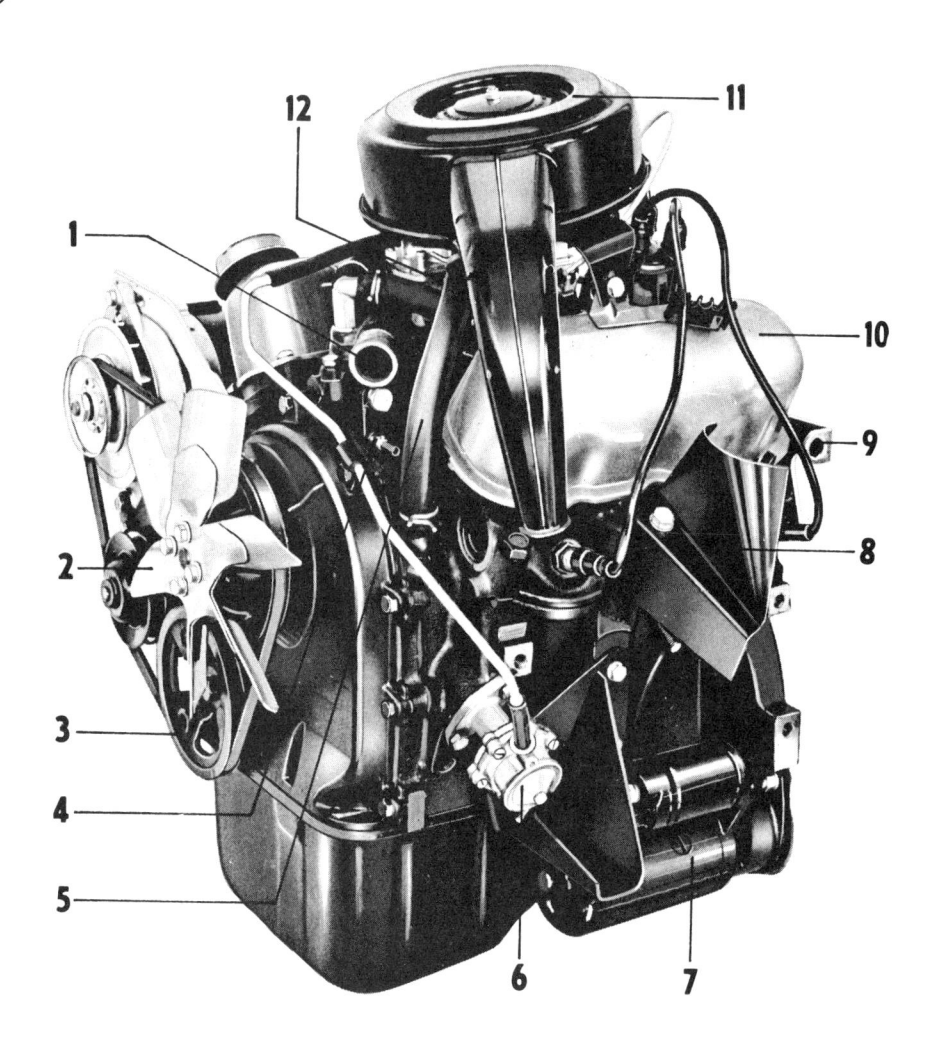

SAAB 95/96 AND SONETT ENGINE
(Left-hand View)

1. Hose connection, upper radiator hose
2. Water pump
3. Balance shaft pulley
4. Temperature transmitter
5. Hose, crankcase ventilation
6. Fuel pump
7. Starter
8. Preheater plate
9. Bracket, engine side stay
10. Valve casing
11. Air filter
12. Carburetor

ENGINE

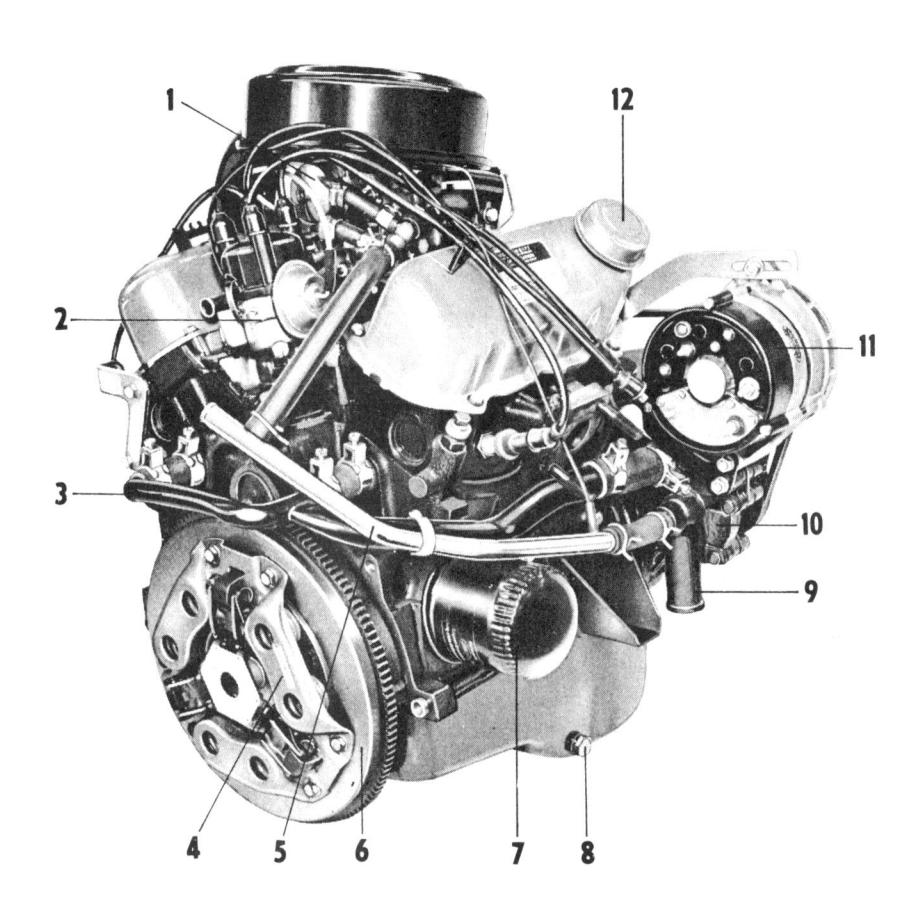

SAAB 95/96 AND SONETT ENGINE
(Right-hand View)

1. Automatic choke
2. Distributor
3. Water distribution pipe
4. Clutch
5. By-pass line
6. Flywheel
7. Oil filter
8. Oil drain plug
9. Hose connection, lower radiator hose
10. Water pump
11. Alternator
12. Oil filler cap

1.7 AND 1.85 INJECTION ENGINE

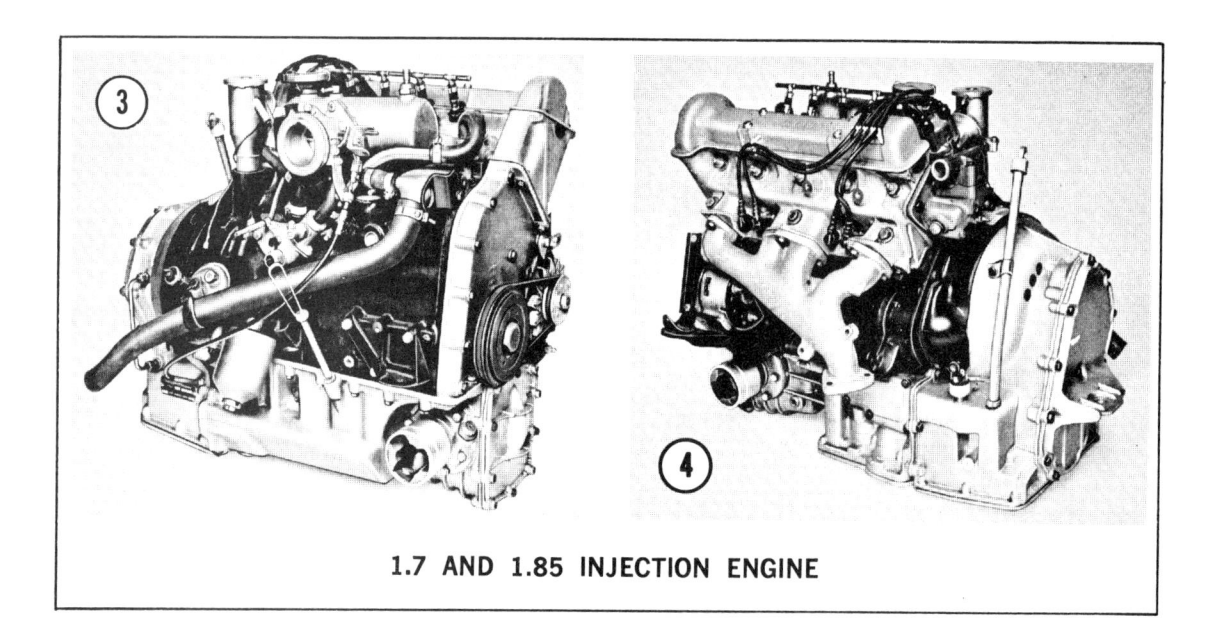

ENGINE

1.7 LITER

1. Air cleaner
2. Oil pressure switch
3. Oil pump
4. Oil filter
5. Oil dipstick
6. Gear control
7. Crankshaft pulley

1.85 LITER

1. Carburetor
2. Crankcase ventilation valve
3. Camshaft cover
4. Alternator
5. Front axle universal joint
6. Engine bracket
7. Transmission
8. Starter
9. Primary gear housing
10. Clutch cover
11. Distributor

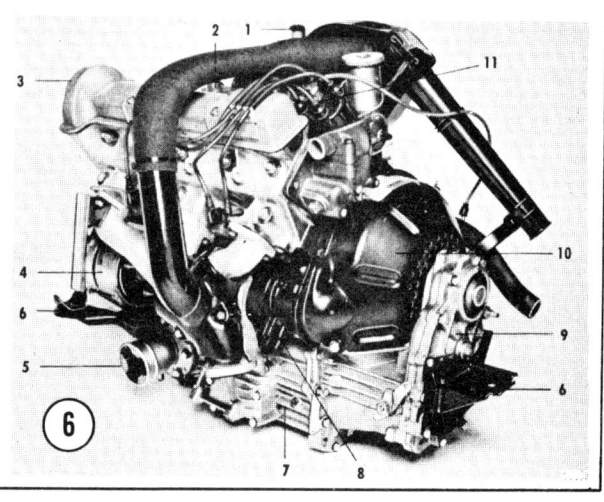

ENGINE

(7)

2.0 CARBURETTED ENGINE
(Automatic Transmission)

(8)

CHAPTER FOUR

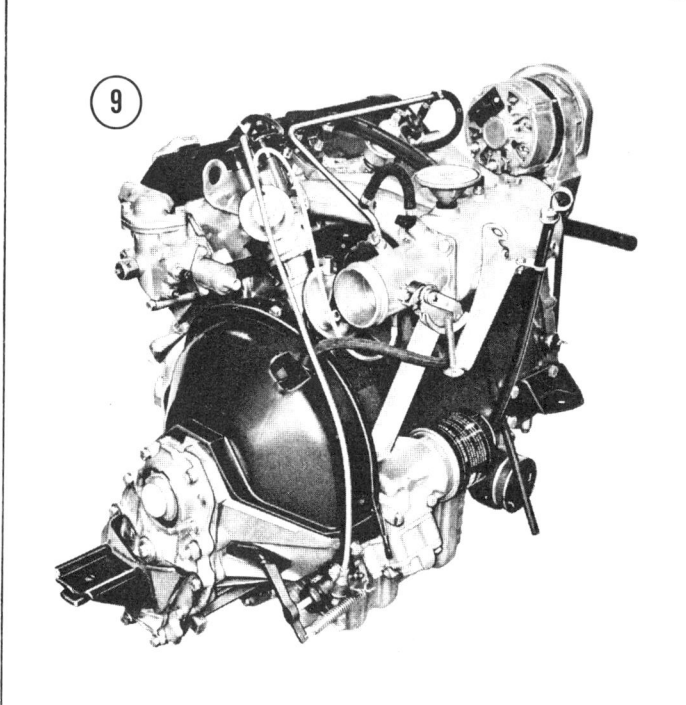

2.0 FUEL INJECTED ENGINE — THROUGH 1974
(Manual Transmission)

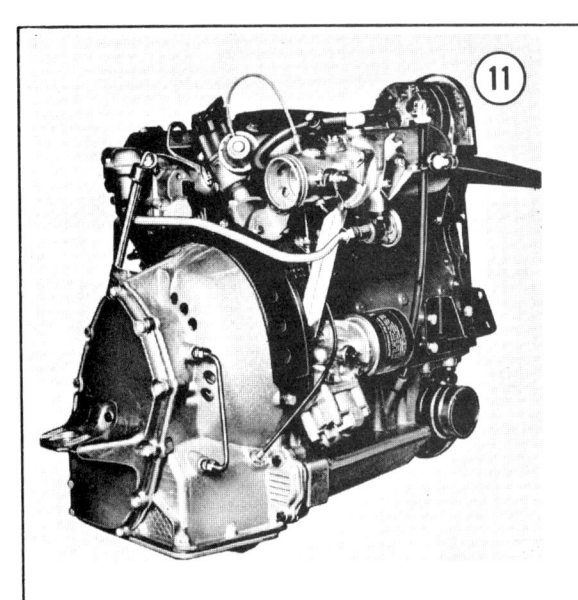

ENGINE

2.0 INJECTION ENGINE WITH AUTOMATIC TRANSMISSION (1975-1976)

10. Raise engine about 2 in. (50mm) with a lifting yoke and separate inner universal joints. See **Figures 13 and 14**. Be sure needle bearings do not separate. Place protective rags over inner universal joints and rubber bellows to prevent dirt from entering.

ENGINE INSTALLATION

1. Be sure inner universal joints are packed with grease.
2. Lower engine into engine compartment far enough to connect starter and alternator cables.
3. Assemble inner universal joints (**Figure 15**).
4. Bolt engine down and reverse all of the removal procedures.

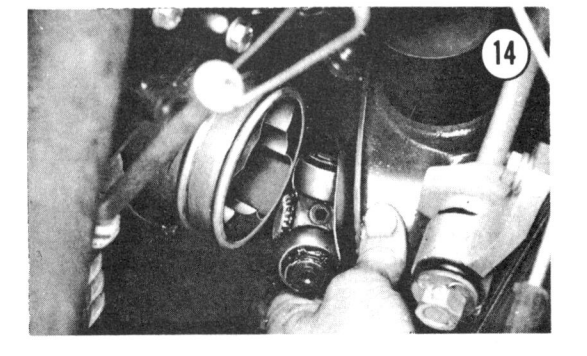

SEPARATING ENGINE AND MANUAL TRANSMISSION

95/96 and Sonett

1. Remove flywheel guard plate from beneath clutch housing.
2. Remove bolts holding engine/transmission together.
3. Remove starter.
4. Separate engine from transmission.
5. To mate engine and transmission reverse preceding steps.

Saab 99

1. Drain engine oil.
2. Remove clutch cover and starter.
3. Remove the alternator and drive belt (1.7 and 1.85 engines only).
4. Withdraw clutch shaft.
5. Remove bolts from release bearing guide sleeve.
6. Back off adjusting bolt and disconnect clutch lever.
7. Remove all bolts in mating flanges of engine and transmission and bolts accessible from under transmission.
8. Lift engine off transmission (**Figure 16**). Remove release bearing guide sleeve.

9. To mate engine and transmission reverse preceding steps.

SEPARATING ENGINE AND AUTOMATIC TRANSMISSION

Saab 99

1. Drain engine oil.
2. Remove bolt inside crankcase (1.7 and 1.85 engines only). This bolt can be reached at an inward angle through the engine oil drain plug opening, using a ½ in. socket and extension. The 1970 model requires a ⅜ in. square grip.
3. Remove flywheel ring gear cover.
4. Remove starter.
5. Remove the alternator and drive belt (1.7 and 1.85 engines only).
6. Disconnect throttle wire from throttle housing (carburetor models).
7. Remove crankcase ventilation device and bolts from mating flanges of engine and transmission.
8. Remove 4 bolts holding flywheel ring gear to torque converter. See **Figure 17**.

9. Turn driver disc so plate angles are horizontal.
10. Lift engine off transmission.
11. Fit torque converter support (tool No. 879025 on models through 1974), No. 8790255 from 1975-1976 models.
12. Mate engine and transmission by reversing preceding steps.

ENGINE DISASSEMBLY/ASSEMBLY

Disassembly (95/96, and Sonett)

1. Install engine on engine stand, if possible.

ENGINE

2. Drain engine oil.

3. Remove distributor cap, ignition cables, distributor vacuum line, and fuel inlet line by applying pressure with a screwdriver behind washers at flexible connections.

4. Remove carburetor.

5. Remove distributor clamping screw and clamp, then remove distributor.

6. Remove fuel pump, pump push rod, and gasket (**Figure 18**). Mark the end of the pump push rod that rests against the camshaft as a guide for reassembly.

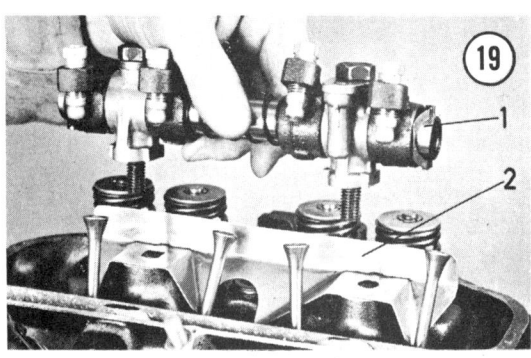

1. Rocker shaft with rocker arms
2. Oil return plate

1. Pump push rod   2. Gasket   3. Fuel pump

7. Remove spark plugs.

8. Remove oil pressure gauge.

9. Remove valve covers. Remove rocker arm assembly by removing bolts and oil return plates (**Figure 19**).

10. Remove push rods (keep in correct order).

11. Remove thermostat housing cap, thermostat, and gasket (**Figure 20**).

12. Remove intake manifold retaining bolts and nuts. (It may be necessary to tap underside of front and rear ends with a plastic or leather

1. Thermostat housing cover
2. Thermostat
3. Gasket

mallet in order to break the seals. Do not pry off with a screwdriver or pry bar).

13. Remove bracket for the side stay.

14. Remove cylinder head bolts. Lift cylinder heads off cylinder block. Inspect head gaskets for damage.

15. Remove tappets with a bent wire (keep in correct order). See **Figure 21**.

16. Remove oil pan retaining bolts, oil pan, and gaskets.

17. Remove balance shaft pulley.

18. Remove transmission cover retaining bolts.

19. Tap rear of water pump with a plastic or leather mallet to loosen transmission cover from intermediate plate. Remove water pump from transmission cover (**Figure 22**).

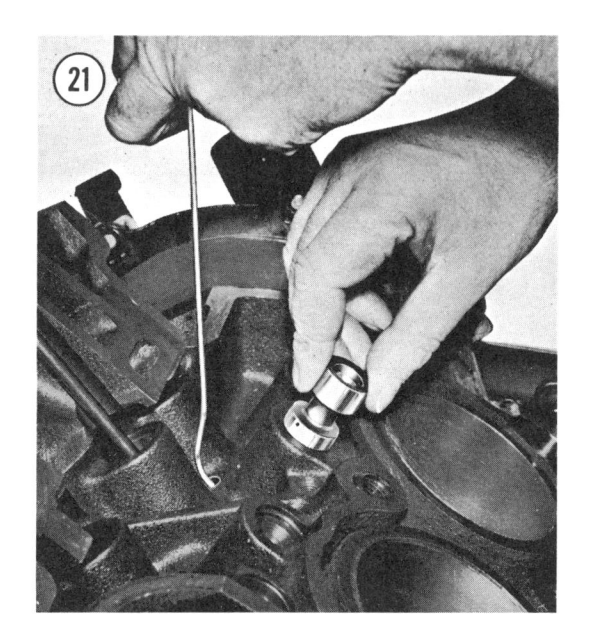

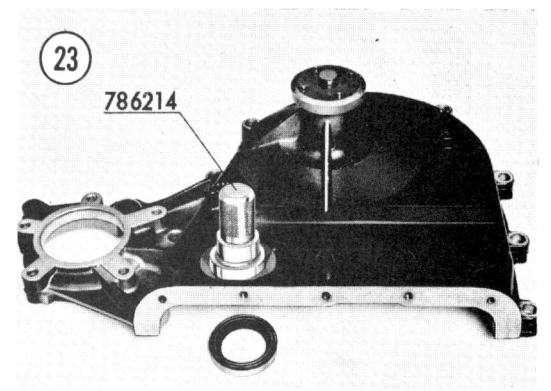

CHAPTER FOUR

20. Remove oil seal for balance shaft from transmission cover with tool No. 786214, or equivalent. See **Figure 23**.

21. Remove oil filter with tool No. 786201 or equivalent (**Figure 24**).

22. Remove oil pump and drive shaft (**Figure 25**).

23. Remove bolt and washer for camshaft drive gear. Remove camshaft gear by hand.

24. Remove balance shaft gear.

25. Remove intermediate plate retaining bolts and plate and gasket (**Figure 26**).

26. Remove camshaft thrust plate, key, and spacer. Pull camshaft out of bearings (toward the front). The bearings have different diameters. Therefore the camshaft can only be removed to the front, even if the rear cover plate has been removed.

27. Remove edges or carbon deposits from upper end of cylinder bores.

ENGINE

(Figure 26)

1. Intermediate plate
2. Retaining bolts, intermediate plate

28. Be sure connecting rods and caps are marked so they can be reinstalled in their original positions (**Figure 27**). Remove nuts and caps. Push pistons with connecting rods out of cylinder bores. Protect crankshaft bearing necks from contact with connecting rod cap screws. The piston and connecting rod with piston pin form an integral unit and must not be further disassembled.

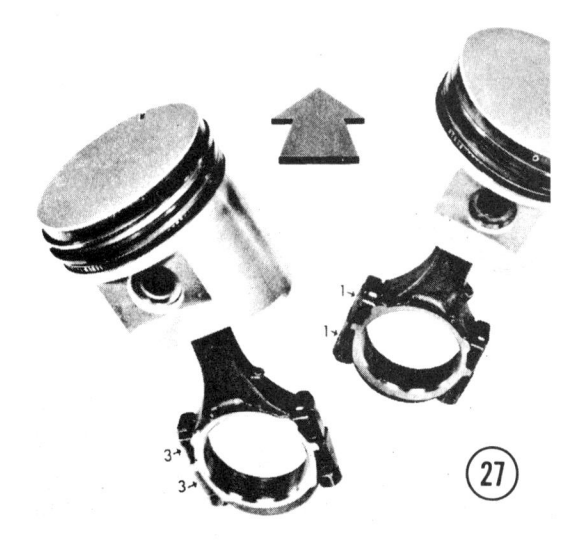

(Figure 27)

29. Remove bearing inserts and caps from connecting rods. Mark them so they can be reinstalled in their original positions. Install caps loosely on connecting rods from which they were removed.

30. Remove crankshaft gear retaining bolt. Remove gear with tool No. 786218 or equivalent (**Figure 28**).

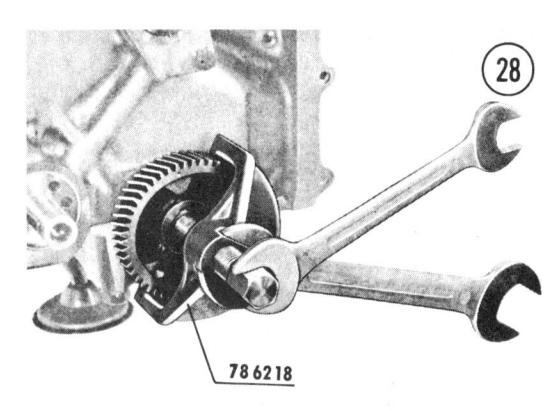

(Figure 28) 786218

31. Mark flywheel and crankshaft flange for ease of installation. Remove flywheel.

32. Drive balance shaft rearward with a plastic or leather mallet until sealing washer is out (**Figure 29**). Remove balance shaft from rear of block.

(Figure 29)

33. Remove main bearing cap bolts. Remove main bearing caps and bearing inserts.
34. Lift crankshaft out of block.
35. Slide oil seal off crankshaft.
36. Remove main bearing inserts and caps from block. Keep in correct order.

Assembly
(95/96, and Sonett)

1. Place all bearing inserts in position in block after coating lightly with engine oil (**Figure 30**).
2. Install crankshaft in bearing seats (**Figure 31**).

CHAPTER FOUR

3. Install main bearing caps over inserted and oiled bearing inserts. Apply a thin coat of sealing compound to rear part of contact surface on rear bearing cap.

> NOTE: *Arrows on center and front main bearing caps must point to the front.*

4. Tighten front and rear bearing main bearing caps to 72 ft.-lb. Install bolts finger-tight for center bearing cap. Refer to Table 1 for torque recommendations at the end of this chapter.

> NOTE: *Don't confuse bolts for cylinder heads and main bearings. They are of same diameter but main bearing bolts are approximately 0.4 in. (10mm) longer.*

5. Press crankshaft forward and pry center bearing cap to the rear. Tighten cap bolts to 72 ft.-lb. while holding crankshaft forward (**Figure 32**).

6. Lubricate inner diameter of new crankshaft seal with engine oil and push seal onto tool No. 786217 or equivalent (**Figure 33**). Drive it into main bearing until it bottoms out.

7. Fit piston rings into cylinder bore as shown in **Figure 34**, one by one. Position the ring in the bore, in the proper attitude by pushing it down into the bore with a piston turned upside down. Remove the piston and measure the piston ring gap with a feeler gauge. The gap should be 0.250-0.500mm (upper and lower compression rings) and 0.380-1.40mm for the oil control ring. If the gap is too small the ring must be trimmed with a special file. The above measurement is on a new or rebored cylinder. When fitting piston rings in a worn cylinder bore the ring gap must be measured in the lower reverse position, as the bore has the smallest diameter at this point.

8. Install new connecting rod bolts (this should be done every time the crankshaft has been disassembled).

9. Coat pistons, rings, and cylinder bores with engine oil. Place piston rings as follows: oil control ring center spring gap 180 degrees from

ENGINE

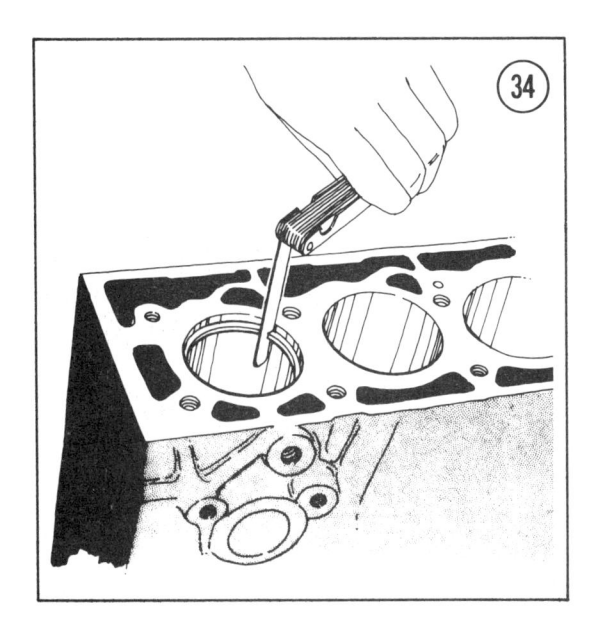

51

mark on top of piston; oil segments with gaps staggered 1 in. (25mm) on either side of center spring gap; lower compression ring gap 150 degrees from one side of center spring gap and upper compression ring gap 150 degrees from other side of center spring gap. Installation of piston rings must be carried out in this manner for optimum sealing and low oil consumption. See **Figure 35**.

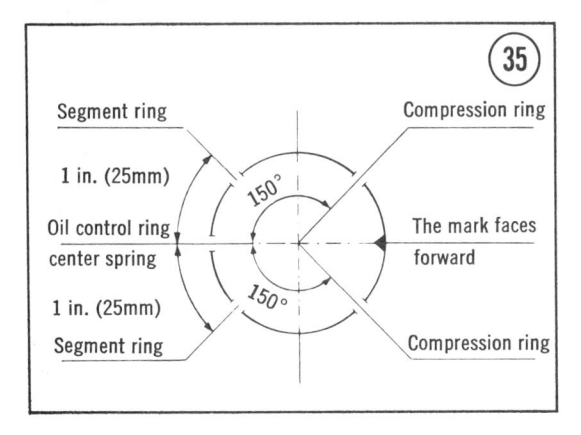

10. Install piston and connecting rod using tool No. 786228 or equivalent (**Figure 36**) and the handle of a hammer to press the piston gently down into the cylinder. Be sure mark on top of piston faces forward.

11. Install bearing inserts dry in the connecting rods. Coat them with engine oil. Put on bearing caps and tighten nuts to 25 ft-lb.

12. Coat balance shaft journals and bearings with engine oil. Install balance shaft from rear end of block (**Figure 37**).

13. Apply a thin coat of sealing compound to tthe new balance shaft sealing washer. Drive it into the block untilt it bottoms out. Install the washer with flat side out (**Figure 38**).

14. Coat the wedge-shaped seals with sealing compound. Press them into rear main bearing cap with a blunt screwdriver (**Figure 39**). The domed side of the seal must be turned to face the main bearing cap.

15. Clean crankshaft flange and flywheel. Install flywheel using new bolts. See **Figure 40**.

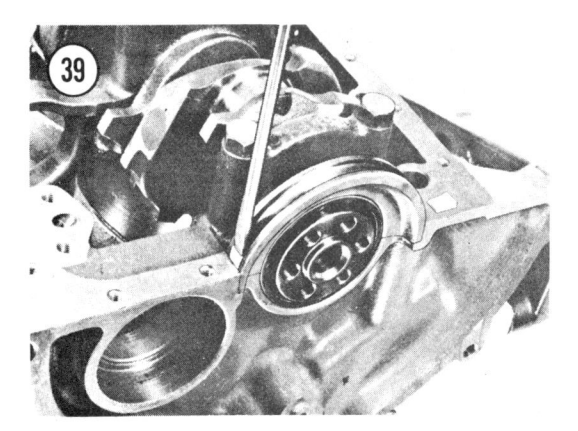

CHAPTER FOUR

17. Coat camshaft bearings with engine oil. Install camshaft in engine block. Install spacer with countersunk side toward camshaft. Insert key. Position thrust plate over front of camshaft so it covers main oil galley hole. See **Figure 42**.

> NOTE: *The spacer is thicker than the camshaft thrust plate. The difference corresponds to the axial play in the camshaft. To indicate size group, the spacers have red or blue markings. When fitting new parts choose a spacer giving correct axial play. A red spacer gives a small clearance and a blue one a larger clearance. Axial play 0.0098-0.0030 in. (0.025-0.076mm).*

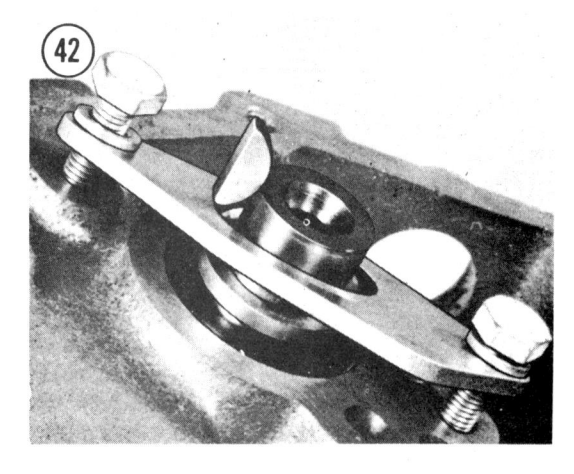

16. Locate crankshaft key. Secure gear on shaft with a bolt and washer. Tighten to 36 ft-lb. See **Figure 41**. Do not tap the gear as this could cause damage to the main bearings.

18. Apply thin coat of sealing compound to mounting surface of intermediate plate on front

ENGINE

of block, and to the block. Position gasket on block and install plate loosely with 2 retaining bolts (**Figure 43**). Temporarily install 2 lower bolts as guide dowels and tighten the 2 retaining bolts. Be sure lower edge of plate is in line with level of the pan. Remove guide bolts.

19. Turn crankshaft until mark on crankshaft gear faces camshaft.

20. Pass camshaft gear onto camshaft so the mark coincides with the mark on the crankshaft gear. Secure camshaft gear with retaining bolt and washer.

21. Install balance shaft gear so mark coincides with mark on crankshaft gear. **Figure 44** shows installation marks.

22. Install new balance shaft pulley and seal in transmission cover using tool No. 786215 or equivalent. See **Figure 45**.

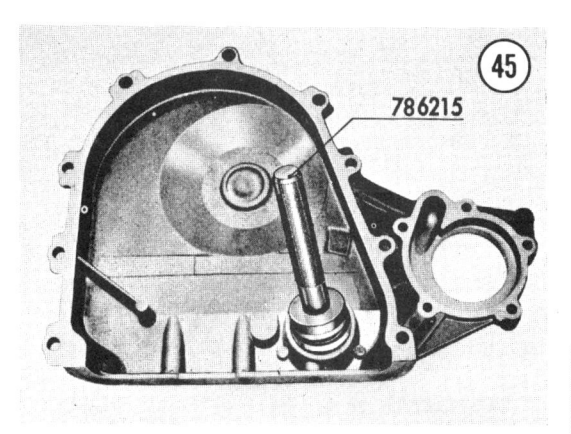

23. Apply thin coat of sealing compound to gasket mounting surfaces on intermediate plate and transmission cover. Position transmission cover gasket against intermediate plate. Center the cover with special pilot tool No. 786214 or equivalent (**Figure 46**) and secure with 9 retaining bolts. The water pump should be secured to transmission cover before this is installed on engine.

1. Transmission cover
2. Centering arbor No. 786214

24. Lubricate inner diameter of balance shaft pulley seal with engine oil. Align pulley keyway with balance shaft key and install pulley, flat washer, and retaining bolt.

25. Insert oil pump drive shaft in block with pointed end first. The stop plate on the shaft

must be positioned 5.02 in. (127.5mm) from blunt end. See **Figure 47**.

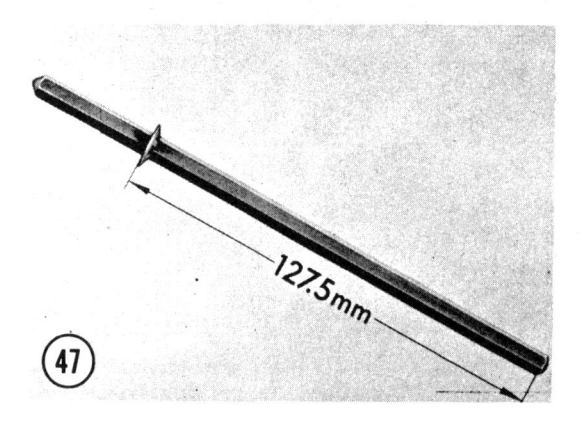

26. Install oil pump and gasket. Tighten actual pump bolts first. Then tighten suction line bolt.
27. Insert rubber seal in groove in rear main bearing cap.
28. Apply thin coat of sealing compound to 2 corner joints where transmission cover, intermediate plate, and oil pan edges meet. Position gasket on block. Insert 2 tabs on cork gasket under recesses in rear bearing cap rubber seal (**Figure 48**).

29. Install oil pan. Position 2 bolts with rubber washers at rear balance shaft bearings. See **Figure 49**.
30. Lubricate tappets and their bores with engine oil. Install tappets in same sequence as they were originally fitted.
31. Install cylinder head gaskets. The gaskets are marked FRONT and TOP. See **Figure 50**.  
32. Install cylinder heads. Insert bolts and tighten them in sequence indicated in **Figure 51**. Tighten to final torque rating in 3 steps: 40 ft.-lb., 50 ft.-lb., and 68 ft.-lb.

NOTE: *The outer rear right-hand cylinder head bolt is specially adapted for engine ground cable.*

33. Install bracket for side stay.

ENGINE

34. Dip push rod ends in engine oil and install pushrods in their original positions in the tappets.

35. Lubricate ends of rocker arms with engine oil. Install oil return plate and rocker arm assembly. See **Figure 52**. Align pushrods under rocker arms. Secure rocker arm assembly by alternately tightening 2 bolts. Be sure oil return plate is not in contact with the valve springs.

1. Rocker shaft with rocker arms
2. Oil return plate

36. Apply sealing compound to cylinder head surfaces as shown in **Figure 53**. Install intake manifold gasket. Make sure protruding part of right-hand cylinder head gasket enters the opening in the intake manifold gasket (**Figure 54**).

37. Fit intake manifold. Tighten bolts and nuts in 2 stages as follows: Stage 1, tighten nuts to 5 ft.-lb. Stage 2, tighten nuts to 15 ft.-lb. Tighten in sequence shown in **Figure 55**.

38. Install thermostat, gasket, and thermostat housing cover in front part of intake manifold, placing thermostat holder at right angles to the longitudinal direction of the engine.

39. Adjust valves (see Chapter Two).

40. Install a new oil filter. Tighten by hand until the oiled rubber seal makes contact with the cylinder block. Then tighten another one-half turn.

41. Install fuel pump pushrod, gasket, and pump. Fit pushrod with same end on cam as originally.

42. Apply sealing compound to threads of oil pressure gauge. Install gauge in block (**Figure 56**).

43. Install clutch after having aligned disc with tool No. 784064 or equivalent.

44. Install carburetor (use a new gasket).

45. Connect carburetor-to-fuel pump fuel lines. Fit hose clamps.

46. Install spark plugs.

47. Install fan belt pulley and fan.

48. Install alternator and alternator bracket. Tighten fan belt.

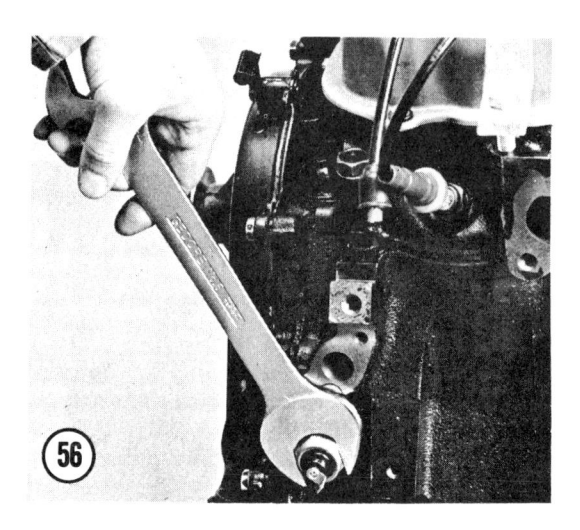

49. Install new valve cover gasket (**Figure 57**). Press the clamp ends of the gasket into notches in valve cover.

> NOTE: *Before valve covers are installed the lubrication of the rocker arm shaft must be checked with engine running.*

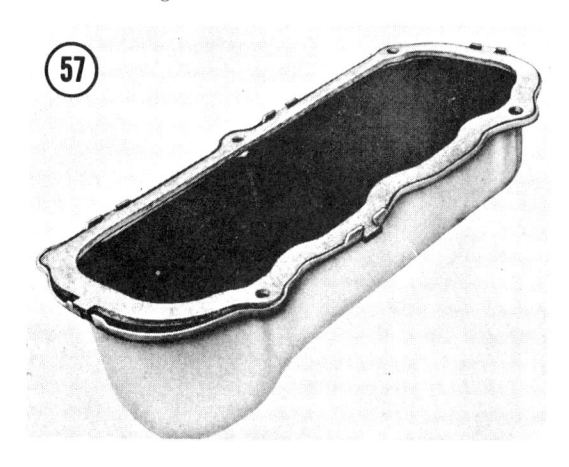

50. Install distributor, and vacuum line to distributor.
51. Install distributor cap and ignition cables.
52. Install oil dipstick and air filter.

Disassembly (Saab 99)

1. Mount engine in an engine stand, if possible.
2. Remove distributor cap and ignition cables.
3. On carbureted engines, remove carburetor. On injection engines (through 1974) disconnect start valve from throttle valve housing and let it hang in its hose. Remove throttle valve housing (**Figure 58**) on the 2.0 engine.

4. Remove hose connections from water pump, bypass system, and crankcase ventilation circuit.
5. Remove valve cover.
6. Remove inlet manifold (1.7 and 1.85 engines).
7. Remove upper engine bracket (1969 1.7 and 1.85 models only).
8. Remove distributor (**Figure 59**).

9. Remove throttle valve housing (1.7 and 1.85 engines).
10. Remove auxiliary air valve (1975-1976 2.0 engines).
11. On 2.0 engines remove inlet manifold (**Figure 60**) and front lifting lug. Also remove alternator bracket on engines with high position alternator.

ENGINE

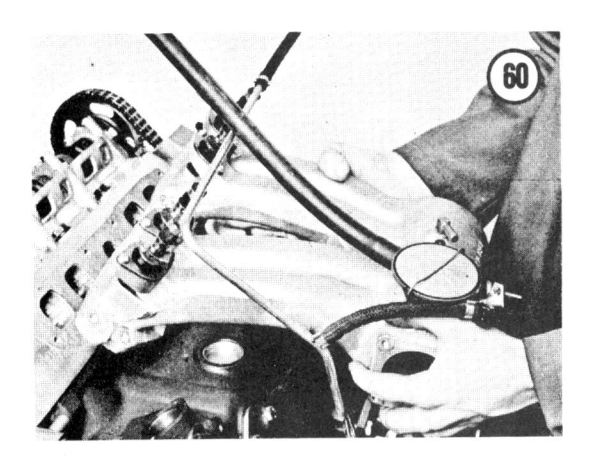

12. Remove fuel pump (remove thermostat housing on injection engine) on the 1.7 and 1.85 engines.

13. Remove cover over oil channels complete with oil pressure transmitter (1.7 and 1.85 engines).

14. Remove vent housing for crankcase ventilation (through 1974 models).

15. Remove oil filter, oil pump (and pump shaft on 1.7 and 1.85 engines), oil pump spacing piece, and suction line to pump.

16. Remove water pump (early models) as follows:

   a. Remove cover
   b. Remove center screw from impeller. Hold impeller with pliers and unscrew clockwise (left-hand thread). Save the washer. See **Figure 61**.

   NOTE: *The impeller must be immobilized while center screw is removed or the gear teeth on the pump shaft and idler shaft could be damaged.*

   c. Fit tapping-out hammer with tool No. 8392136 (2.0 engine) or No. 839057 (1.7 and 1.85 engines) to the water pump shaft and remove pump unit (**Figure 62**).

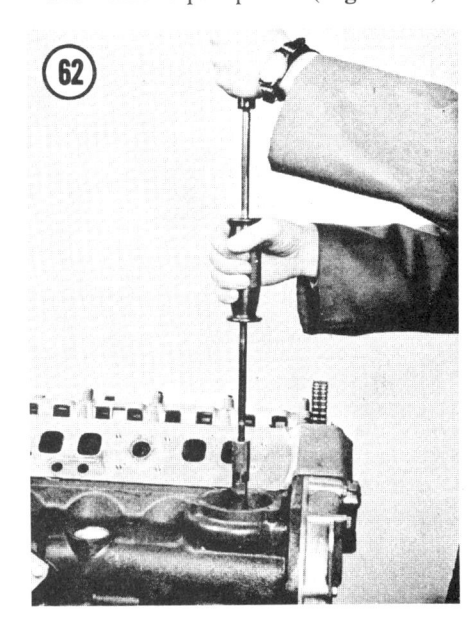

   d. The bearing housing may be left behind in the cylinder block. If so, expel the bearing housing with a tapping out hammer fitted with a nut and flat washer with an O.D. of 1 in. (25mm). See **Figure 63**.

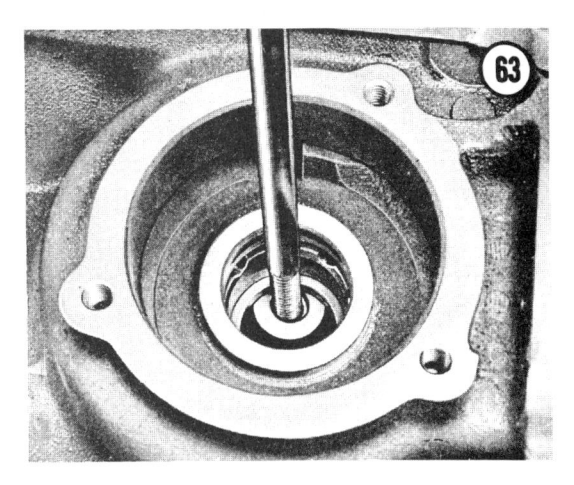

Remove water pump (late model) as follows:
   a. Remove cover.
   b. Position tool No. 8392441 or equivalent (**Figure 64**) over water pump and fit 2 screws without tightening. Turn tool

CHAPTER FOUR

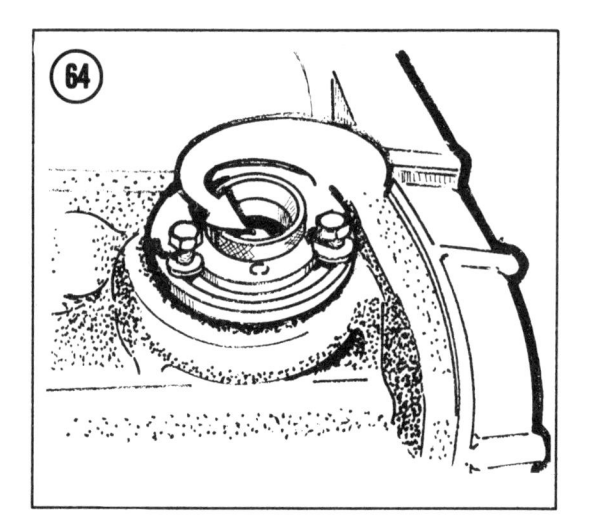

counter-clockwise so peg on tool engages one of the impeller wings. Tighten the 2 screws.

c. Loosen left-hand threaded impeller center nut.

d. Remove water pump using tool No. 8392490 (**Figure 65**). Never use a hammer or similar tool.

e. The bearing housing may be left behind in the cylinder block. If so, extract the bearing housing with a tapping-out hammer fitted with a nut and plain washer with an external diameter of 1 in. (25mm). See Figure 63.

17. Remove thermostat housing (**Figure 66**).

18. Remove exhaust manifold and gasket (2.0 engines) as shown in **Figure 67**.

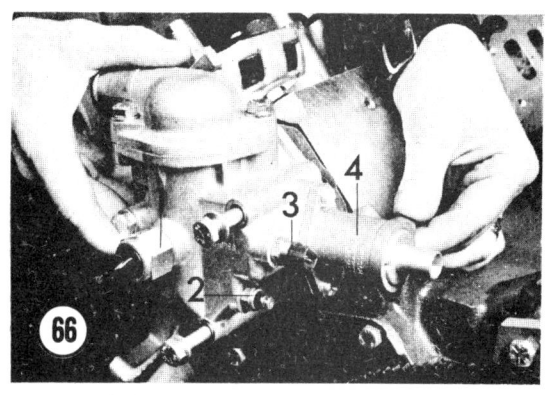

1. Thermoswitch for injection system
2. Temperature transmitter for temperature gauge
3. Temperature transmitter for injection system
4. Auxiliary air regulator

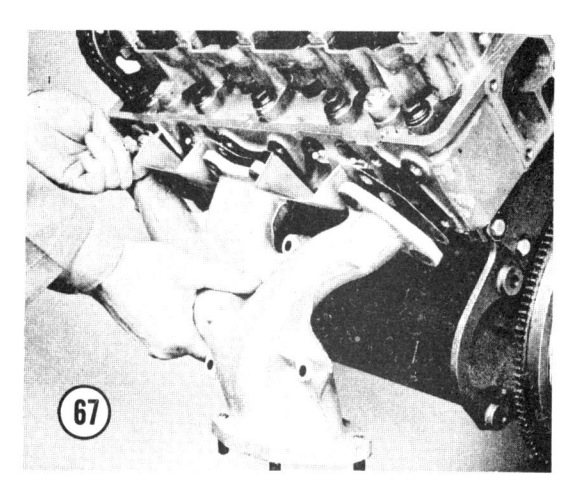

19. Remove camshaft sprocket by turning crankshaft to ignition position for the No. 1 cylinder (**Figure 68**). Screw a nut on the threaded center stud of the crankshaft sprocket and tighten the center stud against the mounting plate.

CAUTION
Tighten nut securely to immobilize center stud. Otherwise chain tensioner will tighten the chain and lock in a new position so that the sprocket cannot be replaced in position.

20. Remove 3 locked retaining bolts from camshaft sprocket. Separate sprocket from camshaft plate until it hangs free on center stud in the mounting plate. See **Figure 69** (1.7 and 1.85 engines illustrated).

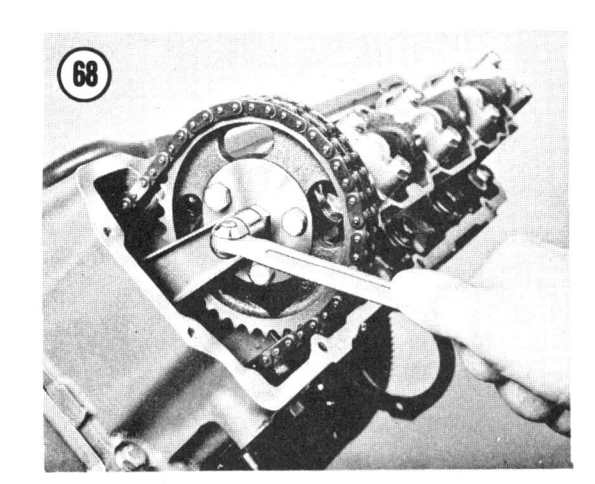

ENGINE

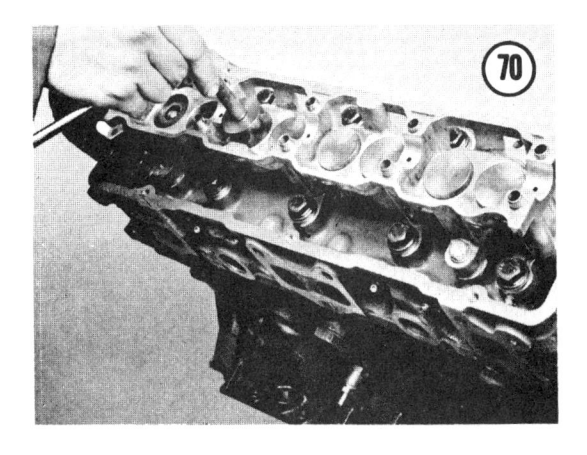

23. Remove camshaft bearing assembly.

24. Remove cylinder head bolts and insert 2 locating pins (No. 839212 on models through 1974 only). Do not forget the bolts in the transmission case.

25. Remove cylinder head and gasket (**Figure 71**).

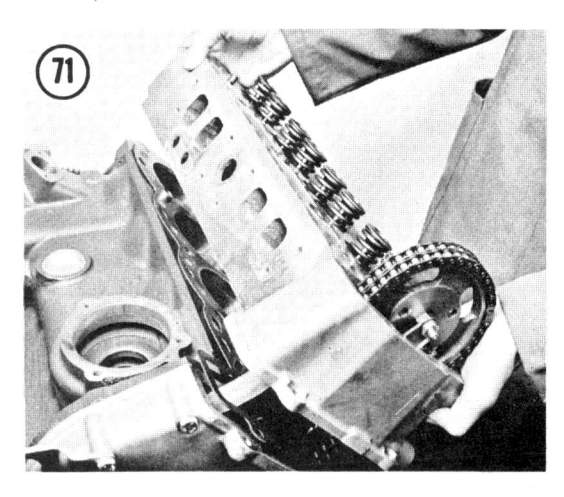

26. Remove belt pulley bolt and pulley using puller No. 839215 on models through 1974, No. 8392151 on 1975-1976 models, or No. 839114 on 1.7 and 1.85 models. See **Figures 72 and 73**.

21. Remove camshaft bearing caps. Lift out camshaft.

22. Remove valve depressors and adjusting pallets (**Figure 70**).

27. Remove chain transmission cover (**Figure 74**).

28. Remove chain tensioner, chain guides, and mounting plate (complete with camshaft sprocket and tranmission chain). See **Figure 75**.

29. Remove crankshaft sprocket. A universal puller may be used (**Figure 76**).

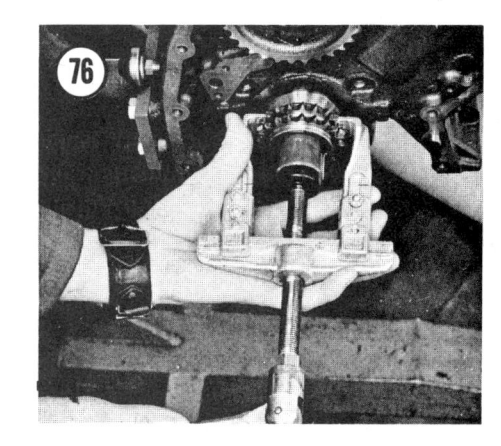

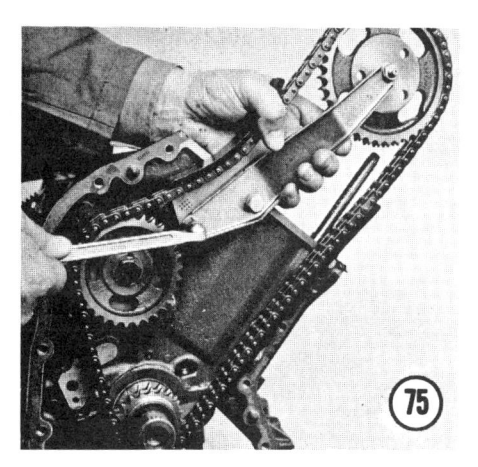

30. Remove idler shaft sprocket (**Figure 77**).

31. Unscrew the idler shaft keeper plate (**Figure 78**). Withdraw idler shaft.

32. Remove residue (carbon, etc.) from top of cylinders.

33. Note markings on connecting rods and big-end bearing caps so they can be reassembled later in their original positions. Remove nuts and bearing caps (**Figure 79**). Push pistons and connecting rods out of cylinders (**Figure 80**). Protect stud threads with pieces of plastic hose when dismantling pistons and connecting rods.

34. Install big-end bearings and caps loosely on connecting rods from which they came.

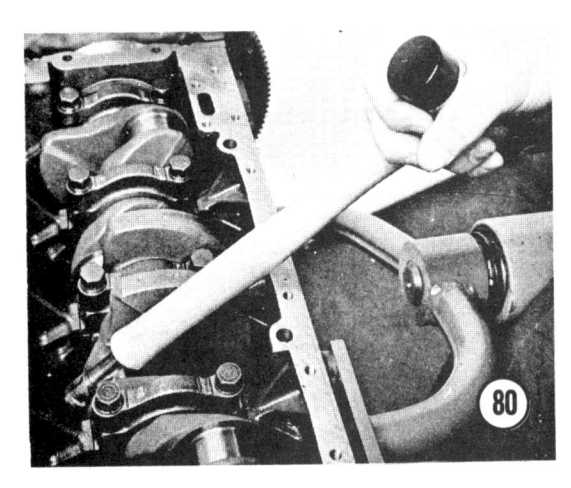

ENGINE

37. Remove bearing halves and thrust bearing washers. Set aside in such a manner that they can be reassembled later in their original positions.

Assembly (Saab 99)

1. Install bearing halves in main bearing journals. Lubricate bearings with engine oil.

2. Place crankshaft in bearing journals. Locate thrust bearing washers (**Figure 82**) so that oil grooves face crankshaft bearing surfaces. Check axial play with a feeler gauge.

35. On the manual transmission, dismantle clutch and flywheel. On the automatic transmission, remove gable plate and shaft seal (**Figure 81**).

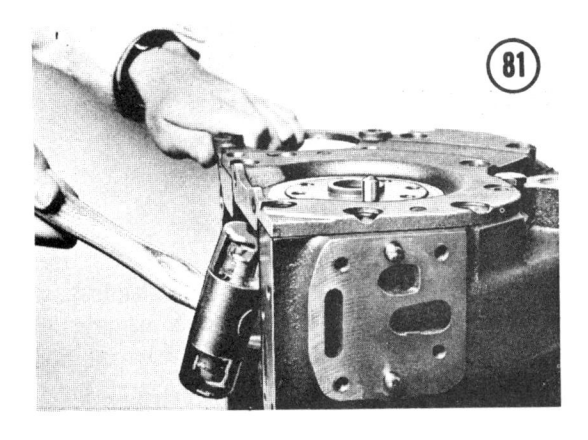

3. Mount main bearing caps with bearing halves in position and oiled. Be sure the markings match. The main bearing caps are numbered (No. 1 goes at the transmission chain end and the others run consecutively to the flywheel end with the bearing locks facing each other). Each number on the bearing cap corresponds to a cast number on the crankcase (**Figure 83**).

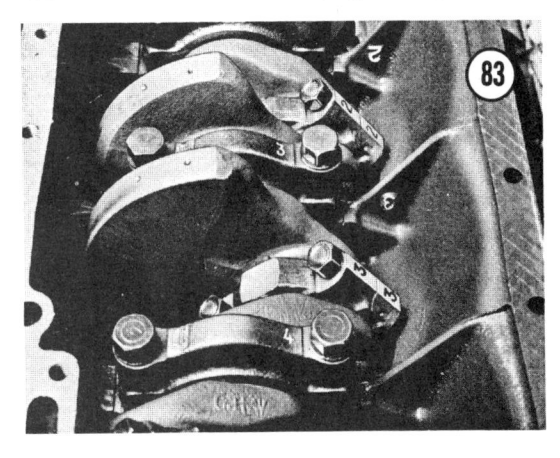

36. Remove main bearing bolts and bearing caps. Lift out crankshaft.

4. Tighten main bearing bolts (**Figure 84**) to 79 ft.-lb. See Table 1 for torque recommendations.

5. Install gable plate with crankshaft seal (**Figure 85**) using guide sleeve No. 839197 (through 1974 models), No. 8391971 (1975-1976 models), or No. 839041 for the 1.7 and 1.85 models.

6. Install flywheel (or driver disc) using new bolts. Apply Loctite pipe sealant 68 or equivalent to the bolt threads. See **Figure 86**. Tighten to 50 ft.-lb.

7. Install pistons and connecting rods using tool No. 786228 (2.0 models through 1974), No. 7862287 (2.0 1975-1976 models), or No. 839036 (1.7 and 1.85 models). See **Figure 87**. Be sure studs are protected by their plastic sleeves. The connecting rods and big-end bearing caps are numbered to match the corresponding cylinders.

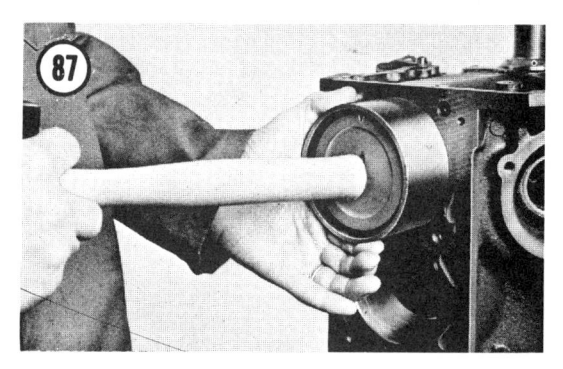

NOTE: *Be sure the groove on the top of the piston faces the transmission end (pistons marked* FRONT *are to be installed with marking nearest the transmission chain end of the engine).* See **Figure 88**.

8. Fit big-end bearing caps so the figures face the same way as those on the connecting rod (away from the idler shaft).

9. Assemble the idler shaft and install keeper plate. On the 1.7 and 1.85 engines turn the shaft until the marked line on the sprocket is horizontal (**Figure 89**).

ENGINE

10. Mount sprocket on idler shaft.

11. Assemble water pump (early models) using a drift pin (**Figure 90**). The impeller must first be removed. Fit the water pump cover and gasket. Assemble the later version. Check the bushing on the engine block, first. The impeller must be removed before pump is fitted. Install the pump unit (**Figure 91**). Press in the bearing housing, O-rings, bearings, shaft, lock ring, and lower and upper seals into the engine block using tool No. 8392490 and mounting sleeve (**Figure 92**). Mount impeller and nut. Position tool No. 8392441 over pump with 2 bolts. Turn tool counter-clockwise so peg on tool engages one of the impeller wings. Tighten the 2 bolts. Tighten the center bolt to 10.8±1.5 ft.-lb. Fit the gasket and pump cover.

12. Mount sprocket on crankshaft. Align 0 degrees mark on flywheel with mark on cylinder block (**Figure 93**).

13. Fit cylinder head gasket (**Figure 94**). Fit 2 locating pins for this operation (tool No. 8392128).

14. Mount cylinder head. Tighten bolts in 2 stages, the first to 43 ft.-lb., the second to 69 ft.-lb. in the order shown in **Figure 95**. (Do final tightening after engine has cooled for about 30 minutes).

15. Mount camshaft bearing assembly.

16. Mount adjusting pallets and valve depressors.

17. Fit camshaft and camshaft bearing caps. Note the marks and guide sleeves.

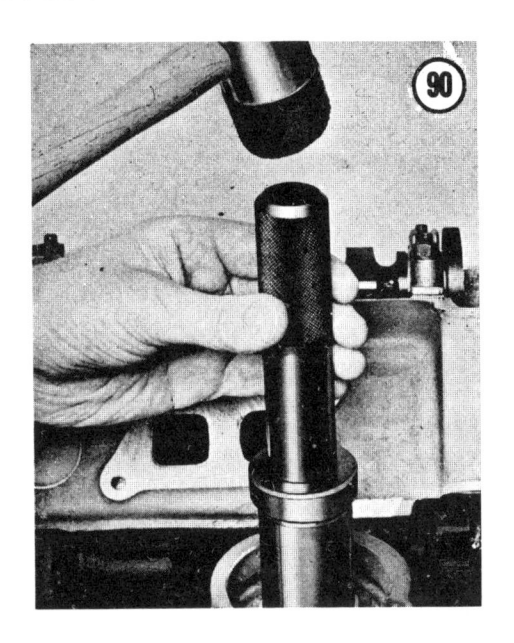

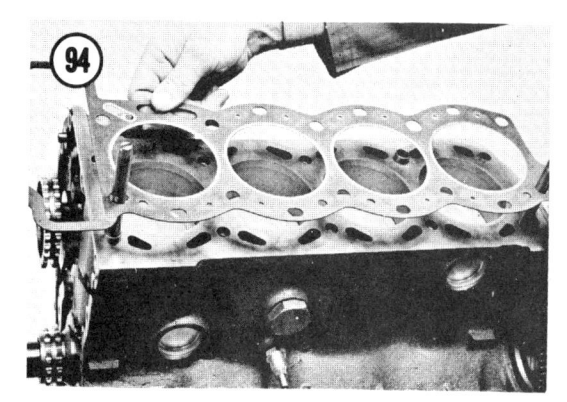

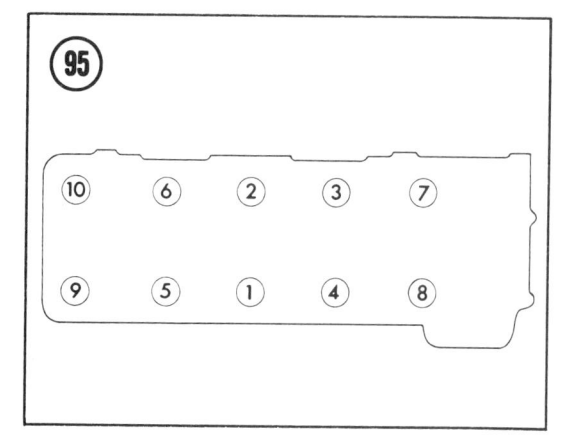

CHAPTER FOUR

18. Mount straight chain guide plate (with the long bolt in the bottom hole on 1.7 and 1.85 models, see **Figure 96**). Also on the 1.7 and 1.85 models, mount curved chain guide plate loosely with a short bolt in the hole nearest idler shaft (**Figure 97**).

19. Check that setting marks on crankshaft, camshaft, and idler shaft are in right position (i.e., ignition position for the No. 1 cylinder). See **Figures 98 and 99** (2.0 engine) and **Figures 100 and 101** (1.7 and 1.85 engines).

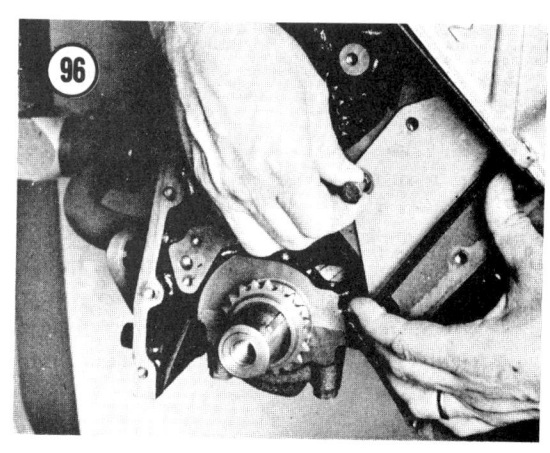

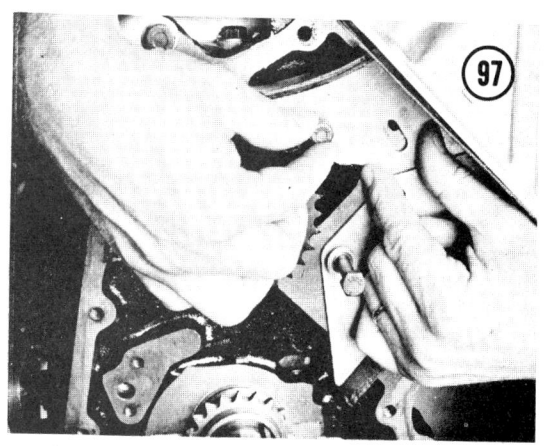

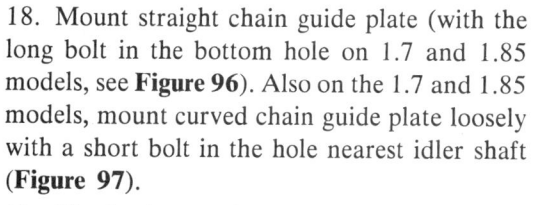

20. Assemble camshaft sprocket and mounting plate (if they have been disassembled). Install

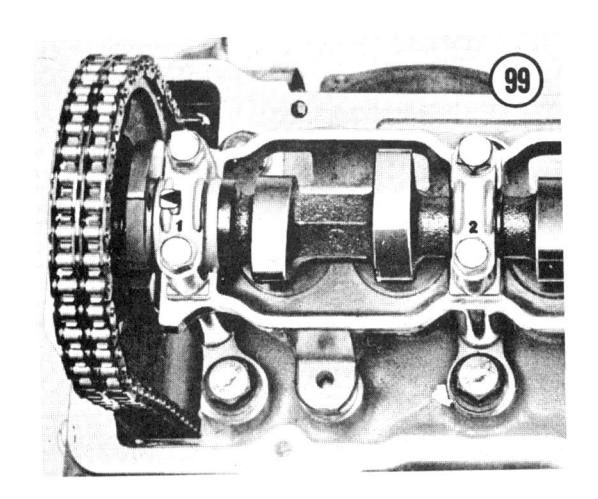

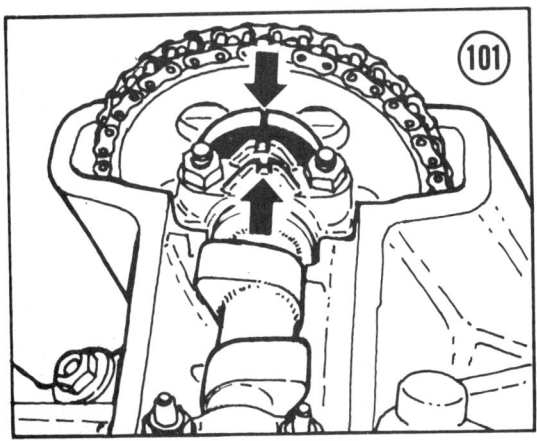

ENGINE

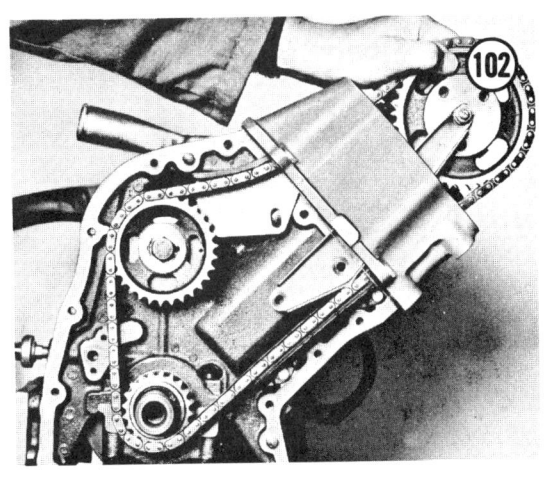

21. Rotate camshaft sprocket until bolt holes match threaded holes in camshaft flange.
22. Install transmission chain over sprockets so that it hangs straight from camshaft to crankshaft.

> NOTE: *The shaft settings must not be changed.*

23. Guide the center stud of the camshaft sprocket into the camshaft. Fit a new locking plate and bolts (**Figure 103**).

24. Mount curved chain guide plate together with mounting plate (the chain guide plate nearest the block) with 2 bolts and stretch the chain somewhat.

25. Install chain tensioner (early version) by first removing tensioner neck from chain tensioner housing (see **Figure 104**). Tension spring by turning ratchet sleeve (actuated by the spring)

transmission chain over camshaft sprocket (**Figure 102**). Lower transmission chain and mounting plate past camshaft flange until center stud of sprocket is lined up with camshaft.

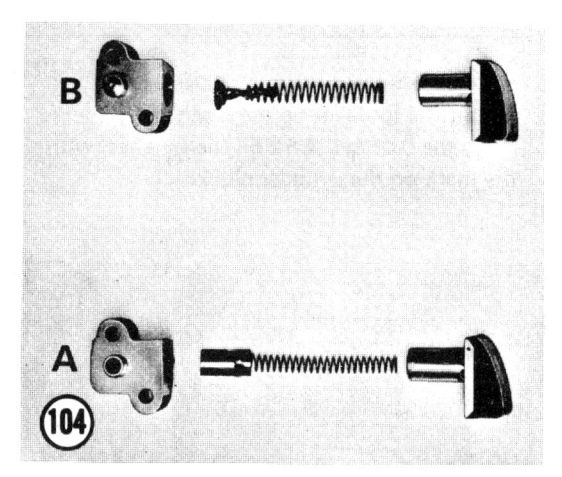

A—Earlier version   B—Later version

clockwise and at same time pushing it until it locks in its innermost position (**Figure 105**). Fit the tensioner neck and spacer piece (**Figure 106**) so that the tensioner neck will not bottom in the chain tensioner housing and release the self-adjuster.

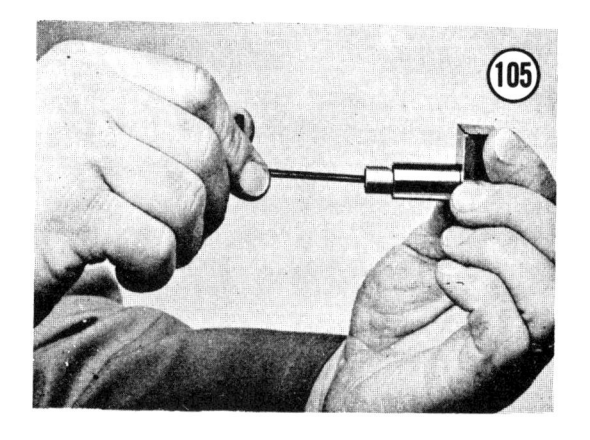

26. Install late model chain tensioner as follows: Place lock washer with spiral rod in the chain tensioner housing. Install spring with smaller diameter against the lock washer. Fit the tensioner neck in the housing by pressing and turning it into its inner position (**Figure 107**). The tensioner neck must be held depressed while chain tensioner is being fitted until the chain has been tensioned.

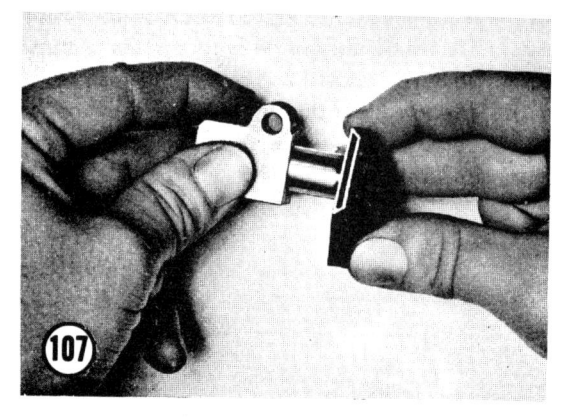

27. On both early and late versions, mount chain tensioner with guide plate on the engine block. Press the curved chain guide against the chain to stretch it. Push tensioner neck against spacer piece. Remove spacer piece while chain is kept tensioned. Adjust to a clearance of 0.02 in. (0.5mm) between housing and tensioner neck (**Figure 108**). Tighten chain guides. Rotate crankshaft one full turn in its normal sense, and check chain tension. The movement of the tensioner neck from its butted position must be at least 0.02 in. (0.5mm) and not more than 0.06 in. (1.5mm).

ENGINE

28. Remove nut from camshaft sprocket center stud.
29. Fit the thrower ring (1.7 and 1.85 models), transmission chain cover, and alternator support.
30. Fit belt pulley.
31. On the 1.7 and 1.85 models, install water pump (**Figure 109**). The clearance between center bolt of the impeller and the cover must be 0.01-0.02 in. (0.25-0.50mm).

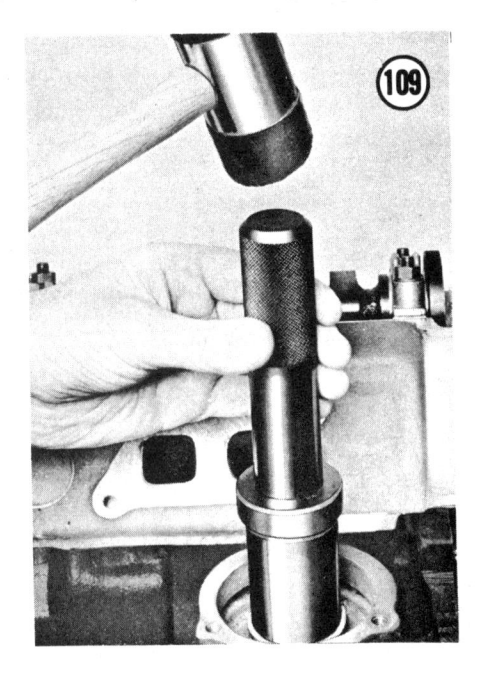

Adjust clearance as follows:
  a. Place washer 0.02 in. (0.5mm) thick between center bolt of the impeller and the pump cover. Use a feeler gauge to measure the gap between cover and block. See **Figure 110**.
  b. Remove washer and fit one or 2 new gaskets corresponding in thickness to the measured gap between cover and block. There are 3 different gaskets to choose from: 0.01, 0.02, and 0.03 in. (0.25, 0.50, and 0.75mm).
  c. Tighten cover.

32. Mount oil pump spacing piece with gasket. (Note the guide pins).
33. Fit the distributor (1.7 and 1.85 engines).
34. Fit the oil pump and suction line. Be sure suction tube gasket is installed correctly.
35. Install oil filter.
36. Install fuel pump (1.7 and 1.85 models).
37. Install intake manifold. Connect water hoses and crankcase ventilation hoses. Screw in the engine lifting eye.
38. On carburetted engines, install carburetor. On injection engines, mount the throttle valve housing and start valve (2.0 engines).
39. Mount thermostat housing (and warm-up regulator on 1975-1976 2.0 engines).
40. Install exhaust manifold. Use new gasket.
41. Install the 2 semicircular rubber seals and camshaft cover.
42. Mount distributor (2.0 engines) with drive shaft for oil pump. Make basic ignition setting (see Chapter Two).
43. Install oil pump (2.0 engines).
44. Mount vent housing for crankcase ventilation (2.0 engines through 1974).
45. Install valve cover (2.0 engines).
46. Install clutch (manual transmission).
47. On 1975-1976 cars for California, install the EGR valve and tube.

Engine specifications and torque tables follow on pages 68-76

CHAPTER FOUR

Table 1   ENGINE SPECIFICATIONS — SAAB 95/96/SONETT

General Data	1967-1970	1971-ON
Engine, type V4	4-stroke, 4 cylinders	4-stroke, 4 cylinders
Power DIN at 4,700 rpm	65 bhp	65 bhp
Max torque at 2,500 rpm	85 ft.-lb. (11.7 kpm)	85 ft.-lb. (11.7 kpm)
Compression ratio	9.0:1	8.0:1
Number of cylinders	4	4
Cylinder bore	3.54 in. (90mm)	3.54 in. (90mm)
Stroke	2.32 in. (58.86mm)	2.63 in. (66.8mm)
Cylinder volume	91.4 cu. in. (1498cc)	104 cu. in. (1698cc)
Firing order	1-3-4-2	1-3-4-2
Placement of cylinders (from front of car):		
Right-hand side	1-2	1-2
Left-hand side	3-4	3-4

Cylinder Block

Type	60° Vee
Material	Cast iron, special alloy
Number of main bearings	3
Cylinder block bores for camshaft bushings:	front: 44.65-44.68mm
	center: 44.27-44.30mm
	rear: 43.89-43.92mm
Cylinder block bores for balance shaft bushings:	front: 54.420-54.445mm
	rear: 57.620-57.645mm
Cylinder bore	90.030-90.040mm
Diameter main bearing bore:	red 60.62-60.63mm
	blue 60.63-60.64mm
Thrust bearing width:	22.61-22.66mm

Pistons

Material	Aluminum
Number of piston rings, on each piston	2 compression and 1 oil control ring
Piston-ring groove width:	upper 2.030-2.055mm
	center 3.030-3.056mm
	lower 5.017-5.042mm
Piston diameter	89.978-90.002mm
Piston clearance	0.0011 in.-0.0024 in. (0.03-0.06mm)

Piston Rings

Upper compression ring	
Thickness	1.978-1.990mm
Width	0.15 in. max (3.76mm)
Piston-ring clearance in groove	0.0394-0.077mm
Ring gap	0.250-0.500mm

(continued)

ENGINE

Table 1 ENGINE SPECIFICATIONS — SAAB 95/96/SONETT (continued)

Piston Rings (continued)
  Lower compression ring:
    Thickness — 2.978-2.990mm
    Width — 0.15 in. max. (3.76mm)
    Piston ring play — 0.040-0.078mm
    Ring gap — 0.250-0.500mm

  Oil control ring
    Thickness (total) — 4.839-4.991mm
    Width (segment) — 3.430-3.580mm
    Piston ring play in groove (total) — 0.026-0.203mm
    Ring gap — 0.380-1.400mm

Connecting Rods
  Big-end diameter — red 56.820-56.830mm
    blue 56.830-56.840mm
  Diameter of crank pins — blue 53.99-53.98mm
    red 54.00-53.99mm
  Main bearings clearance — 0.014-0.054mm

Crankshaft
  Number of main bearings — 3
  Main bearing diameter — red 57.000-56.990mm
    blue 56.990-56.980mm
  Clearance between insert and crank pin — 0.012-0.048mm
  Thrust journal length (center main bearing) — 26.44-26.39mm
  Crankshaft end play — 0.102-0.203mm
  Thrust (axial) bearing insert width — 26.29-26.24mm

Balance Shaft
  Number of bearings — 2
  Clearance in bushing — front 0.02-0.08mm
    rear 0.03-0.07mm
  Balance shaft end float — 0.05-0.15mm
  Inner diameter of bushings — front 50.85-50.88mm
    rear 54.03-54.05mm
  Bearing diameter of balance shaft — front 50.83-50.80mm
    rear 54.00-53.98mm
  Backlash, new drive gear — 0.05-0.14mm
  Backlash, wearing limit — 0.40mm

Camshaft
  Number of bearings — 3
  Insert diameter — front 41.516-41.542mm
    center 41.135-41.161mm
    rear 40.754-40.780mm

(continued)

Table 1   ENGINE SPECIFICATIONS — SAAB 95/96/SONETT   (continued)

Camshaft (continued)

Bearing clearance	all 0.077-0.0025mm
Inner diameter of bushings	front 41.587-41.593mm
	center 41.186-41.212mm
	rear 40.805-40.831mm
Camshaft end float	0.025-0.076mm
Spacer thickness	red 4.064-4.089mm
	blue 4.089-4.114mm
Backlash, new drive gear	0.05-0.20mm
Backlash, wearing limit	0.40mm
Cam lift	0.256 in. (6.490mm)
Cam heel-to-toe dimension	34.201-33.998mm

Valve Mechanism

Angle of seat (intake and exhaust)	45°
Seat width, intake and exhaust	0.059-0.070 in. (1.5-1.7mm)
Stem diameter	
Intake	8.043-8.025mm
Exhaust	8.017-7.999mm
Stem bore (intake and exhaust)	8.063-8.088mm
Clearance between stem and guide	intake 0.020-0.063mm
	exhaust 0.046-0.089mm
Disc diameter	intake 1.46 in. (37mm)
	exhaust 1.26 in. (32mm)
Valve lift	0.38 in. (9.7mm)
Valve clearance, cold engine	
Intake	0.014 in. (0.35mm)
Exhaust	0.016 in. (0.40mm)

	1967 MODEL	1968-ON
Free length of springs	1.78 in. (45.2mm)	1.91 in. (48.5mm)
Fully compressed	1.13 in. (28.6mm)	1.13 in. (28.6mm)
Load for compression to	39-47 lbs.	60-68 lbs.
1.59 in. (40.26mm)	(17.8-21.5kp)	(27.2-30.8kp)
Valve tappet diameter	22.202-22.190mm	22.202-22.190mm
Clearance between tappet and bore	0.023-0.060mm	0.023-0.060mm

Valve Timing

(measured at a valve play of 0.425mm)

Intake opens	21° BTDC
Intake shuts	82° ATDC
Exhaust opens	63° BTDC
Exhaust shuts	40° ATDC

Lubrication System

Oil pan capacity including oil filter	3.3 U.S. quarts (3.3 liters)
Oil pan capacity excluding oil filter	3.0 U.S. quarts (3 liters)
Oil pump	
Clearance rotor to housing	0.012 in. (0.3mm)
Clearance rotor to sealing surface	0.004 in. (0.1mm)

ENGINE

Table 2 ENGINE SPECIFICATIONS—SAAB 99

General Data
Type   4-cylinder, 4-stroke with overhead cam
Power rating, DIN
  1.7 liter carburetor model   80 hp @ 5,200 rpm
  1.7 liter injection model   87 hp @ 5,200 rpm
  1.85 liter carburetor model   88 hp @ 5,000 rpm
  1.85 liter injection model   95 hp @ 5,000 rpm
  2.0 liter carburetor model   115 hp @ 5,200 rpm
  2.0 liter injection model   110 hp @ 5,500 rpm (through 1974)
                                                    115 hp @ 5,500 rpm (1975-1976 Federal)
                                                    110 hp @ 5,500 rpm (1975-1976 California)

Maximum torque, DIN
  1.7 liter carburetor model   94 ft.-lb. @ 3,000 rpm
  1.7 liter injection model   95 ft.-lb. @ 3,000 rpm
  1.85 liter carburetor model   108 ft.-lb. @ 3,000 rpm
  1.85 liter injection model   105 ft.-lb. @ 3,200 rpm
  2.0 liter carburetor model   115 ft.-lb. @ 3,500 rpm
  2.0 liter injection model   123 ft.-lb. @ 3,700 rpm
                                                    119 ft.-lb. @ 3,500 rpm
                                                      (1975-1976 California)

Compression ratio
  1.7 liter   9.0:1
  1.85 liter   9.0:1
  2.0 liter   8.7:1
No. of cylinders   4
Cylinder bore
  1.7 liter   3.288 in. (83.5mm)
  1.85 liter   3.425 in. (87.0mm)
  2.0 liter   3.543 in. (90.0mm)
Stroke   3.071 in. (78.0mm)
Cylinder volume
  1.7 liter   104.2 cu. in. (1709cc)
  1.85 liter   113.1 cu. in. (1854cc)
  2.0 liter   121.0 cu. in. (1985cc)
Order of firing (No. 1 at rear)   1-3-4-2
Engine idling speed
  1.7 liter   800-850 rpm
  1.85 liter   800-850 rpm
  2.0 liter (manual transmission)   800 rpm (through 1974)
  2.0 liter (automatic transmission)   850 rpm (through 1974)
  2.0 liter (all)   850-900 rpm (1975-1976)

Cylinder Block
Material   special alloy
Number of main bearings   5
Cylinder bore
  1.7 liter standard (F)   83.487-83.497mm
      (G)   83.500-83.513mm
      (H)   83.530-83.543mm
  1.85 liter standard (F)   86.987-86.997mm
      (G)   87.000-87.013mm
      (H)   87.030-87.043mm
  2.0 liter standard (A)   90.000-90.010mm
      (B)   90.010-90.020mm

(continued)

Table 2 ENGINE SPECIFICATIONS—SAAB 99 (continued)

Cylinder Head	
2.0 liter, maximum grinding or facing of cylinder head surface	0.4mm
Distance from cylinder head gasket surface to valve cover gasket surface (new cylinder head)	92.75±0.05mm
Pistons	
Material	light alloy
Number of rings per piston	2 compression rings 1 oil scraper (3-piece)
Width of ring grooves	
1.7 liter (top)	2.038-2.064mm
(middle)	3.038-3.064mm
(bottom)	3.988-4.013mm
1.85 liter (top)	1.790-1.810mm (Mahle)
(middle)	2.030-2.050mm (Mahle)
(bottom)	4.000-4.020mm (Mahle)
2.0 liter (top)	1.79-1.81mm
(middle)	2.00-2.05mm
(bottom)	4.01-4.03mm
Piston diameter (measured at lower edge perpendicular to piston pin)	
1.7 liter standard (F)	83.464-83.475mm
(G)	83.475-83.487mm
(H)	83.490-83.503mm
1.85 liter standard (F)	86.962-86.976mm
(G)	86.997-86.991mm
(H)	87.007-87.021mm
2.0 liter standard (AB)	89.980-89.986mm
(C)	89.999-90.010mm
Piston clearance	
1.7 liter	0.013-0.038mm
1.85 liter	0.013-0.038mm
2.0 liter	0.014-0.040mm
Piston withdrawal	From top of block
Piston orientation	
1.7 and 1.85 liter	Marking FRONT (or arrow) facing the engine transmission end
2.0 liter	Groove on top should face engine transmission end
Pin diameter	
1.7 liter	20.635-20.640mm
1.85 liter	22.225mm
2.0 liter	23.996-24.000mm
Fit of pin:	
1.7 and 1.85 liter	0.008±0.007mm (sliding fit under gentle thumb pressure)
2.0 liter	0.005-0.014mm (sliding fit under gentle thumb pressure)
Piston speed	13m/sec. at 5,000 rpm
Piston Rings	
Upper compression ring thickness	
1.7 and 1.85 liter (Hepworth)	1.975-2.000mm
1.7 and 1.85 liter (Mahle)	1.728-1.740mm

(continued)

ENGINE

Table 2 ENGINE SPECIFICATIONS—SAAB 99 (continued)

Piston Rings (continued)	
2.0 liter	1.53-1.65mm
through 1974 models	
2.0 liter	1.73-1.75mm
(1975-1976 models)	
Gap, fitted in new cylinder	
1.7 and 1.85 liter	0.30-0.45mm
2.0 liter	0.35-0.55mm
Piston ring play in groove	0.050-0.082mm
Lower compression ring thickness	
1.7 and 1.85 liter (Hepworth)	2.975-3.000mm
1.7 and 1.85 liter (Mahle)	1.987-1.990mm
2.0 liter	1.78-1.88mm
Gap, fitted in new cylinder	0.30-0.45mm
Piston ring play ingroove	
1.7 and 1.85 liter	0.040-0.063mm
2.0 liter	0.040-0.072mm
Oil scraper thickness	
1.7 and 1.85 liter	0.584-0.635mm
2.0 liter	0.58-0.64mm
Gap fitted in new cylinder	
1.7 and 1.85 liter (Hepworth)	0.40-1.40mm
2.0 liter (Mahle)	0.38-1.40mm
Thickness, middle ring	
1.7 and 1.85 liter (Hepworth)	3.59-3.84mm
2.0 liter (Mahle)	2.63-2.73mm
Connecting rods	
Material	Forged steel
Big-end bore	
1.7 and 1.85 liter	48.146-48.158mm
2.0 liter	56.000-56.019mm
Small-end bushing, installed	
1.7 liter	20.640-20.647mm
1.85 liter	22.232mm
2.0 liter	24.005-24.010mm
Crankshaft	
Number of main bearings	5
Crank pin diameter	
1.7 and 1.85 liter	44.450-44.463mm
2.0 liter	51.981-52.000mm
Main bearing pin diameter	
1.7 and 1.85 liter	53.987-54.000mm
2.0 liter	57.981-58.000mm
Maximum out-of-round	0.05mm
Crankshaft axial play	
1.7 and1.85 liter	0.08-0.25mm
2.0 liter	0.08-0.28mm
Main bearing play	
1.7 and 1.85 liter	0.025-0.064mm
2.0 liter	0.020-0.062mm
Crank bearing play	
1.7 and 1.85 liter	0.020-0.058mm
2.0 liter	0.026-0.062mm

(continued)

Table 2 ENGINE SPECIFICATIONS—SAAB 99 (continued)

Camshaft
Number of bearings	5
Bearing diameter	
1.7 and 1.85 liter	31.75mm
2.0 liter	25.94mm
(through 1974 models)	
2.0 liter	28.94mm
(1975-1976 models)	
Camshaft axial play	
1.7 and 1.85 liter	0.10-0.20mm
2.0 liter	0.08-0.25mm
Valve timing	
Intake Valve	
1.7 liter (carburetor and injection models), and 1.85 liter (carburetor model). Nominal valve clearance, 0.23mm.	Starts 12 degrees BTDC, ends 52 degrees ABDC
1.85 liter (injection model). Nominal valve clearance, 0.23mm.	Starts 16 degrees BTDC, ends 56 degrees ABDC
2.0 liter (through 1974 models). Nominal valve clearance, 0.25mm.	Starts 26 degrees BTDC, ends 70 degrees ABDC
2.0 liter (1975-1976 models). Nominal valve clearance, 0.014 in. (0.35mm).	Starts 10 degrees BTDC, ends 54 degrees ABDC
Exhaust Valve	
1.7 liter (carburetor and injector models), and 1.85 liter (carburetor model). Nominal valve clearance, 0.43mm.	Starts 52 degrees BBDC, ends 12 degrees ATDC
1.85 liter (injection model). Nominal valve clearance, 0.43mm.	Starts 56 degrees BBDC, ends 16 degrees ATDC
2.0 liter (through 1974 models). Nominal valve clearance, 0.45mm.	Starts 70 degrees BBDC, ends 26 degrees ATDC
2.0 liter (1975-1976 models). Nominal valve clearance, 0.22 in. (0.55mm).	Starts 46 degrees BBDC, ends 18 degrees ATDC

Valve Mechanism
Valve grinding angle, intake and exhaust	
1.7 and 1.85 liter	45 degrees
2.0 liter	44.5 degrees
Valve seat angle in cylinder head, intake and exhaust	45.0 degrees
Valve seat width, intake and exhaust	
1.7 and 1.85 liter	2.2-2.5mm
2.0 liter	1.6-2.7mm
(through 1974 models)	
2.0 liter	1-2mm
(1975-1976 models)	
Valve stem diameter	
Intake, 1.7 and 1.85 liter	7.89-7.90mm
Intake, 2.0 liter	7.960-7.975mm
Exhaust, 1.7 and 1.85 liter	7.87-7.88mm
Exhaust, 2.0 liter	7.945-7.960mm
(through 1974 models)	
Exhaust, 2.0 liter	7.955-7.980mm
(1975-1976 models)	
Maximum play, valve stem/valve guide	0.5mm

(continued)

ENGINE

Table 2 ENGINE SPECIFICATIONS—SAAB 99 (continued)

Valve Mechanism (continued)

Valve diameter	
Intake, 1.7 and 1.85 liter	36.6mm
Intake, 2.0 liter	42.0mm
Exhaust, 1.7 and 1.85 liter	32.5mm
Exhaust, 2.0 liter	35.5mm
Valve guides	
Length	
1.7 and 1.85 liter	49mm
2.0 liter (through 1974 models)	49mm
2.0 liter (1975-1976 models)	46.65mm
Outer diameter	13mm
Cylinder head bore for valve guides	
1.7 and 1.85 liter	12.69-12.71mm
2.0 liter	13.000-13.018mm
Valve springs	
Installed length	
1.7 and 1.85 liter	36.3mm
2.0 liter	39.5mm
Free length	
1.7 and 1.85 liter	42.4mm
2.0 liter	44.3mm
Length at full elevation	
1.7 and 1.85 liter	27.9mm
2.0 liter	29.5mm
Load at full elevation	
1.7 and 1.85 liter	110±10 lb.
2.0 liter	178-198 lb.
Valve depressors	
1.7 and 1.85 liter	33.34-33.35mm (diameter) x 27mm (high)
2.0 liter	37.87-37.98mm (diameter) x 33mm (high)
Bore in cylinder head for valve depressors (camshaft bearing assembly)	
1.7 and 1.85 liter	33.37-33.38mm
2.0 liter	38.000-38.016mm
Pallets for valve adjustment	
Diameter	15.5mm
Thickness	1.77-2.89mm (There are 23 pallets of different thicknesses at intervals of 0.050mm)
Valve clearance	
Note: Check valve clearances with engine cold	
Intake	0.008-0.010 in. (0.20-0.25mm)
Exhaust	0.016-0.018 in. (0.40-0.45mm)
Idler shaft axial play (2.0 liter)	0.002-0.005 in. (0.05-0.13mm)
Lubrication System	
Type	Forced-flow circulating oil system, rotary-type or dual-rotor-type oil pump
Pressure lubricated points	Camshaft, crankshaft, idler shaft, connecting rods, transmission chain

(continued)

Table 2 ENGINE SPECIFICATIONS—SAAB 99 (continued)

Lubrication System (continued)

Splash-lubricated points	Piston pins, cylinder walls, valve depressors, and valve spindles
Oil filter	Full-flow type
Oil volume including filter	4.5 U.S. quarts (6 Imperial pints; 3.5 liters)
Oil pump	
Axial clearance between rotor and housing	
Rotary-type	0.001-0.005 in. (0.03-0.13mm)
Dual-rotor type	0.002-0.003 in. (0.05-0.090mm)
Radial clearance between rotor blades and housing (sum of both sides)	Maximum 0.026 in. (0.65mm)
Rotor shaft diameter	0.498-0.499 in. (12.66-12.67mm)
Bore for rotor shaft in pump housing	0.500-0.501 in. (12.70-12.72mm)
Reducing valve spring:	
Free length	2.06 in. (52.3mm)
Compressed length	1.32 in. (33.5mm)
Spring force at compressed length	15-16 lb. (6.8-7.3kp)

Table 3 ENGINE TORQUES — 95/96/SONETT

	ft.-lb.
Balance shaft gear bolt	36
Camshaft gear bolt	36
Camshaft thrust plate bolt	15
Clutch housing-to-engine bolts	30
Connecting rod bearing cap bolts	25
Cylinder head bolts	
Stage 1	40
Stage 2	50
Stage 3	68
Flywheel bolts	50
Front engine cover bolts	15
Intake manifold bolts	
Stage 1	5
Stage 2	15
Intermediate plate bolts	15
Main bearing cap bolts	72
Oil pan bolts	4
Oil pump-to-crankcase bolts	11
Valve cover bolts	4
Water pump connecting bolts	7

Table 4 ENGINE TORQUES — 99

	ft.-lb.
Camshaft bearing caps	13
Chainwheel, camshaft	14
Chainwheel, idler shaft	18
Crankshaft bearing caps	40
Crankshaft belt pulley	137
Cylinder head bolts	69
Exhaust manifold bolts	18
Flywheel bolts	43
Idler shaft keeper plate	14
Intake manifold bolts	13
Main bearing cap bolts	79
Oil pump mounting bolts	13
Sealing end (flywheel side)	14
Spark plugs	20
Thermostat housing	13
Throttle valve housing	13
Valve cover bolts	1.4
Water pump impeller (early version, screw)	18
Water pump impeller (later version, nut)	11

CHAPTER FIVE

FUEL AND EXHAUST SYSTEMS

Saab carburetor equipped engines in the 95/96 and Sonett used Solex carburetors through 1968 (designation 28-32 PDSIT-7 on engines through No. 16100, and 32-PDSIT-4 on engines from No. 16101 onward. FoMoCo carburetors were used from 1969 on. See **Figure 1** (carburetor 28-32 PDSIT-7 is illustrated but the functions described refer to carburetor 32-PDSIT-4 as well).

The carburetor on the 99 is a Zenith-Stromberg. See **Figure 2** for 1.7 and 1.85 engines and **Figure 3** for the 2.0 engine. In 1970, Saab added the 99E electronic fuel injection equipped engines. Both systems were used through 1974 on 1.7, 1.85, and 2.0 liter engines. A mechanical fuel injection system made its appearance on the 1975 99's (2.0 liter only) and the use of carburetors was discontinued. **Figure 4** shows the electronic and **Figure 5** the mechanical fuel injection systems.

Carburetor equipped engines through 1974 used mechanical fuel pumps, driven by a special cam on the idler shaft. The pump is located on the left-hand side of the engine. Fuel passes through a nylon filter in the pump. The earlier fuel pump has an external lever for manual fuel feed (**Figure 6**). **Figure 7** shows the later design.

Fuel injected engines use electric fuel pumps. **Figure 8** shows the pump used on the electric fuel injection system through 1974. The 1975-1976 pump for the mechanical fuel injection system is mounted inside the fuel tank.

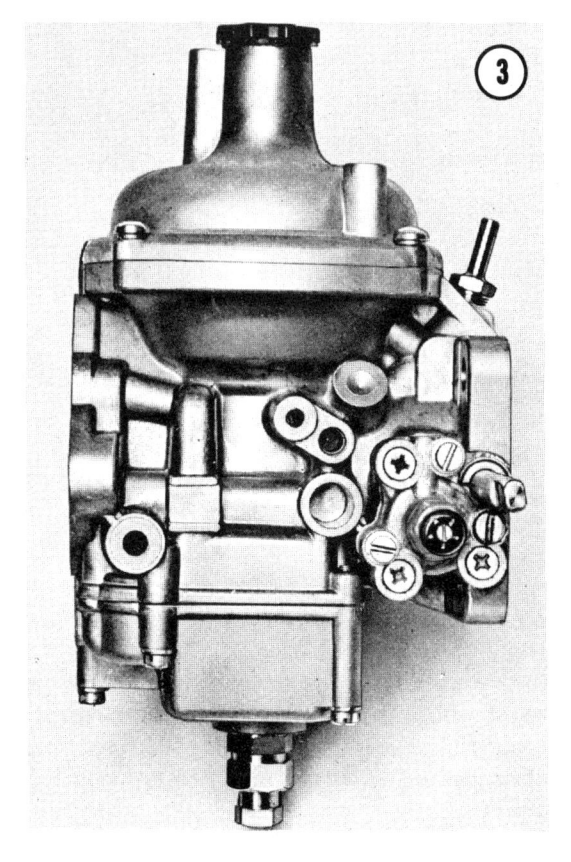

The fuel tank is located between the rear wheels on all models.

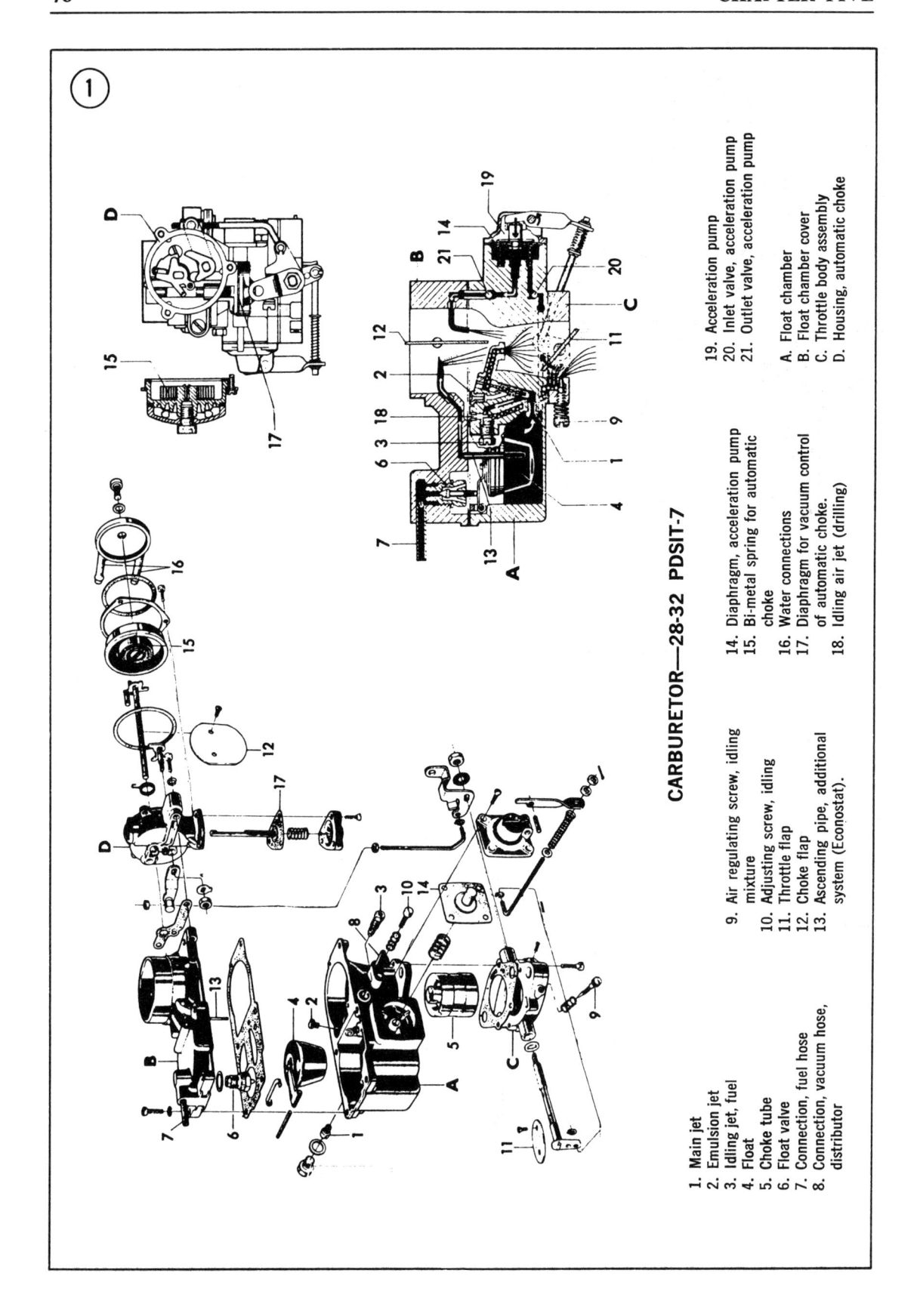

CHAPTER FIVE

CARBURETOR—28-32 PDSIT-7

1. Main jet
2. Emulsion jet
3. Idling jet, fuel
4. Float
5. Choke tube
6. Float valve
7. Connection, fuel hose
8. Connection, vacuum hose, distributor
9. Air regulating screw, idling mixture
10. Adjusting screw, idling
11. Throttle flap
12. Choke flap
13. Ascending pipe, additional system (Econostat).
14. Diaphragm, acceleration pump
15. Bi-metal spring for automatic choke
16. Water connections
17. Diaphragm for vacuum control of automatic choke.
18. Idling air jet (drilling)
19. Acceleration pump
20. Inlet valve, acceleration pump
21. Outlet valve, acceleration pump

A. Float chamber
B. Float chamber cover
C. Throttle body assembly
D. Housing, automatic choke

FUEL AND EXHAUST SYSTEMS

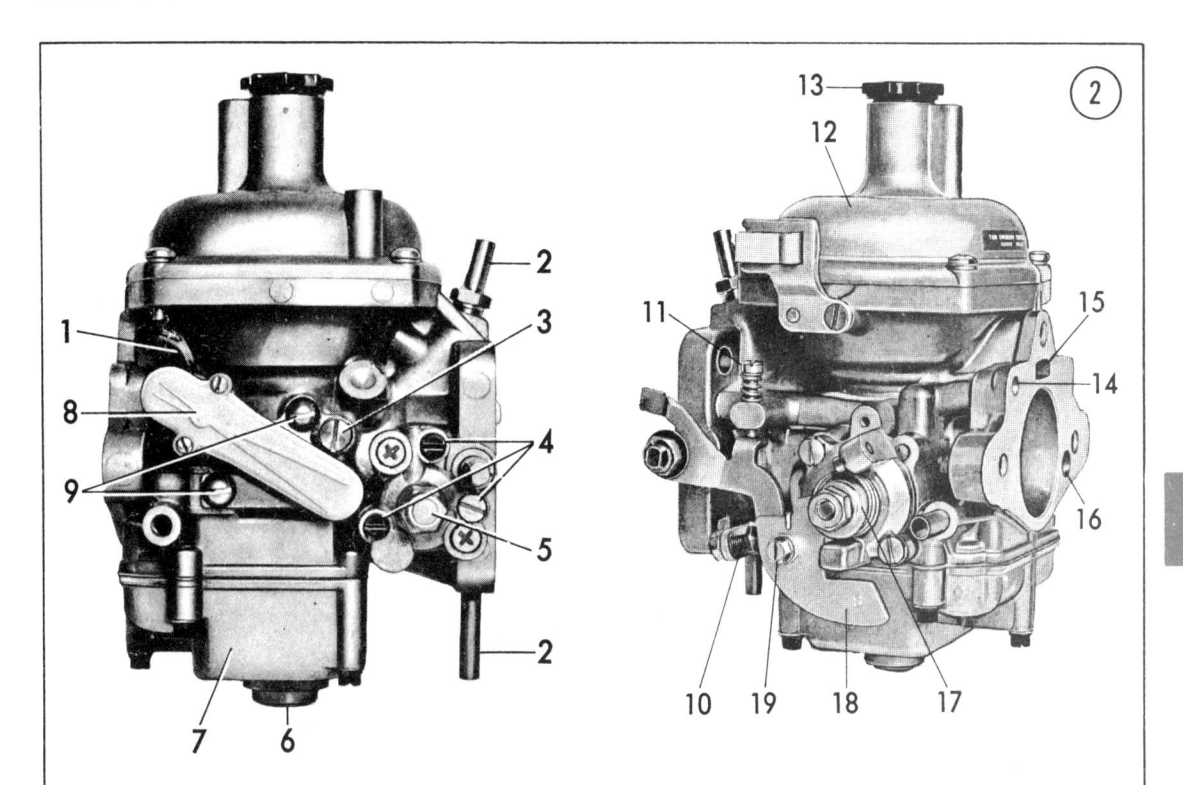

CARBURETOR, 1.7 AND 1.85 LITER ENGINES
(Saab 99 through 1974)

1. Clip, choke control wire
2. Vacuum chamber cover
3. Damper cap
4. Air channel, float chamber ventilation
5. Channel, air to space under diaphragm
6. Channel, air to temperature compensator
7. Choke
8. Fast idling cam
9. Connection, choke control wire
10. Adjusting screw, fast idling
11. Idling screw
12. Vacuum chamber cover
13. Damper cap
14. Air channel, float chamber ventilation
15. Channel, air to space under diaphragm
16. Channel, air to temperature compensator
17. Choke
18. Fast idling cam
19. Connection, choke control wire

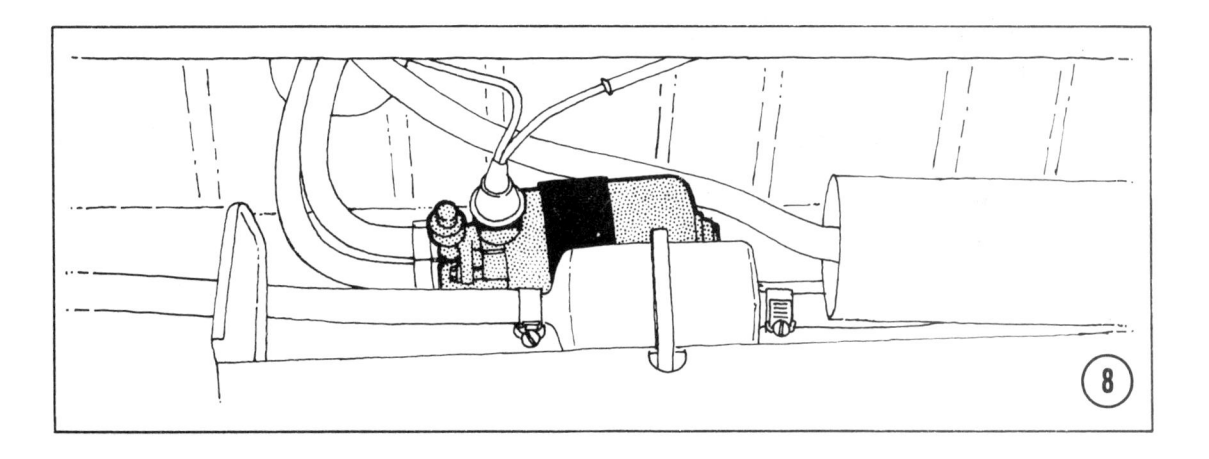

CHAPTER FIVE

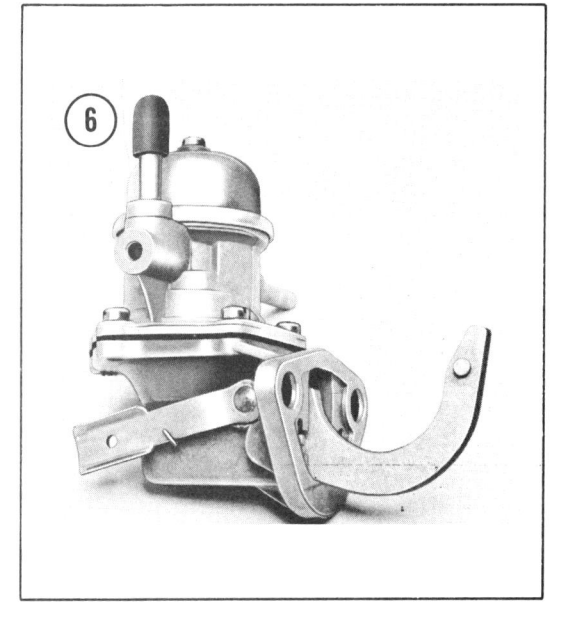

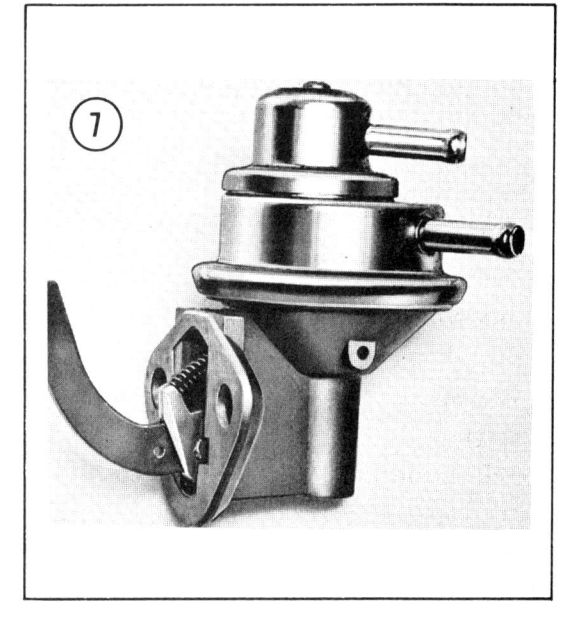

FUEL AND EXHAUST SYSTEMS

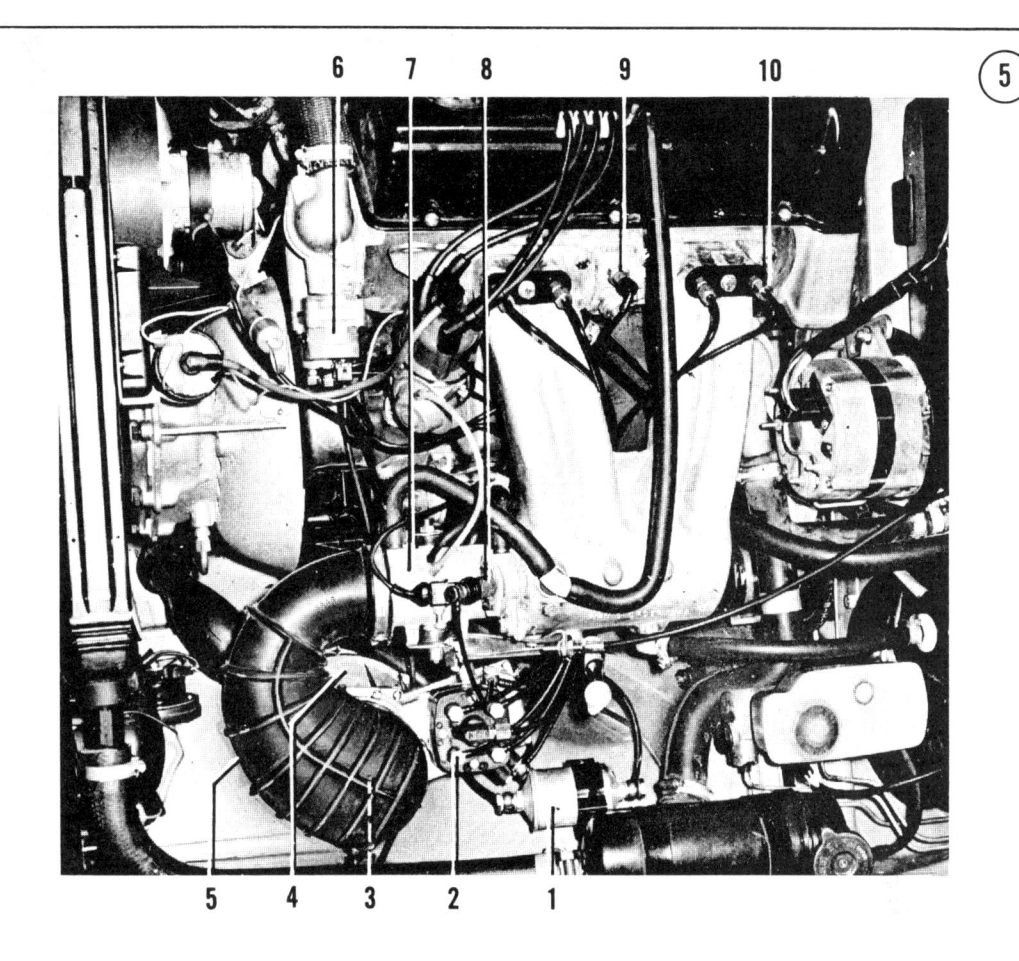

1975 MECHANICAL FUEL INJECTION SYSTEM

1. Fuel filter
2. Fuel distributor
3. Air flow sensor
4. Air cleaner
5. Rubber bellows
6. Warm-up regulator
7. Throttle valve housing
8. Cold start valve
9. Thermo-time switch
10. Injection valve

CARBURETOR

Removal/Installation

1. Drain off cooling water (95/96 and Sonett).

2. Remove air cleaner and preheater hose.

3. Disconnect water hoses from automatic choke (95/96 and Sonett).

4. Disconnect fuel line, throttle and choke controls, and distributor vacuum line.

5. Remove retaining nuts and lift off carburetor.

6. On the 32 PDSIT-4 carburetor disconnect hose from valve cover and remove intermediate flange. Cover opening in induction pipe.

7. Install by reversing preceding steps. Always use new gasket.

8. For carburetor adjustment see Chapter Two.

FUEL INJECTION SYSTEM

Due to the complexity of the fuel injection system it is recommended that service or replacement of any part of the fuel injection system be left to a qualified dealer, with the exception of the fuel and air filters (see Chapter Two).

MECHANICAL FUEL PUMP

Removal/Installation

1. Remove fuel line from pump.
2. Remove retaining bolts and washers. Remove pump and old gasket.
3. To install reverse preceding steps. Always use new gasket. See **Figure 9**.

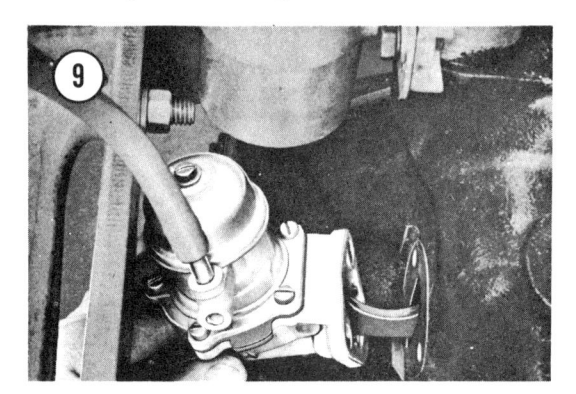

Disassembly

Refer to **Figure 10**.

1. Remove cover bolt. Unscrew cover and remove gasket and filter.
2. Mark flanges of top and bottom halves of pump housing so no mistake can be made during reassembly.
3. Remove flange bolts. Separate the 2 halves of housing.
4. Hold bottom half of housing and push down on the diaphragm. Twist ¼ turn to the right to disengage the diaphragm rod from pump lever. Remove diaphragm rod and spring. The top half of the pump containing the valves, and the bottom half containing the lever and manual priming lever cannot be disassembled further.

Assembly

1. Hold bottom half of pump and insert diaphragm with spring and rod so that rod slips into the slot in the lever.
2. Give diaphragm ¼ turn to the left. Be sure the rod has hooked on to lever.

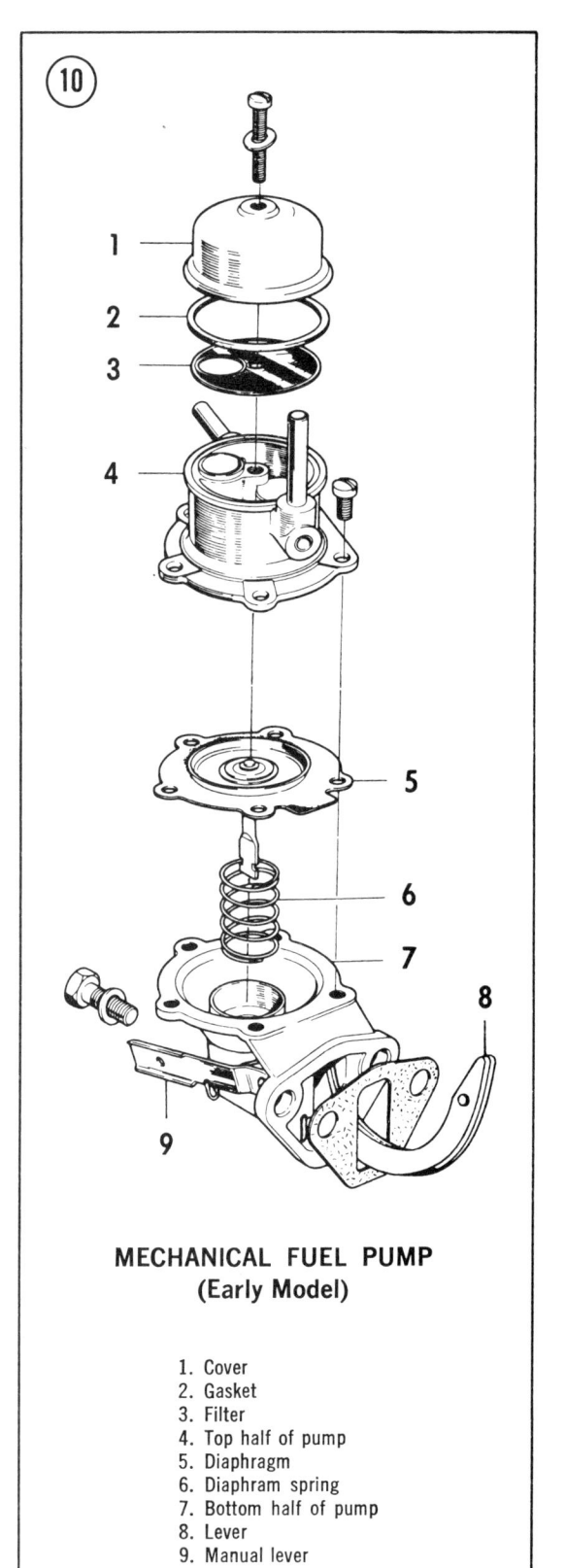

**MECHANICAL FUEL PUMP
(Early Model)**

1. Cover
2. Gasket
3. Filter
4. Top half of pump
5. Diaphragm
6. Diaphram spring
7. Bottom half of pump
8. Lever
9. Manual lever

FUEL AND EXHAUST SYSTEMS

3. Push in lever to relieve tension on the diaphragm. Align the top half of the pump by the flange markings. Insert screws in this position. Screw the 2 halves together.

4. Fit new gasket and filter. Screw on cover and install cover bolt.

> NOTE: *The late model mechanical fuel pump cannot be dismantled or repaired. Replace entire pump if faulty. The cover can be removed and the filter replaced or cleaned. A new gasket should always be used. Refer to* **Figure 11**.

MECHANICAL FUEL PUMP (Late Model) — Figure 11
- Cover
- Filter
- Gasket

Figure 12

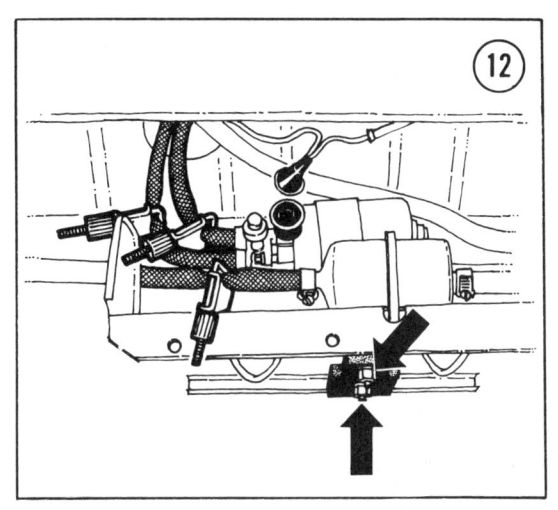

Installation

1. Install fuel hoses in the following sequence: suction side (23/64 in. [9mm] connection); pressure side (center conection); return side. Be sure you do not connect hoses wrong.

2. Fit pump together with the rubber pads.

3. Connect electrical plug.

ELECTRIC FUEL PUMP
(1975-1976)

Removal

1. Roll carpet back in trunk compartment. (On the 99 Wagonback remove rear floor cover and panel in trunk). Remove circular cover plate on top of pump mounting.

2. Disconnect battery to prevent risk of fire when fuel pump is opened.

3. Disconnect electric terminals at pump and fuel line. Hold pump with an open end wrench. See **Figure 13**.

4. Turn the pump mounting anticlockwise to the nearest groove to unlock bayonet socket. Use Saab tool No. 8392433 or equivalent (**Figure 14**). Lift unit out (**Figure 15**).

5. Cover the tank opening.

> **CAUTION**
> *Extreme care should be exercised when removing and installing the fuel pump due to fumes escaping from the open gas tank during this operation. Be certain no open flame or electrical apparatus is in the immediate vicinity.*

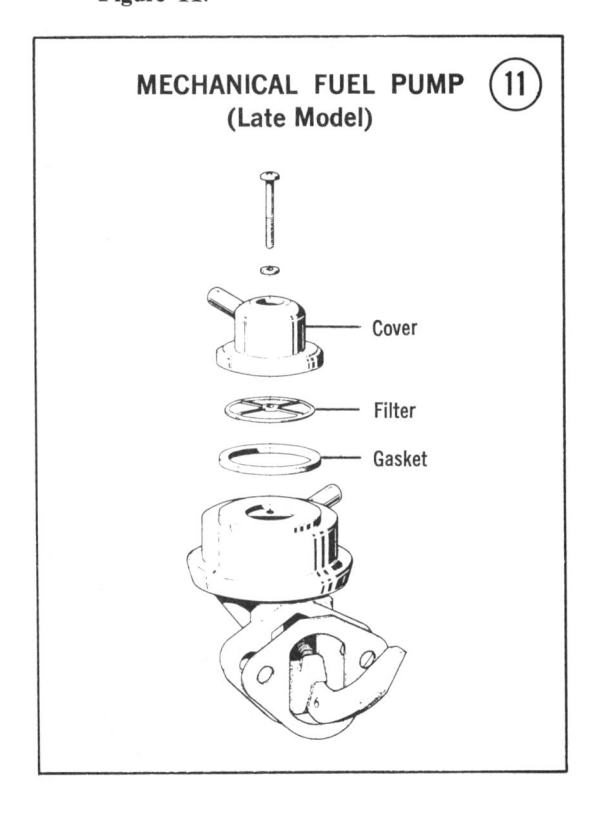

ELECTRIC FUEL PUMP
(1974 and Earlier)

Removal

1. Refer to **Figure 12**. Pinch off the 3 fuel hoses on the pump with clamps.

2. Disconnect electrical plug.

3. Loosen 2 fastening nuts (arrows, Figure 12) with a 13/32 (10mm) socket wrench.

4. Remove fuel pump, rubber pads, and fuel hoses together in an upward direction.

5. Open hose clamps. Pull fuel hoses off pump.

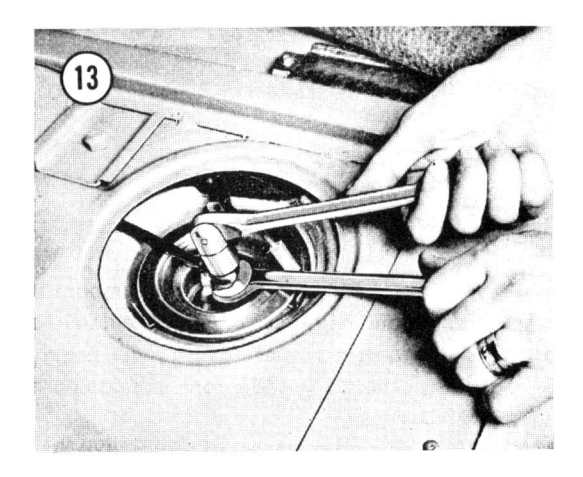

CHAPTER FIVE

others. The wider tongue is equipped with a locking groove.

2. Tighten pump with Saab tool No. 8392433 (Figure 14) or equivalent.

3. Connect fuel line. Use new sealing washers. Connect electric cables. Hold fuel pump with an open-end wrench when conection is loosened (Figure 13).

4. Connect battery.

5. Fit cover plate for pump opening in floor. Fit carpet. On the Wagonback fit the floor panel and rear floor cover.

FUEL TANK

Removal

1. Jack up rear of car.
2. Drain tank. (On the Sonett detach the lower fuel pump hose and drain fuel into a suitable container).
3. Remove rear seat, cushion, backrest, and sheathing over tank (95) or the right seat and sheathing (Sonett). On the 96 lift out spare wheel. Remove flooring where necessary.
4. Disconnect battery ground cable. Disconnect electrical, hose, and line connections on tank.
5. Loosen clips for vent and filler tubes under rear fender. Remove tubes.
6. Remove tank retaining straps (**Figure 16**).
7. Remove tank and rubber seal in wheel house well.

Installation

1. Be sure rubber seals are undamaged and correctly fitted around opening of fuel level transmitter, vent, and filler tubes.
2. Mount straps. Cover tank openings with masking tape.
3. Clamp wires to top of tank. Lift tank into position and suspend it in 2 straps. Center tank and tighten nuts (Figure 16). Remove masking tape from openings.
4. Connect fuel line hose and filler pipe. Position rubber seal.
5. Connect vent hose and upper filler pipe (from 1970 models onward also on top of the tank). Connect fuel level transmitter wires.

Installation

1. Place O-ring over tank opening and mount fuel pump. The pump fits in one position only because the bayonet socket tongue is wider than

FUEL AND EXHAUST SYSTEMS

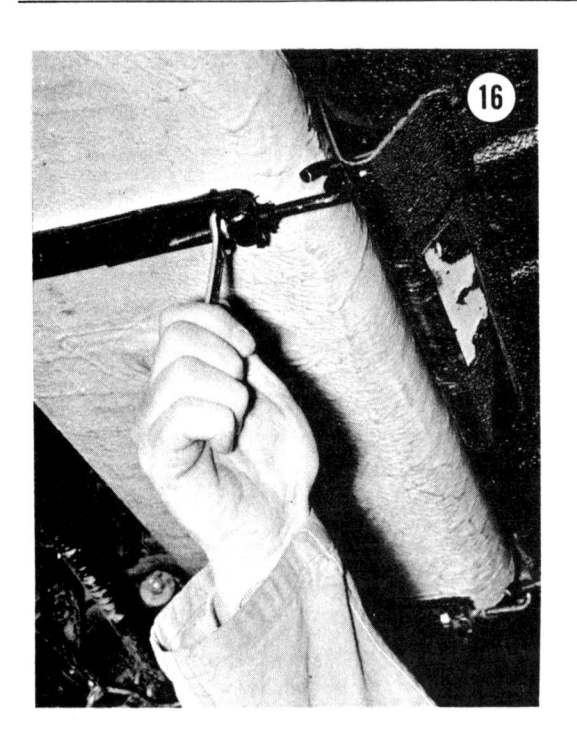

6. Replace the fuel lever transmitter access panel and the flooring, seats, and cushion, as necessary.

7. Replace wheel (96).

8. Lower car to ground.

EXHAUST SYSTEM

Front Muffler Removal/Installation (95/96 and Sonett)

1. Remove hood.

2. Jack up front of car and support with jackstands.

3. Disconnect battery cable.

4. Disconnect starting motor cables. Remove starter motor if necessary.

5. Remove nuts from engine connections. Remove binding clips from inlet pipe of muffler (at the engine brackets). Remove spacers and flame guard. See **Figure 17**.

6. Loosen exhaust pipe clamp. Separate exhaust pipe from muffler.

7. Remove muffler by lowering it and pulling the right side inlet pipe out through engine compartment floor. Turn the right side pipe forward between front panel and bumper. Then the left pipe can be removed.

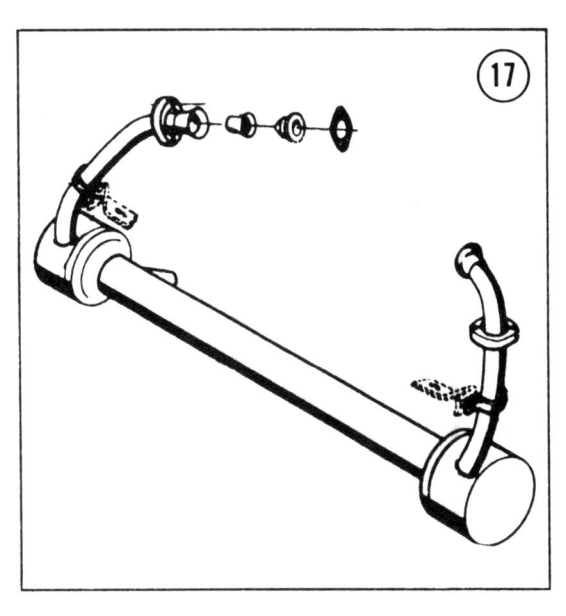

8. Install by reversing preceding steps. Always use new gaskets.

Rear Muffler Removal/Installation (95/96 and Sonett)

1. Jack up the right side of the car. Remove rear wheel.

2. Loosen exhaust pipe clamp at rear muffler (**Figure 18**).

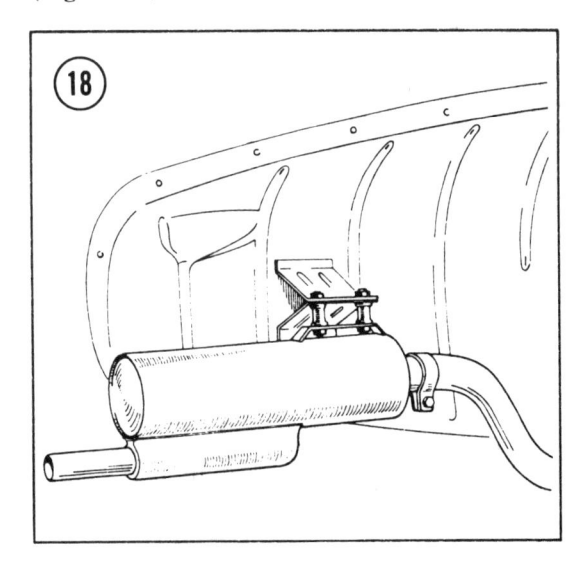

3. Loosen 2 upper nuts by which muffler is suspended.

4. Detach muffler from exhaust pipe.

5. Install by reversing preceding steps.

Muffler Removal/Installation (99, through 1974)

1. Jack up front of car. Support on jackstands.
2. Remove preheater casing. Remove bolts securing front exhaust pipe to exhaust manifold (**Figure 19**).
3. Remove clamps holding connecting ring at the joint with the middle exhaust pipe. Unhook rubber suspension from front exhaust pipe and separate the pipes.
4. Detach rubber suspensions and clamps in order to remove muffler and other sections of pipe.
5. Install by reversing preceding steps.

> NOTE: *After installing check exhaust system for leaks and contact with the body, heat shield, or fuel filler extension hose. Pipe clamps are to be fitted with plate washer pointing 45 degrees downward. Effective with the 1971 1.7 liter engine No. JB 85583 and 1.85 liter engine No. JE 77539* (**Figure 20**) *the exhaust manifold is fitted with 2 outlets and the front muffler with 2 pipes. The exhaust system used on chassis No. 99722012428 onward is shown in* **Figure 21**.

Muffler Removal/Installation (99, 1975-1976)

1. Jack up car. Support on jackstands.
2. Remove bolts holding front exhaust pipe to exhaust manifold (**Figure 22**).
3. Remove clamp holding connecting ring at joint with middle exhaust pipe. Separate pipes.
4. Remove rear muffler and other sections of pipe by detaching rubber suspensions and clamps from the part to be removed. Be sure to check for leaks and contact with the body after installation is completed.

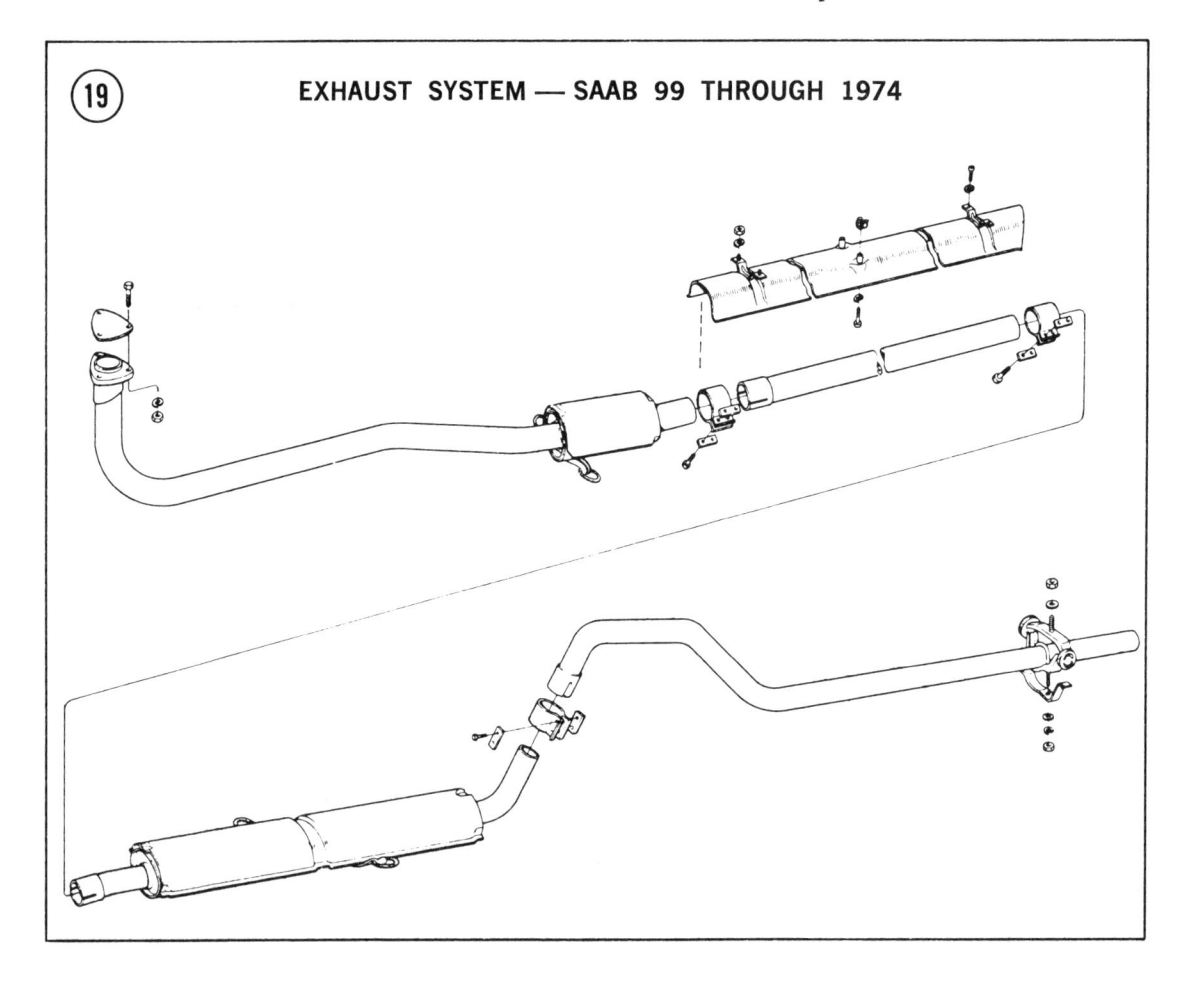

(19) EXHAUST SYSTEM — SAAB 99 THROUGH 1974

FUEL AND EXHAUST SYSTEMS

EXHAUST SYSTEM — SAAB 99 THROUGH 1974

1.7 LITER (Engine No. JB 85583 Onward) and
1.85 LITER (Engine No. JE 77539 Onward)

(20)

CHASSIS No. 99722012428 ONWARD

(21)

88 CHAPTER FIVE

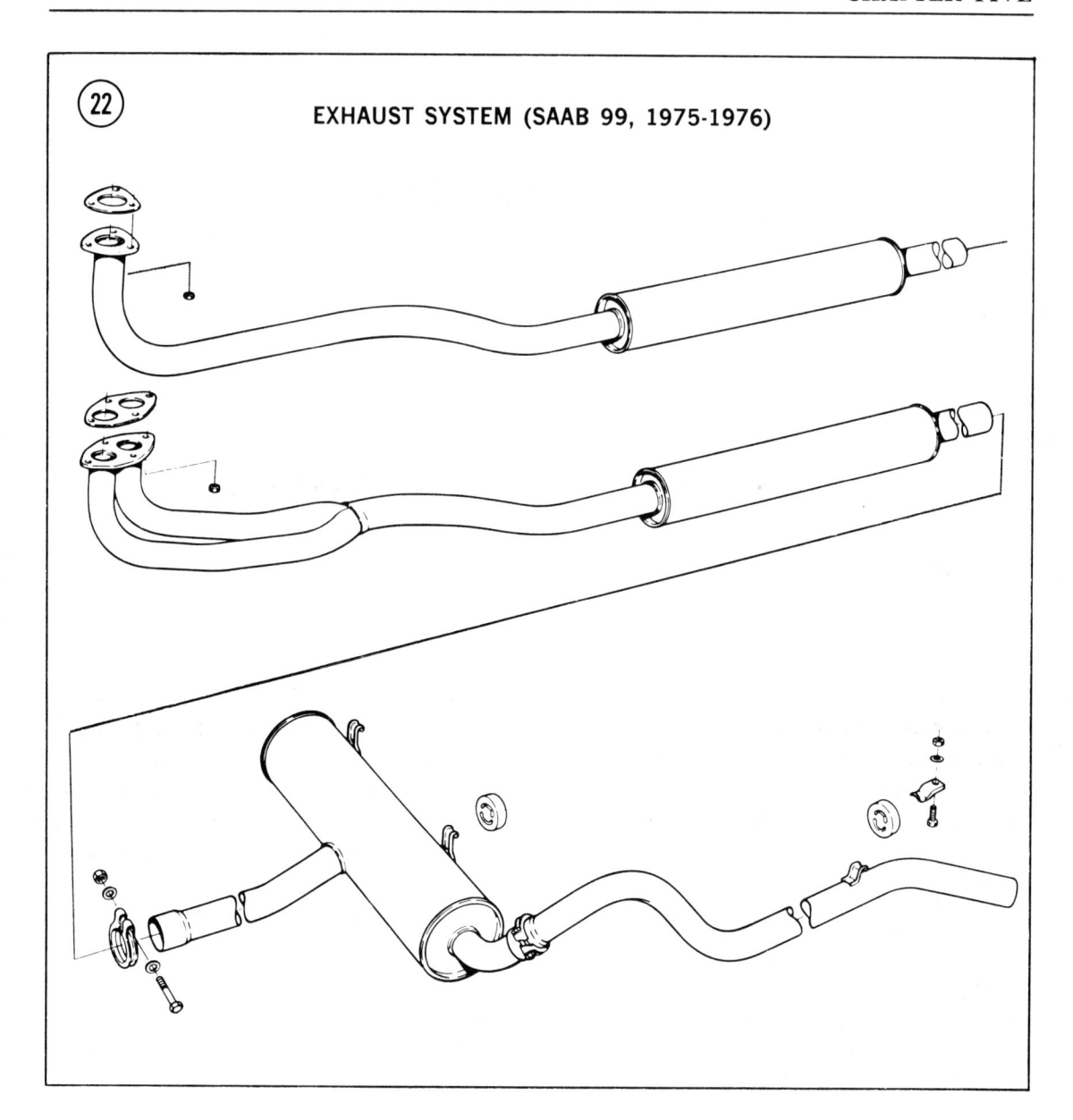

22 EXHAUST SYSTEM (SAAB 99, 1975-1976)

CHAPTER SIX

COOLING AND HEATING SYSTEMS

The pressurized cooling system incorporates a crossflow radiator and expansion tank. The impeller type water pump is driven by a belt from the balance shaft pulley which also drives the fan on the 95/96 and Sonett models. The fan on the 99 is electrically driven and controlled by a thermostat.

A conventional thermostat controls the passage of the cooling water through the cylinder block, cylinder head, inlet manifold, and heater.

Figures 1 and **2** show the cooling systems used on the various 95/96 models; **Figure 3** the system for the Sonett; and **Figures 4, 5, 6, and 7** the systems for the various 99 models.

RADIATOR

Removal/Installation (95/96 and Sonett)

1. Remove hood.
2. On the Sonett jack up the car and place jackstands under the front edge of the sills.
3. Remove horns (Sonett only).
4. Remove bolts holding upper and lower front stays together (Sonett only). Bend upper stay out of way to provide access to upper retaining bolts of the radiator.
5. Disconnect upper and lower hoses from radiator and expansion tank hose from the tank.
6. Remove radiator retaining bolts. Remove radiator by lifting out (95/96) or by pulling it out right side first (99, see **Figure 8**), then rearward and inward so as to release the left-side pipe.
7. Install by reversing preceding steps.

Removal/Installation (Saab 99)

1. Drain coolant.
2. Disconnect water hoses.
3. Disconnect wiring for radiator fan and thermoswitch.
4. Remove front sheet and radiator (**Figure 9**).
5. Install by reversing preceding steps.

EXPANSION TANK

Removal/Installation

1. Remove water hose.
2. Remove tank retaining bolts.
3. Remove tank.
4. Install by reversing preceding steps.

CHAPTER SIX

SAAB 95/96 COOLING SYSTEM (through 1969)

→ Water
⇨ Warm air
⇒ Cold air

1. Water pump
2. Radiator
3. Radiator cap
4. Expansion tank
5. Pressure cap
6. Fan
7. Temperature transmitter
8. Thermostat
9. By-pass
10. Water jacket, automatic choke
11. Heater core
12. Bleeding nipple
13. Fan motor
14. Side defroster hose
15. Defroster jet
16. Collector box
17. Cold air intake
18. Defroster pipe
19. Fan wheel
20. Air distributor
21. Thermostat valve
22. Drain valve
23. Drain plugs (1 on each side)

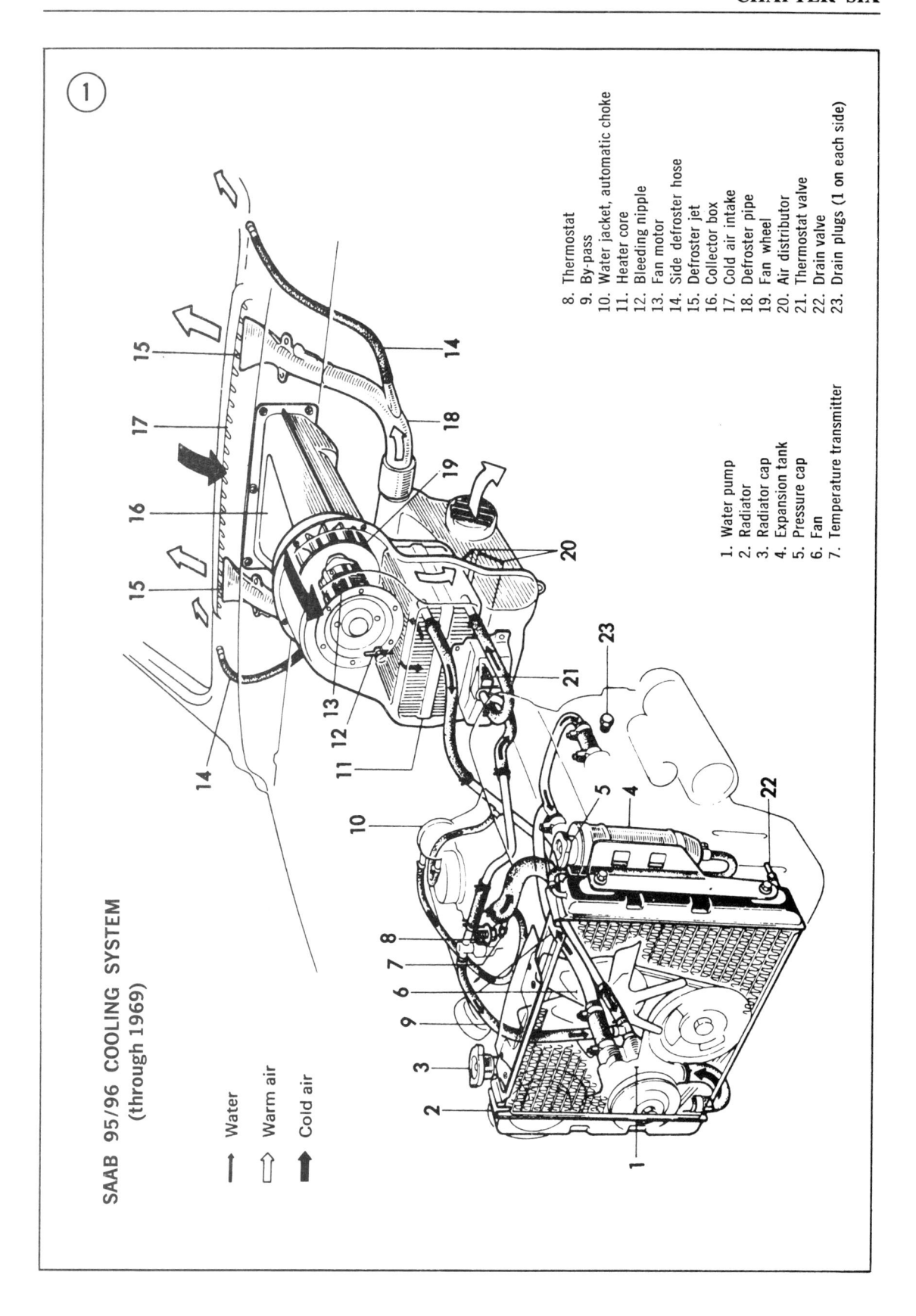

COOLING AND HEATING SYSTEMS

SAAB 95/96 COOLING SYSTEM
(from 1970 onward)

→ Water
⇧ Warm air
⬆ Cold air

1. Water pump
2. Radiator
3. Radiator cap
4. Expansion tank
5. Pressure cap
6. Fan
7. Temperature transmitter
8. Thermostat
9. By-pass
10. Water jacket, automatic choke
11. Heat exchanger
12. Bleeding nipple
13. Fan motor
14. Side defroster hose
15. Defroster jet
16. Collector box
17. Cold air intake
18. Defroster pipe
19. Fan wheel
20. Air distributor
21. Thermostat valve
22. Drain valve
23. Drain plugs (1 on each side)

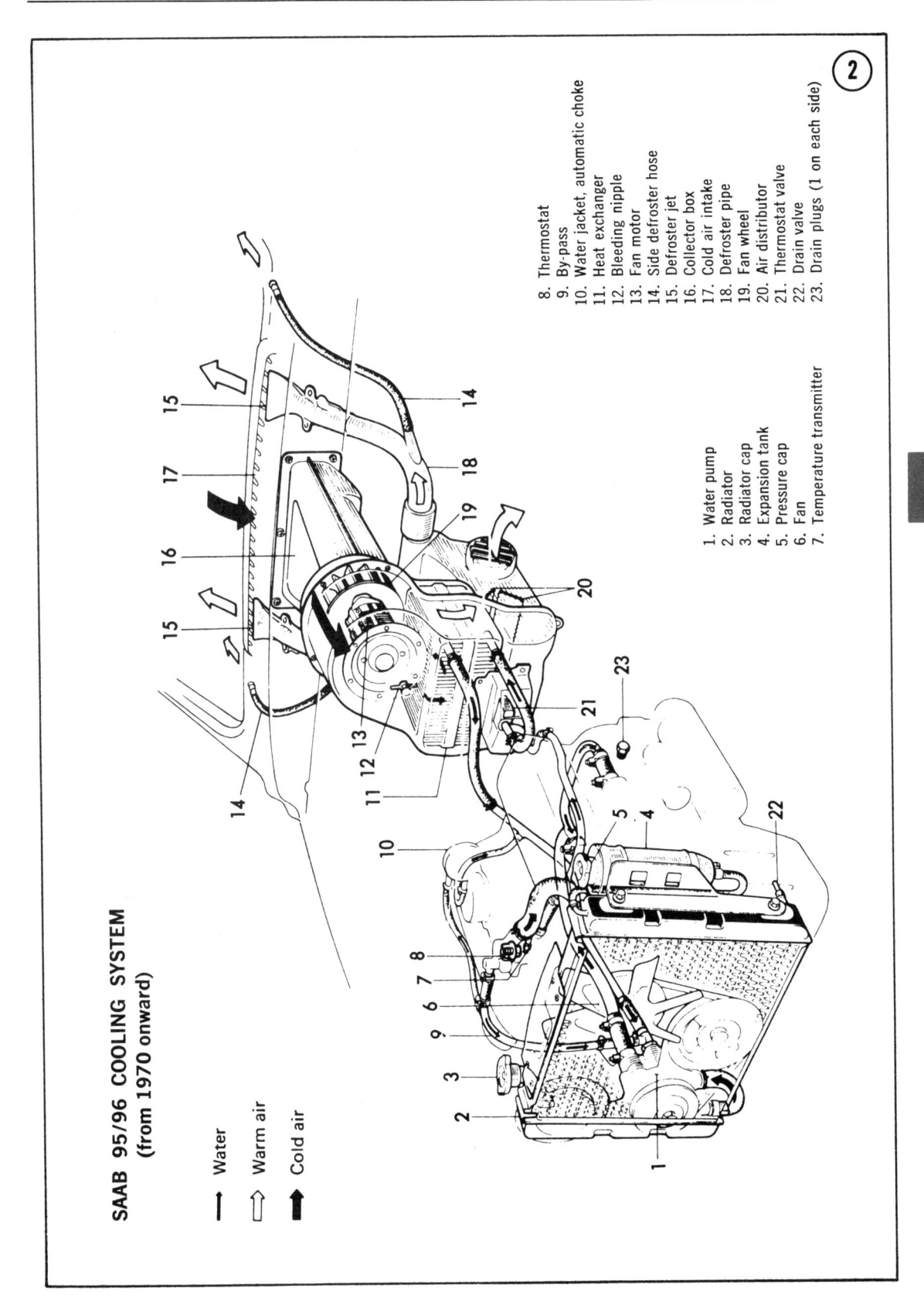

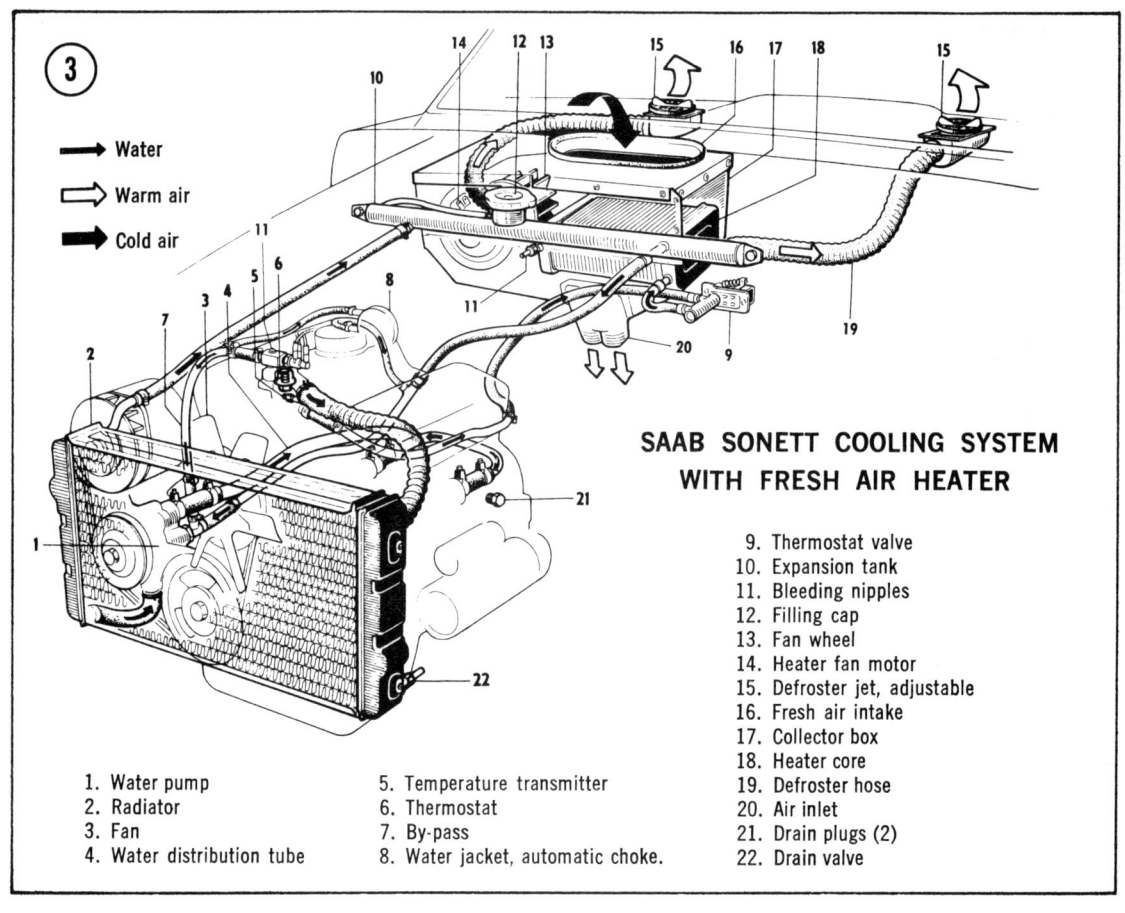

SAAB SONETT COOLING SYSTEM WITH FRESH AIR HEATER

→ Water
⇨ Warm air
⇒ Cold air

1. Water pump
2. Radiator
3. Fan
4. Water distribution tube
5. Temperature transmitter
6. Thermostat
7. By-pass
8. Water jacket, automatic choke.
9. Thermostat valve
10. Expansion tank
11. Bleeding nipples
12. Filling cap
13. Fan wheel
14. Heater fan motor
15. Defroster jet, adjustable
16. Fresh air intake
17. Collector box
18. Heater core
19. Defroster hose
20. Air inlet
21. Drain plugs (2)
22. Drain valve

SAAB 99 COOLING SYSTEM THROUGH 1970 MODELS

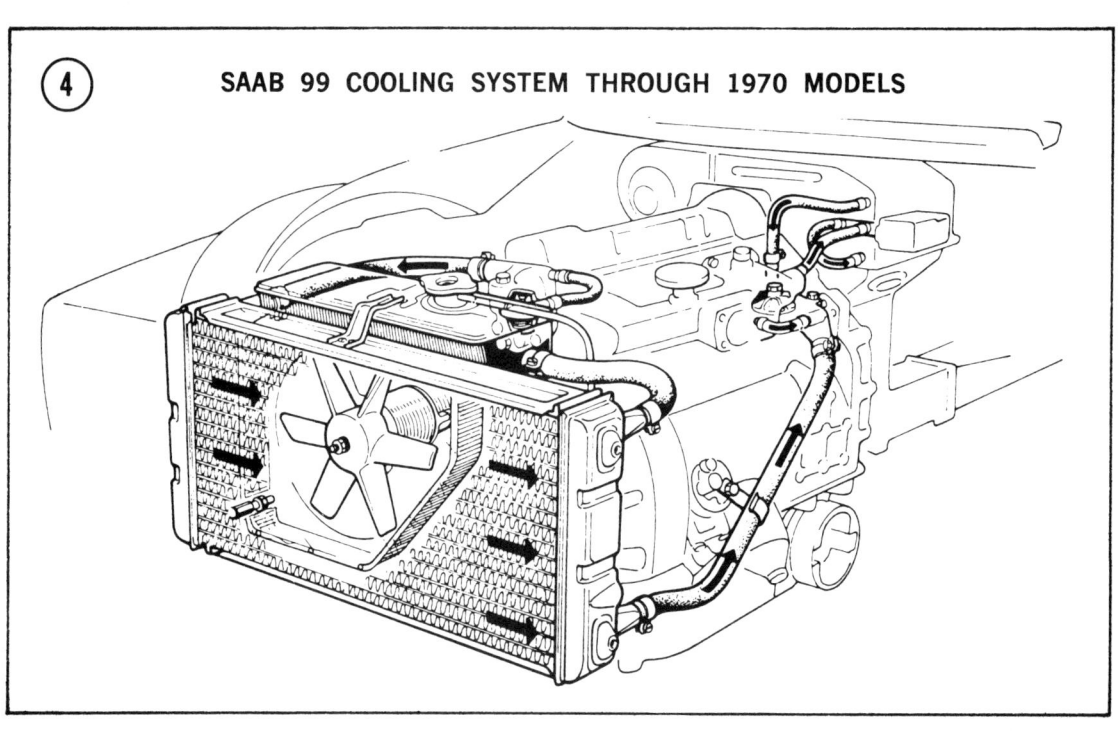

COOLING AND HEATING SYSTEMS

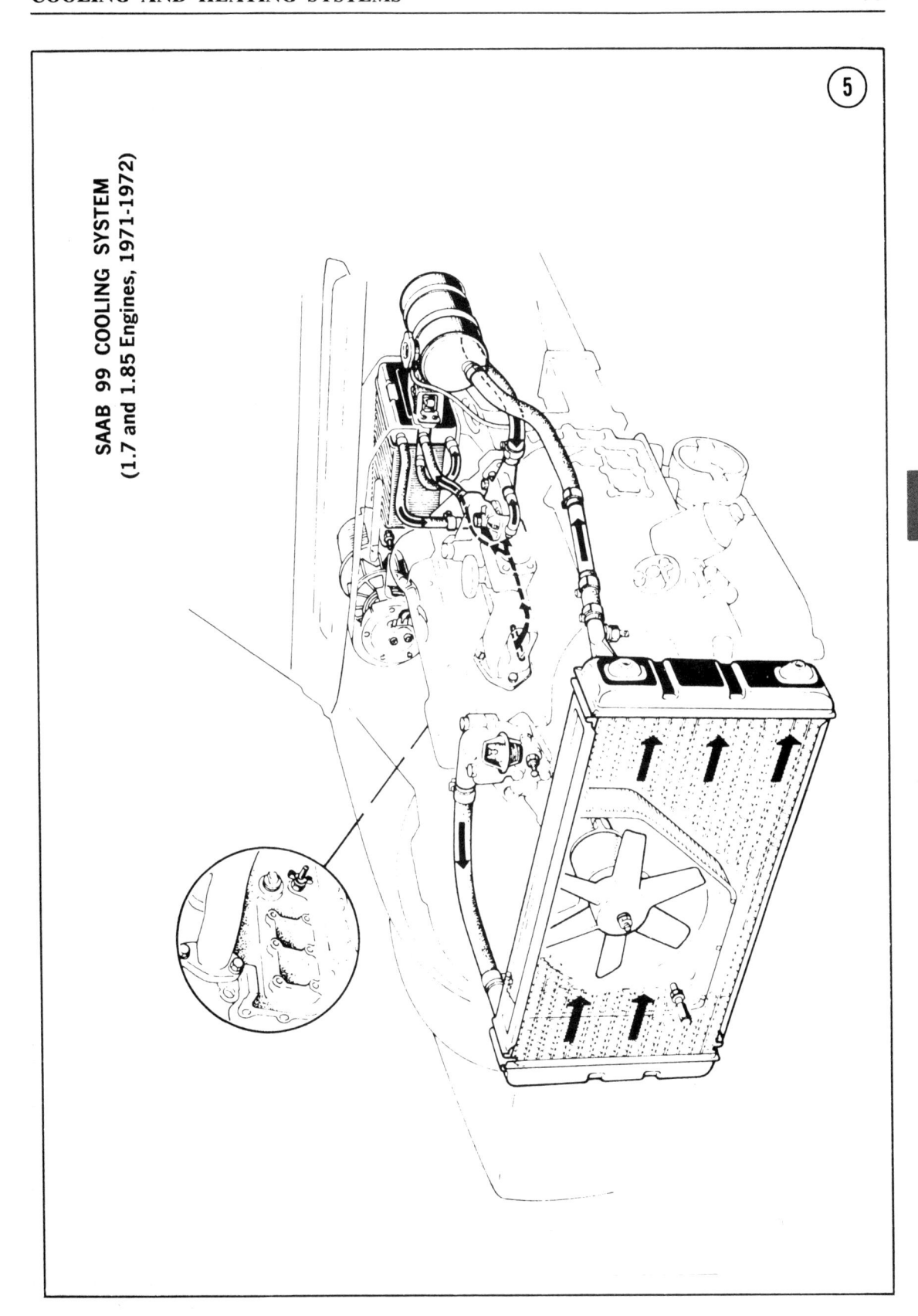

SAAB 99 COOLING SYSTEM
(1.7 and 1.85 Engines, 1971-1972)

(5)

CHAPTER SIX

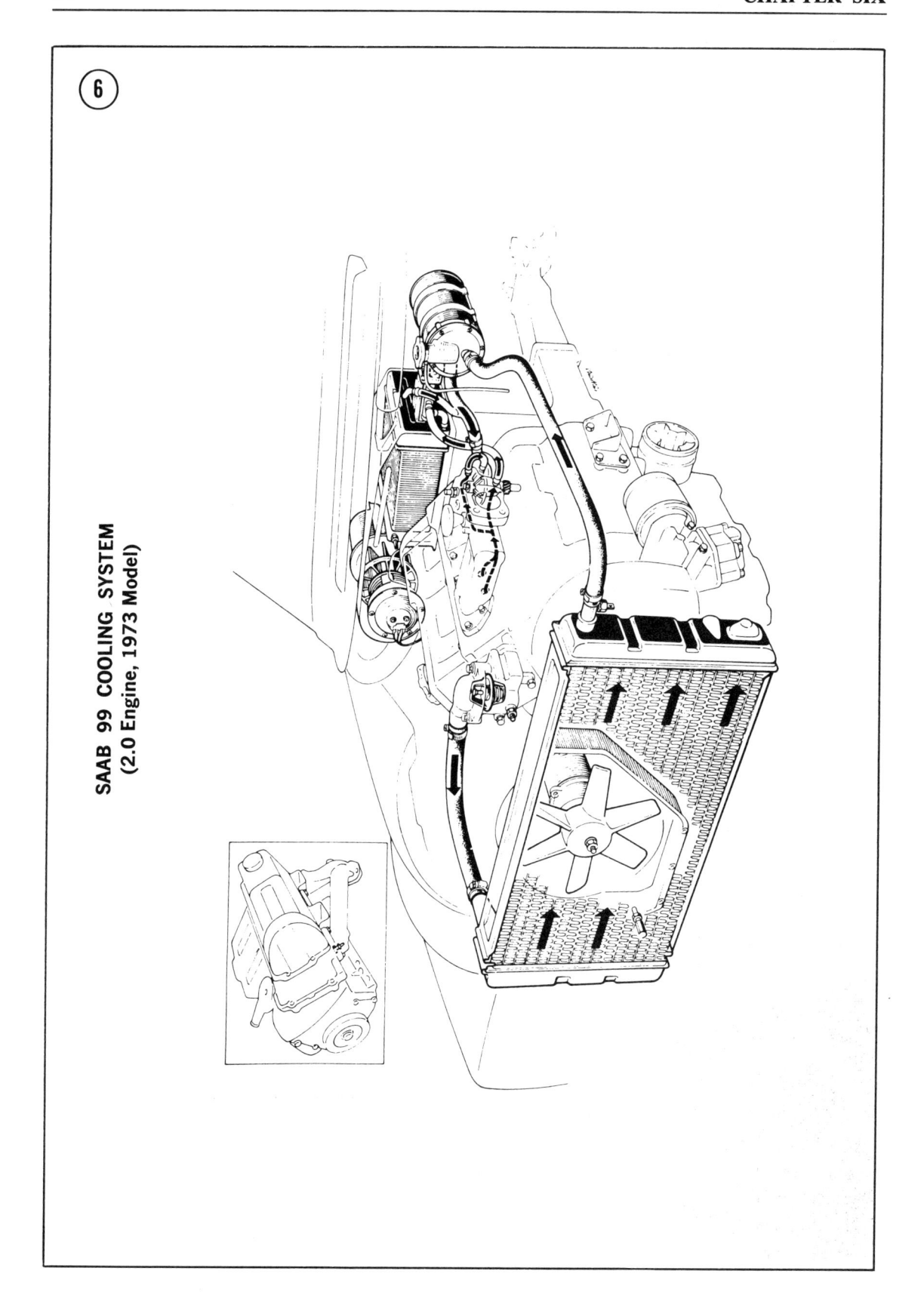

SAAB 99 COOLING SYSTEM
(2.0 Engine, 1973 Model)

COOLING AND HEATING SYSTEMS

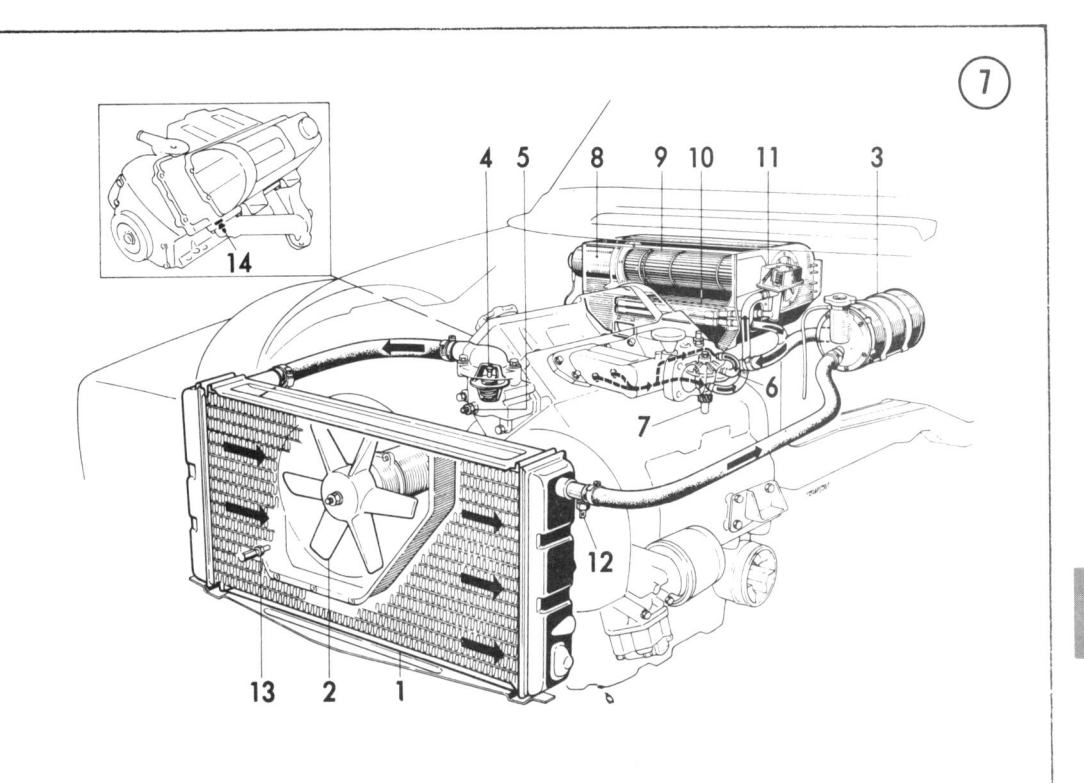

95

SAAB 99 COOLING SYSTEM
(2.0 Engine, 1974 onward)

1. Radiator
2. Radiator fan
3. Expansion tank with pressure cap
4. Thermostat
5. Temperature transmitter
6. By-pass line
7. Coolant pump
8. Fan motor
9. Impeller
10. Heater core
11. Thermostat controlled valve
12. Thermostat switch, radiator fan
13. Radiator drain cock
14. Engine drain cock

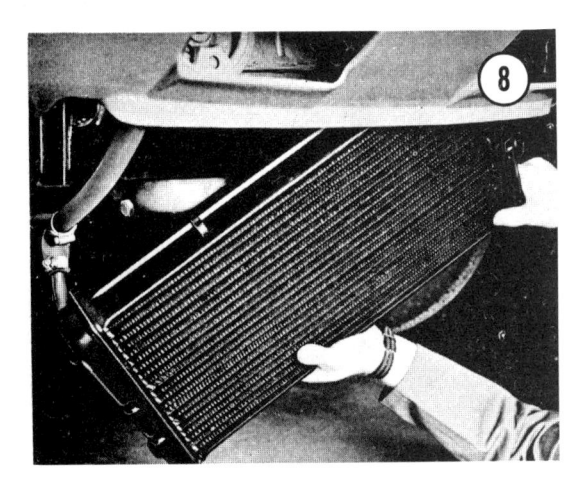

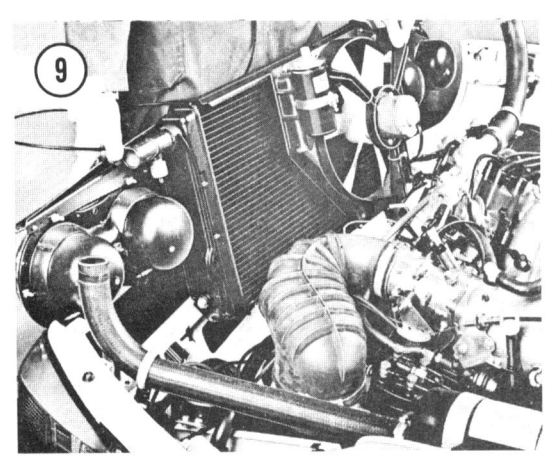

WATER DISTRIBUTION PIPE AND WATER HOSES

Removal
(95/96 and Sonett)

1. Drain coolant.
2. Loosen 3 hose clamps. Allow hoses to remain on water distribution tube. See **Figure 10**.

3. Loosen clamp holding water pipes together.
4. Remove water distribution tube from engine together with hoses.

Installation
(95/96 and Sonett)

1. Wet hoses and push onto water distribution pipe.
2. Hold distribution pipe over engine connection tailpieces. Slide hoses on.
3. Tighten hose and pipe clamps.
4. Fill cooling system and bleed it (see *Changing Coolant* this chapter).

WATER PUMP

Removal/Installation
(95/96 and Sonett)

1. Drain coolant.
2. Remove alternator and its bracket.
3. Remove belt.
4. Loosen water pump retaining bolts but allow them to remain in transmission cover. Remove water pump (**Figure 11**).
5. Install new gasket.
6. Install rebuilt water pump by reversing preceding steps.

Removal/Installation
(Saab 99)

Special tools are required to replace the water pump on the 99. It is recommended that this be left up to an authorized Saab dealer.

THERMOSTAT

Removal
(95/96 and Sonett)

1. Drain coolant (see *Changing Coolant*, this chapter).
2. Remove air filter and carburetor.
3. Disconnect water hoses.
4. Remove bolts and lift upper part of thermostat housing off (**Figure 12**). Remove thermostat.

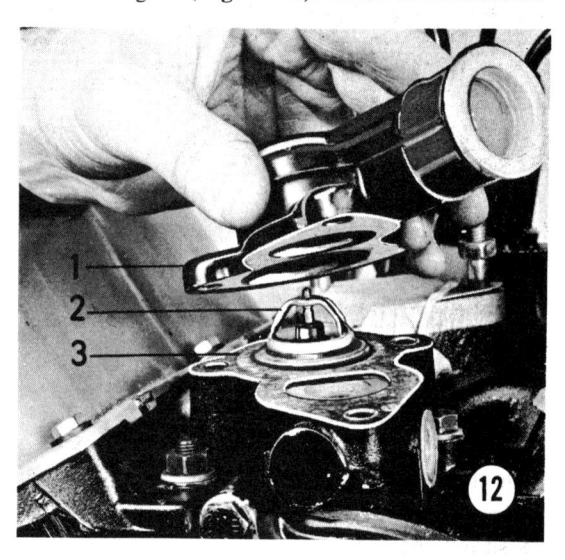

1. Thermostat housing cover   2. Thermostat   3. Gasket

COOLING AND HEATING SYSTEMS

Installation
(95/96 and Sonett)

1. Clean thermostat housing gasket surface to remove residual gasket material.

> NOTE: *The thermostat retaining bracket must be perpendicular to the longitudinal axis of the car. Otherwise the bracket will be squeezed by the water outlet tailpiece.*

2. Install new thermostat and gasket and screw on the upper part. See **Figure 13**.
3. Connect water hoses.
4. Install carburetor and air filter.
5. Fill system with coolant (see *Changing Coolant*, this chapter).

Removal/Installation
(Saab 99)

1. Drain coolant (see *Changing Coolant*, this chapter).
2. Disconnect water hose.
3. Remove bolts and lift upper part of thermostat housing off. **Figure 14** shows housing with thermostat, water outlet pipe, and valve body, as used through 1970 model 99's; **Figure 15** shows the thermostat and water outlet pipe used from 1971 on).
4. Clean thermostat housing gasket surface to remove residual gasket material.
5. Install new gasket and thermostat by reversing preceding steps.

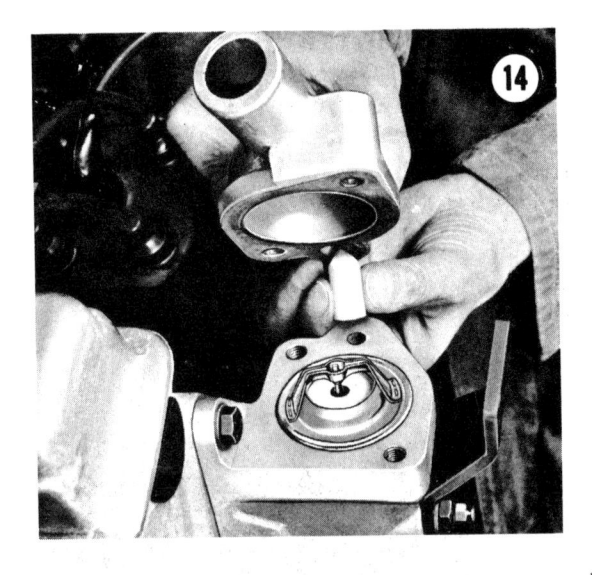

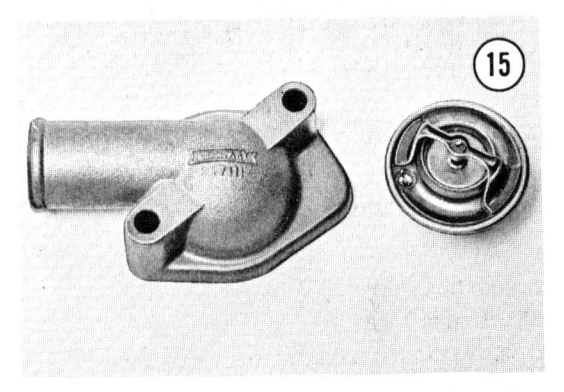

CHANGING COOLANT

1. Unscrew radiator and expansion tank caps.
2. Drain coolant through radiator and engine block drain cocks. Open heater core bleeder nipple and set the heater control to maximum.
3. Close drain cocks and fill the system with fresh coolant.

> NOTE: *Use at least a 50/50 mixture of ethylene glycol and water even if you live in a climate which does not require this degree of freeze protection; the anti-freeze makes a good rust inhibitor. Use more anti-freeze if temperatures in your area require it.*

4. Start the engine and let it run at moderate speed with heater control set to maximum heat until coolant overflows from the heater core bleeder nipple with no air bubbles.

5. Close bleeder nipple. Stop engine and top up with more coolant if necesary. (Use only clean liquid for filling).

FAN MOTOR

Removal/Installation

1. Remove battery.
2. On models up to and including 1970 loosen expansion tank and lay to one side (**Figure 16**).
3. Disconnect electric wires from ignition coil and fan. Disconnect cable harness from fan housing.
4. Remove headlight wiper motor (1971 onward).
5. Loosen fan housing with the fan. Lift it out.
6. Remove nut on fan motor shaft. Remove the fan.
7. Remove 2 retaining screws. Remove fan motor.
8. Install by reversing preceding steps. Check operation of radiator fan by grounding connecting wire to the thermoswitch.

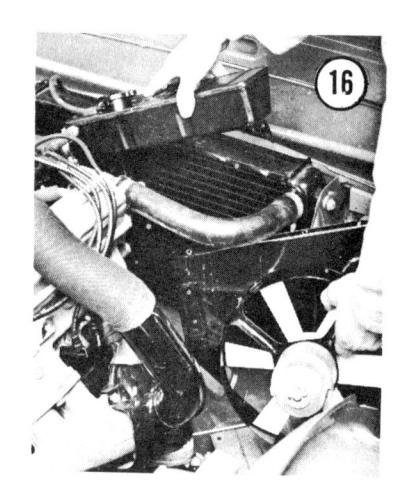

CHAPTER SEVEN

EMISSION CONTROL SYSTEM

The 1970 V4 engines used in the 95/96 and Sonett models were the first ones fitted with an emission control system consisting of a deceleration valve, modified carburetor, an altered distributor advance curve, an air cleaner incorporating a thermostatically controlled valve assembly, and enclosed crankcase ventilation system (later models).

Further refinement of the emission control system was achieved in 1971 when an evaporative loss control unit was added to the fuel system. The unit prevents fuel tank vapors from being discharged directly into the atmosphere.

The 99 inline engine uses the same emission control system with the addition of a fully enclosed crankcase ventilation system.

To further reduce emission, 1975-1976 models have an exhaust emission control system (EGR), which reintroduces some of the exhaust gas into the intake manifold and reburns it.

Very little maintenance is required on emission control systems. When trouble does occur it is generally best left to factory trained Saab specialists to handle.

DECELERATION VALVE

Refer to **Figure 1**. The deceleration valve provides satisfactory combustion of fuel during engine deceleration. An intermediate plate is used to connect the deceleration valve assembly to the inlet manifold. A spring loaded diaphragm is fitted into the valve body and held in place by the bottom cover. Manifold vacuum acts on the top side of the diaphragm and atmospheric pressure on the bottom side via a bleed hole in the cover.

During deceleration manifold vacuum is sufficient for the diaphragm to overcome the spring loading and lift the deceleration valve off its seat. The fuel and air needed for combustion is supplied to the engine through a connecting hose between the deceleration valve and the decelerating section of the carburetor.

Inspection

1. Allow the engine to idle until it reaches normal operating temperature.
2. With the air cleaner in place check that the deceleration valve is not working at idle. This can be achieved by disconnecting the hose between the deceleration valve and the carburetor. If the valve is open (vacuum passing the valve) the adjusting screw on the deceleration valve must be screwed in until the valve is closed. Connect the hose.
3. Connect a tachometer and adjust the idle speed to 900 rpm. Advance the engine speed to 3,000 rpm with the throttle. Release the

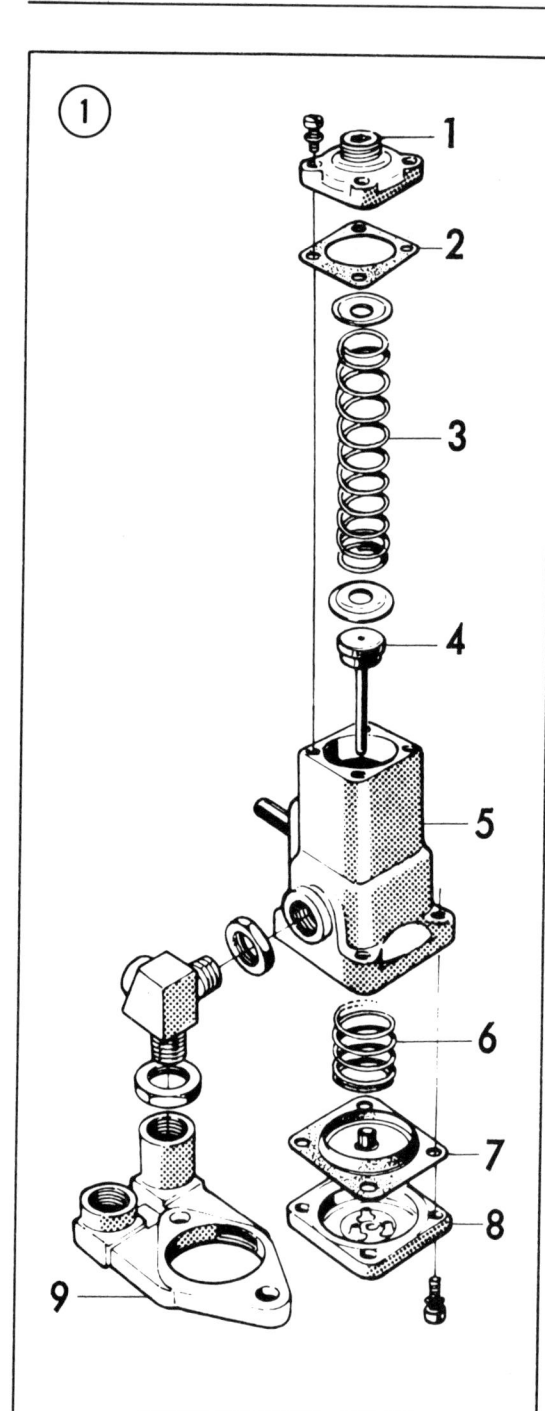

throttle quickly and allow the engine speed to drop to idle. Time the drop from 3,000 rpm to idle. A correctly adjusted deceleration valve should drop the engine speed to idle in 7 to 8 seconds.

Adjustment

After checking the deceleration valve and determining that it needs adjusting, remove the air cleaner and proceed as follows:

1. If the engine speed drops from 3,000 rpm to idle in more than 7 to 8 seconds, screw the deceleration valve adjusting screw in until the desired time is reached. If the time is less than 7 to 8 seconds the adjusting screw should be screwed out until the desired time is reached.

2. Install the air cleaner and recheck the time. If necessary repeat the procedure until the correct time is achieved.

> NOTE: *Irregular idling or stalling could be the result of diaphragm failure in the deceleration valve (allowing air to pass from the bleed hole in the cover through the diaphragm and straight into the inlet manifold, which would result in a weak fuel/air mixture). If both the carburetor and ignition settings are correct, check the diaphragm by covering the bleed hole. If idling is restored replace the deceleration valve.*

Removal

1. Disconnect the inlet pipe to the deceleration valve.

2. Remove the nuts holding the deceleration unit to the inlet manifold. Lift the unit off.

Disassembly/Reassembly

1. Remove the retaining screws holding the cover to the body. Lift off the cover and diaphragm slowly to release spring pressure.

2. Replace the diaphragm, carefully positioning it on the end of the valve stem.

3. Set the cover in place and insert the retaining screws. Tighten them evenly to avoid distortion of the cover.

DECELERATION VALVE

1. Adjusting screw
2. Gasket
3. Spring
4. Valve
5. Body
6. Spring
7. Diaphragm
8. Bottom cover
9. Intermediate plate

EMISSION CONTROL SYSTEM

Installation

1. Install the deceleration valve on the inlet manifold. Tighten the retaining nuts evenly.
2. Connect the inlet pipe.

> NOTE: *An abnormally high idling speed (1200-1400 rpm) which cannot be eliminated by normal adjustment could be caused by a permanently open deceleration valve. Remove the valve unit (see Removal, Disassembly/Reassembly, and Installation procedures above). Check the bottom cover and diaphragm (remember that it is spring-loaded, be careful). If the valve is open, clean the parts and replace the entire deceleration valve assembly if necessary. Do not attempt to free the valve.*

CARBURETOR

The deceleration section of the carburetor requires no maintenance. However, should the fuel pickup tube be damaged the upper body casting must be replaced.

The deceleration section senses high manifold vacuum when the deceleration valve opens, drawing a metered amount of fuel and air from the fuel pick-up tube and air bleed which flows from the outlet tube through the deceleration valve into the manifold. This extra fuel and air, coupled with the rest of the emission control system workings, provide improved combustion within the engine cylinders which considerably reduces exhaust emissions. Refer to **Figure 2**.

Adjustment

1. With the engine idling and warmed to normal operating temperature, connect a tachometer and set the throttle adjusting screw to obtain 900 rpm.
2. If the correct rpm cannot be obtained check the deceleration to be sure that it is working correctly.

AIR CLEANER

The air cleaner is designed to provide the carburetor with air warmed to a temperature above 90 degrees F during normal operation.

The air cleaner utilizes a valve assembly comprised of a metal box fed by 2 air inlets, one drawing in normal, unheated air, the other drawing in hot air from a separate heat stove surrounding the exhaust pipe. A spring-loaded flap valve is installed in the metal box which pivots to control the amount of incoming hot and cold air. A thermostat is connected via a spring linkage to this flap valve to regulate incoming air.

During engine warm up air is drawn through the hot air intake over the thermostat and into the air cleaner. When air temperature reaches approximately 90 degrees F the thermostat forces the flap valve down. This allows cold air

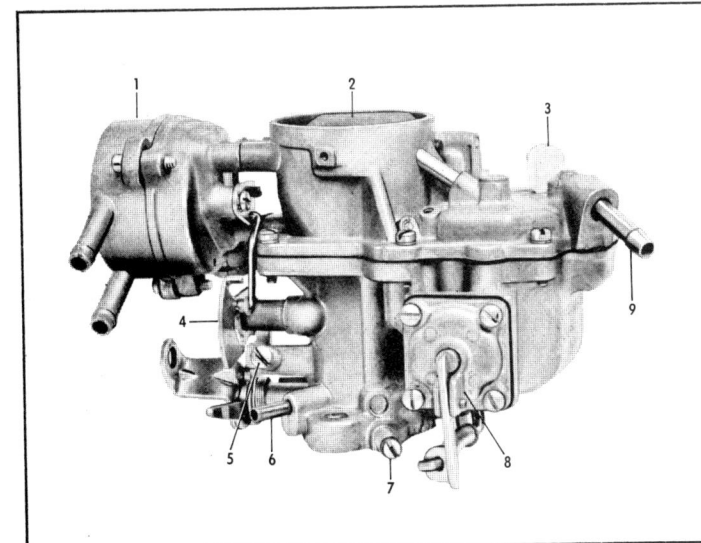

CARBURETOR SAAB 95/96 AND SONETT 1971 ONWARD

1. Automatic choke housing
2. Choke plate
3. Connection for float chamber vent
4. Step cam
5. Idle adjusting screw
6. Vacuum nipple
7. Idle mixture control screw
8. Accelerating pump
9. Fuel supply tube

to enter the duct and valve assembly, mix with hot air, and travel on to the engine. When the air temperature increases still more the valve plate moves toward the back position and shuts off the hot air intake if the temperature reaches 95-105 degrees F.

Adjustment

1. Remove the front hose. With the engine cold, the valve assembly in position, and the ambient temperature in the engine compartment 85 degrees F or less, the flap valve should be in the forward position, shutting off the cold air intake.
2. Let the engine run at fast idle for 2-6 minutes. If ambient temperature is approximately 50-70 degrees F, the valve plate should move toward the middle or back position.
3. If the flap valve does not meet the requirements in Steps 1 and 2, above, remove the unit by unscrewing the 3 screws and check for possible breakage or wear of flap valve or linkage.
4. Check the thermostat by placing the flap valve under running water with a temperature of 82-85 degrees F. See **Figure 3**. Note the angle of approximately 15 degrees.
5. Release the flap valve after a minute. It should remain in the same position (**Figure 4**).
6. Allow the water temperature to rise to 87-90 degrees F. The flap valve should move to the central position as shown in **Figure 5**.
7. When the temperature of the water reaches 95-105 degrees the flap valve should move to the left as shown in **Figure 6**.

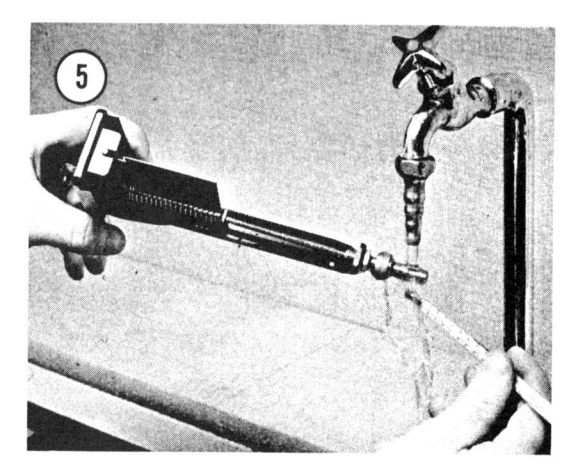

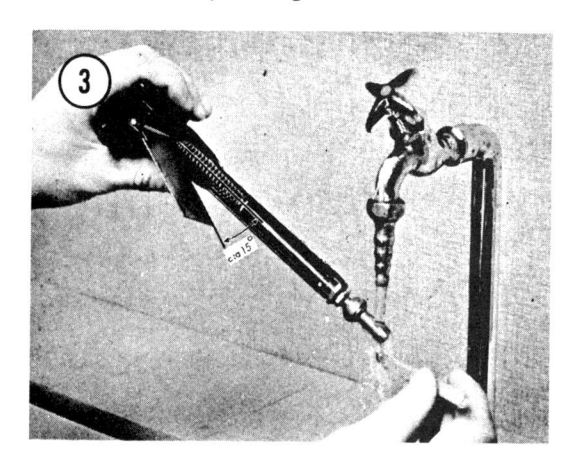

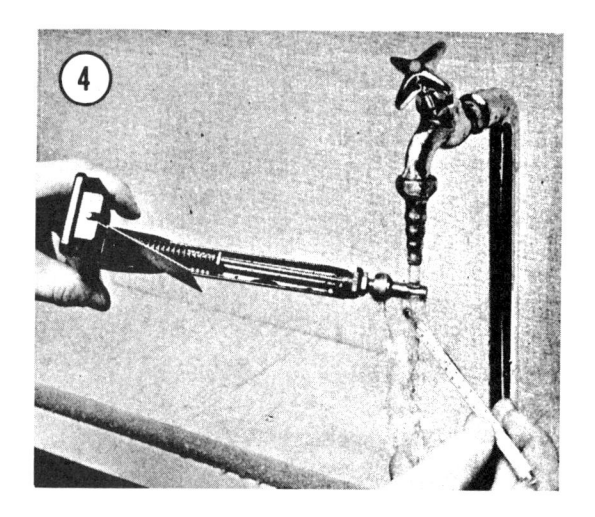

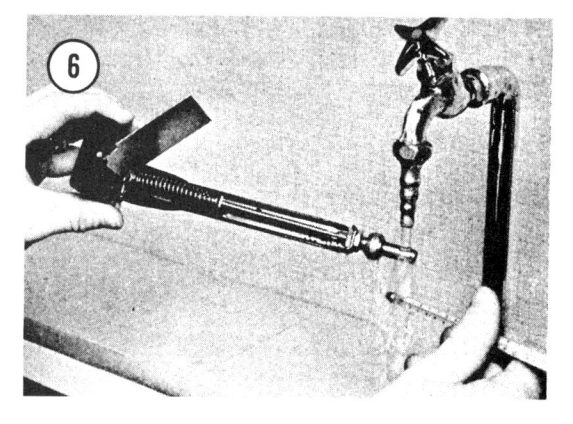

If these requirements are not met the thermostatic unit should be replaced.

EVAPORATIVE LOSS SYSTEM

From 1971 on, the fuel tank allows internal expansion of the fuel and fuel tank ventilation.

EMISSION CONTROL SYSTEM

Refer to **Figure 7**. When fuel is poured in, the tank will not completely fill. The level will rise only slightly above the lower opening on the venting tube. The tank is designed this way so that an air cushion is formed above this level and prevents further filling of the tank. This is accomplished by means of a spring loaded valve located in the filler pipe blocking the upper opening on the vent tube from the upper side of the tank. When the tank cap is screwed on a lever is actuated which opens the valve, venting the upper part of the tank to the surrounding air via the vent hose which runs out under the rear fender. The fuel, which increases in volume as the temperature rises, expands inside the tank instead of being forced up and out of the filler pipe. As the fuel level becomes lower air is drawn into the tank via the vent hose.

A charcoal filter located in the engine compartment absorbs vapor from the fuel tank. It is connected to the vent hose of the fuel tank and with a hose to the air cleaner. When the engine is running fresh air draws the fumes from the charcoal filter into the carburetor. **Figures 8, 9, and 10** show the evaporative loss system as installed on the 95/96, Sonett, and 99 models, respectively.

The canister should be replaced every 24,000 miles (30,000 miles effective with the 1975 models).

CRANKCASE VENTILATION

Early V4 engines are equipped with semi-enclosed crankcase ventilation (see **Figure 11**). The air is admitted through the oil filler cap on the right-hand valve cover. It passes through the crankcase to an air filter via a hose. From the filter it continues on to the carburetor without passing the air filter insert.

Later V4 engines used a totally enclosed crankcase ventilation (**Figure 12**). The air enters

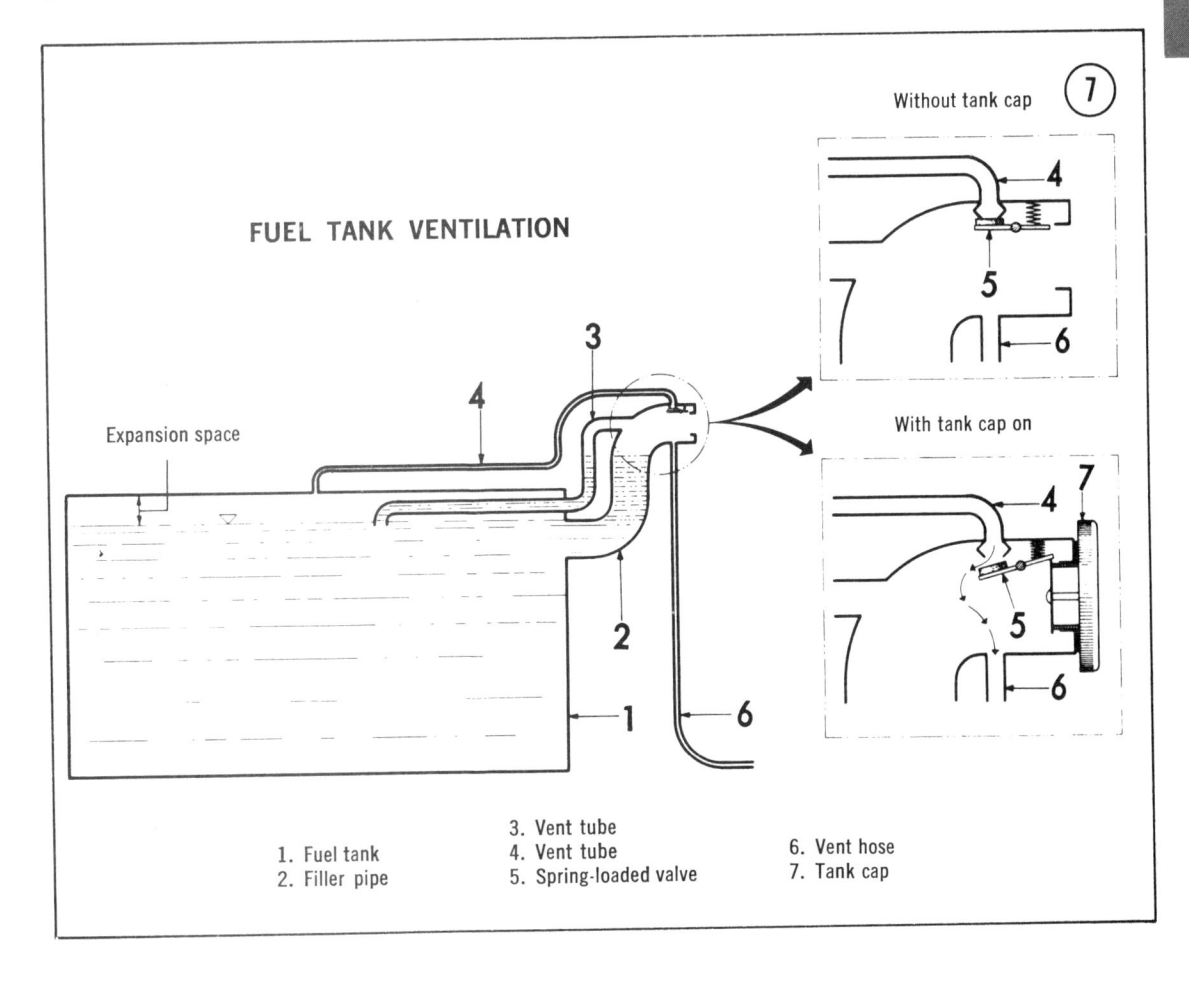

FUEL TANK VENTILATION

1. Fuel tank
2. Filler pipe
3. Vent tube
4. Vent tube
5. Spring-loaded valve
6. Vent hose
7. Tank cap

**FUEL SYSTEM
(Saab 95/96, 1971 onward)**

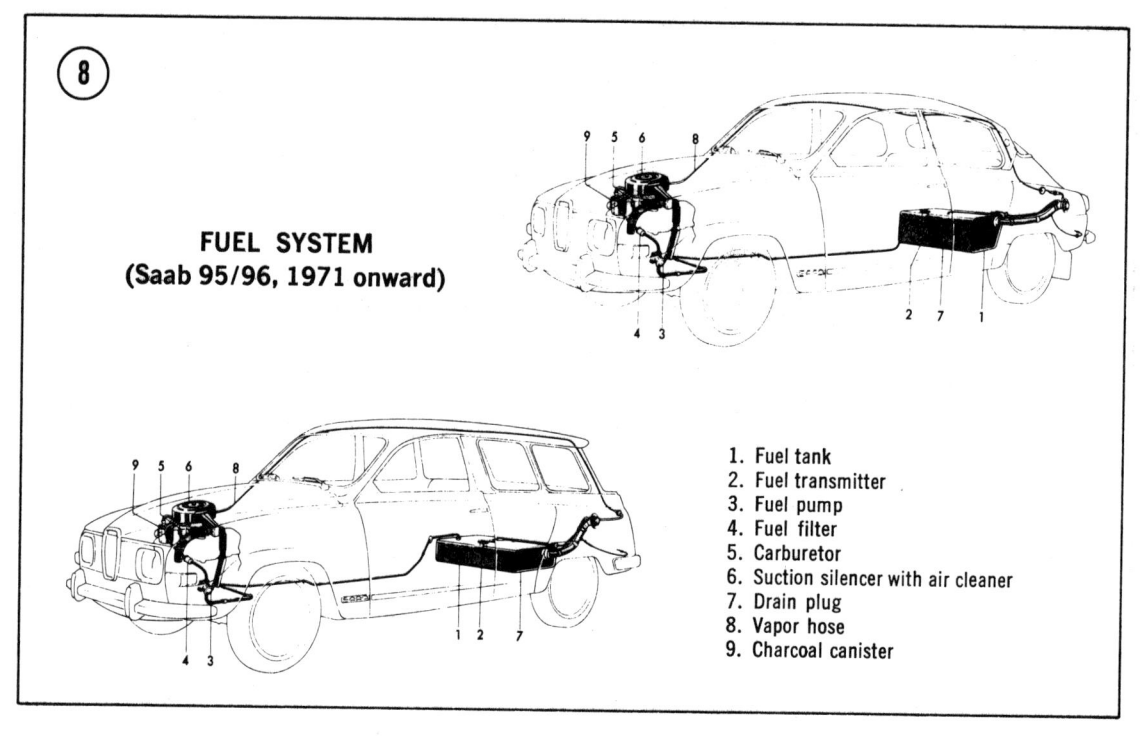

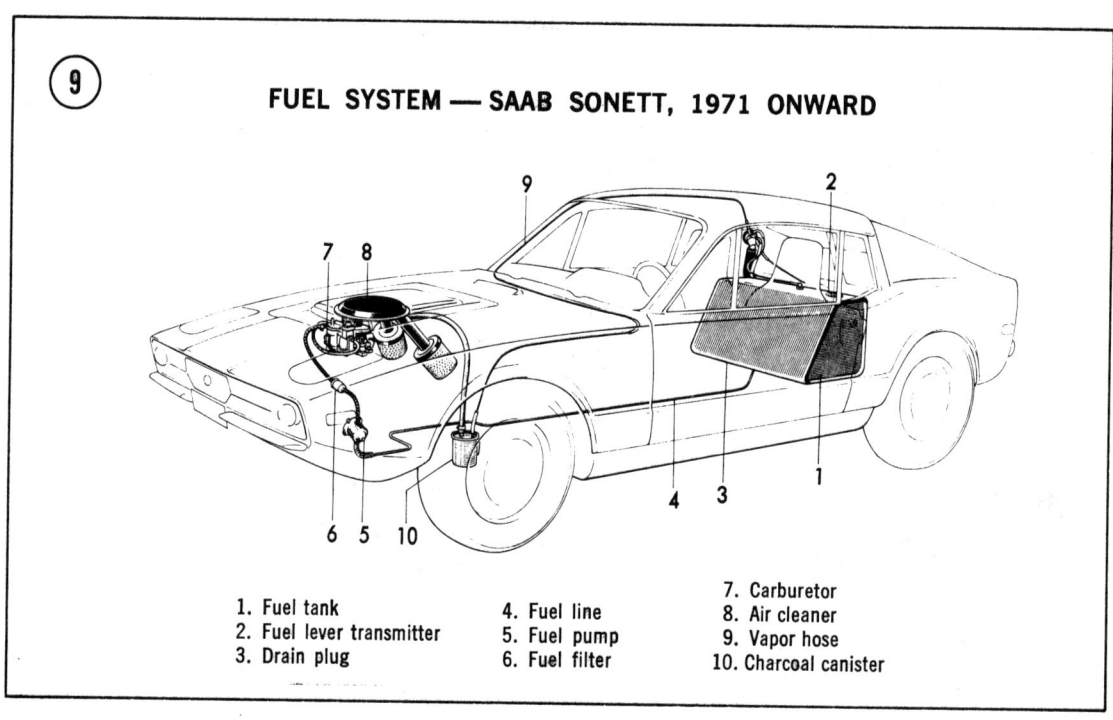

1. Fuel tank
2. Fuel transmitter
3. Fuel pump
4. Fuel filter
5. Carburetor
6. Suction silencer with air cleaner
7. Drain plug
8. Vapor hose
9. Charcoal canister

FUEL SYSTEM — SAAB SONETT, 1971 ONWARD

1. Fuel tank
2. Fuel lever transmitter
3. Drain plug
4. Fuel line
5. Fuel pump
6. Fuel filter
7. Carburetor
8. Air cleaner
9. Vapor hose
10. Charcoal canister

through the air filter, passes to the filter insert, and via a flame guard and hose into the right-hand valve cover. It passes through the crankcase and into the left-hand valve cover via a hose and on to an intermediate flange beneath the carburetor. A valve in the intermediate flange regulates the flow of air through the crankcase.

Early 99 models featuring the inline 4-cylinder engine (1.7, 1.85, and 2.0 liter engines

EMISSION CONTROL SYSTEM

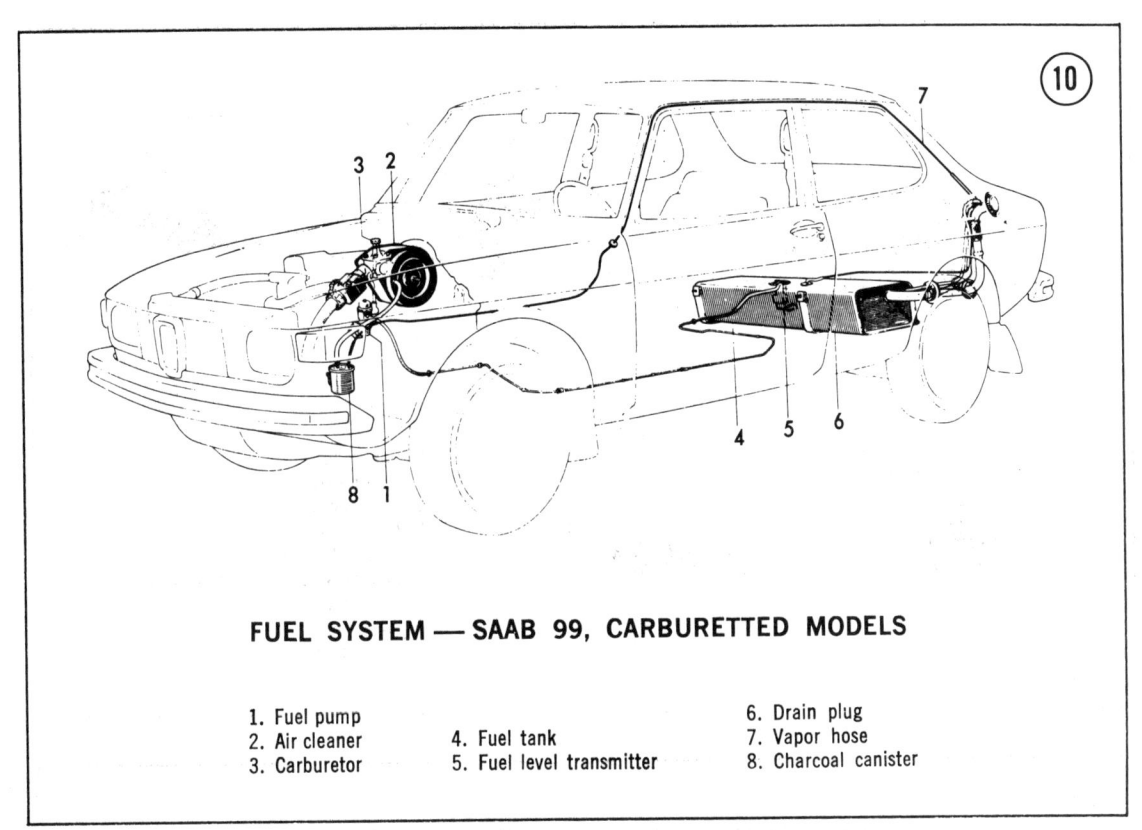

FUEL SYSTEM — SAAB 99, CARBURETTED MODELS

1. Fuel pump
2. Air cleaner
3. Carburetor
4. Fuel tank
5. Fuel level transmitter
6. Drain plug
7. Vapor hose
8. Charcoal canister

SEMI-ENCLOSED CRANKCASE VENTILATION SYSTEM
(Early V4)

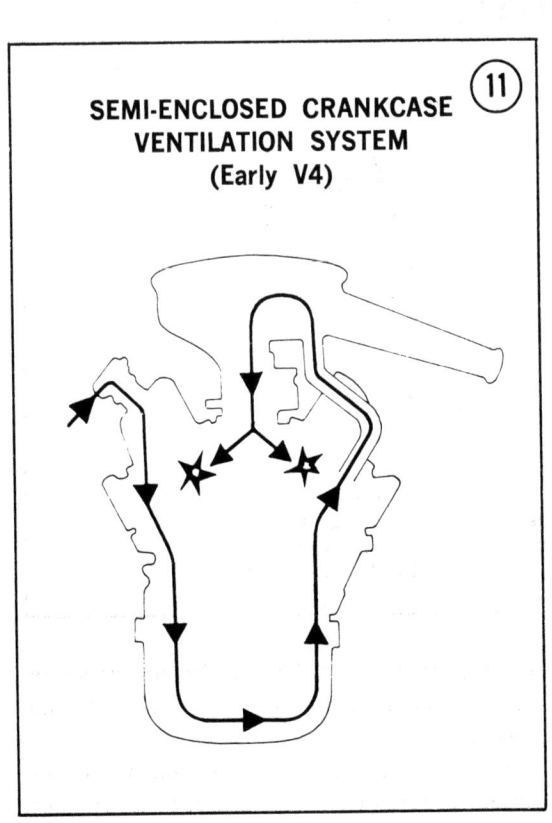

FULLY ENCLOSED CRANKCASE VENTILATION SYSTEM
(Later V4)

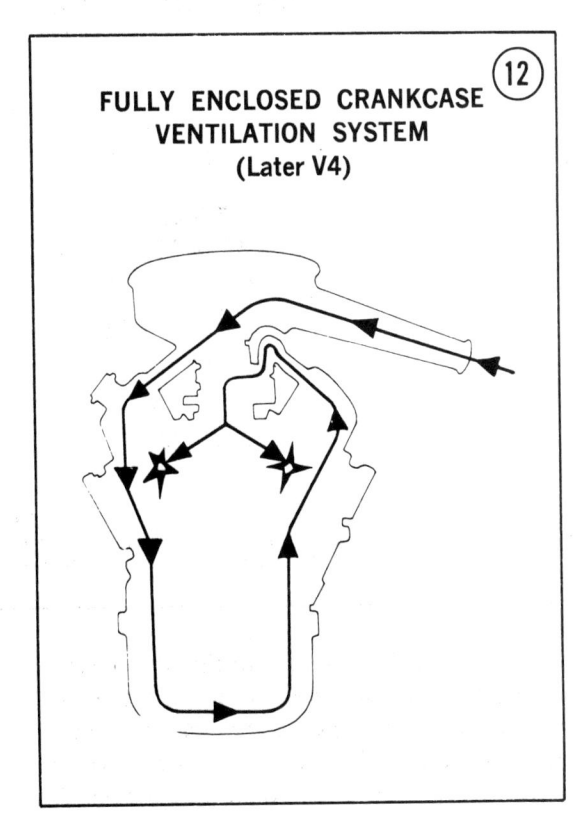

through 1973) use a fully enclosed crankcase ventilation system (**Figure 13**). Air is drawn through the air cleaner and on the 1.7 and 1.85 liter engines enters the oil filler tube via a flame guard and hose. The 2.0 liter engines have a special connection housing with a built-in flame guard which passes air along to the engine block. The air flows from the crankcase into the valve cover and through oil traps, then out through a hose to a Smith valve, which regulates the vacuum in the crankcase. The air then flows from the Smith valve to the inlet manifold.

The 2.0 liter fuel injection, beginning with the 1974 model, uses a slightly different fully enclosed crankcase ventilation (**Figure 14**). The crankcase pressure is regulated by a T-nipple connected to the intake manifold. A hose from the camshaft cover and a hose from the air cleaner lead to this nipple, which contains an orifice plate with a bore designed to give the crankcase proper vacuum. When the pressure gets too high the air flow goes from the camshaft cover via a T-nipple to the intake manifold. When the pressure gets too low, air is drawn from the air cleaner via the T-nipple and into the intake manifold.

EXHAUST EMISSION CONTROL SYSTEM

All 1975-1976 models are fitted with a continuous fuel injection system fitted with a deceleration valve. In addition an exhaust emission control system, which is comprised of an exhaust gas recirculation system (EGR) and an air injection system, provides clean emissions into the atmosphere.

Two types of EGR system are used, an EGR on-off type which is used on all automatic transmission models sold in the United States, and a

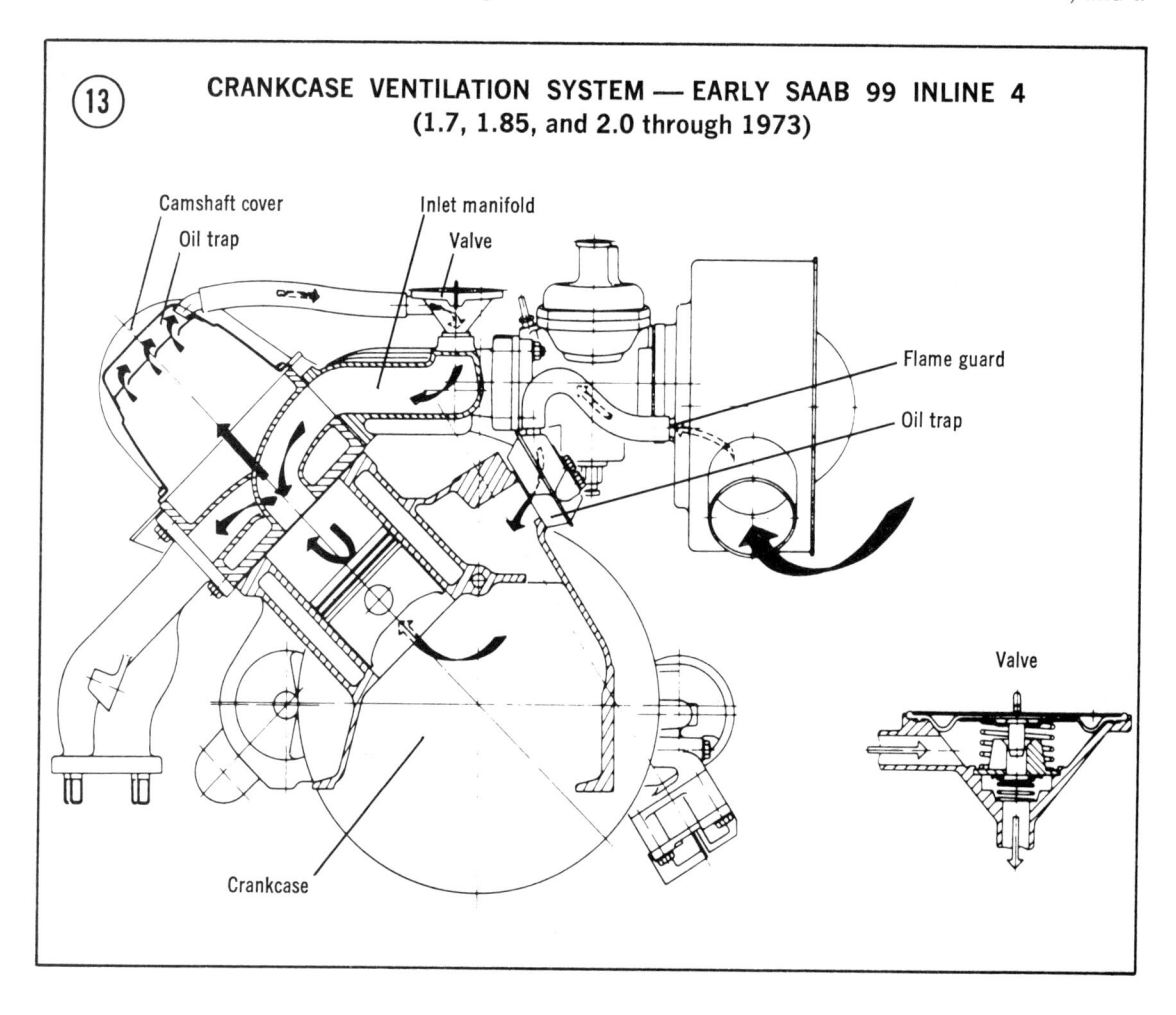

CRANKCASE VENTILATION SYSTEM — EARLY SAAB 99 INLINE 4 (1.7, 1.85, and 2.0 through 1973)

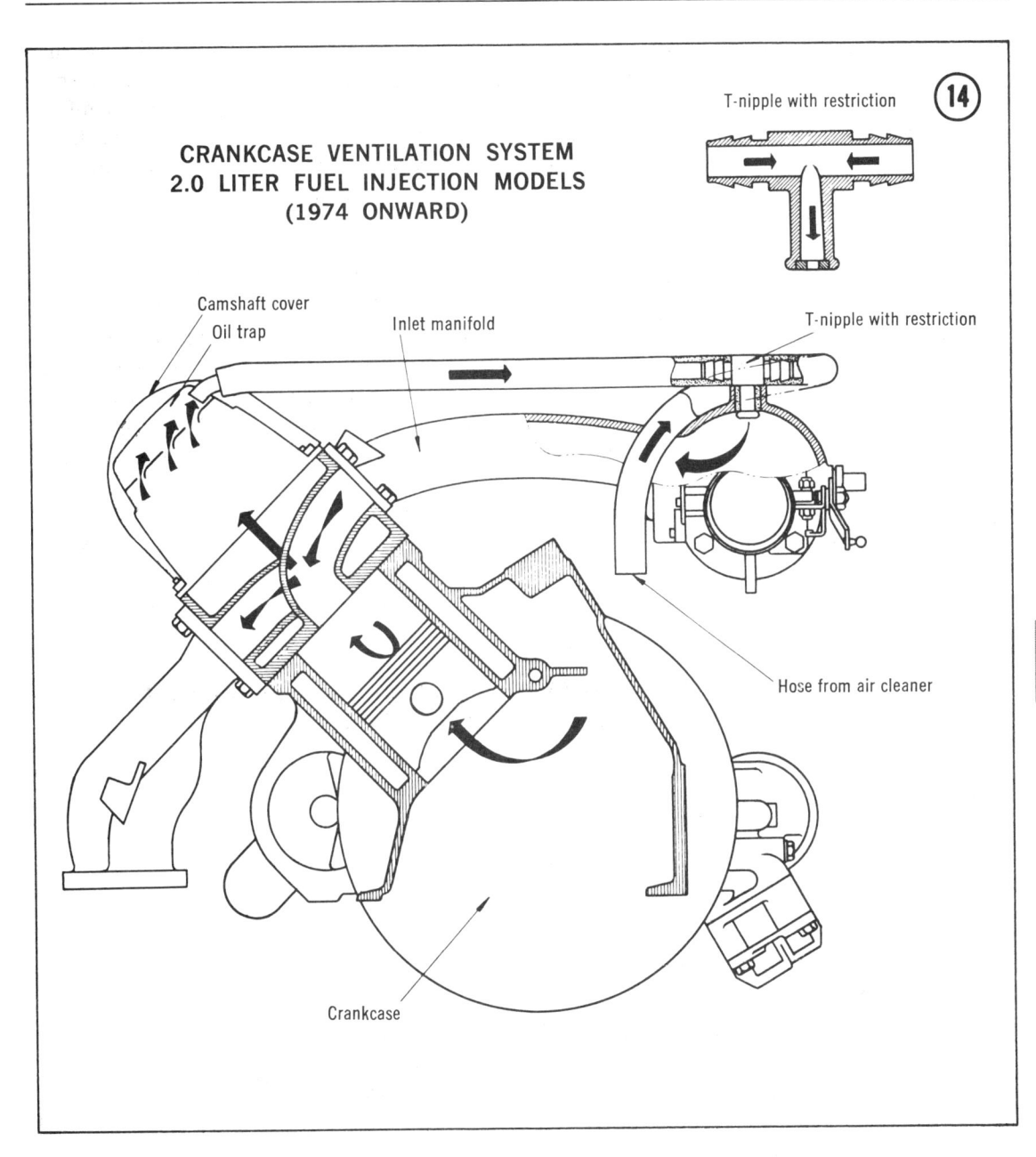

EMISSION CONTROL SYSTEM

**CRANKCASE VENTILATION SYSTEM
2.0 LITER FUEL INJECTION MODELS
(1974 ONWARD)**

T-nipple with restriction

Camshaft cover
Oil trap
Inlet manifold
T-nipple with restriction
Hose from air cleaner
Crankcase

EGR proportional type on both manual and automatic transmission models sold in California.

In addition, California models require a one-branch exhaust manifold in place of the two-branch manifold used for the rest of the United States.

The EGR on-off system includes an EGR valve, PVS valve, exhaust manifold with 0.16 in. (4mm) diameter metering orifice, EGR crosspipe, and vacuum hoses. See **Figure 15**. When the EGR valve opens a small quantity of exhaust gases flows via the metering orifice into the exhaust manifold, EGR crosspipe, and EGR valve to the inlet manifold. The EGR valve is controlled by vacuum from the throttle valve housing. The vacuum hole is situated relative to the throttle valve so that a vacuum signal is obtained when engine speed is 1,800 rpm or higher. Even during light engine load a sufficiently strong vacuum is created to open the valve completely. At full throttle (or slightly below) the vacuum is so weak that the valve does not open. The PVS

CHAPTER SEVEN

EGR ON-OFF SYSTEM

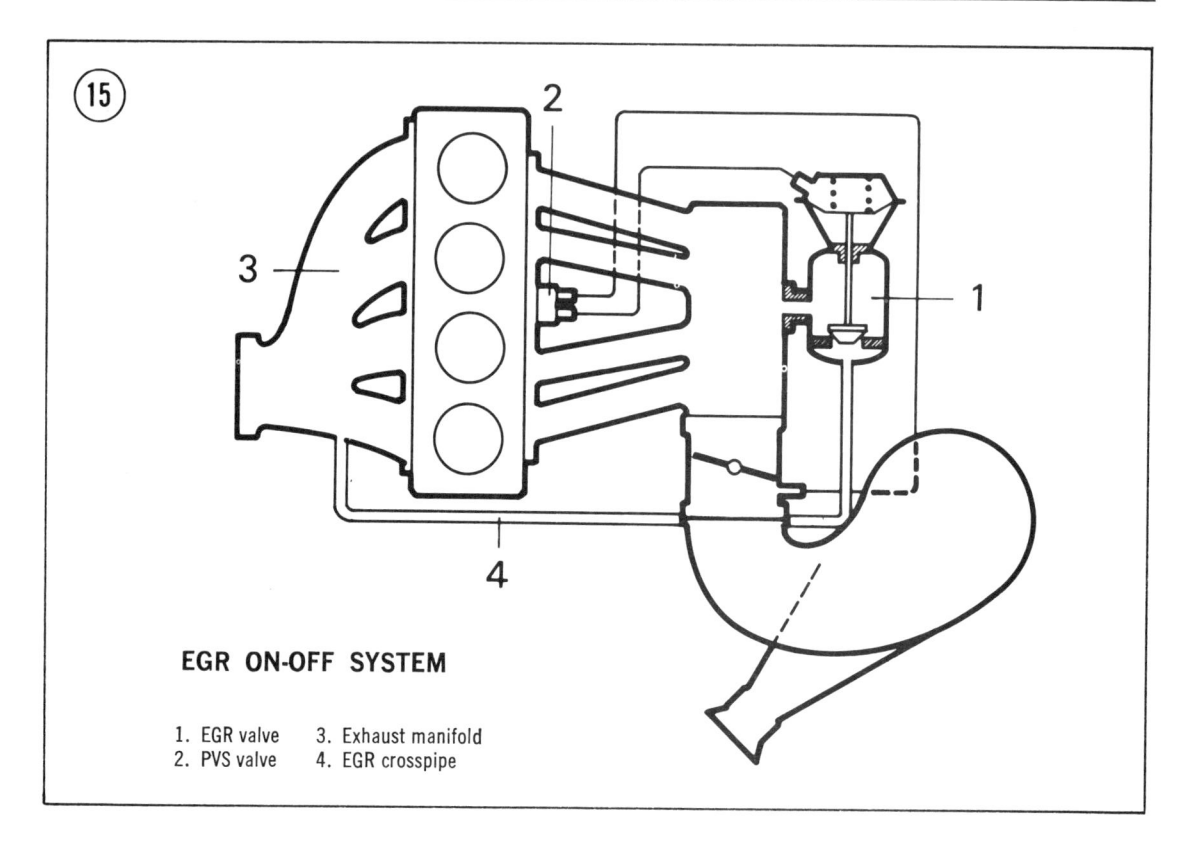

1. EGR valve
2. PVS valve
3. Exhaust manifold
4. EGR crosspipe

valve senses the temperature of the coolant and cuts out the vacuum at temperatures lower than 100 degrees F., which means that improved performance is obtained immediately after starting with a cold engine.

The EGR proportional system includes an EGR valve, PVS valve, EGR crosspipe, venturi and venturi tap, amplifier, vacuum reservoir, vacuum signal switch, and vacuum hoses. See **Figure 16**. The EGR valve is controlled by a vacuum regulator. A small quantity of exhaust gas is recirculated through the EGR crosspipe and the EGR valve to the intake manifold when the valve opens. When the air passes through the venturi a venturi signal, which is proportional to the total air flow, is obtained. The signal is transmitted to the EGR vacuum amplifier which amplifies the signal 14 times via a manifold vacuum reservoir. The amplified signal goes via the vacuum signal switch and the PVS valve to the EGR valve. The vacuum signal switch cuts out the EGR signal at engine speeds below 2,400 rpm, or at a somewhat higher speed. This is accomplished by means of a hole drilled through the throttle valve housing. The PVS valve senses the temperature of the coolant and cuts out the EGR signal at temperatures lower than 100°F, which results in improved performance with a cold engine. At wide-open throttle the vacuum in the manifold vacuum reservoir disappears after a few seconds and the EGR valve closes.

EGR Maintenance

1. See **Figures 17 and 18**. Remove the throttle valve housing, EGR crosspipe, and EGR valve.

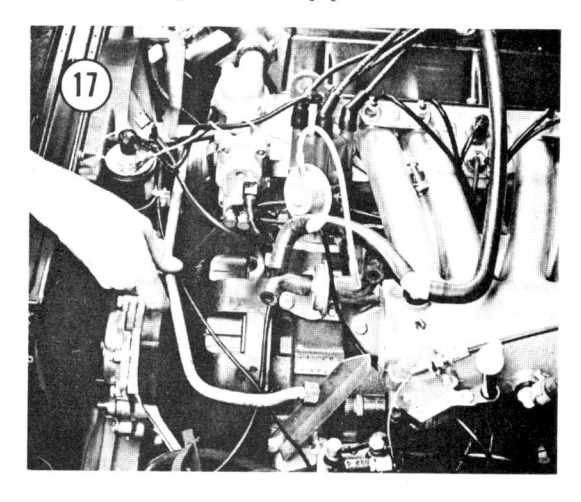

EMISSION CONTROL SYSTEM

EGR PROPORTIONAL SYSTEM

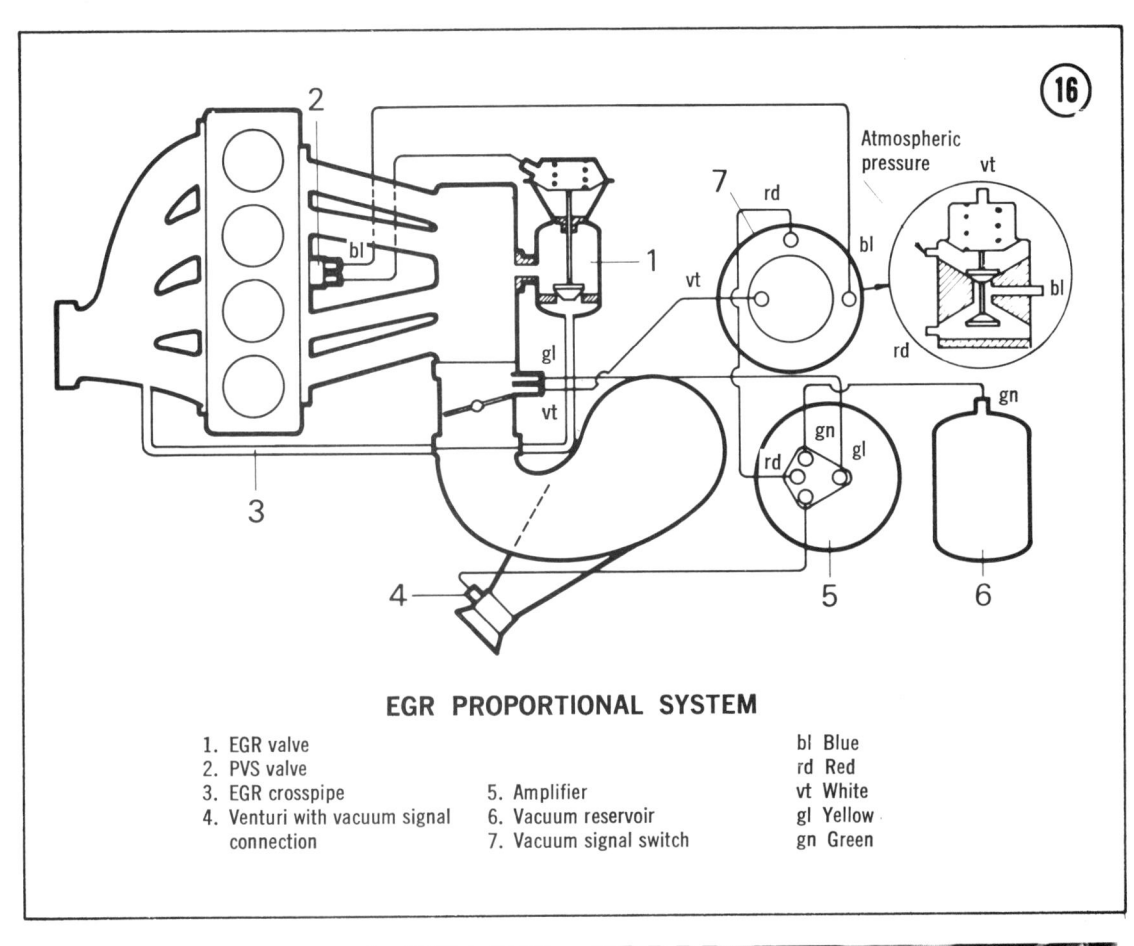

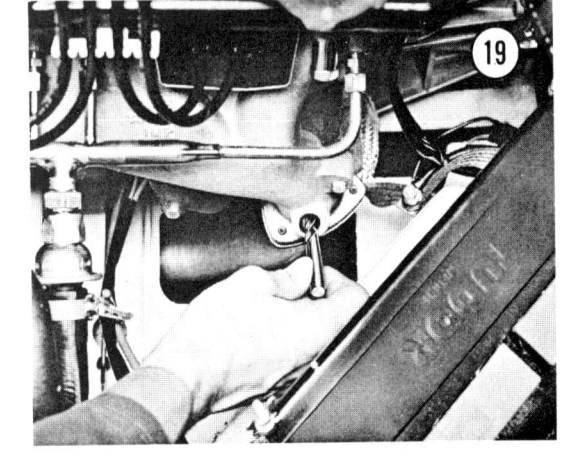

1. EGR valve
2. PVS valve
3. EGR crosspipe
4. Venturi with vacuum signal connection
5. Amplifier
6. Vacuum reservoir
7. Vacuum signal switch

- bl Blue
- rd Red
- vt White
- gl Yellow
- gn Green

2. On the EGR on-off system, clean the calibrated hole at the exhaust manifold with a 0.16 in. (4mm) drill bit. See **Figure 19**.

3. On the EGR proportional system, clean the hole at the exhaust manifold with a 0.39 in. (10mm) drill bit.

4. Clean the EGR crosspipe by flushing with solvent. Pipes with thicker deposits should be cleaned with a piece of wire, then blown clean.

5. Clean the inlet and outlet of the EGR valve with a rotary wire brush (**Figures 20 and 21**). Be careful you do not damage the valve stem.

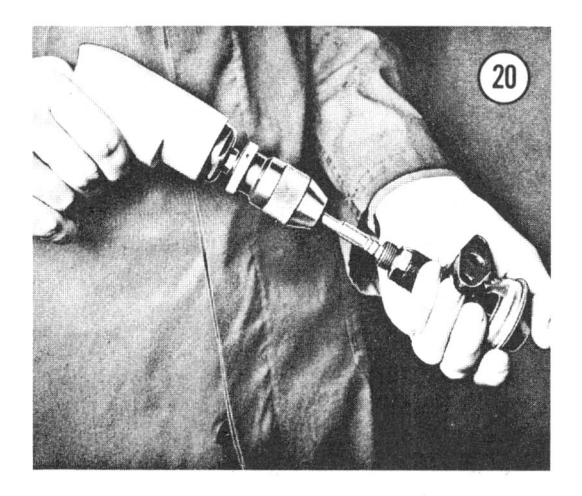

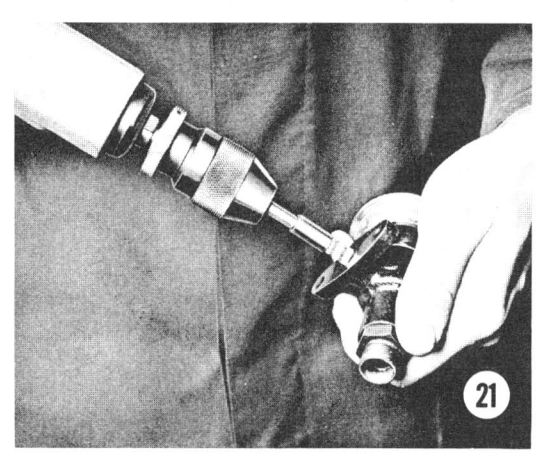

CHAPTER SEVEN

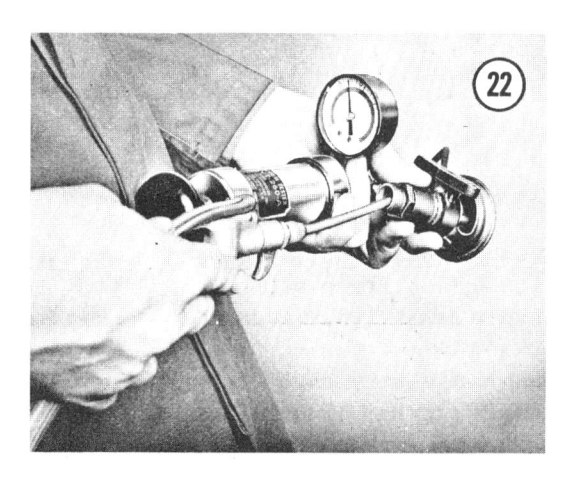

7. Clean the inlet manifold wall with a 0.39 in. (10mm) drill. See **Figure 23**. Remove any deposits which may have formed inside the manifold.

6. Flush out the valve with solvent. If a vacuum tester is available, create a vacuum in the vacuum connection to open the valve and at the same time blow compressed air through the valve (**Figure 22**). Check the opening and closing of the valve with a vacuum tester.

8. Fit a new gasket to the EGR valve. Connect the hose from the PVS valve.

9. Fit the EGR crosspipe to the exhaust manifold and EGR valve. Clamp the pipe at the throttle valve housing. Be sure no hoses or electric cables come into contact with the EGR crosspipe.

10. Mount the throttle valve housing, using a new gasket. Connect the rubber bellows, vacuum hoses, and throttle cable.

11. Start the engine. Check for leaks in the system.

12. Set the EGR counter to zero by removing the left-hand screen below the instrument panel and the cover of the counter. See **Figure 24**. Press the button (**Figure 25**). Replace the cover and fit the screen below the instrument panel.

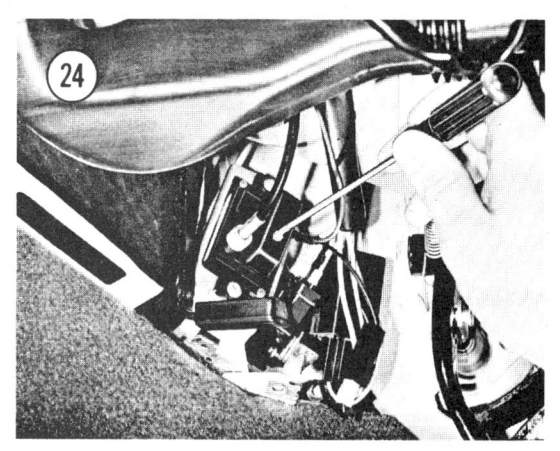

EMISSION CONTROL SYSTEM

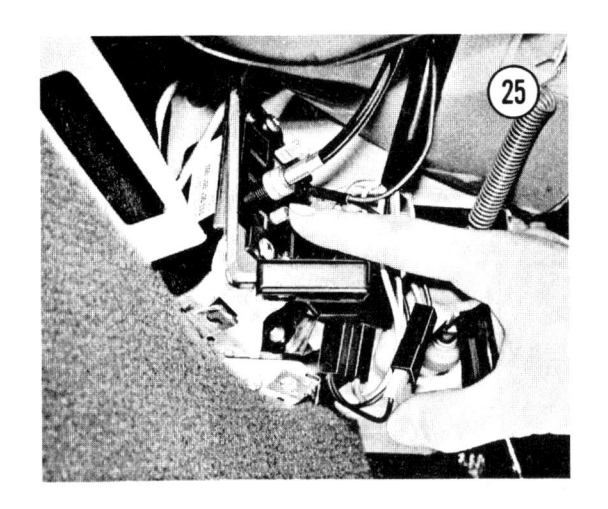

AIR INJECTION SYSTEM

The function of the air injection system is to create after-burning in the exhaust pipes and exhaust manifold. The system includes an air pump, air inlet hose, check valve, and air distribution pipe with injection tubes. See **Figure 26**. The air pump is driven by a V-belt from the crankshaft pulley. Air is drawn into the pump via a labyrinth seal at the pulley and pumped into the air hose and distribution pipe. A relief valve opens if the pressure in the distribution pipe becomes too great.

The function of the check valve is to prevent exhaust gases from entering the air pump should the V-belt break.

The air distribution pipe connects the check valve with the 4 injection tubes. The ends of the injection tubes are located at the hottest part of the exhaust passage in order to achieve a maximum afterburning effect.

Pump noise is partly absorbed by the labyrinth seal and partly by a small silencer located above the relief valve. Insulation is also glued to the dash panel behind the pump.

Air Injection Maintenance

1. Remove the air pump drive belt.
2. Remove the 3 pulley retaining screws. Remove the air pump pulley.

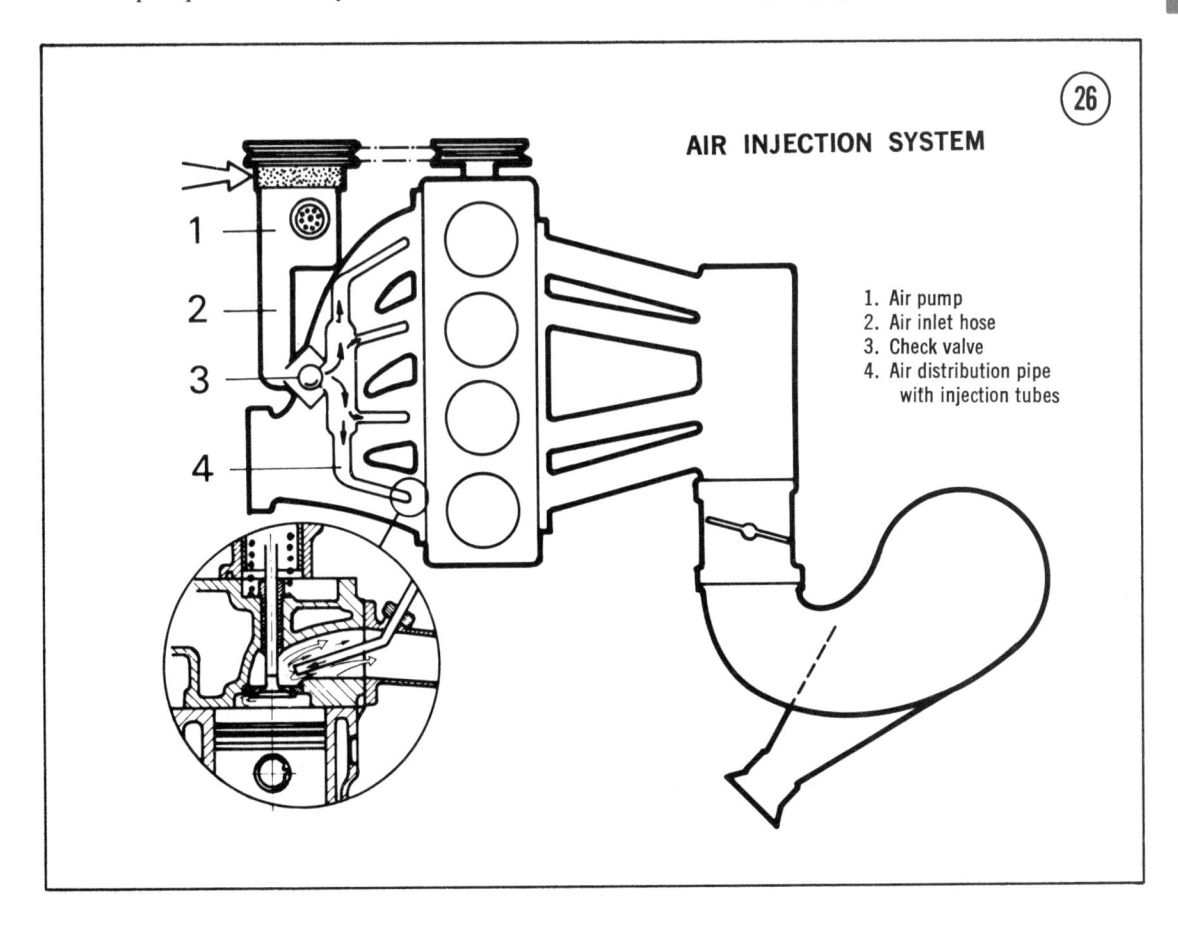

AIR INJECTION SYSTEM

1. Air pump
2. Air inlet hose
3. Check valve
4. Air distribution pipe with injection tubes

3. See **Figure 27**. Clean the pulley, paying attention to the recess for the centrifugal cleaner.
4. Fit the pulley and V-belt.

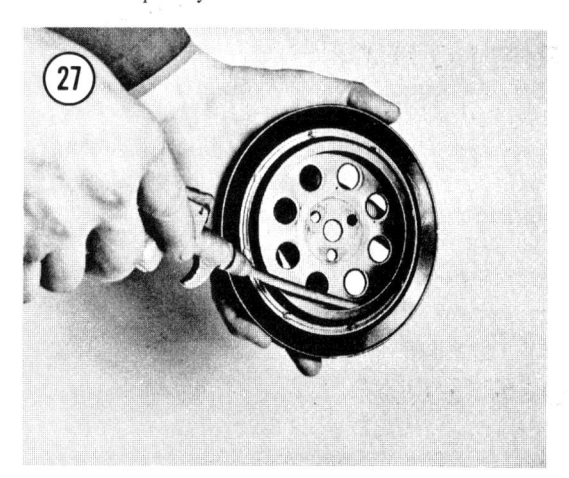

5. See **Figure 28**. Remove the air inlet hose and check the check valve at the air distribution pipe.
6. Check and fit the air inlet hose.

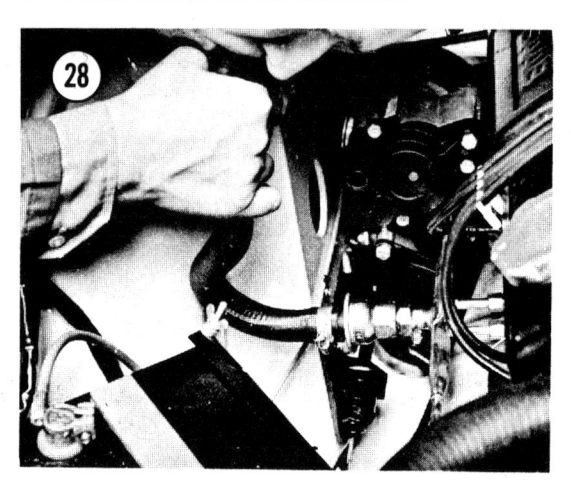

> NOTE: If you own a 1977 or later model, first check the Supplement at the back of the book for any new service information.

CHAPTER EIGHT

ELECTRICAL SYSTEM

This chapter includes service procedures for the battery, charging system, starter, and ignition system.

BATTERY

Removal/Installation

CAUTION
The engine must be stopped before disconnecting the battery terminals or the alternator may be damaged.

1. Disconnect the negative (ground) cable to prevent shorting.
2. Disconnect the positive cable.
3. Unscrew the 2 wing nuts from the battery hold-down hooks. Lift battery out of car.
4. Install by reversing preceding steps. Be sure battery terminals and case are clean. Coat the terminals and clamps with Vaseline. For additional battery maintenance see Chapter Two.

CAUTION
Use care when installing battery cables on terminals. Even momentary wrong connections will ruin the alternator rectifier. The positive cable must connect to the negaitve post. The battery must not be disconnected while engine is running. When quick-charging the battery be sure to first disconnect the positive cable.

Charging

The state of charge of the battery is determined by measuring the specific gravity of the electrolyte with a hydrometer. A full charge has a specific gravity of approximately 1.28, a half charge 1.21, and discharge 1.12.

Charging must be adjusted to the battery's capacity. The battery is fully charged when the voltage per cell has reached 2.5-2.7 volts, without load, and has remained constant during the last 3 hours of charging.

The filler caps must be removed from the cells while charging is in process.

ALTERNATOR

All models use an alternator which generates alternating current (AC) which is converted to direct current (DC) by silicon diodes. Bosch and SEV alternators are used. The 1971-1972 electronic fuel injection engines use a Bosch alternator with a cooling device consisting of a hose attached to the bottom of the radiator which conducts cool air to a hood mounted on the rear of the alternator (**Figure 1**). **Figure 2** shows the Bosch alternator wiring connections for the 95/96 and Sonett used through chassis No. 95/47295 and 96/443386; **Figure 3** the one used from chassis No. 95/47296 and 96/443381 onward. **Figure 4** shows alternator

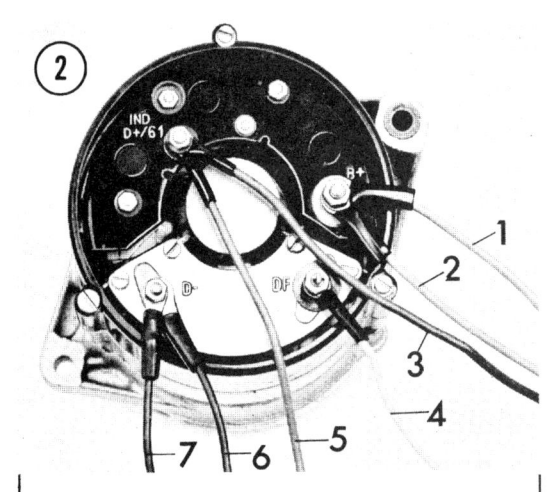

CHAPTER EIGHT

1. 85 grey to B+ (battery connection)
2. 74 grey to B+ (battery connection)
3. Black to ground (1970 model only)
4. 73 yellow to DF (exciter coil connection; and for DF of regulator)
5. 72e red to D+ (exciter diodes output; connection of regulator D+)
6. 49 black to D— (connected to regulator via a cable in the 3-pole connector)

1. 85 grey to B+ (battery connection)
2. 74 grey to B+ (battery connection)
3. 72 red to D+/61 (exciter diodes output; connection of regulator D+; and of charge indicator light)
4. 73 yellow to DF (exciter coil input; connection of regulator DF)
5. 61 red to D+/61 (exciter diodes output; connection of regulator D+; and of charge indicator light)
6. 49 black to D— (ground, connection to regulator D—)
7. 47 black to D— (ground, connection to regulator D—)

wiring connections for the 99 Bosch and SEV alternators (the Bosch is illustrated; the connections are the same for both makes).

> NOTE: *The alternator requires very little maintenance because carbon brushes and commutators are not needed for the output current. Periodical maintenance is not required. Repair of the alternator should be made by a specialist in alternator overhaul and/or maintenance.*

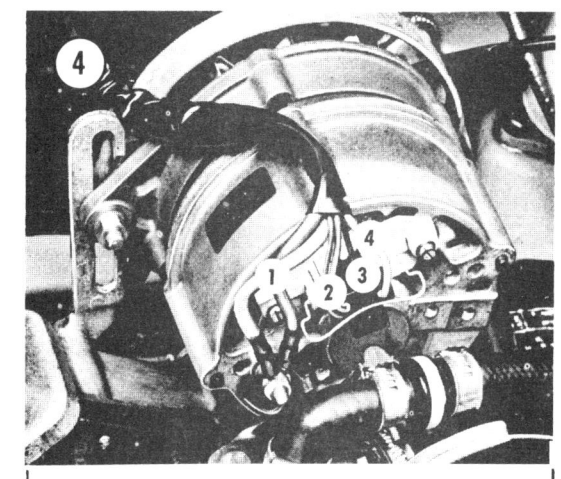

1. 74 gray to B+ (battery connection)
2. 72 red to D+ (exciter diode output; terminal for regulator D+)
3. 49 black to D— (connected to regulator via a cable in the 3-pole connector)
4. 73 yellow to DF (terminal to exciter winding; and for regulator DF)

ELECTRICAL SYSTEM

Removal/Installation

1. Disconnect the negative battery cable.

CAUTION
The engine must be stopped before disconnecting the battery terminals or the alternator may be damaged.

2. Remove right valve cover (Sonett).

3. On the Sonett remove the windshield washer from its holder and detach the throttle control spring from the control arm shaft. Remove the 2 retaining screws holding the expansion tank. Lift the tank to one side so that the hose is not in the way.

4. Remove the alternator cables and retaining and adjusting bolts.

NOTE: *On the Sonett, removal and installation is easier if the bolt for the retaining bracket by the water pump is loosened, then opened up.*

5. Remove the drive belt. (On earlier cars equipped with the 55A alternator remove the cooling hose).

6. Install the alternator by reversing the preceding steps. (On the Sonett use a new gasket when installing the valve cover).

7. Adjust drive belt tension so the belt can be depressed about 0.3 in. (7mm) on the 95/96 and Sonett, or 0.4 in. (10mm) on the 99, under a pressure of 3.5 lbs. See **Figure 5**.

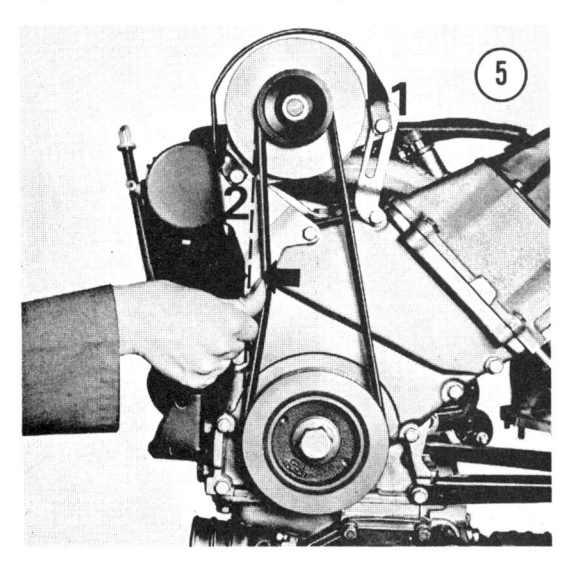

1. Adjusting bolt   2. Retaining bolt

VOLTAGE REGULATOR

The voltage regulator on all models requires neither service nor adjustment. If defective, replace it.

STARTER

Removal/Installation

1. Disconnect negative battery cable. On cars equipped with 55A alternator loosen the cooling hose.
2. Disconnect starter wiring.
3. Disconnect positive battery cable.
4. Remove flywheel cover retaining bolts, then the cover (99).
5. Loosen nuts holding starter in place. Remove starter.
6. To install reverse preceding steps.

Brush Replacement

Refer to **Figure 6**.

1. Remove 2 bolts from protective cap.

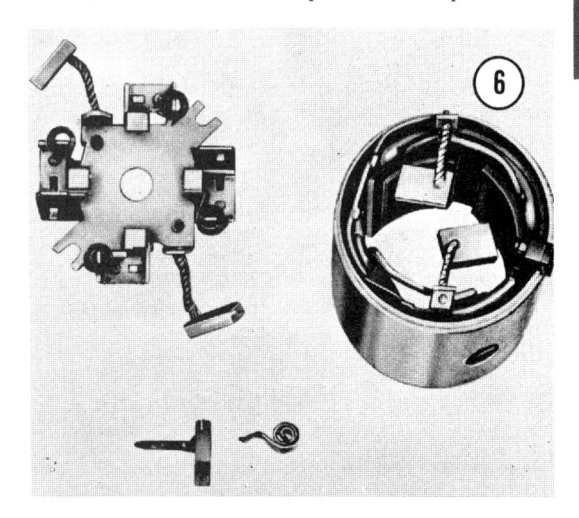

2. Remove protective cap, U-washer, shims, and rubber gasket.
3. Remove bolts securing commutator bearing housing. Remove housing.
4. Lift brush springs from holders with a piece of wire. Remove brushes and brush holder plate.
5. Unsolder brush wiring connections from brush holder plate and field winding. Solder new brushes in place.

6. Install brush holder plate in position. Lift brush springs with a wire hook and insert the brushes.

7. Mount commutator bearing housing. Be sure notches are above feed cables rubber insulation.

8. Fit rubber gasket, shims, and U-washer.

9. Position protective cap and secure with 2 bolts.

10. Insert and tighten bearing housing bolts.

STARTER SOLENOID

Removal

1. Disconnect cable.

2. Remove retaining bolts and solenoid.

Installation

1. Hook solenoid to engaging lever arm. Secure with 2 bolts.

2. Connect cable.

IGNITION SYSTEM

Ignition Coil Removal/Installation

1. Disconnect wiring from coil (**Figure 7**).

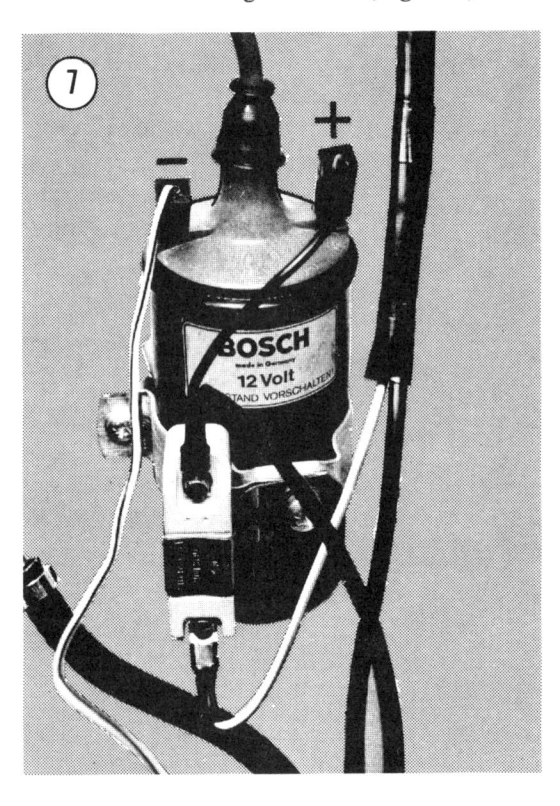

2. Remove clamping screws and coil.

3. Install by reversing preceding steps.

Distributor Removal

1. Disconnect ignition cables.

2. Release spring clips and remove distributor cap.

3. Disconnect low voltage wire from ignition coil.

4. Remove vacuum hose.

5. Crank engine over until rotor and distributor housing marks are aligned on the 95/96 and Sonett (**Figure 8**). This is the ignition position for the No. 1 cylinder (6 degrees BTDC). On the 99, crank engine over until flywheel marking is at ignition position for the No. 1 cylinder (**Figure 9**).

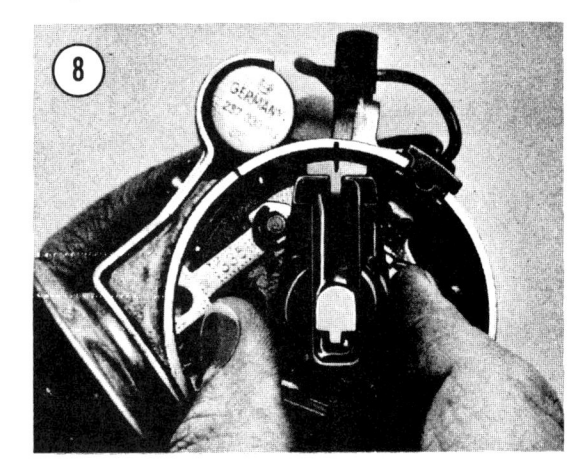

6. Remove bolts holding distributor to engine block and remove distributor. Refer to **Figure 10** (the 95/96 and Sonett distributor is illustrated).

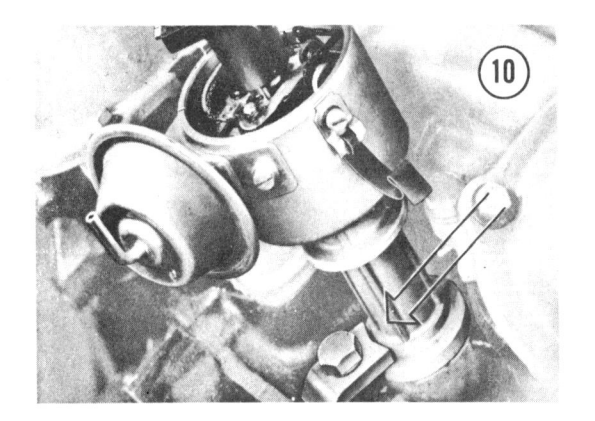

ELECTRICAL SYSTEM

Distributor Installation

1. On the 99, check flywheel position (Figure 9) which corresponds to ignition position on the No. 1 cylinder.

2. On the 99 carburetor equipped engines, turn distributor shaft until rotor points away from flywheel along fore-and-aft line of engine (**Figure 11**). On 99 fuel injected engines, rotate distributor shaft until rotor points approximately 50 degrees clockwise from the mark on the edge of the distributor housing which indicates the firing position for the No. 1 cylinder (**Figure 12**). On the 95/96 and Sonett models turn the distributor shaft until rotor is directly opposite the mark on the distributor housing (Figure 8).

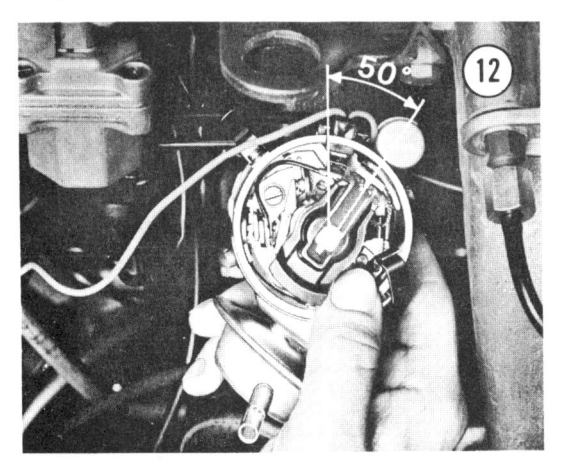

3. On the 99, place distributor in engine block with vacuum control unit facing flywheel. As distributor is inserted into engine the rotor turns counterclockwise (25-30 degrees on carburetor equipped engines; approximately 50 degrees on fuel injected engines). Be sure gears mesh properly.

> NOTE: *When distributor is fully inserted in the engine the marks on the distributor housing and rotor should be aligned (Figure 8, Saab 95/96 and Sonett;* **Figure 13**, *Saab 99).*

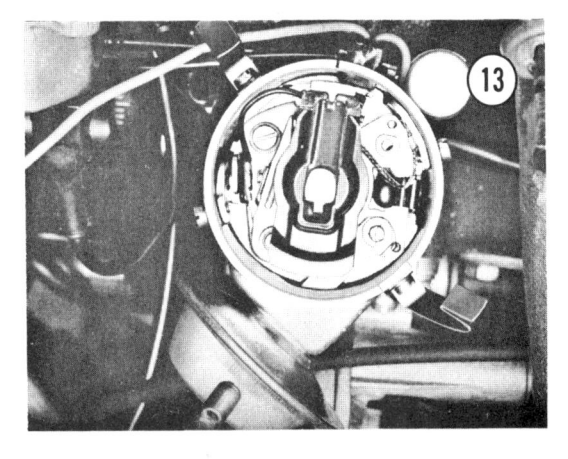

4. On the 95/96 and Sonett, be sure pulley mark is aligned with the 6 degrees mark on the transmission cover which is the firing position for the No. 1 cylinder (**Figure 14**).

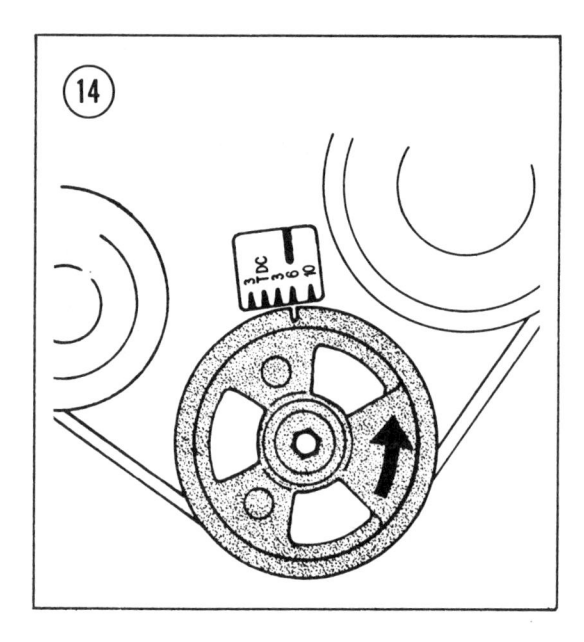

5. Install by reversing preceding steps. Do not tighten retaining bolts completely until ignition timing has been adjusted.

6. Adjust ignition timing. See Chapter Two.

**Vacuum Regulator Removal
(1974 and Earlier 99)**

1. Use a drift pin and knock out cotter pin in the distributor drive gear. Pull the gear off the shaft.

2. Lift out shaft assembly and rotor arm.

3. Remove condenser retaining screw. Disconnect ground lead.

4. Disconnect breaker arm lead by pulling cable shoe out of the insulated contact plate on the breaker arm.

5. Remove breaker plate lock ring. Lift out the plate.

6. Loosen both vacuum regulator retaining screws. Remove the unit.

**Vacuum Regulator Installation
(99, 1974 and Earlier)**

1. Attach the ground lead to a screw and screw the vacuum regulator to the distributor housing (2 screws).

2. Mount the breaker plate and lock ring. Be sure the arm of the vacuum control unit hooks into the hole in the breaker plate and that the ground lead is not caught between the plate and housing.

3. Attach the ground lead to the condenser retaining screw.

4. Attach the breaker arm lead by pushing the cable shoe into the insulated contact plate on the breaker arm. (The pressure of the leaf spring will hold the cable shoes in place).

5. Oil the distributor shaft. Insert the shaft assembly and rotor into the housing.

6. Fit the spacer and push the drive gear onto the shaft until the cotter pin hole is aligned.

7. Tap the cotter pin into position. The distributor shaft must be supported properly during this operation.

**Vacuum Regulator Removal/Installation
(1975-1976 Saab 99)**

See **Figure 15**.

1. Remove distributor cap. Disconnect vacuum hose leading to vacuum regulator.

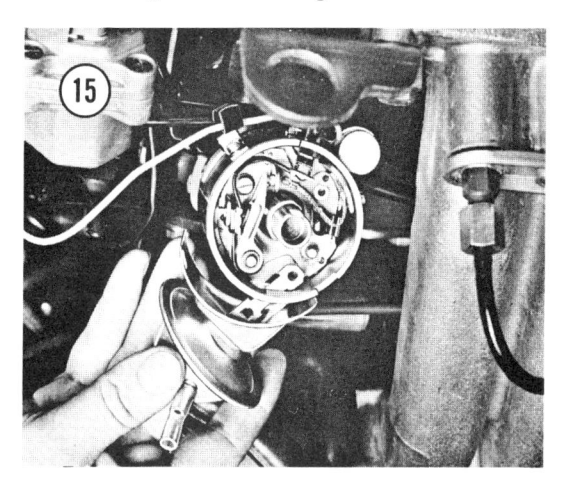

2. Remove 2 vacuum regulator retaining bolts. One bolt retains the distributor retaining springs.

3. Remove lock ring from bearing pin of regulating arm.

4. Remove vacuum regulator.

5. Install by reversing preceding steps.

**Impulse Contact Point Removal/Installation
(99 Fuel Injected Models)**

1. Remove the distributor (see *Distributor Removal, All Models*, this chapter).

ELECTRICAL SYSTEM

2. Remove vacuum regulator retaining screws and retaining screws from the impulse contact points.

3. Lift the vacuum regulator slightly and remove the impulse contact points (**Figure 16**).

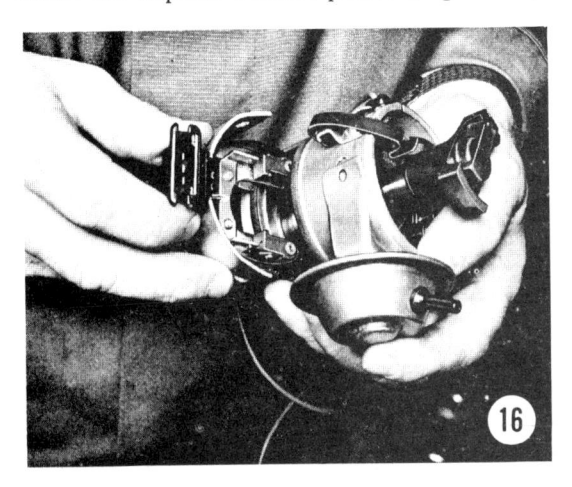

4. Install by reversing preceding steps. Before fitting lubricate with light grease. Do not adjust contacts in any way.

Distributor Cap Removal/Installation

1. Remove ignition cables with rubber protective boots from distributor cap.

2. Push spring clips aside. Remove distributor clip.

3. Install by reversing preceding steps. Be sure ignition cables are attached in correct firing order. See **Figure 17** (1975-1976 Saab 99 illustrated).

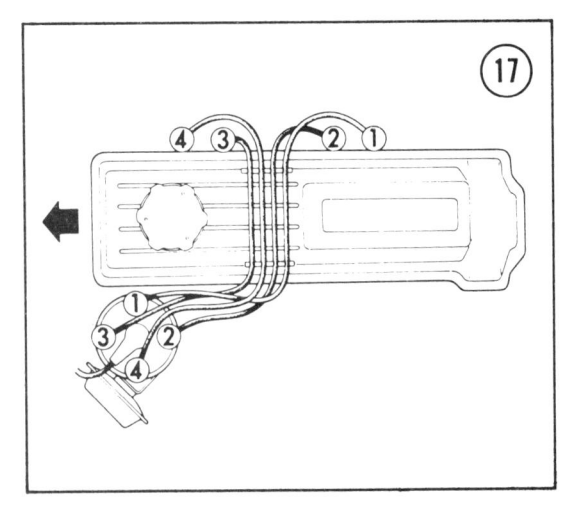

Contact Point Replacement and Adjustment

Refer to Chapter Two.

Spark Plug Inspection and Service

Refer to Chapter Two.

NOTE: If you own a 1977 or later model, first check the Supplement at the back of the book for any new service information.

CHAPTER NINE

CLUTCH, TRANSMISSION, AND DIFFERENTIAL

The Saab is fitted with a single dry plate clutch of the diaphragm spring type as shown in **Figure 1**. The components are the disc, pressure plate assembly, and release bearing (**Figure 2**). The clutch disc consists of a resilient steel plate attached to a hub which slides on the clutch shaft splines. The clutch linings are riveted to both sides of the disc.

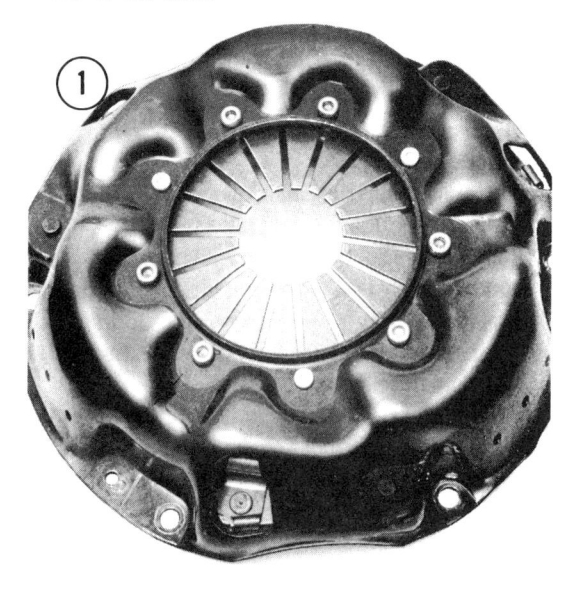

The pressure plate assembly consists of a pressure plate under pressure from coil springs and housing. The spring acts as a lever and pressure spring.

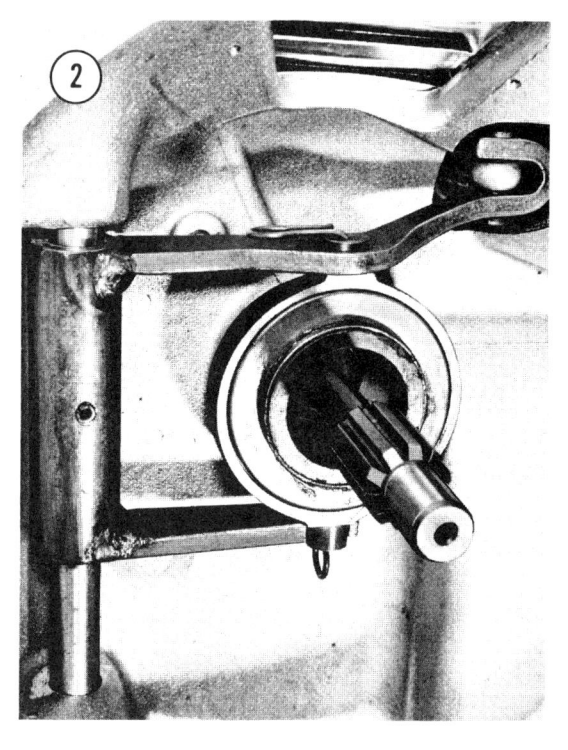

The release bearing is a ball bearing with an elongated outer ring that pushes directly against the diaphragm spring when the clutch is engaged. It is mounted on a guide sleeve screwed to the transmission case. Effective with transmission No. 45459 a new release bearing incorporating an O-ring bearing on the guide sleeve is used.

CLUTCH, TRANSMISSION, AND DIFFERENTIAL

Operation of the clutch is hydraulic. The clutch pedal actuates a master cylinder (**Figure 3**) connected via a hose to a slave cylinder which is mounted on the transmission. Refer to **Figure 4** (Saab 99) **and Figure 5** (95/96 and Sonett). The action of the slave cylinder is transmitted to the release bearing via a clutch lever in the transmission case.

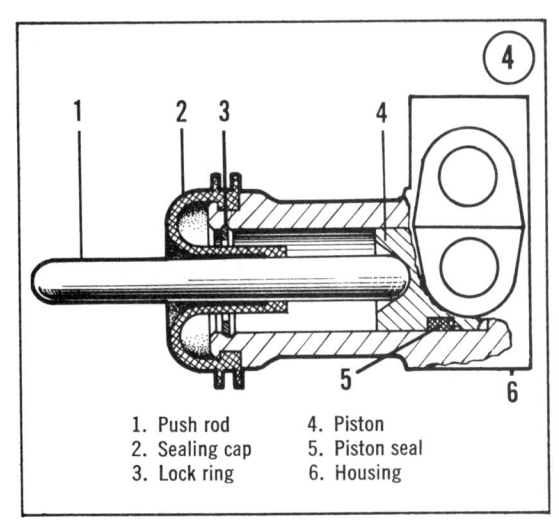

1. Push rod
2. Sealing cap
3. Lock ring
4. Piston
5. Piston seal
6. Housing

CLUTCH

Removal
(Saab 99)

1. Drain the radiator.
2. Remove the hood.
3. Disconnect battery cable, wiring for radiator fan housing, ignition coil, oil pressure switch, temperature transmitter, and fan thermal switch. 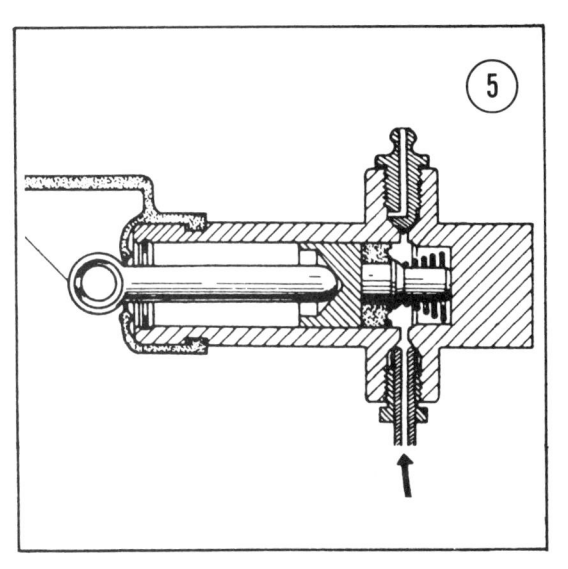
4. Disconnect radiator hoses.
5. Remove grille, front sheet, and radiator.
6. Remove clutch cover after removing retaining bolts.
7. Remove slave cylinder spring.
8. Slacken clutch adjustment by backing adjusting screw off. Lower clutch lever.
9. Remove lock ring and seal cap from clutch shaft.
10. Remove clutch shaft with tool No. 8390270 (1975-1976 models) or No. 839027 (through 1974) and joint No. 8390015 (1975-1976) or No. 839001 (through 1974) as shown in **Figure 6**.

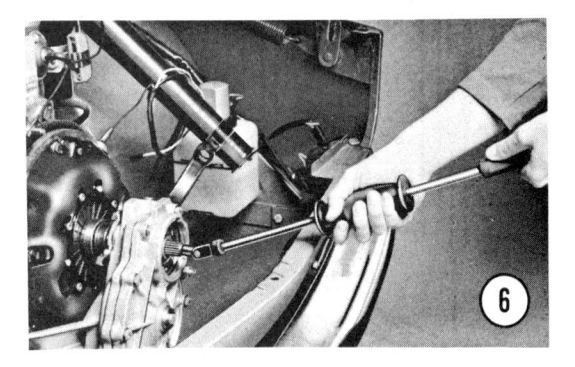

12. Remove clutch retaining bolts, except the upper 2, which should be left to prevent clutch from slipping down.
13. Remove 3 retaining bolts holding release bearing guide sleeve.

14. Fit clutch tool No. 8392078 (1975-1976 models) or No. 839207 (through 1974). See **Figure 7**. Clamp clutch and release bearing together. The pressure plate assembly, clutch disc, and guide sleeve can now be removed.

NOTE: *The pressure plate assembly should never be disassembled.*

Installation
(Saab 99)

1. Position the clutch disc in the flywheel. Press the clutch and release bearing together with tool No. 8392078 (1975-1976 models or No. 839207 (through 1974). Refer to Figure 7. Use guide spindle No. 8790412 (1975-1976) or No. 879041 (through 1974) as shown in **Figure 8** to center the release bearing. Check the guide sleeve seal and place the guide sleeve with new gasket in the release bearing. Place clutch assembly in position.

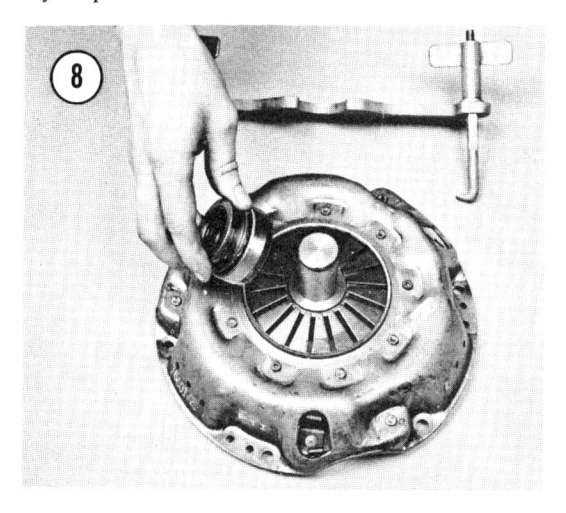

2. Center clutch disc by mounting clutch shaft. Be sure the clutch slips onto locating pin. Lightly tighten top bolts.

3. Slide guide sleeve on so that the seal centers against the sealing surface. Be sure that the upper primary gear is correctly installed so that its sealing surface projects as far as possible.

NOTE: *The gasket is not symmetrical.*

4. Tighten the 3 guide sleeve retaining bolts.
5. Remove clutch tool. Tighten clutch retaining bolts.
6. Fit the plastic propeller and O-ring (1975-1976 models) or the clutch shaft center bolt with washer and O-ring (through 1974) to the clutch shaft.
7. Fit sealing cap and lock ring at the clutch shaft.
8. Mount the slave cylinder. Be sure clutch lever is correctly positioned. Fit the spring.
9. Tighten adjusting bolt so that clutch is released when clutch pedal is depressed. See **Figure 9**. Adjust clearance between diaphragm spring and release bearing by turning the adjusting bolt. Tighten locknut. Clearance should be 0.06 in. (1.5mm) which corresponds to 0.12 in. ± 0.02 in. (3 ± 0.5mm) when clearance is measured at outer end of clutch lever.
10. Mount clutch cover.
11. Mount front sheet and radiator. Connect coolant hoses.
12. Connect electric wiring.
13. Fill radiator with coolant.
14. Fit engine hood.
15. Check headlight alignment.

Removal
(95/96 and Sonett)

1. Remove engine. See Chapter Four.
2. Remove 6 bolts holding pressure plate assembly to flywheel.
3. Remove pressure plate assembly and clutch disc.

NOTE: *Disassembly of pressure plate assembly requires special press. Work should be done by authorized Saab dealer.*

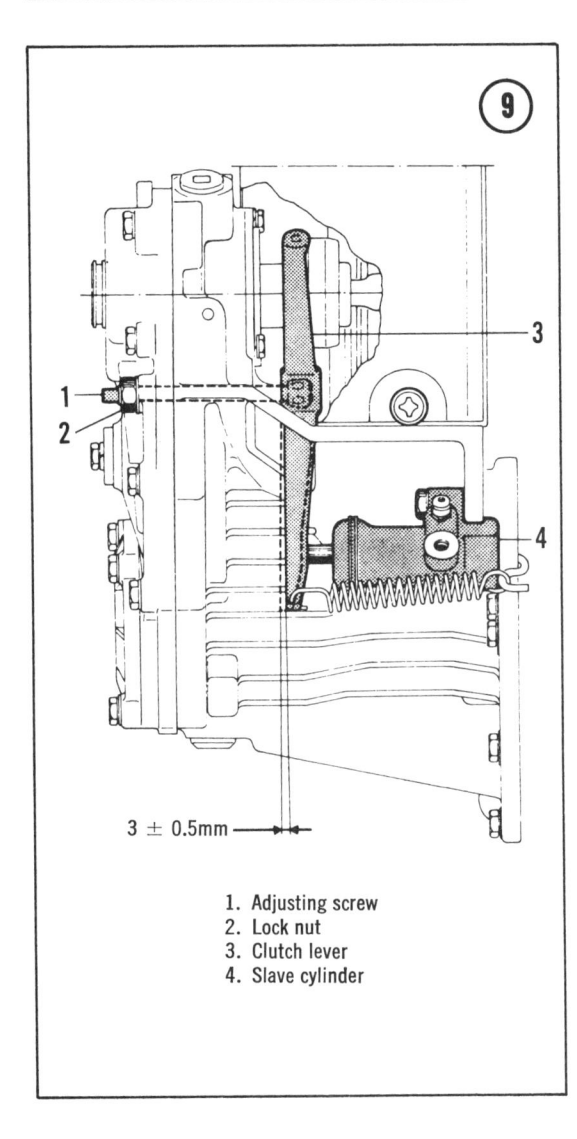

CLUTCH, TRANSMISSION, AND DIFFERENTIAL 123

stalling clutch (see *Clutch Removal* and *Clutch Installation*, preceding).

Release Bearing Removal/Installation (95/96 and Sonett)

1. Refer to Figure 2. Remove engine (see *Engine Removal*, Chapter Four).

2. Move clutch lever forward and remove 2 spring clips holding release bearing in the fork.

3. Remove release bearing.

4. Install by reversing preceding steps.

> NOTE: *If release bearing is provided with a graphite ring the ring must not be worn with its retainer. Always be sure spring clips are correctly located.*

Pressure Plate Assembly Inspection

1. Check pressure plate for cracks and scratches. Be sure plate surface is not cambered (use a ruler and feeler gauge as shown in **Figure 10**). A gap of not more than 0.0012 in. (0.03mm) is allowed at inner edge of friction surface, but there must be no gap at all between the rule and outer edge of the friction surface. Check at several points. Be sure pressure spring is not cracked or damaged. Be sure release bearing turns freely when rotated under slight axial pressure.

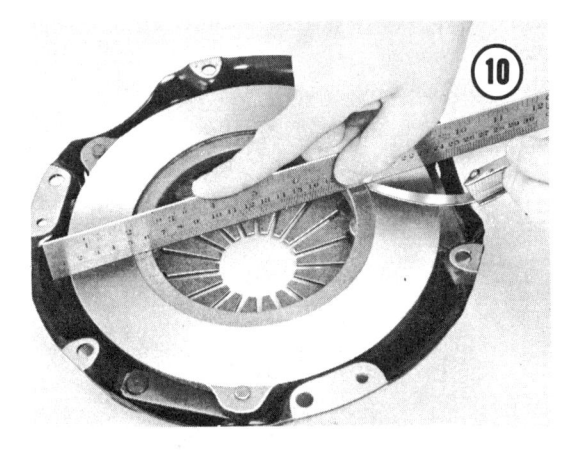

2. Inspect flywheel where clutch disc makes contact. If there are any deep scratches, machine flywheel down or replace.

3. Check release bearing for noise, wear, etc.

4. Check disc for wear. Replace if necessary.

3 ± 0.5mm

1. Adjusting screw
2. Lock nut
3. Clutch lever
4. Slave cylinder

Installation (95/96 and Sonett)

1. Insert clutch disc and pressure plate assembly in flywheel.

2. Center clutch disc with tool No. 784064 or equivalent, which fits into clutch-disc bearing in crankshaft end.

3. Tighten 6 retaining bolts evenly.

4. Install engine (see *Engine Installation*, Chapter Four).

Release Bearing Removal/Installation (Saab 99)

To remove and install release bearing proceed in same manner as when removing and in-

CLUTCH CONTROL

Clutch Adjustment

Clutch play (the clearance between the release bearing and diaphragm spring) is checked by measuring the gap at the outer end of the clutch lever (refer to Figure 9). Check by pressing the slave cylinder connection to the clutch arm (**Figure 11**). The gap should be 0.12 ± 0.02 in. (3 ± 0.5mm) for the 99; 0.16 in. (4mm) for the 95/96 and Sonett. The gap can be adjusted by backing off the adjusting bolt threaded into the transmission case (**Figure 12**).

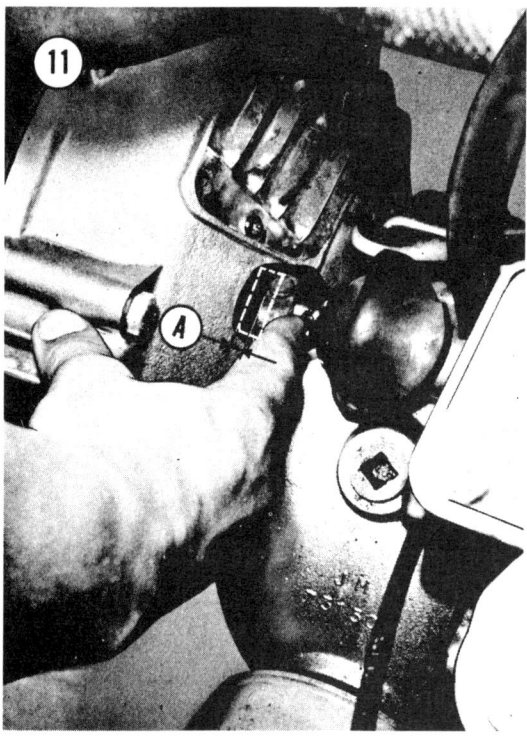

A = 0.16 in. (4mm)

Clutch Pedal Removal/Installation (95/96 and 99)

1. Remove cotter key and washer. Pull out shaft bolt for master cylinder push rod.

2. Disconnect clutch pedal return spring.

3. Remove axle bolt or cotter key and washer from pedal shaft. Remove pedal (and spring if necessary).

4. Lubricate pedal bearing with chassis grease before reassembling.

5. To install reverse preceding steps.

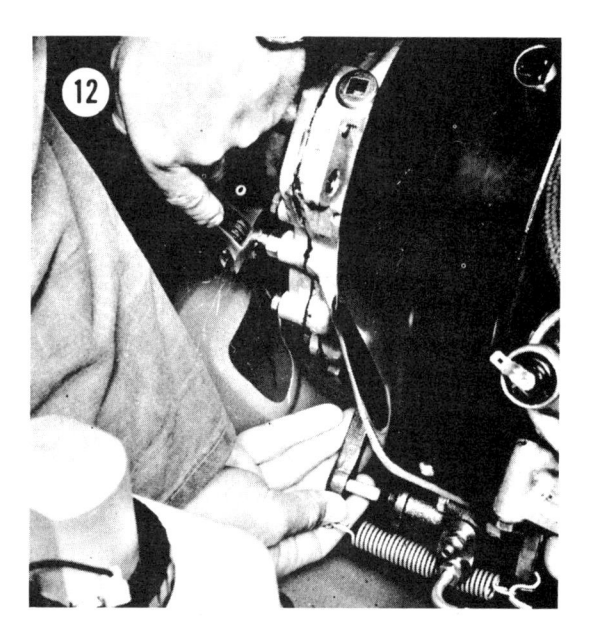

Clutch Pedal Removal/Installation (Sonett)

Each pedal can be removed separately if pedal shaft is removed.

1. Remove floor mat, wallboard panels, gear lever knob, and rubber boot. Remove gear lever cover (4 screws).

2. Remove screws securing pedal plate. Lift pedal plate out.

3. Release clutch pedal push rod by removing cotter key and shaft bolt.

4. Release brake and clutch pedal return springs.

5. Push out slotted pins. Remove pedal shaft (**Figure 13**).

6. Disconnect push rod from the rubber boot. This enables the brake pedal to be separated from the master cylinder. (When pedal is lifted out it will be accompanied by the push rod.)

7. To install reverse preceding steps.

CLUTCH MASTER CYLINDER

Removal

1. Disconnect hose from slave cylinder. Pump fluid into a clean container.

2. Disconnect clutch pedal push rod by removing cotter key, plain washer, and pin or bolt. Remove left front wheel (Sonett only).

CLUTCH, TRANSMISSION, AND DIFFERENTIAL

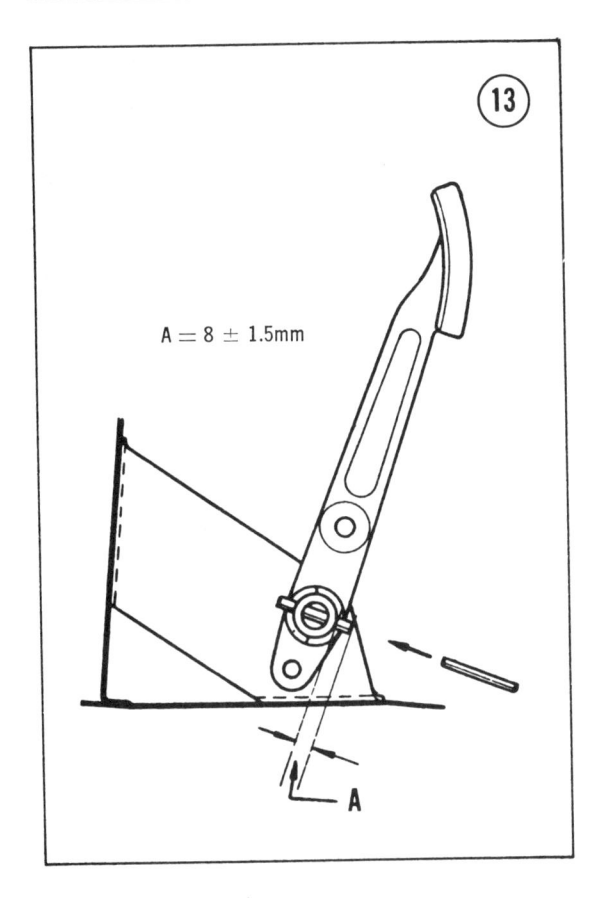

$A = 8 \pm 1.5\text{mm}$

3. Remove retaining bolts. Remove master cylinder.

Installation

1. Mount master cylinder.
2. Connect clutch pedal push rod by inserting shaft bolt or pin through the holes in the push rod fork and the clutch pedal hole. Refit the plain washer (if used) and secure with the cotter key. Install left front wheel (Sonett only).
3. Connect the hose and bleed the system (see *Bleeding*, following).

Bleeding

1. Connect a hose (about ¼ in. or 6mm I.D.) to the slave cylinder bleeder nipple. Place the free end of the hose in a clean container partly filled with brake fluid.
2. Fill the master cylinder reservoir with brake fluid.
3. Open the bleed nipple a half turn and depress clutch pedal. Close bleed nipple just before the bottom position and release the pedal. Repeat procedure until no air bubbles can be seen in the container of brake fluid. (Be sure reservoir remains full during this operation.)
4. After all air has been expelled from the system close the bleed nipple firmly.

SLAVE CYLINDER

Removal

The slave cylinder is bolted to the clutch cover. The inner assembly consists of a push rod, lock ring, and piston. The open end of the cylinder is protected by a rubber dust cover. A bleed nipple is located in the bleeder opening. See Figures 4 and 5.

1. Disconnect hose. Pump fluid into a clean container.
2. Remove retaining bolt for the cylinder.
3. Separate the cylinder from the pushrod and clutch housing.

Installation

1. Place the slave cylinder on the clutch housing. Insert the push rod through the hole in the rubber dust cover.
2. Insert and tighten retaining bolt.
3. Connect hose.
4. Bleed the system (see *Bleeding*, this chapter).

MANUAL TRANSMISSION

The transmission is designed for front wheel drive and is constructed so that all shafts with gears, free wheel (on engines up to 1.7 liter only), differential, and inner universal joints form an integral unit. The transmission features 4 synchronized forward speeds plus reverse. **Figure 14** shows the transmission used through chassis No. 99722003498; **Figure 15** the transmission used from chassis No. 99722003499 on.

For removal/installation procedures refer to *Engine Removal*, Chapter Four.

AUTOMATIC TRANSMISSION

The automatic transmission (**Figure 16**) consists of a 3-element hydrokinetic torque converter and a hydraulically operated gearbox

CHAPTER NINE

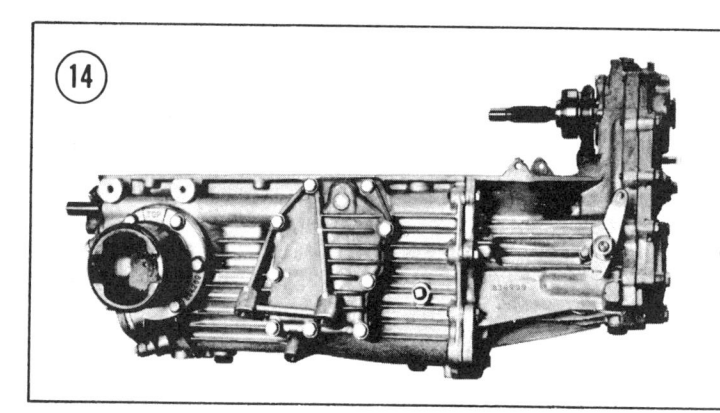

MANUAL TRANSMISSION
(to Chassis No. 99722003498)

MANUAL TRANSMISSION
(from Chassis No. 99722003499)

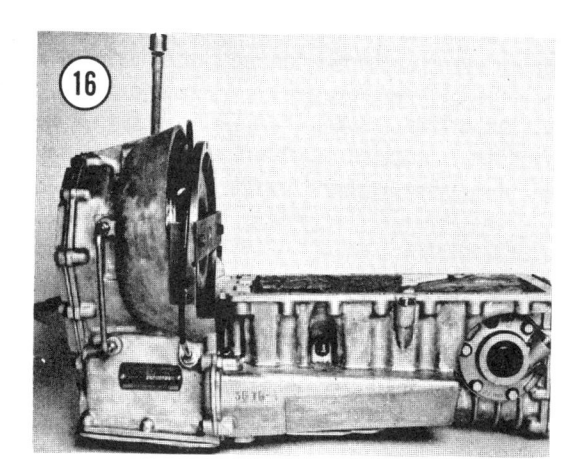

comprising a planetary gear set providing 3 forward ratios and reverse.

For removal/installation procedures refer to *Engine Removal*, Chapter Four.

FREE WHEEL

Free wheeling is provided in cars equipped with engines up to 1.7 liter capacity only. If repairs are needed to the free wheel it is usually necessary to renew the hub and rollers only. If the free wheel shaft is damaged, the free wheel shaft must be exchanged as a unit.

NOTE: *The power plant need not be removed when removing the free wheel.*

Removal/Installation

1. Remove hood.
2. Disconnect battery cables and lift out battery.
3. Drain coolant.
4. Disconnect cable connections to radiator fan, thermostat contact, headlamps, and headlamp cleaner motor.
5. Detach radiator hoses.
6. Remove 4 fastening bolts from front sheet.
7. Remove headlamp decor frames.
8. Remove 4 lower bolts holding headlamps (2 bolts each lamp).
9. Detach hood lock operating cable.
10. Remove front sheet.

CLUTCH, TRANSMISSION, AND DIFFERENTIAL

11. Remove front engine bracket (1970 model onwards).

12. Loosen 3 exhaust pipe bolts.

13. Detach throttle control linkage and throttle control damper.

14. Raise power plant about 4 in. (100mm) at the front.

15. Remove lock ring and clutch shaft sealing cover.

16. Remove clutch shaft center screw, washer, and O-ring.

17. Fit tapping hammer No. 839027 or equivalent and joint No. 839001 or equivalent in the clutch shaft end. Pull clutch shaft out.

18. Separate primary gear case from bearing housing by inserting wrench No. 879032 or equivalent into splines of the free wheel drive hub. Twist hub to the right, pulling it outward at same time until rollers project half their length. Fit sleeve No. 879031 over rollers and keep tool pressed against the free wheel shaft. Twist hub to the right with the wrench while pulling hub into the tool sleeve.

19. To install reverse preceding steps.

DIFFERENTIAL

The differential assembly consists of 2 differential gears and 2 front driveshaft gears, 1 for each front axle. All have straight beveled teeth. The axle gears are splined to the ends of the inner U-joints and driveshafts. The ring gear, which is driven from the transmission by the pinion shaft, is bolted to the differential case.

Universal Joints

The inner universal joint consists of a driveshaft journaled in the differential housing and splined into the differential side gear. See **Figure 17** (through 1969 models) **and Figure 18** (1970 models on). It is locked to the differential side gear by a resilient lock ring fitting into a groove inside the side gear. When the driveshaft is inserted or withdrawn the ring expands into the groove. The outer end of the driveshaft is in the form of a fork in which the driveshaft is journaled in needle bearings. When the car is moving the driveshaft can slide axially as well as being jointed. The joint is packed with grease and shielded by rubber bellows. Lubrication is needed only when the joint is reconditioned or removed. Special Saab chassis grease must be used.

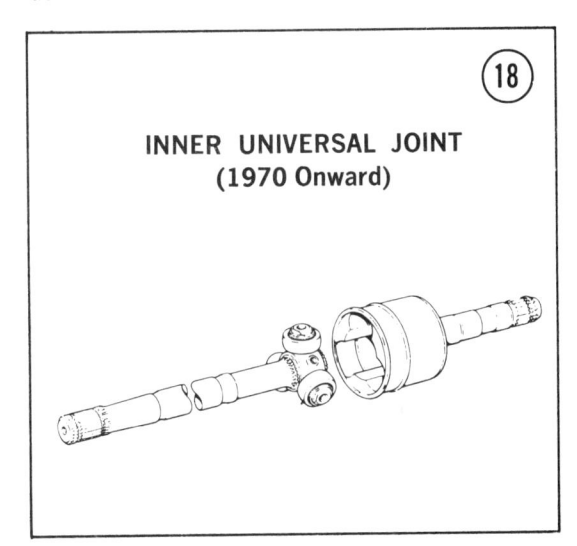

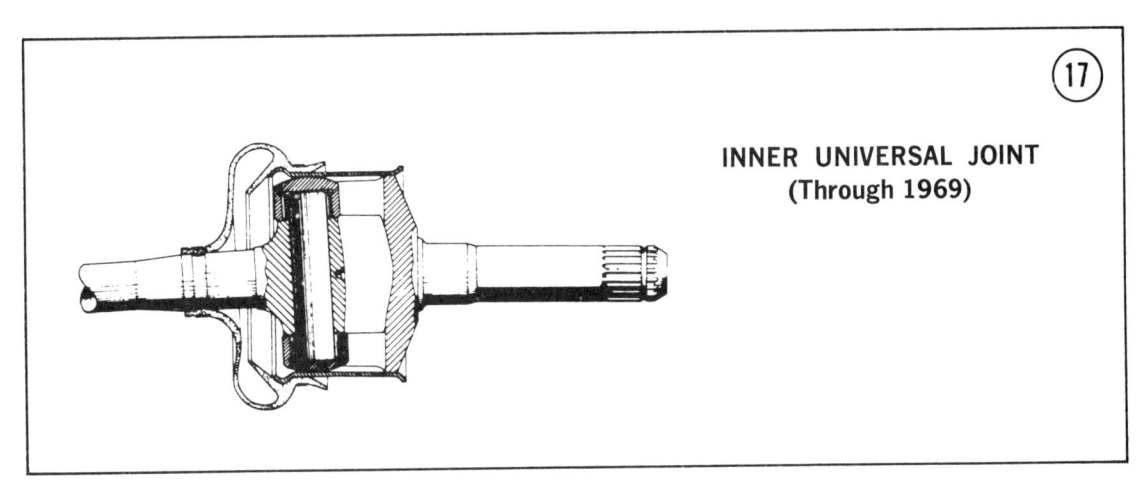

INNER UNIVERSAL JOINT
(1970 Onward)

INNER UNIVERSAL JOINT
(Through 1969)

CHAPTER NINE

The outer universal joint (**Figure 19**) driveshaft terminates in a bell housing with a spherical track in which 6 balls transmit driving power from a hub. The inner driveshaft is splined into the hub and located by a resilient lock ring. To mount the shaft in the hub the lock ring is first compressed with a special tool and the shaft inserted.

NOTE: *Special tools are required to change the complete outer drive shaft assembly (which is a complete unit). Its component parts are individually matched and not interchangeable.*

The joint needs lubricating only in conjunction with reconditioning or disassembly. Special Saab chassis grease must be used.

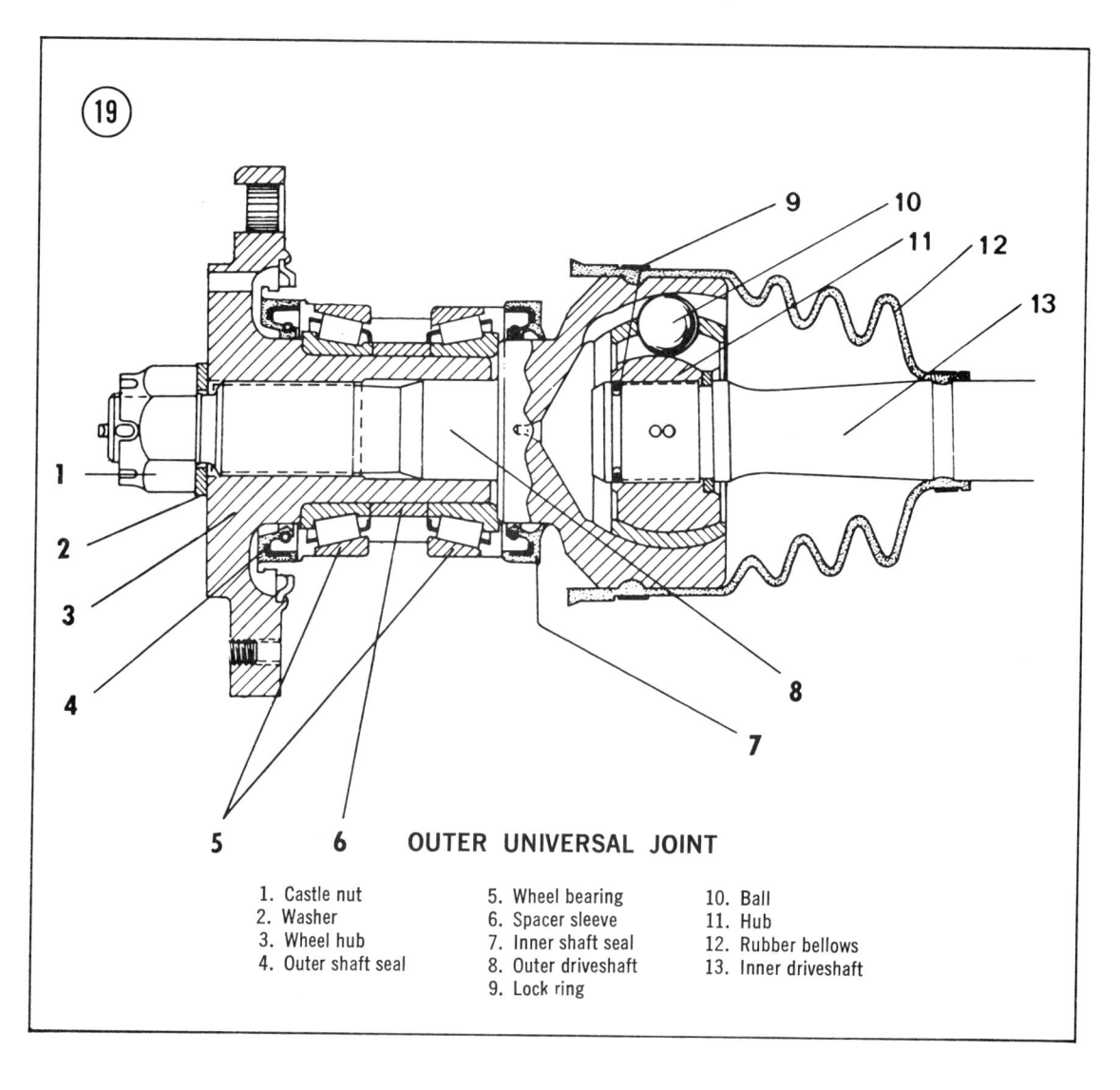

OUTER UNIVERSAL JOINT

1. Castle nut
2. Washer
3. Wheel hub
4. Outer shaft seal
5. Wheel bearing
6. Spacer sleeve
7. Inner shaft seal
8. Outer driveshaft
9. Lock ring
10. Ball
11. Hub
12. Rubber bellows
13. Inner driveshaft

CHAPTER TEN

FRONT SUSPENSION, WHEELS, AND STEERING

The front suspension features coil springs, transverse rubber bushed control arms, and double-acting hydraulic shock absorbers. Each front wheel is attached to the steering knuckle, which is suspended via ball-joints. Vertical wheel travel is limited by rubber bumpers. **Figure 1** shows the front suspension for the 95/96 and Sonett; **Figure 2** shows the front suspension for 99 models through 1972. On these models the coil springs are compressed between fixed seats. The lower seat is secured by 2 screws to the upper control arm in the 1969 model and welded to it in the 1970-1972 models. The top seat in the 1969-72 models consists of a steel cone welded to the wheel housing with a rubber buffer screwed to the cone. The rubber buffer acts as a stop, limiting the upward stroke of the suspension.

Figure 3 shows the front suspension on 1973-76 Saab 99 models. The lower spring seat is attached by a rubber bearing to the control arm. The seat is thus articulated (pivoted). The top seat consists of a steel cone held in place in the wheel housing by the pressure of the spring itself and located in a pressed boss in the wheel housing that fits inside rim of the cone. The downward stroke is limited by 2 rubber bumpers attached to the bodywork. The shock absorbers are attached by rubber bushings at both ends, to the bodywork at the top and to the lower control arms at the bottom.

BALL-JOINT REPLACEMENT

See **Figure 4** (99) **and Figure 5** (95/96 and Sonett).

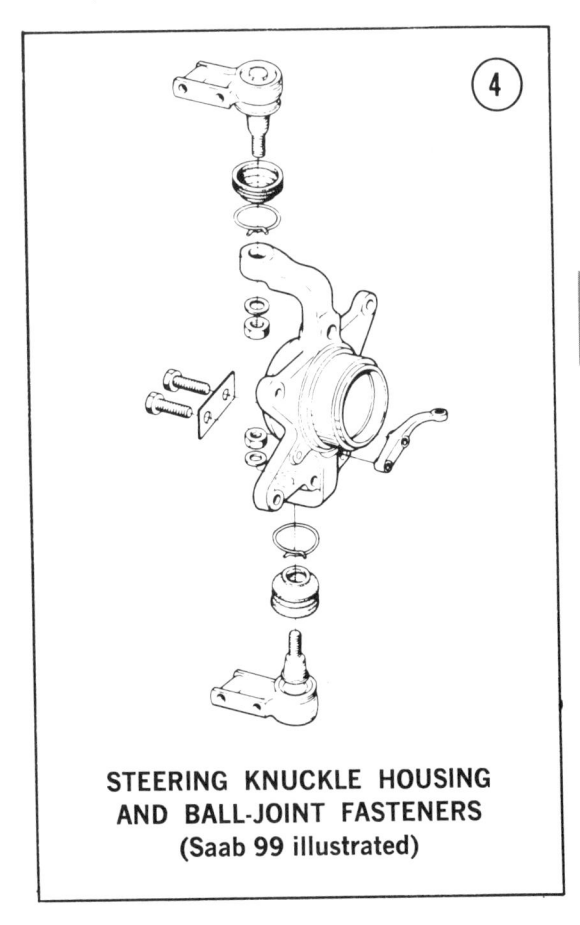

STEERING KNUCKLE HOUSING AND BALL-JOINT FASTENERS
(Saab 99 illustrated)

CHAPTER TEN

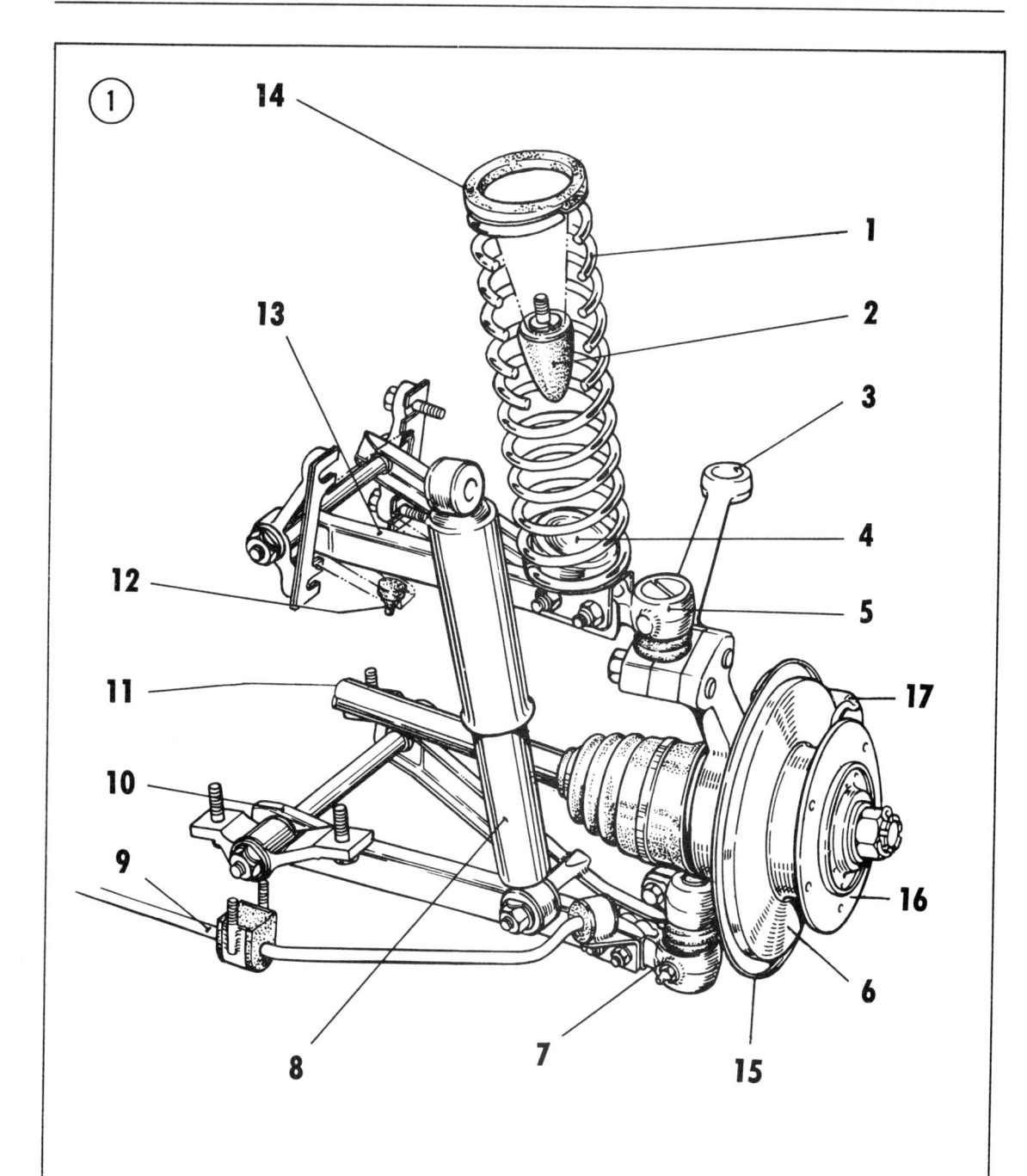

FRONT SUSPENSION (SAAB 95/96 AND SONETT)

1. Coil spring
2. Rubber bumper
3. Steering arm
4. Spring support
5. Upper ball-joint
6. Brake disc
7. Lower ball-joint
8. Shock absorber
9. Stabilizer bar
10. Lower control arm
11. Inner drive shaft
12. Rubber bumper
13. Upper control arm
14. Rubber spacer
15. Protective shield
16. Hub
17. Brake housing

FRONT SUSPENSION, WHEELS, AND STEERING

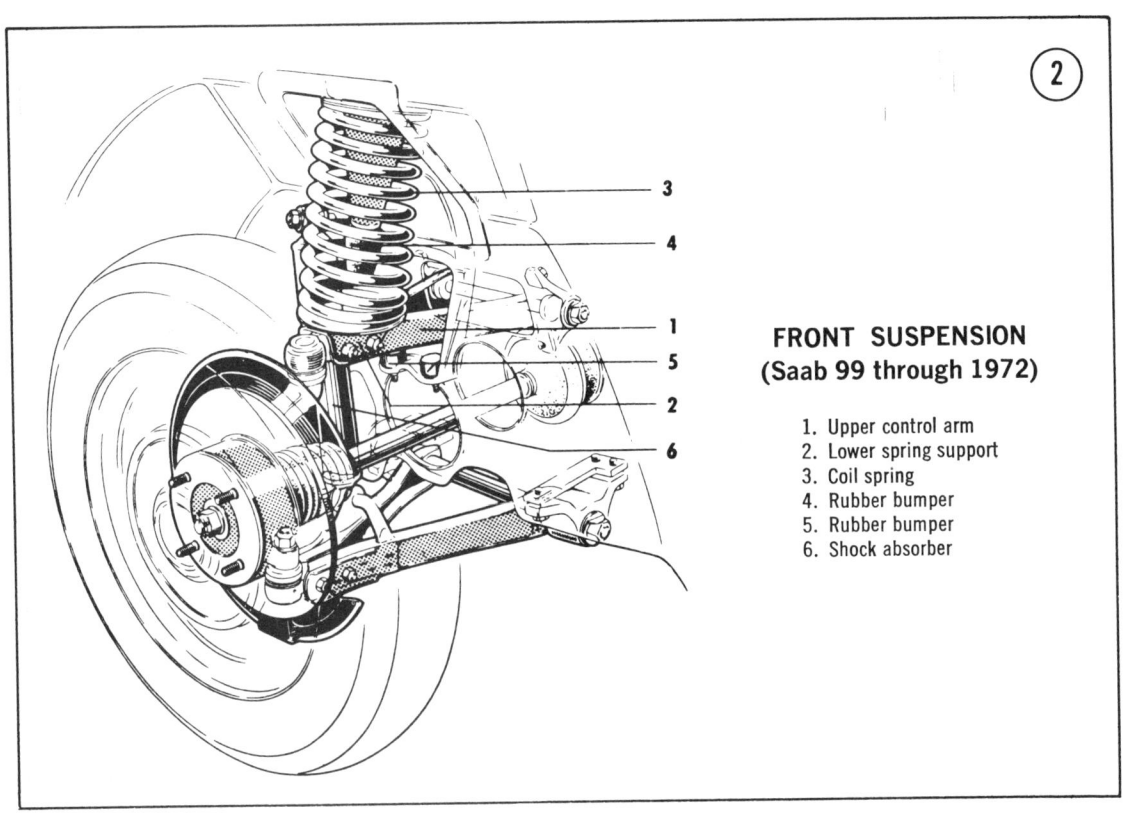

FRONT SUSPENSION
(Saab 99 through 1972)

1. Upper control arm
2. Lower spring support
3. Coil spring
4. Rubber bumper
5. Rubber bumper
6. Shock absorber

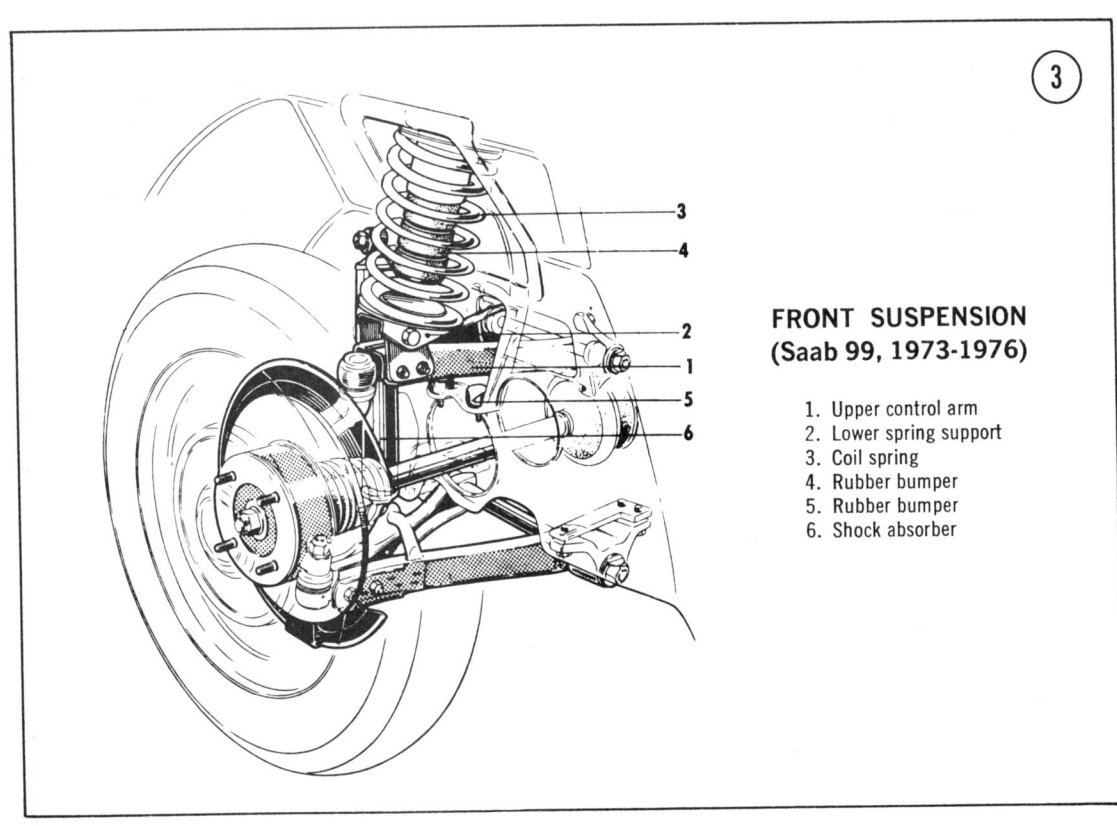

FRONT SUSPENSION
(Saab 99, 1973-1976)

1. Upper control arm
2. Lower spring support
3. Coil spring
4. Rubber bumper
5. Rubber bumper
6. Shock absorber

STEERING KNUCKLE AND BALL-JOINT ATTACHMENT
(Saab 95/96 and Sonett illustrated)

spring compressor tool No. 784082 or equivalent (**Figure 6**). The clamp must be fitted as shown. On the 99 models (**Figure 7**) compress the spring with tool No. 8995839 (tools No. 899506 and 899502 for the 1969 Saab 99, **Figure 8**).

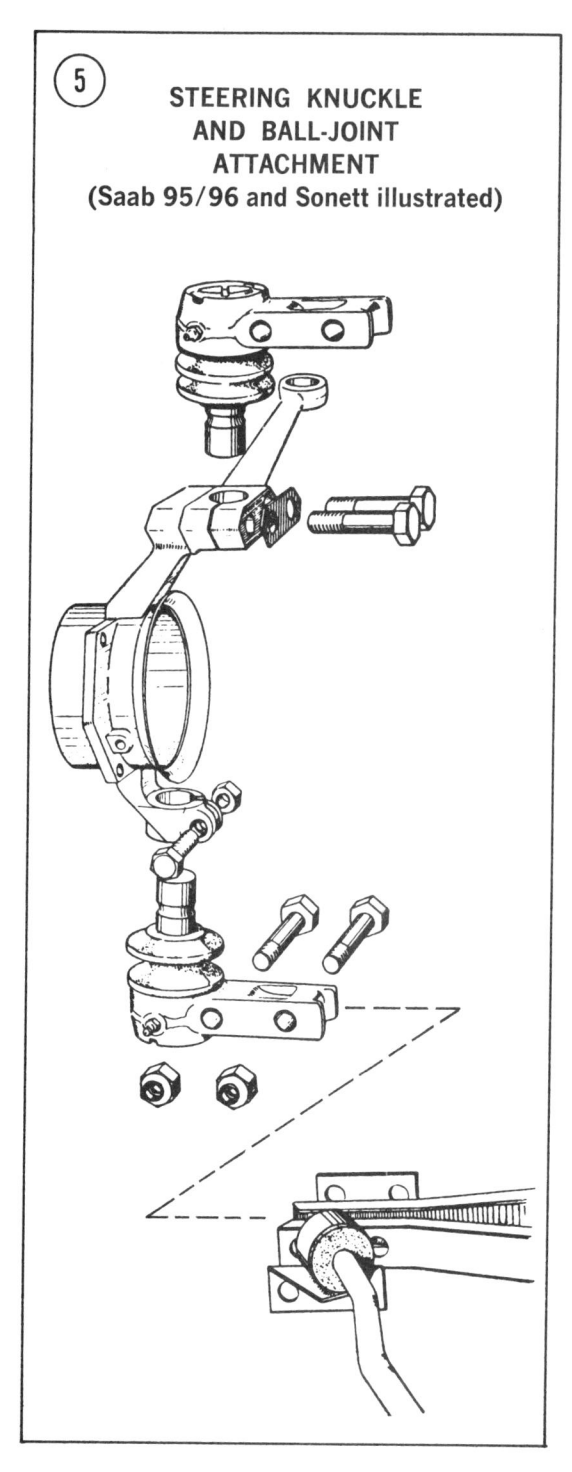

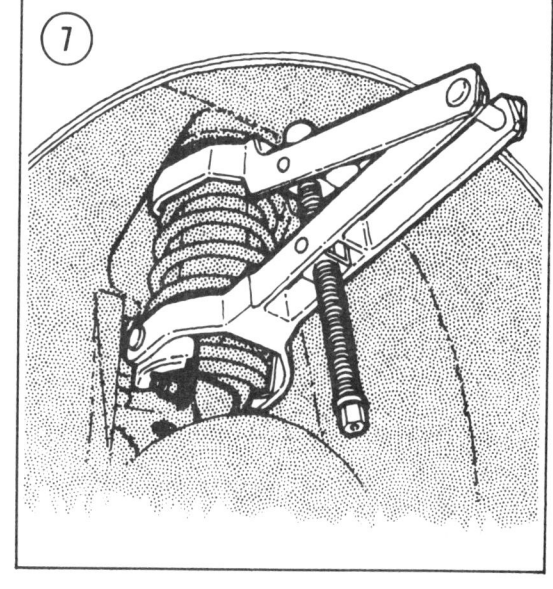

1. Jack up the car and support it with jackstands. Remove the wheels and wash the ball-joint and adjacent parts clean.

2. If the upper ball joint is to be changed (95/96, and Sonett) compress the spring with

FRONT SUSPENSION, WHEELS, AND STEERING

3. On 99 models unscrew the brake housing and hang it up so that the brake hose or pipe cannot be damaged.

4. Remove the ball-joint from the steering knuckle by loosening the nut holding the ball bolt in the steering knuckle housing and removing the bolt using tool No. 899540 (99 models through 1974), or tool No. 8995409 (1975-1976 models). See **Figure 9**. No special tools are needed for the 95/96, and Sonett models (Figure 5). Simply loosen the bolts (2 bolts on the upper ball-joint, one on the lower one).

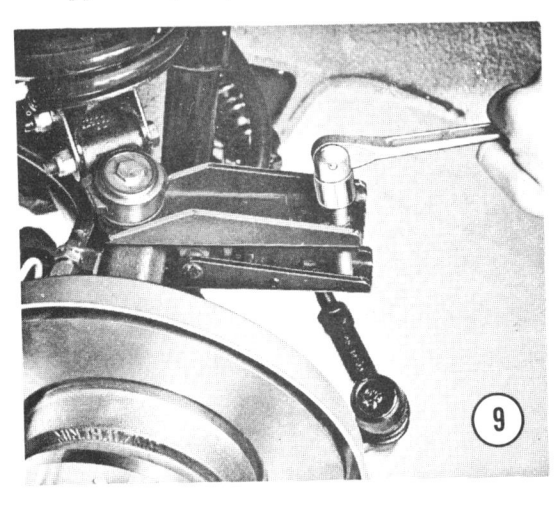

5. Remove the ball-joint from the control arm.
6. Mount a new ball-joint. Connect the bolt to the steering knuckle housing and tighten the nut (99 models). On the 95/96, and Sonett, set the pivot pin of the ball-joint in the steering knuckle hole (refer to Figure 5) and install the nuts and bolts.

7. Secure the ball-joint to the control arm, using new locknuts. Release the spring compressor.

8. Mount the brake housing (99 models).

9. Install the wheel and lower the car to the ground.

STEERING GEAR

The steering gear is accurately adjusted at the factory and should not be disassembled unless absolutely necessary. Proper lubrication is vital (refer to Chapter Two). See **Figure 10**.

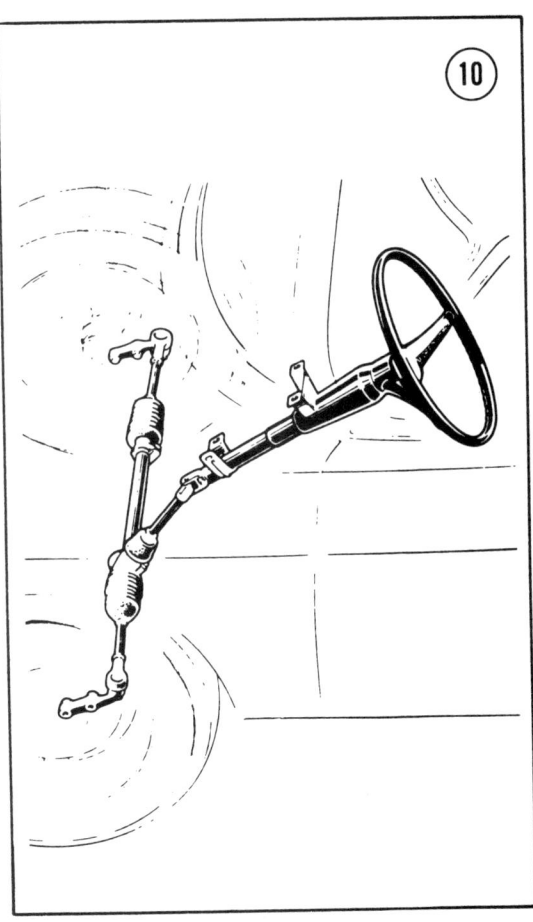

Changing Tie Rod Ends

The tie rod end assemblies cannot be disassembled and must be exchanged as a complete unit.

1. Jack up the car and support on jackstands. Remove wheels.

2. Remove the nut holding the tie rod end to the steering arm. Use puller No. 899540 (through 1974) or No. 8995409 (1975-1976) to disconnect ball bolt from steering arm (**Figure 11**). Do not knock ball bolt out as damage could result.

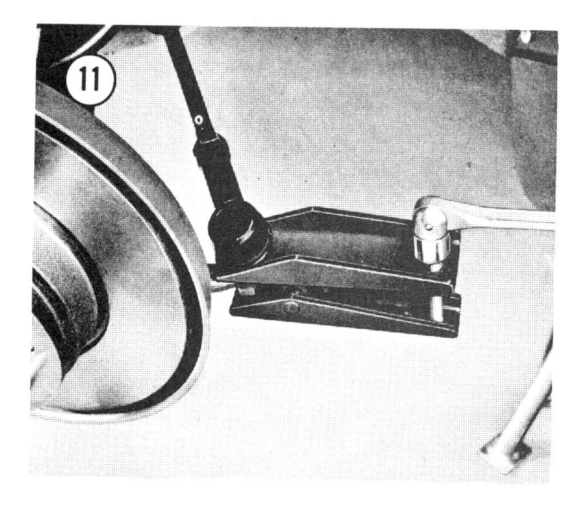

3. Loosen the nut that locks the tie rod end assembly to the tie rod. Unscrew the end assembly from the tie rod.

4. Thread a new end assembly onto the tie rod (but do not lock it by tightening the nut).

5. Connect the ball bolt to the steering arm. Install the nut and tighten to 25-36 ft.-lb.

6. Mount the wheels and lower the car to the ground.

7. Have toe-in adjusted at a front end alignment shop.

Changing Rubber Bellows

Each ball-joint is protected by a rubber bellows. If damaged it no longer makes a tight seal and should be exchanged as follows:

1. Perform Steps 1 and 2 under *Changing Tie Rod Ends*, preceding.

2. Remove damaged bellows from ball bolt. Fit new bellows.

3. Connect ball bolt to steering arm. Install nut and tighten to 25-36 ft.-lb.

4. Mount the wheels and lower car to ground.

FRONT END ALIGNMENT

Front end alignment requires special tools and knowledge and should be performed by your dealer or a front end alignment specialist.

SHOCK ABSORBERS

Shock absorbers contribute greatly to good roadholding and steering characteristics. Shock absorbers on the same axle should be exchanged in pairs.

Removal/Installation

1. Jack up car and support on jackstands. Remove wheels.

2. Remove retaining nuts, washers, and rubber insulators, and remove shock absorber units. See **Figure 12**.

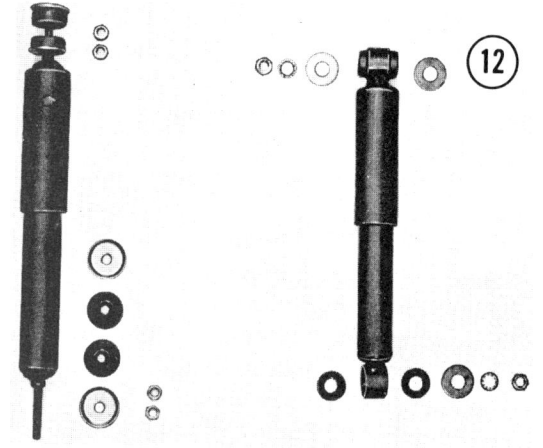

3. Before installing the new shock absorber(s), expel any air from the unit by holding it upright in the same position as when installed and pump it up and down for a few full strokes. Install in car.

4. Fit new rubber insulators and washers. Tighten nuts firmly.

WHEELS

The wheels are riveted and welded pressed sheet steel units mounted via 5 studs. Bent or broken wheels should be replaced immediately. See **Figure 13**.

FRONT SUSPENSION, WHEELS, AND STEERING

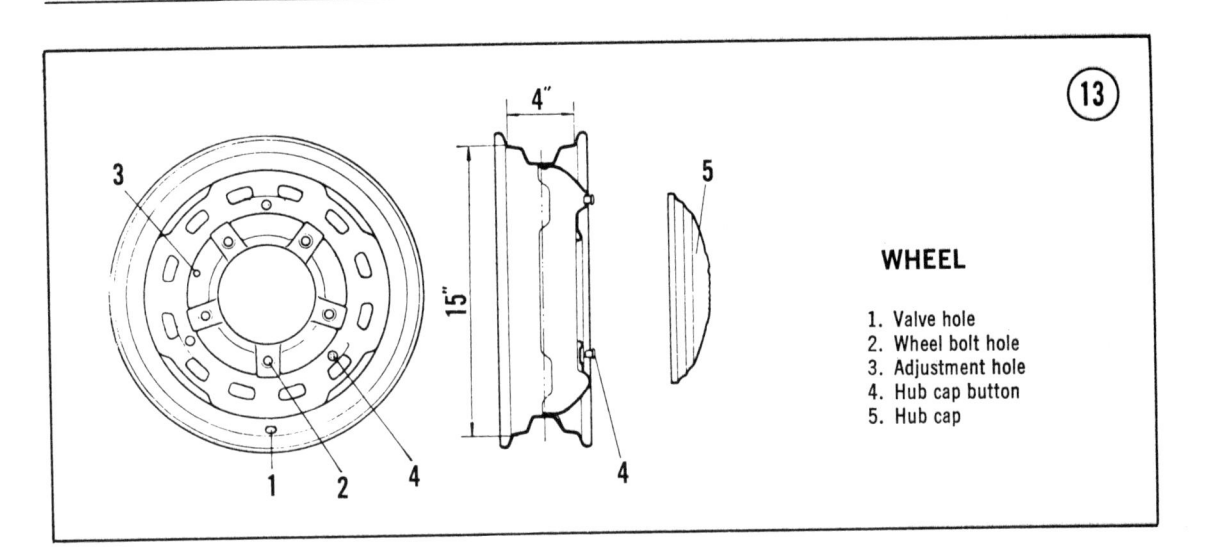

WHEEL

1. Valve hole
2. Wheel bolt hole
3. Adjustment hole
4. Hub cap button
5. Hub cap

CHAPTER ELEVEN

REAR SUSPENSION

The rear axle on the 95, 96, and Sonett is attached to the body at 3 points via rubber-bushed bearings. The axle tube is swept back at the ends and fitted with end plates to carry press-fitted stub axles. Wheel hubs and brake drums are carried in ball bearings on the stub axles, while the backplates and rear brakes bolt to the outside of the end plates.

At the center the rear axle is attached to the car body through a rubber-bushed bearing bracket. It is also braced at the sides via longitudinal side links attached to both the body and rear axles by means of rubber-bushed bearings.

The lower coil spring seats are bolted to the stub axle extension on the inside of the rear axle end plates; the upper seats for these springs are connected to the body via spring isolators and are combined with rubber buffers which limit upward travel of the rear axle. Wheel travel rebound is limited by the stop straps.

The 95 rear shock absorbers are of the arm type, bolted to the body and connected to the rear axle by links. See **Figure 1**.

Saab 96 models utilize telescopic rear shocks (**Figure 2**) connected to the body by rubber bushed bearings and to the rear axle at the bottom of the shock absorber by rubber bushed bearings.

Saab 99 models use a rear suspension comprised of a rigid axle with coil springs and double-acting telescopic shock absorbers. The rear axle tube carries end pieces into which the stub axles are force-fitted. Wheel hubs are journaled to the stub axles on conical roller bearings. Disc brake shields are bolted to the outside of the end pieces.

The rear axle is attached to the body by 2 spring links, their front ends journaled to the body, their rear ends connected by 2 rubber bushings of the rear axle tube. Two links also connect the end pieces of the rear axle and the body behind the rear axle. These links take torsional stresses in the axle. Lateral forces are handled by a cross bar with one end journaled in a rubber bearing in a bracket fixed to the underbody. The other end of the bar attaches to the right end piece of the rear axle. See **Figure 3** for an illustration of the rear suspension used on 99 models through 1973.

The 1974 Saab 99 introduced a new cross bar, attached to the body somewhat more forward than previous rear suspensions; its attachment to the rear axle is on a bracket on the axle tube. See **Figure 4**. The spring links carry seats for the lower ends of the coil springs, the upper seats being attached by spring insulators to the body. Rear wheel travel is limited by

REAR SUSPENSION

137

① REAR SUSPENSION (Saab 95)

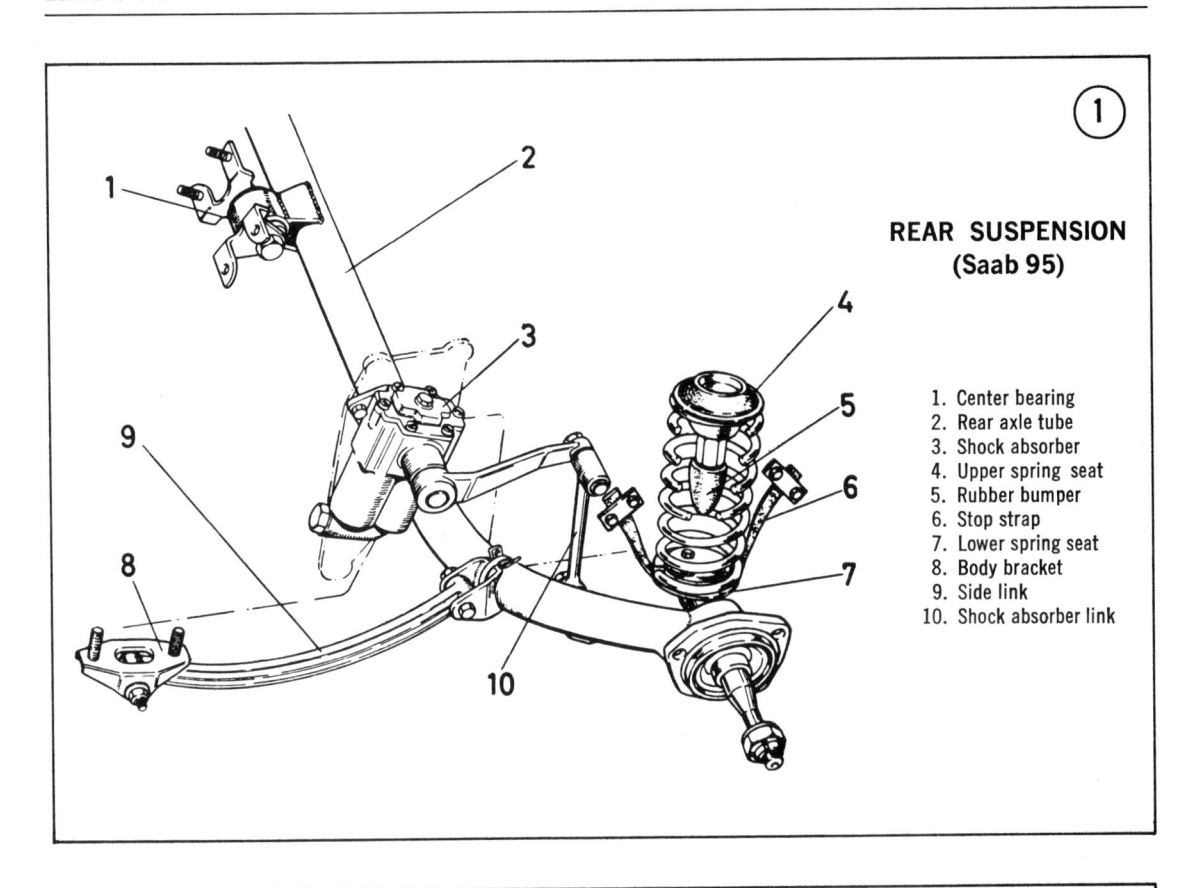

1. Center bearing
2. Rear axle tube
3. Shock absorber
4. Upper spring seat
5. Rubber bumper
6. Stop strap
7. Lower spring seat
8. Body bracket
9. Side link
10. Shock absorber link

② REAR SUSPENSION (Saab 96)

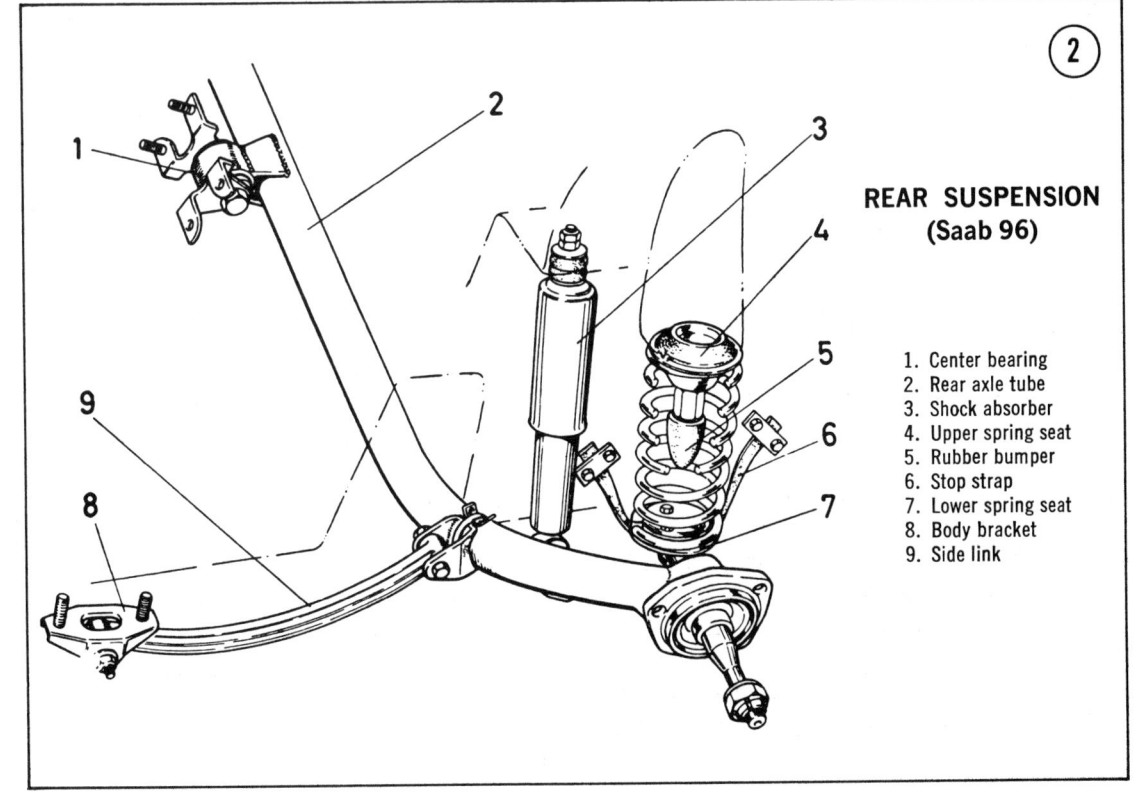

1. Center bearing
2. Rear axle tube
3. Shock absorber
4. Upper spring seat
5. Rubber bumper
6. Stop strap
7. Lower spring seat
8. Body bracket
9. Side link

**REAR SUSPENSION
(Saab 99 through 1973)**

1. Rear axle
2. End piece
3. Stub axle
4. Spring links
5. Rear links
6. Cross bar
7. Spring seat
8. Coil spring
9. Spring insulator
10. Rubber bumper
11. Stop
12. Shock absorber

**REAR SUSPENSION
(Saab 99, 1974-1976)**

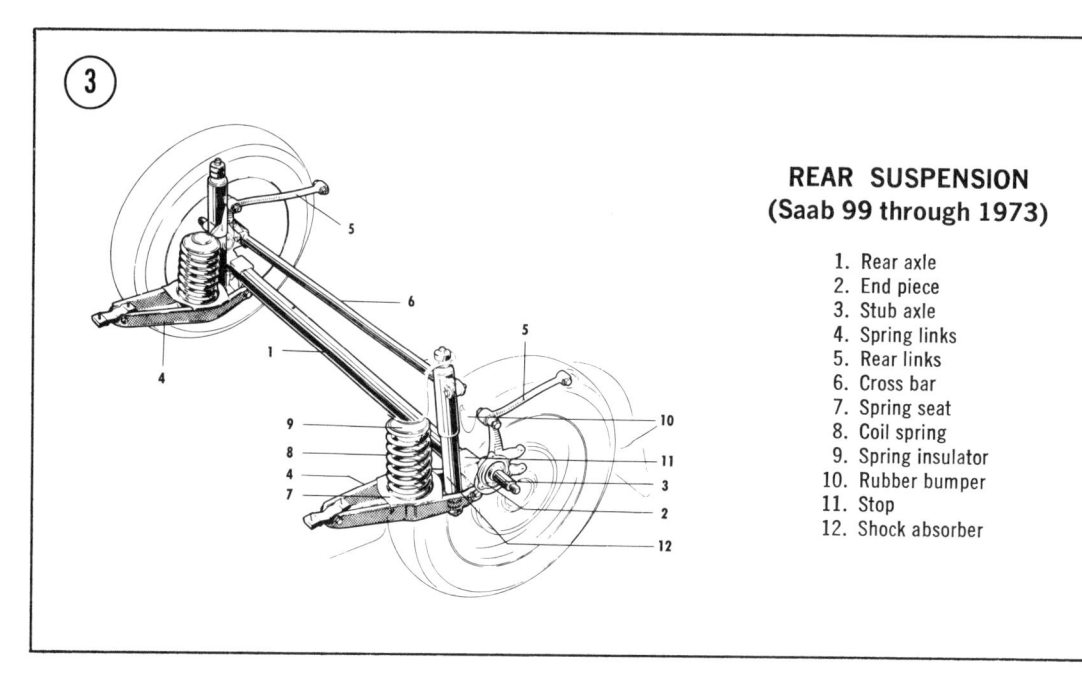

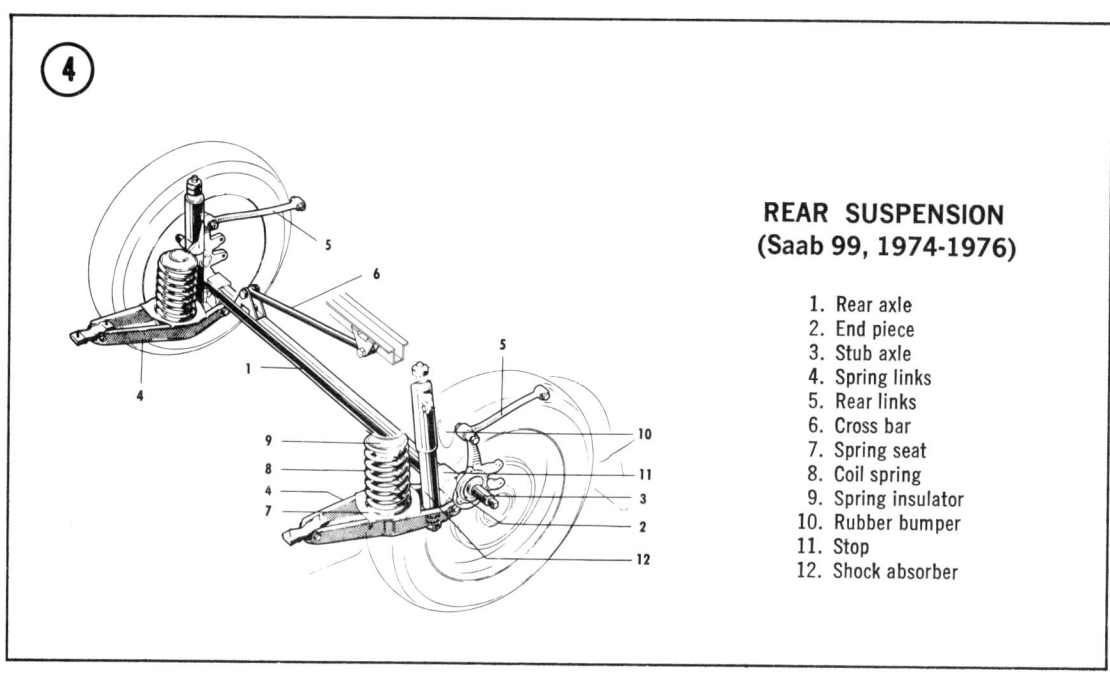

1. Rear axle
2. End piece
3. Stub axle
4. Spring links
5. Rear links
6. Cross bar
7. Spring seat
8. Coil spring
9. Spring insulator
10. Rubber bumper
11. Stop
12. Shock absorber

rubber buffers screwed into the body which, at extreme spring compression, strike a stop on the rear axle. Downward movement is limited by the shock absorbers.

The rear shock absorbers are journaled in rubber bearings at both ends, the upper end being attached to the body and the lower end to the back axle spring links.

REAR SPRINGS AND RUBBER BUMPERS

Removal
(95, 96, and Sonett)

1. Jack up one side of the car (with the jack in the appropriate place under the rear end of the sill) and remove the rear wheel.

REAR SUSPENSION

2. Unfasten stop strap at rear bracket in order to lower axle so that spring can be removed without the use of tools. See **Figure 5**.

NOTE: *On the 95, first remove the shock absorber unit.*

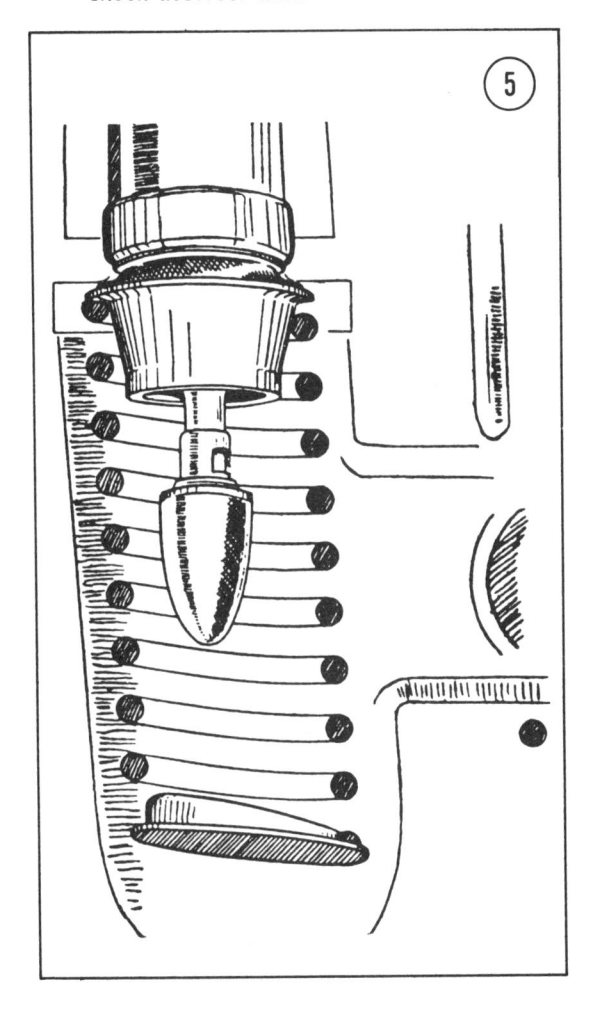

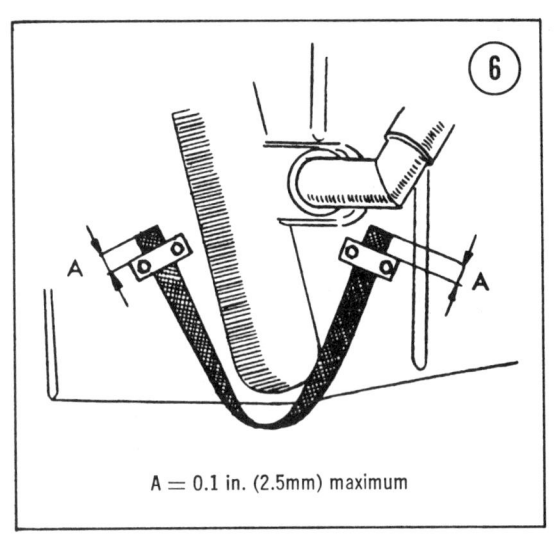

A = 0.1 in. (2.5mm) maximum

2. Fit the spring in position with the unground end facing downward. Turn it until it is correctly located in the lower spring seat.

3. Fasten a new stop strap to the front bracket if old one has been removed. Bear in mind that the ends should project 0.6 in. (15mm) beyond the bracket (Figure 6).

4. Install the rear wheel and tighten the nuts evenly. Lower the car to the floor with the jack.

5. Secure the stop strap at the rear end, again keeping in mind that the ends of the strap should extend 0.6 in. (15mm) beyond the bracket (Figure 6).

**Removal
(Saab 99)**

1. Apply handbrake. Remove rear hub cap and loosen wheel lug nuts. Jack car up and place a rigid support under the side where the spring is to be removed.

3. If rubber bumper needs replacement unscrew it with a pair of pliers, gripping the steel washer at its thick end.

4. Check condition of stop strap to see if a new one is required. (Be sure that the ends of the new rear axle stop strap project 0.6 in. [15mm] beyond the brackets). See **Figure 6**.

CAUTION
The jack must not be placed under rear axle, as this could deform the axle.

2. Remove wheel. Place a jack under the spring link and disconnect the lower end of the shock absorber. See **Figure 7**. Remove the 2 nuts under the rear seat that hold the front spring link bearing to the body. (On 99 models from 1974 on, remove the lock nuts from underneath.)

**Installation
(95, 96, and Sonett)**

1. Screw a new rubber bumper in place if old one has been removed. Be sure to fit the retaining washer between the bumper and its seat.

3. Carefully lower the spring link so that the spring can be removed. From 1974 on, the

CHAPTER ELEVEN

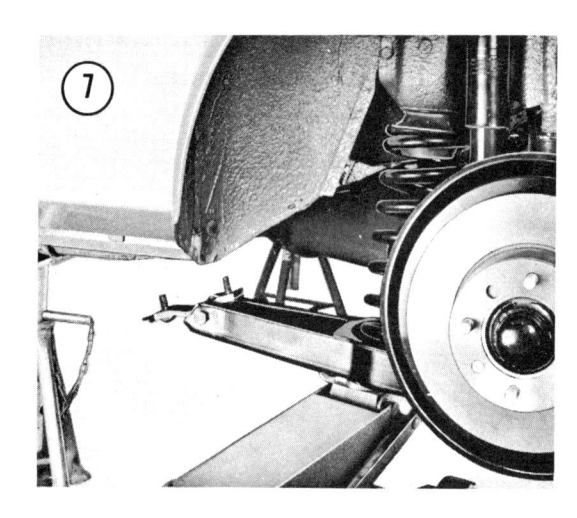

upper spring support is held in place by spring tension and is to be removed together with the spring. Refer to **Figure 8**.

Installation
(Saab 99)

Install the coil springs by reversing the removal steps. Be sure that the unmachined end of the spring is at the bottom and securely seated in the lower spring seat (through 1973). See Figure 8.

> NOTE: *Effective with 1974 models the upper end of the spring is unmachined and is, instead, provided with an upper rubber spring support. The locknuts at the front spring link bearing attachment in the body are to be exchanged.*

REAR AXLE
Removal
(95, 96, and Sonett)

1. Remove rear seat and back cushions.
2. Loosen rear wheel lug nuts. Jack rear of car up and remove wheels.
3. Disconnect rear muffler and exhaust pipe from wheel house and floor.
4. Disconnect brake hoses from body.
5. Unscrew rear stop straps brackets. Remove coil springs (no tools required).
6. "Suspend" the axle in the stop straps.
7. Disconnect shock absorbers (on the 95 unfasten at rear axle; on the 96 disconnect at upper connection).
8. Detach brake cable clamps from the shaft and the wire connections from rear brake levers.
9. Disconnect rear axle center bearing bracket from the body (see **Figure 9**).

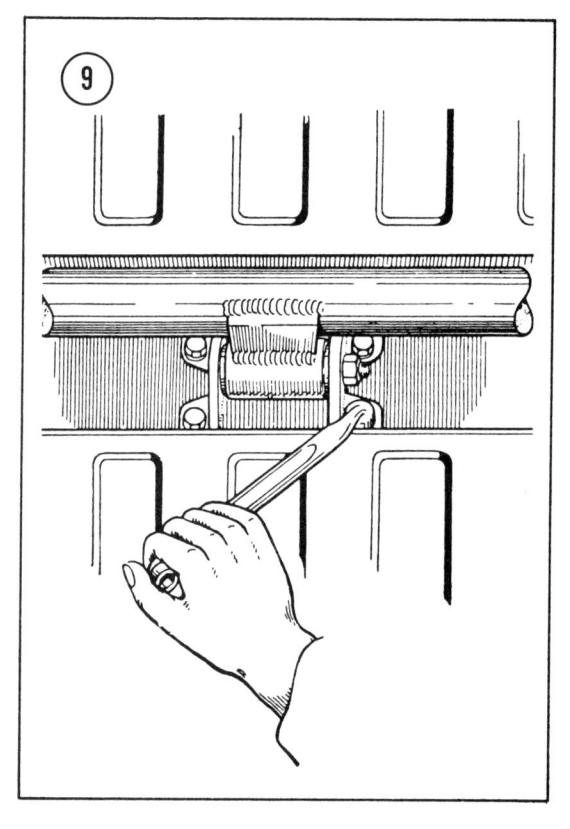

10. Unfasten side link body brackets (nuts are accessible from inside the car under the rear seat cushion). See **Figure 10**.

REAR SUSPENSION

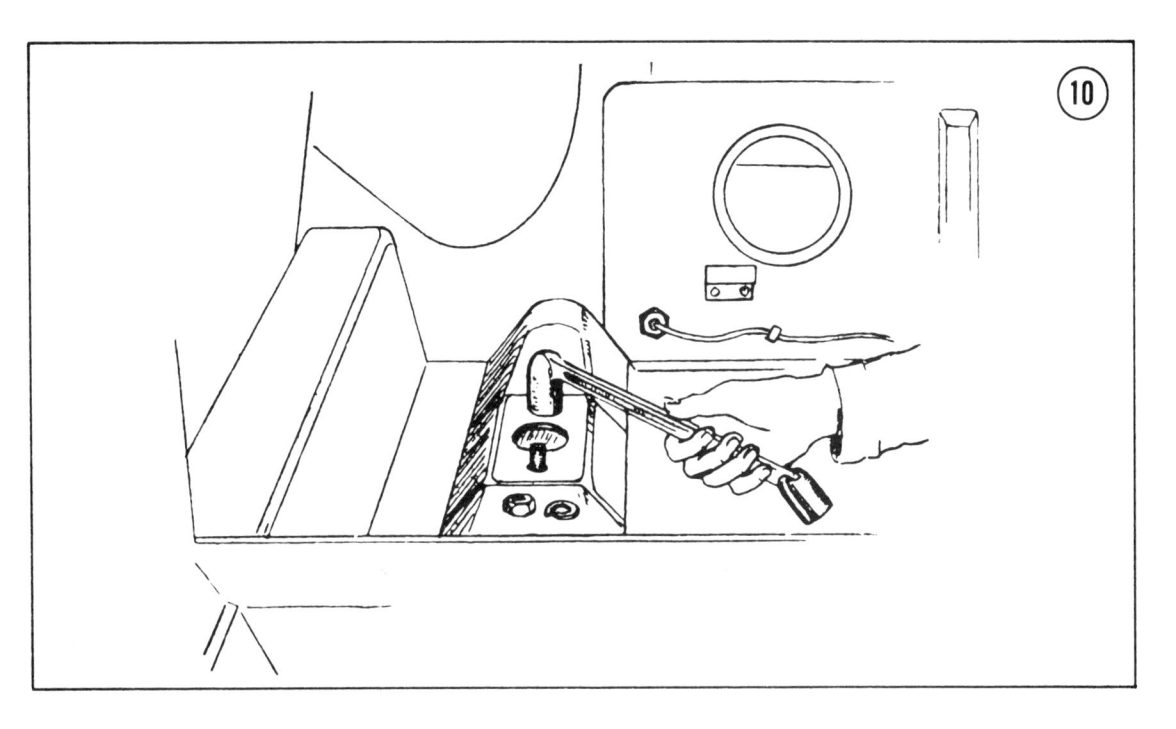

11. Unfasten stop straps again and remove rear axle assembly.

Installation
(95, 96, and Sonett)

Installation is accomplished by reversing the removal steps. Clean parts thoroughly and renew all worn or damaged parts.

> NOTE: *The rubber bushed bearings must be fitted so that no stress occurs when car is resting on the wheels (i.e., such bearings must not be tightened at the axle and body brackets until car has been lowered to floor). The ends of the stop straps should project 0.6 in. (15mm) beyond the brackets. Refer to Figure 6.*

Removal
(Saab 99)

1. Set the handbrake. Loosen rear wheel lug nuts. Jack up rear of car and place 2 rigid supports under the body. Remove the rear wheels.

> WARNING
> *Do not jack up the car with the jack applied directly to the rear axle.*

2. Disconnect brake hoses in front of rear axle.

3. Place jack under rear axle. Lower the axle carefully and lift out the rear springs.

4. Remove the spring link rear bushing screws. Lift away the rear axle asembly.

Installation
(Saab 99)

Installation is accomplished by reversing the removal steps. Clean parts thoroughly and renew all worn or damaged parts.

> NOTE: *The jack is not to be placed on the center of the rear axle. Use 2 jacks or rigid supports at one side when the other is lifted to the correct position with the jack. The rubber bearings must be fitted so that no stress occurs when the weight of the car is supported on its own wheels (i.e., the rubber bearings must be drawn tight only when the car is resting on its 4 wheels, unladen).*

> CAUTION
> *On models through 1973 the screw at the cross bar attachment to the body must be installed with the nut facing backward; from 1974 on the nut faces forward.*

Bleed the brakes (see Chapter Twelve).

CENTER BEARING

The entire rear axle assembly should be removed in order to replace the center bearing bushing. However, it is possible to change the bushing while the axle remains in place.

Bushing Replacement (95, 96, and Sonett, Axle on Car)

1. Jack up rear part of car.
2. Disconnect rear muffler and exhaust pipe brackets from wheel house and floor.
3. Remove the bolt through the center bearing.
4. Lower rear axle and place an assembly bar across the tunnel between body and axle on either side of center bearing.
5. Remove rubber bushing. See **Figure 11**. 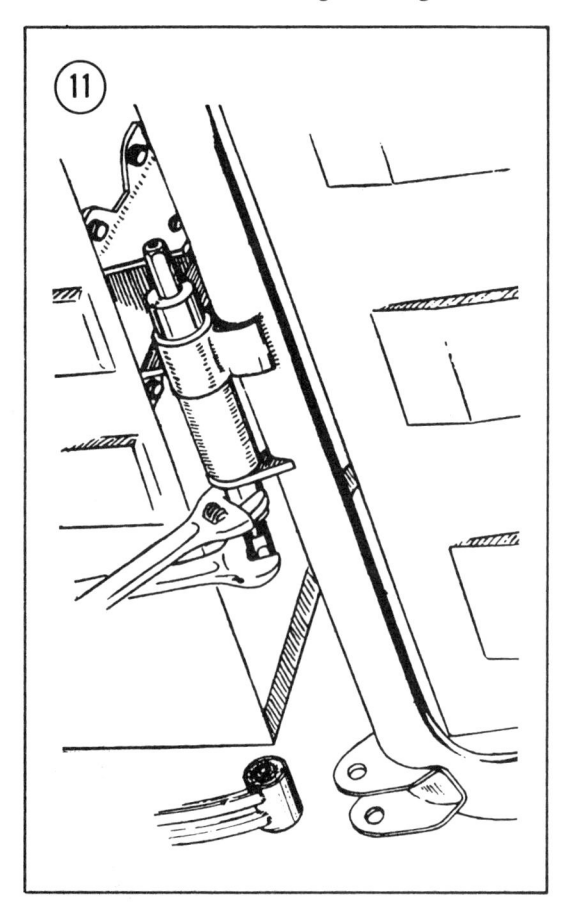
6. Press a new bushing in. Locate the bushing in the exact center of the bearing. Refit the center bearing but do not tighten the nut until car has been lowered to the floor.
7. Reinstall the rear muffler and exhaust pipe.
8. Lower the car to the floor. Tighten the nut on the rear axis center bearing bolt.

SIDE LINKS

Rubber Bushings Replacement (95, 96, and Sonett)

1. Disconnect links from brackets on rear axle. Detach body brackets from links.
2. Gently heat the link bearing sleeves with a torch or other suitable heat source. Carefully drive the bushings off with Saab special tool 784076, or equivalent. See **Figure 12**. 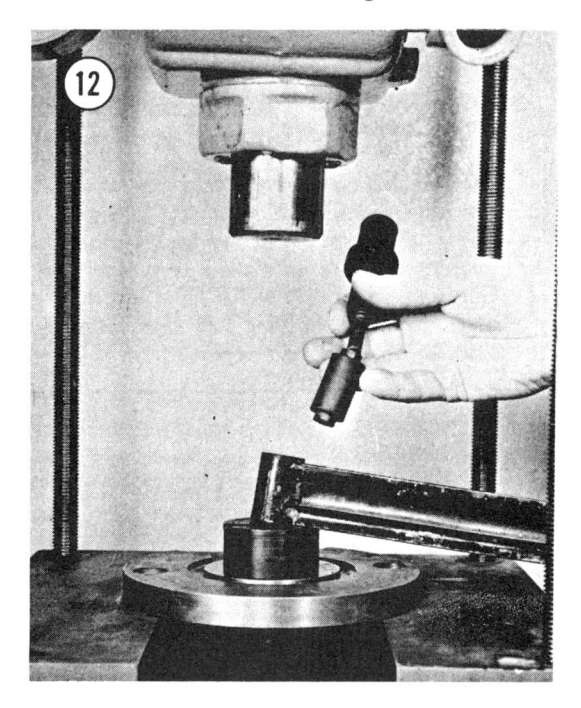
3. Reinstall body brackets to links, noting that the angle between the link and bracket should be 4 degrees (see **Figure 13**) when the bushing is tightened.
4. Reinstall links to rear axle (do not tighten nuts until car is resting on its wheels). Insert bolts from the outside toward the center bearing.
5. Lower car to floor. Tighten nuts on the side link rear bearing brackets.

> NOTE: *Elastic retaining nuts can lose their gripping power after several tightenings. It is a good idea to replace elastic nuts when in doubt.*

REAR SUSPENSION

13

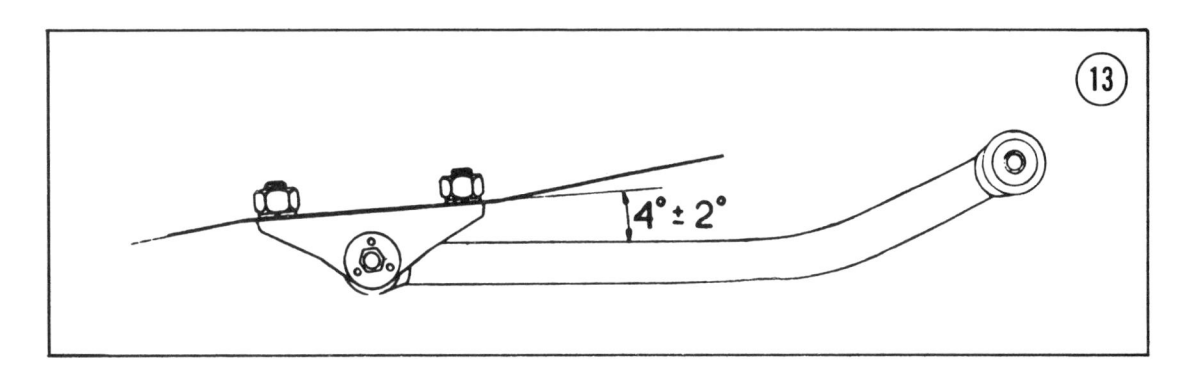

$4° \pm 2°$

SHOCK ABSORBERS

Removal
(Saab 95)

1. Loosen rear wheel lug nuts. Jack car up and support with rigid jack stands. Remove rear wheels.

2. Refer to Figure 1. Disconnect the arm of the shock absorber from the shock absorber link.

3. Remove shock absorber mounting bolts. Remove shock absorber.

Installation
(Saab 95)

To install the rear shock absorbers, reverse the removal procedure.

Removal
(96, Sonett, and 99)

1. Loosen rear wheel lug nuts. Jack car up and support with rigid jack stands. Remove rear wheels.

2. Disconnect shock absorber from upper and lower brackets (refer to **Figure 14** for 96 and Sonett; **Figure 15** for 99).

3. Remove shock absorber, being careful not to lose any washers or rubber items.

Installation
(96, Sonett, and 99)

1. Install rubber bushings and washers (replace with new ones whenever possible).

> NOTE: *Before installing shock absorbers any air in the units must be expelled. Accomplish this by pumping each shock absorber up and down several times.*

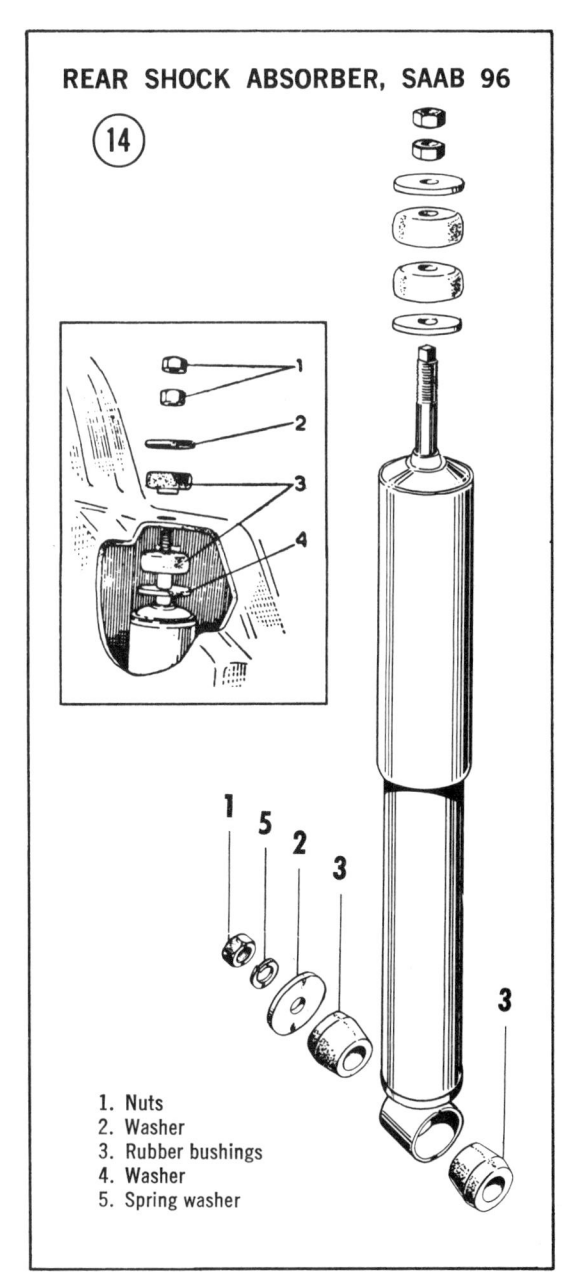

REAR SHOCK ABSORBER, SAAB 96

14

1. Nuts
2. Washer
3. Rubber bushings
4. Washer
5. Spring washer

Figure 15

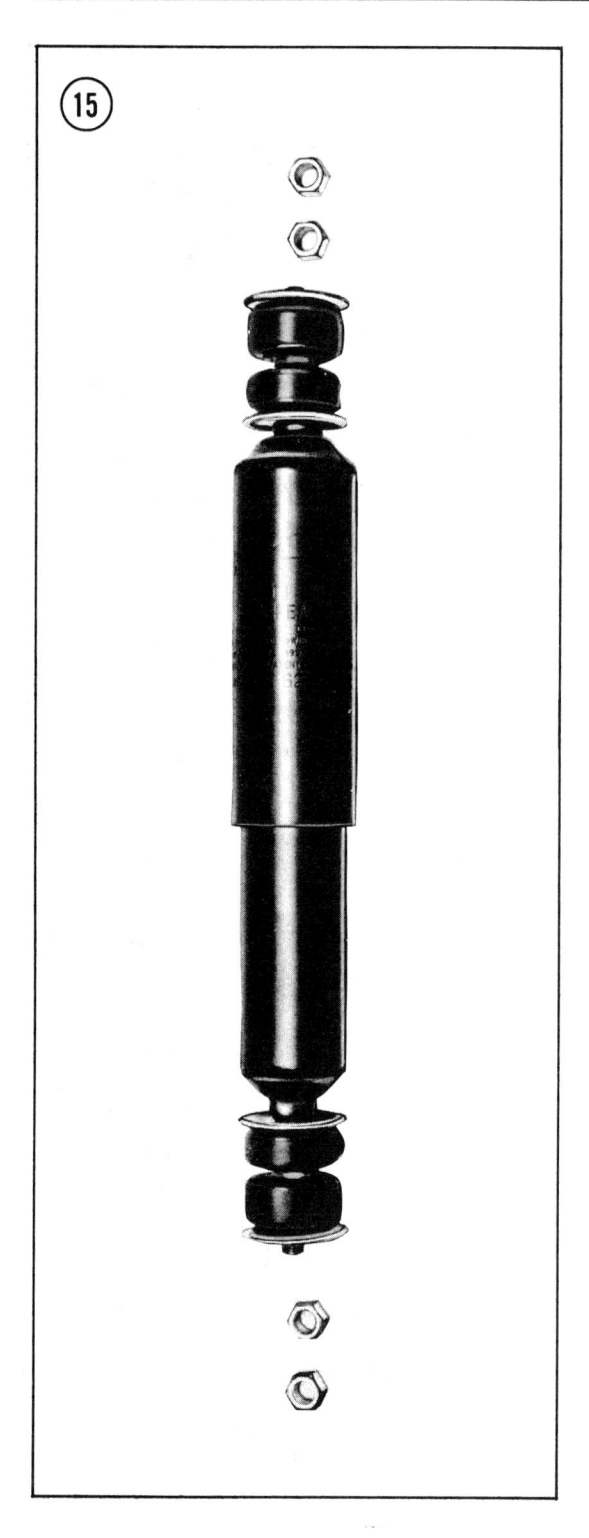

2. Be certain rubber bushings in upper connection are located correctly. Ease upper bushing flange into the hole in the body so that the shock absorber is centered in the hole.

3. Coat the pin threads with grease. Screw nuts on and tighten enough to provide suitable tension against the rubber bushings.

HUBS/WHEEL BEARINGS

The hub and brake drum on the rear wheels of the 95, 96, and Sonett are an integral casting. Refer to **Figure 16**. Ball bearings are fitted into the rear wheel hubs. These, together with the shaft seal, accompany the hub when it is removed.

The rear wheel hub on 99 models is journaled on 2 identical tapered roller bearings. Refer to **Figure 17**. The hub is removed complete with bearings and shaft seal.

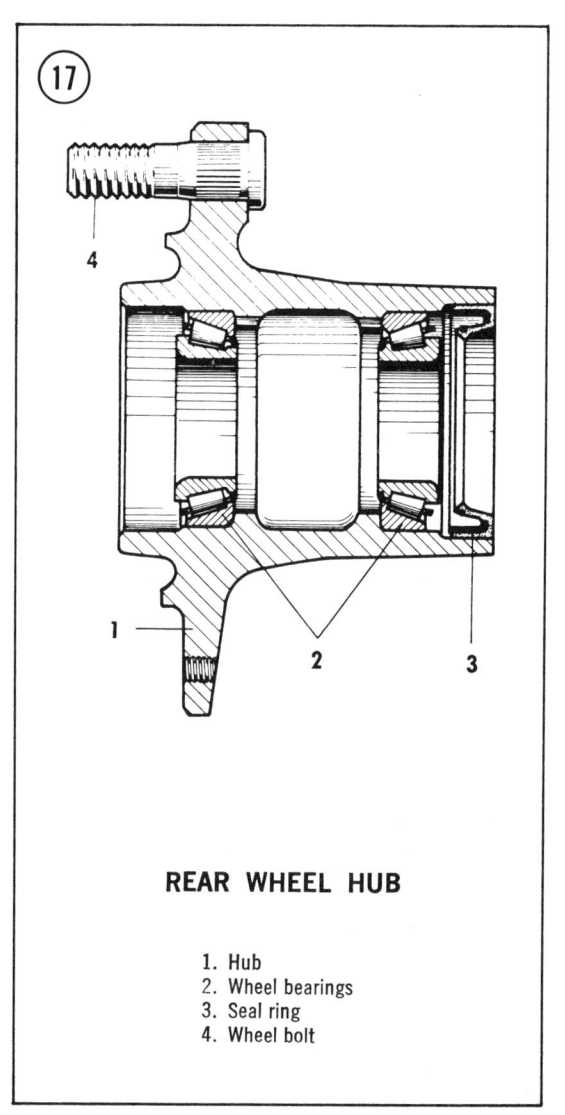

Figure 17

REAR WHEEL HUB

1. Hub
2. Wheel bearings
3. Seal ring
4. Wheel bolt

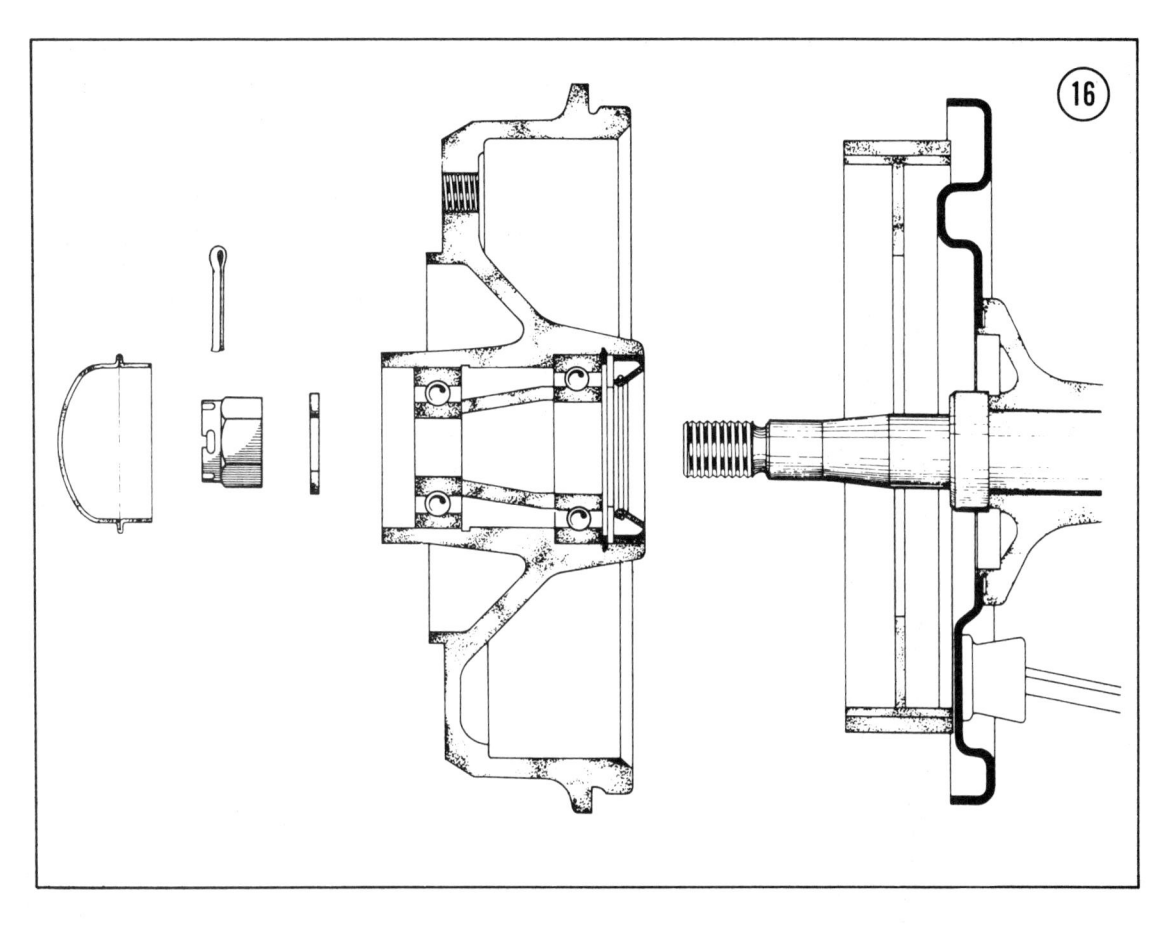

REAR SUSPENSION

Hub Removal
(95, 96, and Sonett)

1. Clean dirt away from under fenders before starting work, so that no dirt falls into bearings.

2. Remove hub cap and loosen rear wheel lug nuts. Remove dust cap, cotter pin, castle nut, and washer.

3. Jack rear of car up and support it on rigid jack stands.

4. Release handbrake and back off brake adjusting bolts. Remove rear wheel.

5. Remove brake housing and hang it on wheel housing so that the brake hose cannot be damaged. Remove cotter pin, crown nut, and washer.

6. Install a hub puller (**Figure 18**) and pull hub.

Wheel Bearing Removal
(95, 96, and 99)

1. Perform Steps 1 through 6 under *Hub Removal, 95, 96, and Sonett Models,* preceding.

2. Remove shaft seal and lock ring (see **Figure 19**).

3. From outside the brake drum, press out both bearings.

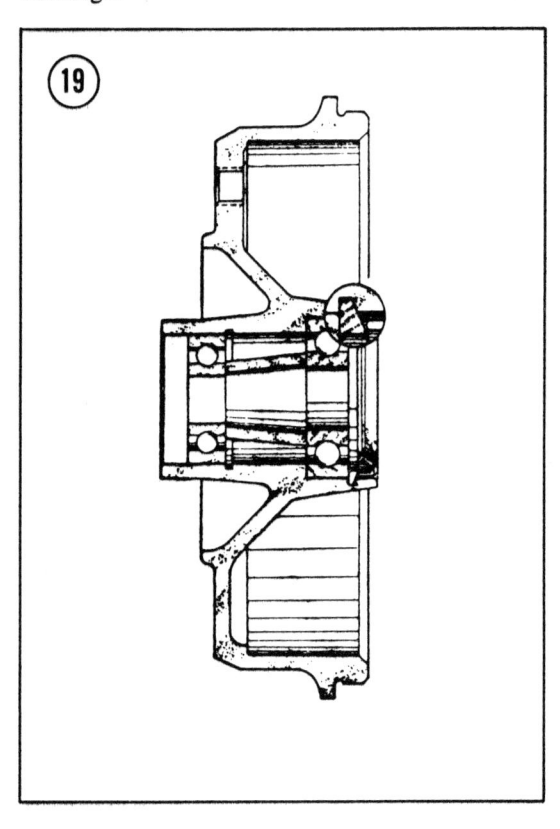

Figure 19

Wheel Bearing Installation
(95, 96, and 99)

1. Clean components and renew any worn parts. Fit a new shaft seal.

2. Pack ball bearings with Saab special chassis grease or equivalent.

3. Press in small bearing 0.5 in. (12mm) from the edge, using Saab tool 784033 or equivalent (see **Figure 20**).

4. Turn hub over. Fill brake drum with enough Saab special chassis grease (or equivalent) to occupy approximately half the space between bearings. Too much grease could ooze out onto the brake linings.

5. Insert spacer sleeve. Press in big bearing (**Figure 21**) with Saab tool 784032 or equivalent.

6. Install lock ring.

7. Fit new sealing ring.

Hub Installation
(95, 96, and Sonett)

After new wheel bearings have been installed (see *Wheel Bearing Installation, 95, 96, and Sonett Models*, preceding), install the hub as follows:

1. The axle stub sliding surface for the seal must be flawless. If damaged, polish with very fine emery cloth. Grease the sliding surface with Saab special chassis grease (or equivalent).

2. Install the brake drum and tighten the castle nut to 65 ft.-lbs. torque. Secure with cotter pin.

3. Install the dust cap.

4. Install the rear wheel and lower the car to the floor.

Hub Removal
(Saab 99)

1. Clean dirt from under fenders before starting work, so no dirt falls into bearings.

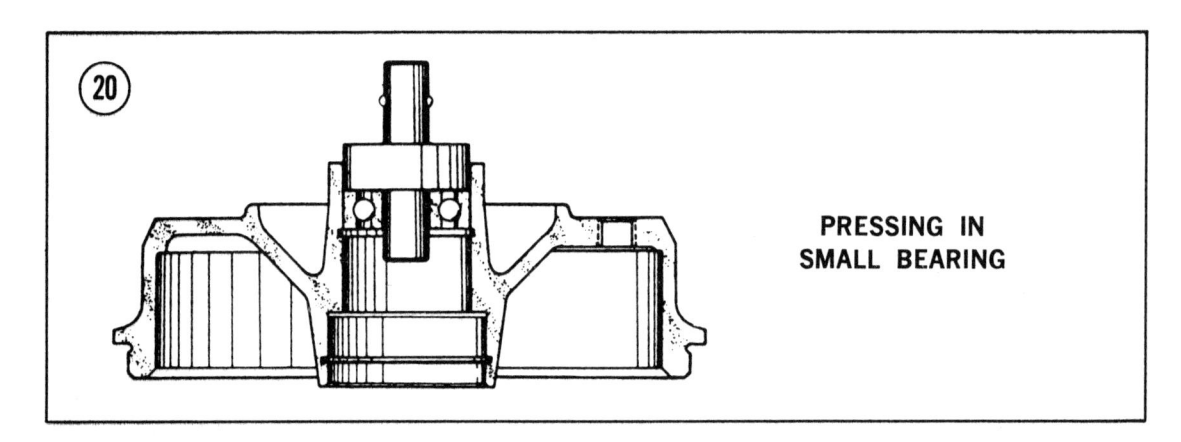

Figure 20 — PRESSING IN SMALL BEARING

REAR SUSPENSION

PRESSING IN BIG BEARING

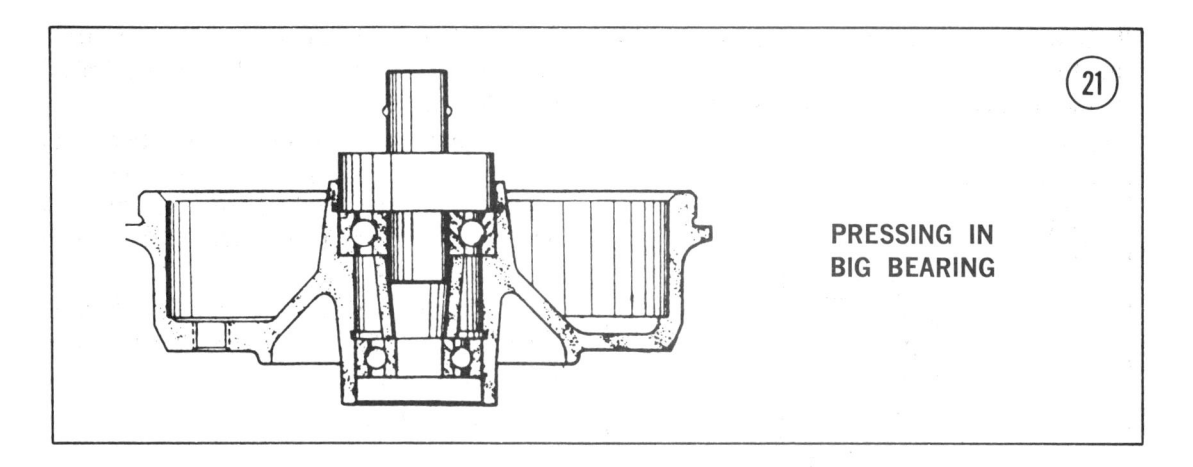

2. Loosen rear wheel lug nuts. Jack rear of car up and support it on rigid jack stands.

3. Remove brake housing and brake disc. The housing must be supported to avoid damaging the brake pipe (see **Figure 22**).

4. Pry out the cap with a screwdriver. Remove the nut and washer (carlier cars are provided with a castle nut secured with a split pin; later cars with a lock nut).

5. Pull the hub (if necessary use Saab hub puller 819518 or equivalent).

Wheel Bearing Removal
(Saab 99)

1. Perform Steps 1 through 5 under *Hub Removal, Saab 99 Models,* preceding.

2. Remove the seal ring with a screwdriver (it cannot be removed intact; break it out). Remove both inner rings.

3. Drive out the outer bearing rings with a drift pin placed in the 3 milled hub recesses. (It is advisable to place a wooden board under the hub to avoid deforming the end faces during this operation.)

Wheel Bearing Installation
(Saab 99)

1. Clean components and renew any worn parts. Fit a new shaft seal ring.

> NOTE: *Although both tapered roller bearings are identical, the inner and outer bearings must not be interinterchanged as they wear themselves into a given fit after a time in service.*

2. Press outer rings of the bearings into the hub using Saab drift 899516 (or equivalent). See **Figure 23**.

3. Fill half the space between outer rings with Saab special chassis grease (or equivalent). Grease inner rings.

4. Fit a new shaft seal to the inner ring of the inner bearing, after lubricating the seal with grease or thick oil. See **Figure 24**.

5. The bearing surface for the seal ring on the stub axle must be perfectly smooth. If not, polish with very fine emery cloth. Lubricate the bearing surface with grease.

Hub Installation
(Saab 99)

After new wheel bearings have been installed (see *Wheel Bearing Installation, Saab 99 Models,* preceding), install the hub as follows:

CHAPTER ELEVEN

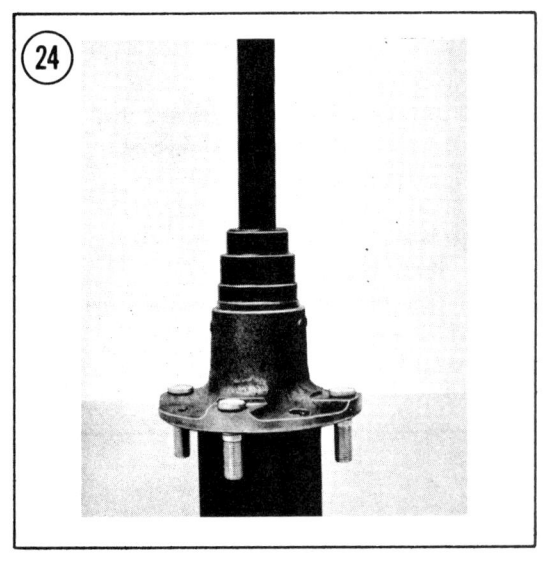

1. Fit the hub to the stub axle. Insert inner ring of outer bearing. Mount the washer and nut (on earlier models tighten the castle nut until the wheel begins to bind when rotated, then back off slightly until the wheel turns freely and the washer is loose, but without play. Mount the split pin. On later models, tighten the locknut to 36 ft.-lb. torque, then slacken nut completely. Finally, tighten the nut again to 1.4-2.9 ft.-lb. (If the old securing nut at the flange is at the locking groove, change the nut.)

2. Secure the lock nut by deforming the flange in the locking groove, using a round drift so that cracks will not occur when securing (see **Figure 25**).

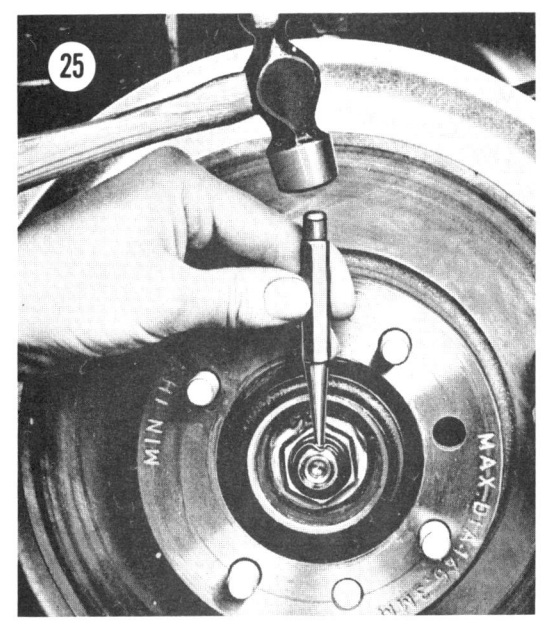

3. Install the cap.

4. Mount the brake disc, brake housing, wheel, and wheel lug nuts. Lower the car, retighten the wheel lug nuts, and fit the hub cap.

CHAPTER TWELVE

BRAKES

All Saab models use a dual circuit hydraulic system on all 4 wheels, one circuit operating the left front and right rear wheels, the other circuit the right front and left rear wheels. Should one circuit malfunction the remaining circuit will stop the car in a reasonably straight line. Failure of a circuit is revealed by excessive pedal travel and a tendency for the car to pull toward the side at which brake pressure remains on the front wheel when the brakes are applied. Models from 1969 on employ a vacuum operated servo unit linked directly to the master cylinder.

The 95/96 and Sonnett models are fitted with self-adjusting front disc brakes and adjustable rear drum brakes; 99 models use self-adjusting disc brakes on all 4 wheels. A warning light indicates a leak in the brake system.

A cable operated mechanical parking brake acts on the 2 front wheels on the 95/96 and Sonnett models, and the 2 rear wheels on the 99 models. Refer to **Figures 1, 2, 3, 4, and 5**.

MASTER CYLINDER (95/96 THROUGH 1968)

Removal

1. Disconnect brake lines from master cylinder.
2. Remove the rubber boot from the push rod. Back off the locking nut and unscrew the push rod from the brake pedal fork.
3. Remove the 2 master cylinder retaining bolts. The lower one is a stud bolt; the nut is accessible from the engine compartment. The upper one is a screwbolt, accessible from inside the car.
4. Remove the master cylinder.

Installation

1. Cover openings to prevent dirt from entering the cylinder during installation.
2. Attach brake cylinder.
3. Install rubber boot on the push rod. Reassemble the push rod if it has been disassembled.
4. Reconnect outlet brake lines. Refill the system with brake fluid.
5. Adjust the brake pedal free movement. Refer to *Brake Pedal,* this chapter.
6. Bleed the brake system. Refer to *Brake Bleeding,* this chapter.

MASTER CYLINDER (SONETT)

Removal/Installation

1. Remove the clutch master cylinder (refer to Chapter Nine, *Clutch Master Cylinder, Removal*).
2. Disconnect stop light switch cables.

CHAPTER TWELVE

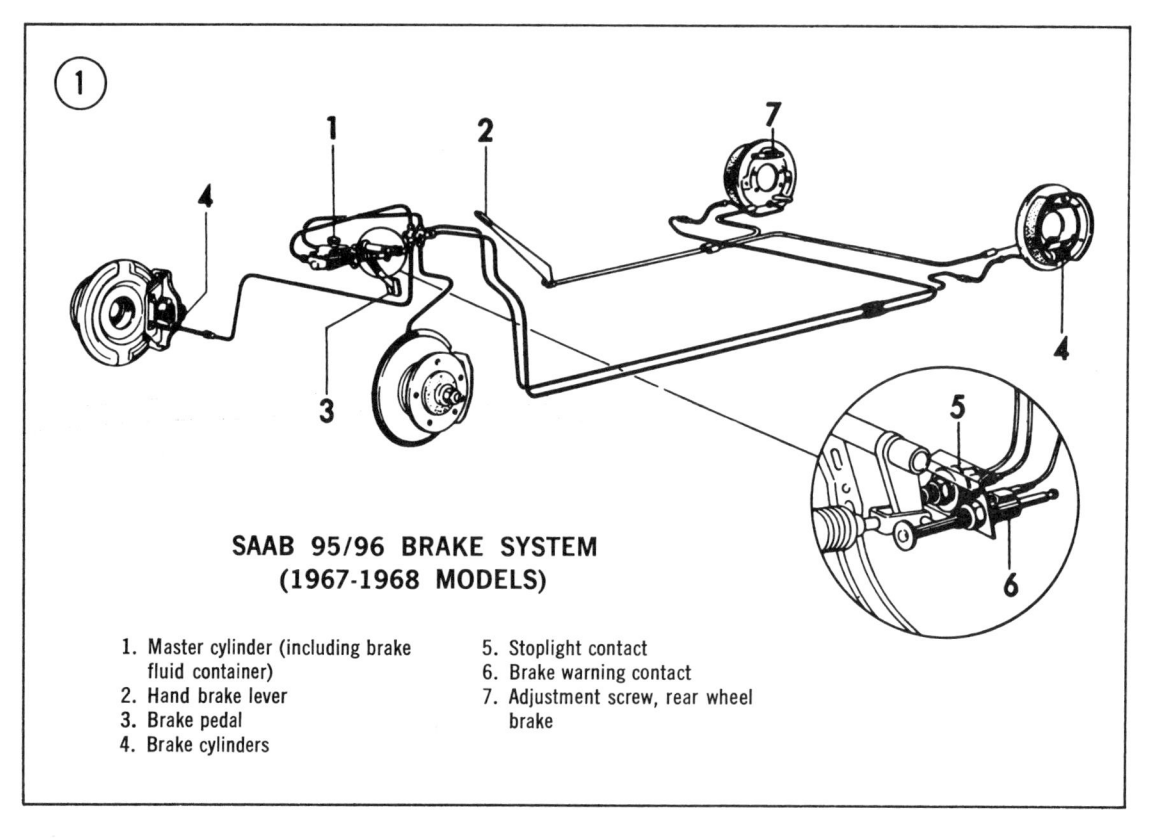

SAAB 95/96 BRAKE SYSTEM (1967-1968 MODELS)

1. Master cylinder (including brake fluid container)
2. Hand brake lever
3. Brake pedal
4. Brake cylinders
5. Stoplight contact
6. Brake warning contact
7. Adjustment screw, rear wheel brake

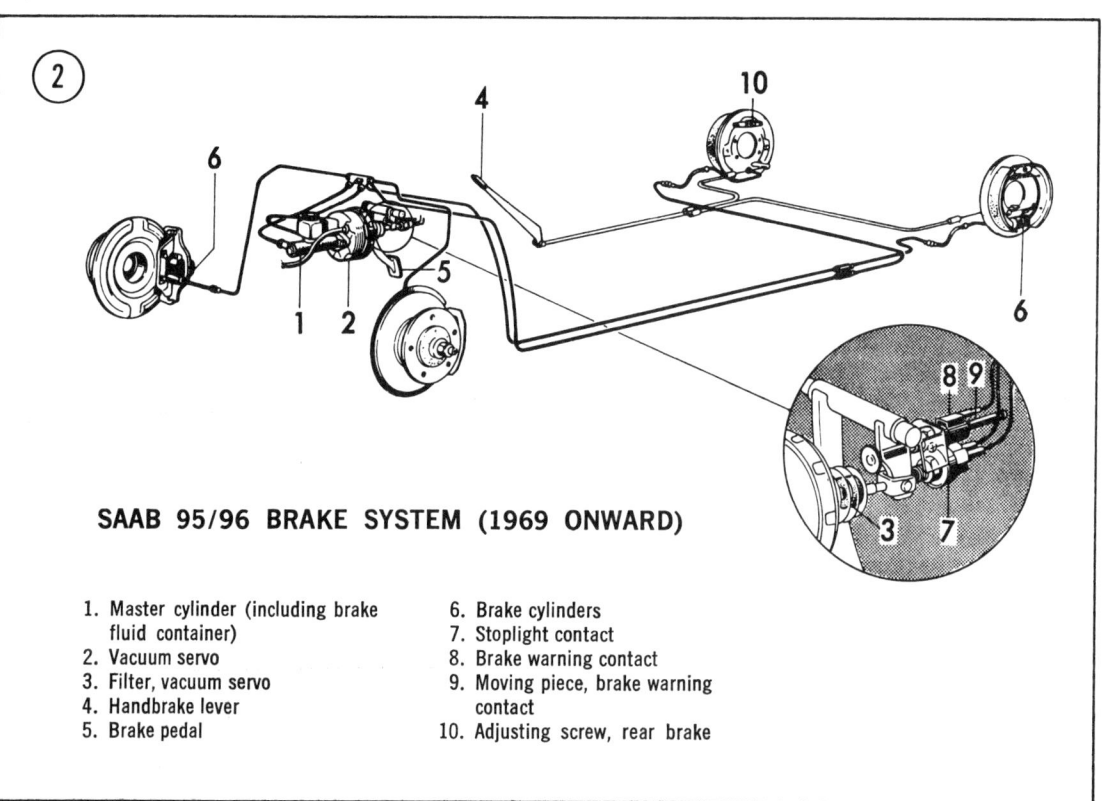

SAAB 95/96 BRAKE SYSTEM (1969 ONWARD)

1. Master cylinder (including brake fluid container)
2. Vacuum servo
3. Filter, vacuum servo
4. Handbrake lever
5. Brake pedal
6. Brake cylinders
7. Stoplight contact
8. Brake warning contact
9. Moving piece, brake warning contact
10. Adjusting screw, rear brake

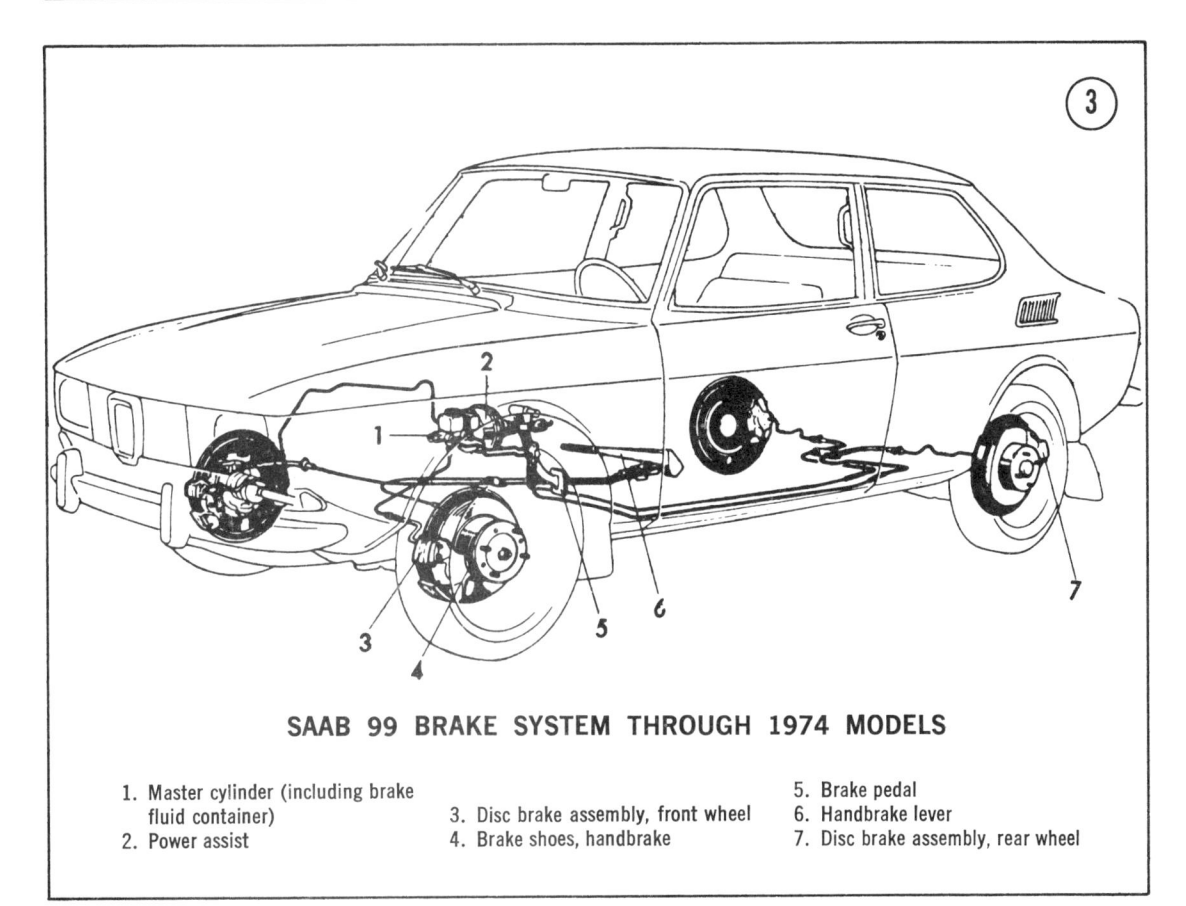

BRAKES

SAAB 99 BRAKE SYSTEM THROUGH 1974 MODELS

1. Master cylinder (including brake fluid container)
2. Power assist
3. Disc brake assembly, front wheel
4. Brake shoes, handbrake
5. Brake pedal
6. Handbrake lever
7. Disc brake assembly, rear wheel

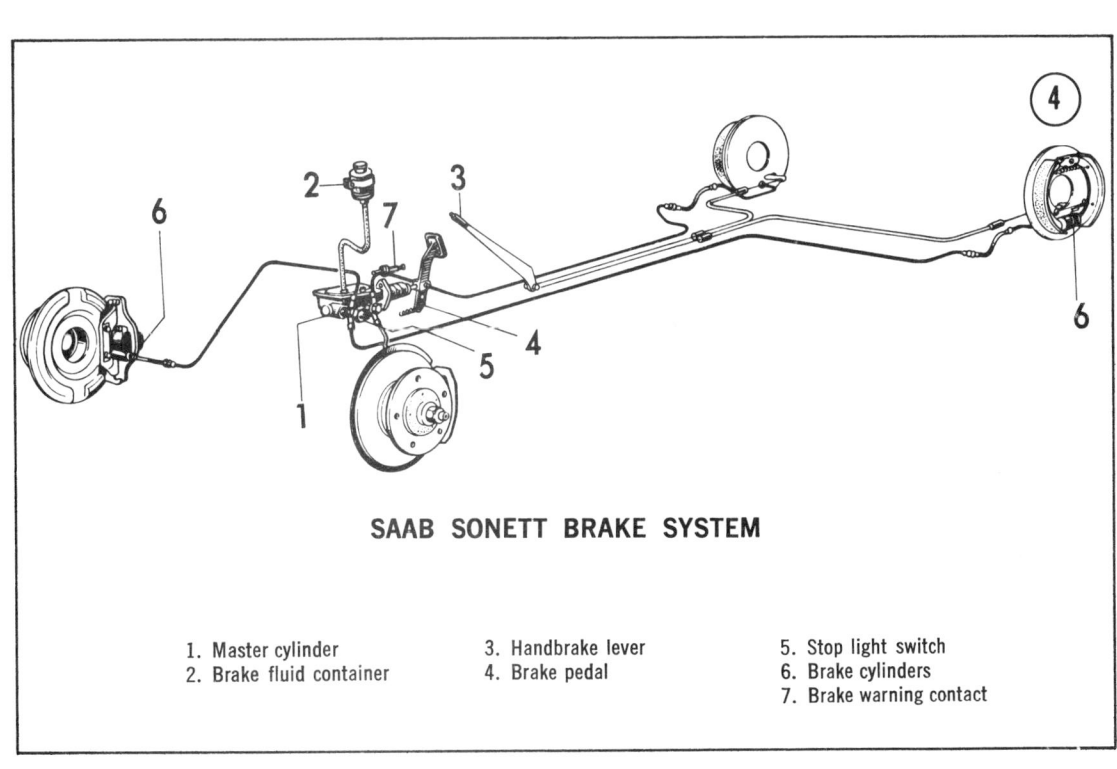

SAAB SONETT BRAKE SYSTEM

1. Master cylinder
2. Brake fluid container
3. Handbrake lever
4. Brake pedal
5. Stop light switch
6. Brake cylinders
7. Brake warning contact

CHAPTER TWELVE

SAAB 99 BRAKE SYSTEM (1975-1976 MODELS)

1. Brake pedal
2. Servo unit
3. Master cylinder
4. Brake housing, front wheel
5. Brake housing, rear wheel
6. Brake discs
7. Handbrake lever

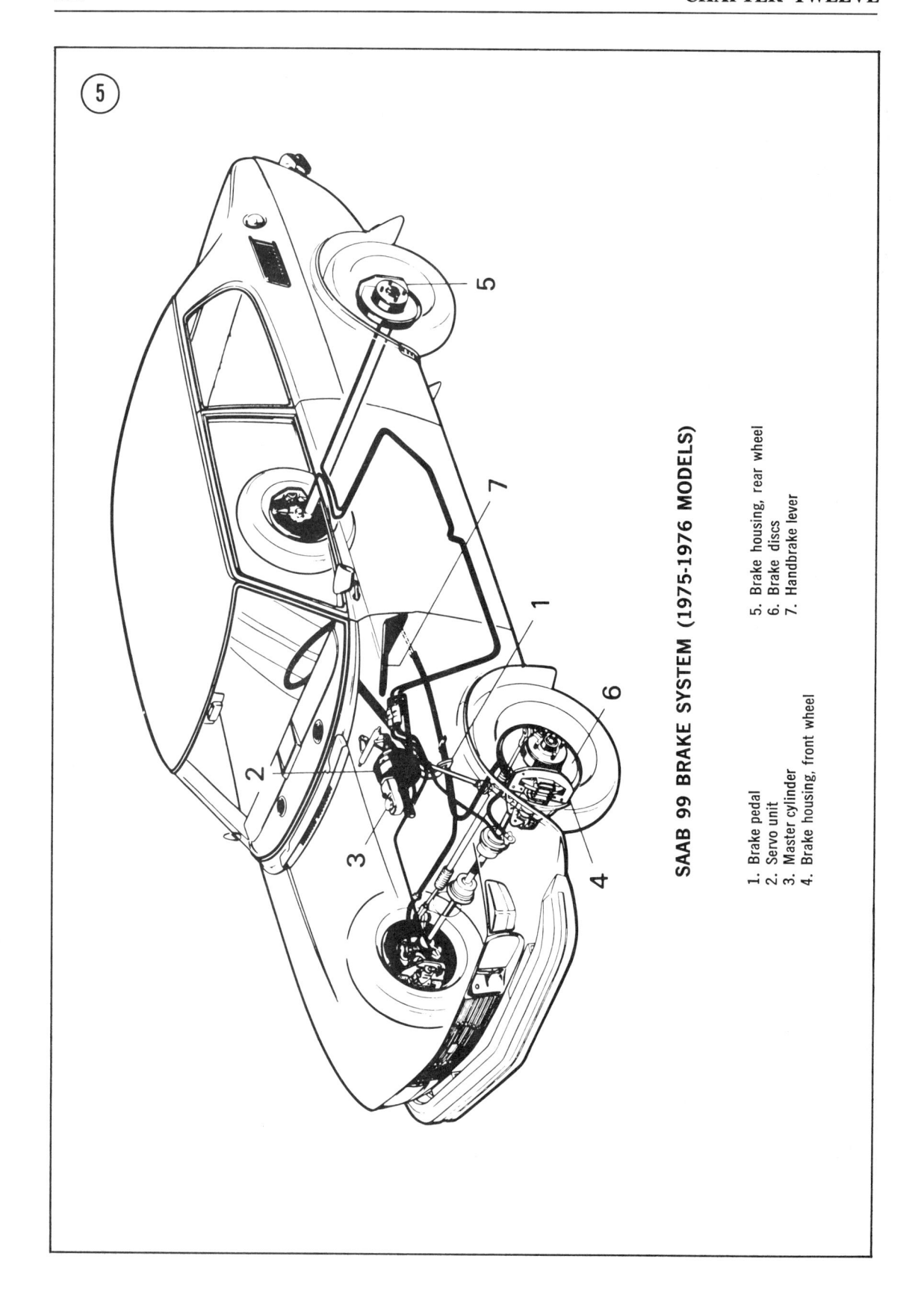

BRAKES

3. Remove screws for primary and secondary circuits.
4. Release filler hose connection to the cap.
5. Remove retaining bolts for master brake cylinder. Lift cylinder out.
6. Install master cylinder by reversing preceding steps.
7. Bleed brake system. See *Brake Bleeding*, this chapter.

MASTER CYLINDER
(95/96, 1969-1973 AND 99, 1967-1974)

**Removal/Installation
(Master Cylinder With
Vacuum Servo Unit)**

1. Remove protective steering wheel shaft cover (95/96 only).
2. Remove air cleaner (where necessary).
3. Remove clip holding speedometer cable to power assist unit (where applicable).
4. Disconnect brake lines from master cylinder. Disconnect vacuum hose from vacuum servo unit.
5. Detach push rod at brake pedal.
6. Loosen the 4 retaining nuts holding vacuum servo unit to dash panel (nuts are accessible from inside the car). Remove master cylinder.
7. Install by reversing Steps 1 through 6.
8. Bleed the brake system. See *Brake Bleeding*, this chapter.

**Removal/Installation
(Master Cylinder Only)**

It is not necessary to remove the vacuum servo unit when removing and installing the master cylinder. Use following procedure:

1. Disconnect brake lines from master cylinder.
2. Remove the 2 retaining nuts connecting the master cylinder to the vacuum servo unit.
3. Lift master cylinder off the servo unit.
4. Install master cylinder by reversing Steps 1 through 3.
5. Bleed brake system. Refer to *Brake Bleeding*, this chapter.

MASTER CYLINDER
(1975-1976 SAAB 99)

Removal/Installation

1. Remove upper circlip on brake pedal push rod.
2. Disconnect 2 electric cables from brake light switch.
3. Remove vacuum hose from non-return valve on servo unit.
4. Disconnect electrical connection for brake warning switch, the hose from a fluid reservoir to the clutch master cylinder, and the 2 brake line connections to the master cylinder.
5. Remove the servo unit, master cylinder, and bracket. (The bracket fastens to the dash panel via 4 screws, 3 accessible from the passenger compartment after removal of the screen section and parts of the dash panel insulation felt below the instrument panel, the fourth from the engine compartment by the bracket).
6. Remove the 2 nuts holding the master cylinder and bracket to the vacuum servo unit.
7. Install by reversing Steps 1 through 6.
8. Bleed the brake system. Refer to *Brake Bleeding*, this chapter.

BRAKE LINES AND HOSES

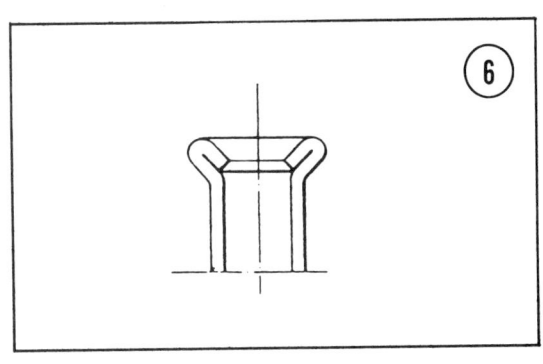

Brake lines, hoses, and connections should be checked periodically for signs of chafing or other deterioration. It is important that pipes and hoses are not allowed to rub against each other as they will quickly wear through and a leak will result. Be certain that the copper gaskets in the brake lines are flawless. The lines are flanged and fitted with compression nuts. Brake lines for connection to brake hoses are flanged as shown in **Figure 6**, other pipes are flanged as shown in **Figure 7**. All connections must be properly tightened to ensure a leak-free joint. Never stretch a badly fitted pipe by overtightening a compression nut, and never bend an already fitted pipe. The result of either could be leakage, pipe fracture, or stripped threads.

> **CAUTION**
> *The brake system incorporates 2 front and 2 rear brake hoses. The hoses are of different lengths and must not be confused. The front wheels should point straight ahead and be freely suspended when installing the brake hoses. When tightening the brake lines, hold the hose nipple (not the locking nut) to prevent the hose from twisting. The front hoses should form a curve downward when properly installed.*

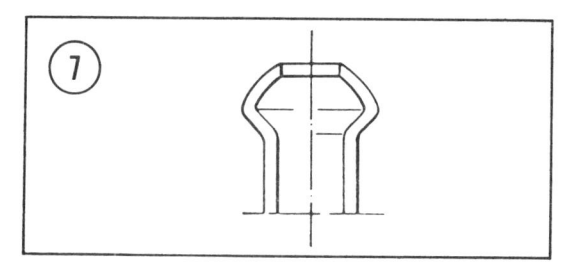

Removal

1. Clean all connections before loosening the connecting nuts and clips.
2. Insert plastic plugs in the open ends of the brake lines and hoses after removing them.

Installation

1. Clean the brake lines and hoses by blowing clean, moisture free compressed air through them.
2. Remove the plastic plugs and position the brake lines and hoses. Tighten the connecting nuts.
3. Bleed the brake system (see *Brake Bleeding*, this chapter).

REAR WHEEL CYLINDERS (95/96 AND SONETT)

The 95 is equipped with larger wheel cylinders at the rear than the 96 prior to 1970 (rear wheel cylinders from 1970 on are the same dimension on both models).

A locating pin is used on the rear wheel cylinder (see **Figure 8**) to firmly position the cylinder on the backplate. The location of the pin is different on the 95 and 96 prior to 1970 to avoid fitting a cylinder of the wrong dimension.

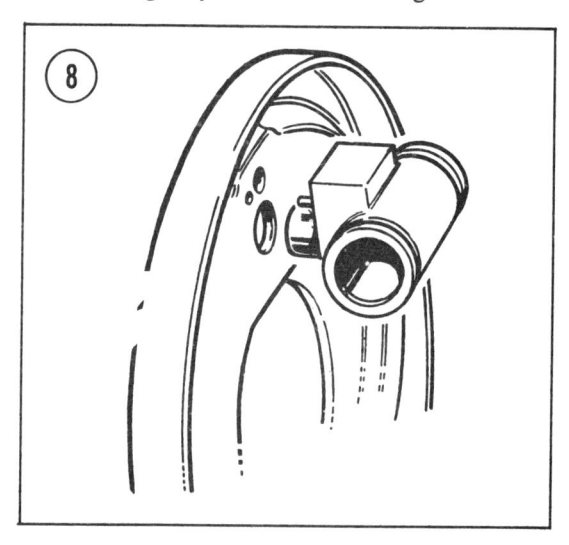

Refer to **Figures 9 and 10** for sectional and exploded views of the rear wheel cylinder.

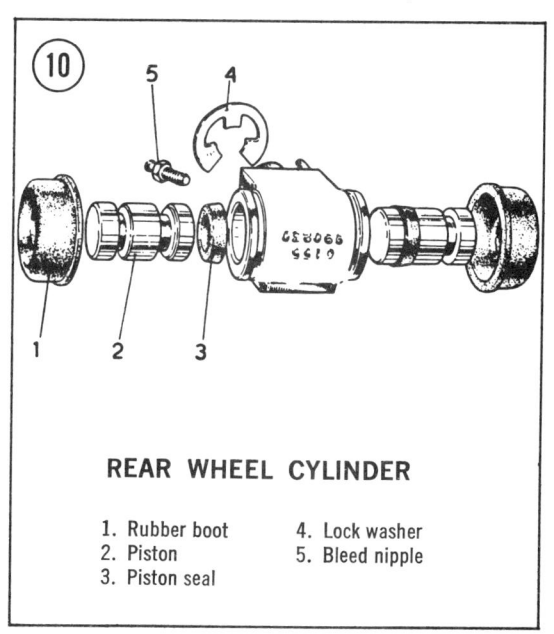

REAR WHEEL CYLINDER

1. Rubber boot
2. Piston
3. Piston seal
4. Lock washer
5. Bleed nipple

Removal

1. Remove the rear wheels, brake drums, and brake shoes.

BRAKES 155

REAR WHEEL CYLINDER

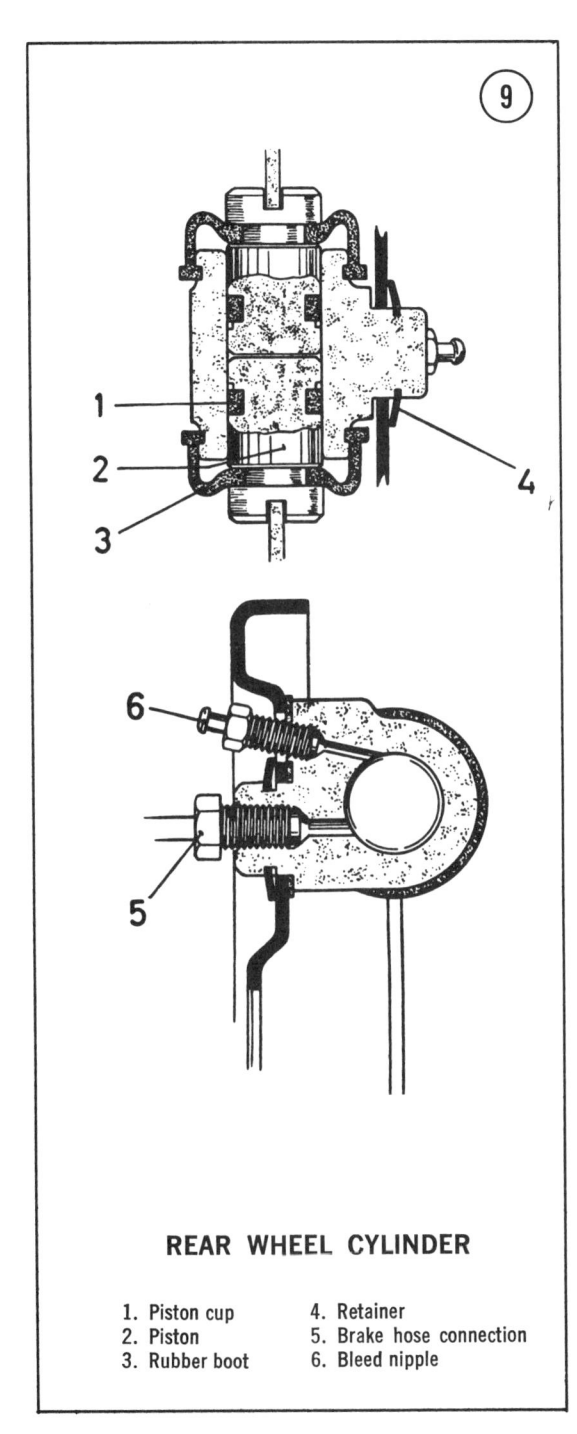

1. Piston cup
2. Piston
3. Rubber boot
4. Retainer
5. Brake hose connection
6. Bleed nipple

2. Disconnect the handbrake cable from the levers.
3. Disconnect the brake line from the backplate.
4. Remove the wheel cylinder retaining ring and the bleed nipple from the backplate.
5. Remove the wheel cylinder.

Installation

1. Refer to Figure 8. Fit the cylinder to the backplate, making certain that the locating pin fits correctly.
2. Connect the brake line. Fit the brake shoes, brake drum, and wheel, taking care not to damage the axle seal.
3. Connect the handbrake cable. The lever must be installed with the bent part facing upward. See **Figure 11**.

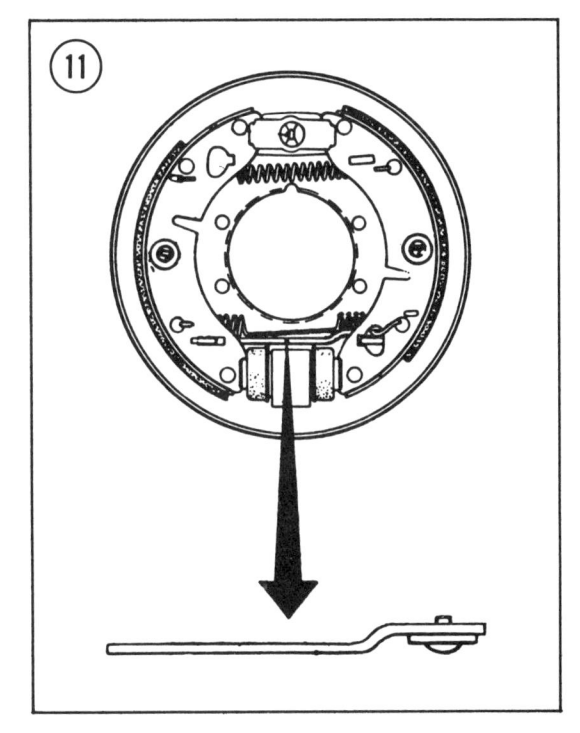

4. Bleed the brake system (see *Brake Bleeding*, this chapter).

FRONT WHEEL CYLINDERS AND BRAKE HOUSINGS (95/96 AND SONETT)

Removal

1. Remove the brake pads (see *Brake Pad Removal*, this chapter).
2. Remove the 2 brake retaining bolts from the steering knuckle housing after bending up the retaining plate. Lift the brake away from the brake disc.
3. Disconnect the brake hose from the brake cylinder. Plug the hose to prevent the escape of

brake fluid and the entry of foreign matter into the brake system.

4. Remove the 2 springs holding the cylinder in place. Remove the cylinder.

5. Clean the entire brake housing thoroughly. Check for brake wear, particularly on the hinge pin. See **Figure 12**.

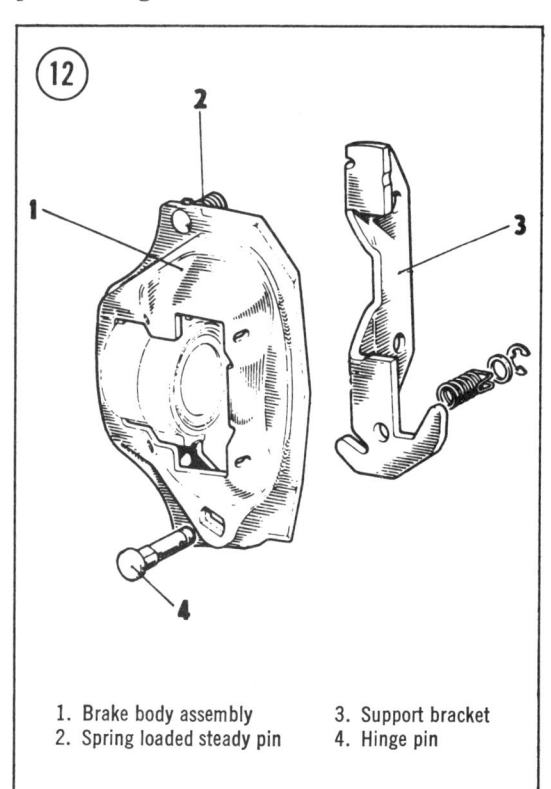

1. Brake body assembly
2. Spring loaded steady pin
3. Support bracket
4. Hinge pin

Disassembly/Assembly

Should it be necessary to replace the brake body assembly or support bracket, use the following procedure:

1. Refer to Figure 12. Remove the brake from the steering knuckle housing (Step 2 under *Removal*, preceding).

2. Compress the hinge pin spring and remove the lock washer and spacer.

3. Remove the spring. Lift the support bracket from the hinge.

4. Assemble by reversing the preceding steps.

Installation

1. Insert the brake cylinder in the brake body assembly and fit the springs.

2. Remove the plug from the brake hose. Fit a new copper washer and tighten the hose securely in the cylinder.

3. Position the brake housing and tighten the retaining bolts. Secure the bolts with the retaining plate.

> CAUTION
> *If the brake hose is not mounted in a neutral position loosen its attachment at the wheel housing, position it correctly, and retighten the attachment.*

4. Install the brake pads, spring, and new cotter pins as described in *Brake Pad Installation*, this chapter.

5. Bleed the brake system (see *Brake Bleeding*, this chapter).

FRONT BRAKE PISTONS AND SEALS (95/96 AND SONETT)

For this job, Saab tool No. 786043 or equivalent (see **Figure 13**) is required.

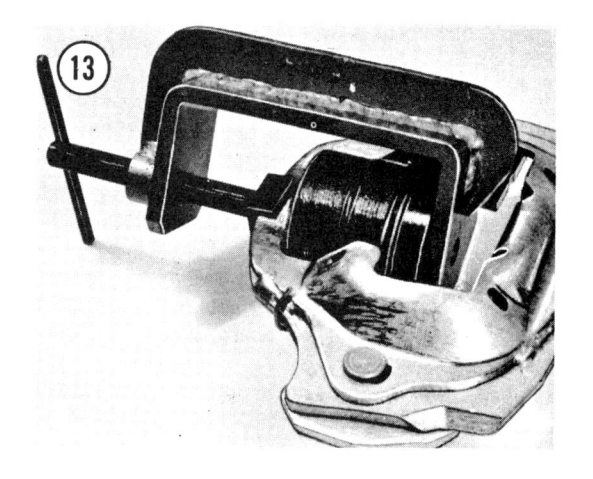

1. Remove the brake pads as described in *Brake Pad Removal*, this chapter.

2. Bend the retaining plates up and remove 2 retaining bolts holding the brake housing to the steering knuckle housing. Lift the brake housing away from the brake disc. Do not disconnect the brake hose. Place the brake housing so that the brake hose does not get stretched.

3. Gently press the brake pedal down far enough to force the piston out until it can be

BRAKES

taken off by hand. Use a clean jar to catch the brake fluid when the piston is removed.

4. Disconnect the brake hose from the brake cylinder. Plug the brake hose to prevent brake fluid from escaping and foreign matter from entering the brake system.

5. Remove the 2 springs holding the cylinder in place. Remove the cylinder.

Disassembly

1. Replace the piston seal (if necessary) by removing it from its groove in the cylinder.

2. Remove the wiper seal (if necessary) with a screwdriver.

Assembly

1. Coat a new seal with disc brake lubricant and position it carefully in its groove in the cylinder. Make sure it is properly seated.

2. Coat the piston and cylinder with disc brake lubricant. Press the piston into the cylinder. Be sure that the recess in the contact surface facing the brake pad is pointing downward. The later pistons have a ground contact surface facing the brake pad. The damping shim has been altered so that the piston has the corresponding part facing the friction pad. Do not press the piston fully in. Leave about 0.4 in. (10mm) outside the cylinder.

3. Smear disc brake lubricant on a new wiper seal and place it in the retainer with its groove turned toward the piston. See **Figure 14**.

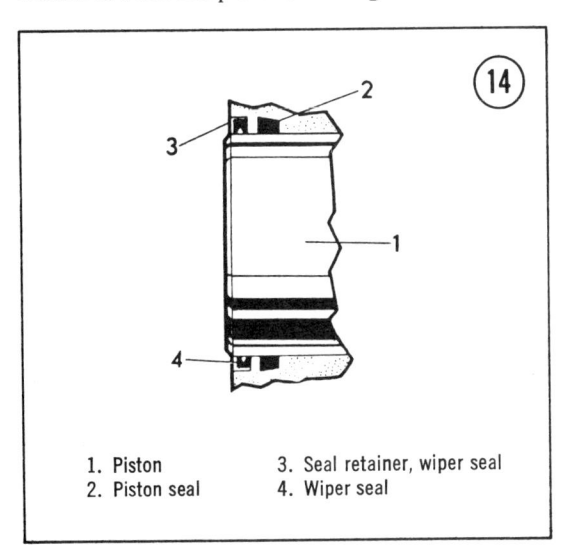

1. Piston
2. Piston seal
3. Seal retainer, wiper seal
4. Wiper seal

4. Press the retainer and seal in with Saab tool No. 786043 or equivalent (see Figure 13).

Installation

1. Position the brake cylinder in the brake body assembly. Refit the springs.

2. Remove the plug from the brake hose. Fit a new copper washer and tighten the hose securely in the cylinder.

3. Position the brake housing and tighten the retaining bolts. Secure the bolts with the retaining plate.

> **CAUTION**
> *If the brake hose is not mounted in a neutral position loosen its attachment at the wheel housing, position it correctly, and retighten the attachment.*

4. Install the brake pads, spring, and new cotter pins as described in *Brake Pad Installation*, this chapter.

5. Bleed the brake system as described in *Brake Bleeding*, this chapter.

WHEEL CYLINDERS AND DISC BRAKE HOUSINGS (SAAB 99 THROUGH 1974)

For this job, Saab tool No. 784132 or equivalent (see **Figure 15**) is required.

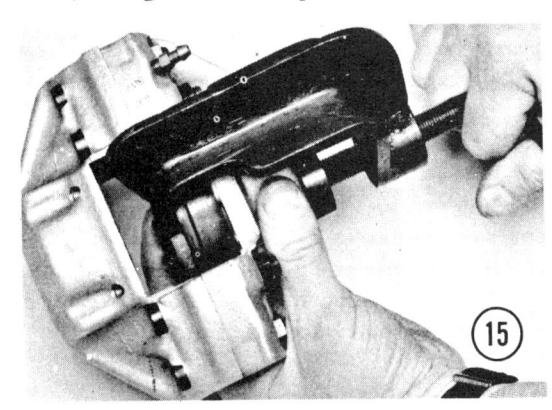

1. Jack up the front or rear of the car. Remove the wheel.

2. Remove the guard plate with a screwdriver. Use a drift pin to knock out the lock pins. Remove the retaining spring and brake pads. See **Figure 16**.

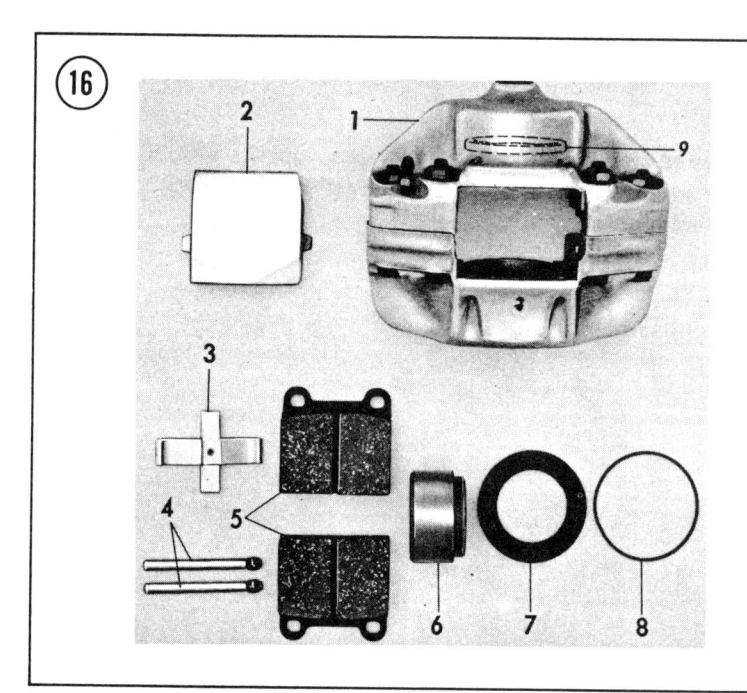

BRAKE HOUSING COMPONENTS

1. Brake housing
2. Guard plate
3. Retaining spring
4. Lock pins
5. Brake pads
6. Piston
7. Dust gasket
8. Seal retainer
9. Piston seal

3. Unscrew the brake housing from the steering knuckle housing. Disconnect the brake line from the housing.

4. Lift brake housing off the brake disc. The 2 halves of the brake housing need not be separated.

5. Clean the outside of the brake housing.

Disassembly

1. Use Saab tool No. 784132 or equivalent (Figure 15) and compressed air (in the brake line connection) to force the piston out. Be sure the piston does not fall and suffer damage.

> NOTE: *When the piston has been removed care must be taken to ensure that no foreign matter enters the brake system.*

2. Use a blunt tool to pry the seal out of the cylinder (see **Figure 17**). Be careful not to damage the seal groove or cylinder. Clean the cylinder with brake fluid.

Assembly

1. Apply disc brake lubricant to a new, dry seal. Place the seal carefully in its groove in the cylinder and rotate it with your fingers to seat it properly.

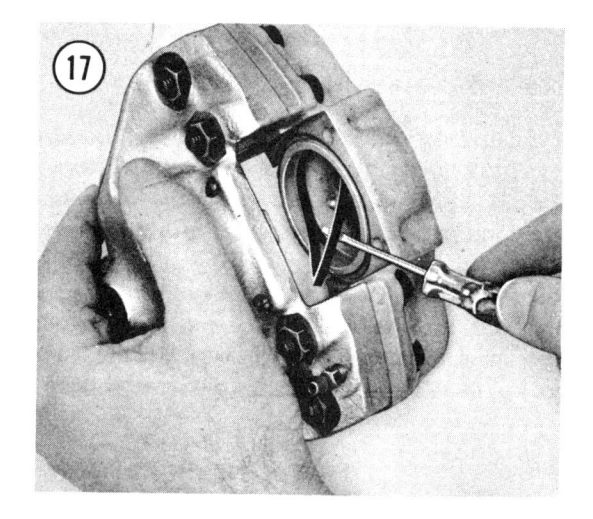

2. Coat the piston with disc brake lubricant and locate it so that the recess in the contact surface with the brake pad is turned the correct way. Use Saab template No. 899534 or equivalent (**Figure 18**). If the piston must be rotated after insertion, use Saab tool No. 899536 or equivalent (**Figure 19**). Push the piston into the cylinder. Be sure it does not jam.

3. Coat a new dry dust gasket with disc brake lubricant. Press the gasket retainer and brake piston in place with Saab tool No. 784132 or equivalent (Figure 15).

BRAKES

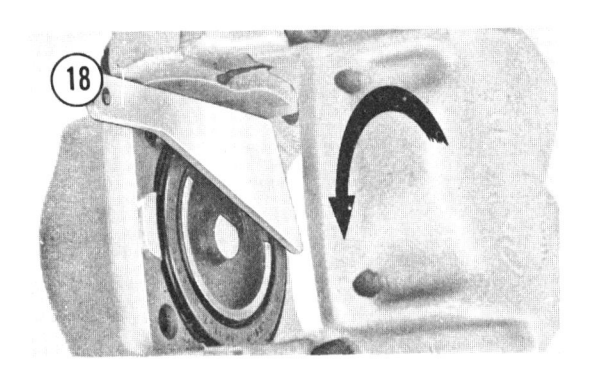

Arrow indicates wheel rotation when driving forward

Installation

1. Connect the brake line to the housing. Screw the brake housing to the steering knuckle housing. Apply a new locking plate. Clean the brake disc with trichoroethylene.

2. Install the brake pads (see *Brake Pad Installation*, this chapter).

> NOTE: *On the rear wheel brakes a washer is placed between the brake pad and brake piston. The washer recess prevents the piston from rotating.*

3. Bleed the brakes. See *Brake Bleeding*, this chapter.

WHEEL CYLINDERS AND DISC BRAKE HOUSINGS (99, 1975-1976)

Removal
(Front Brake Housing)

1. Refer to **Figure 20**. Remove brake pads (see *Brake Pad Removal*, this chapter).

2. Disconnect handbrake cable from brake housing (**Figure 21**).

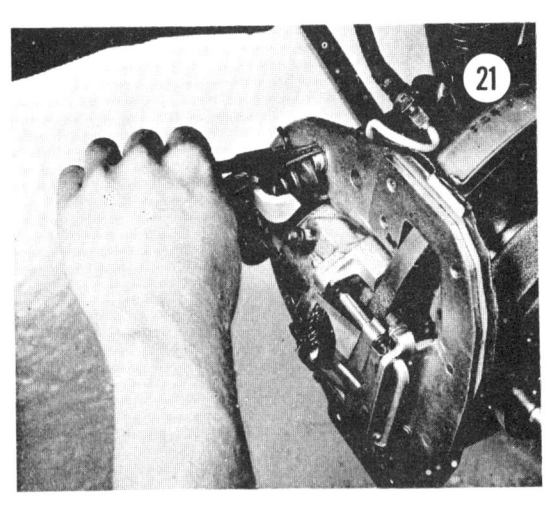

3. See **Figure 22**. Unscrew brake lines from brake housing. Plug the connection to avoid brake fluid loss and to keep foreign matter from entering the brake system.

4. Remove the 2 screws holding the brake housing to the steering knuckle housing.

Disassembly
(Front Brake Housing)

1. Clean the brake housing. Mount it in a vise.
2. Remove the handbrake lever return spring.
3. See **Figure 23**. Remove the brake housing yoke. Remove the spring and the handbrake lever.

CHAPTER TWELVE

FRONT BRAKE HOUSING

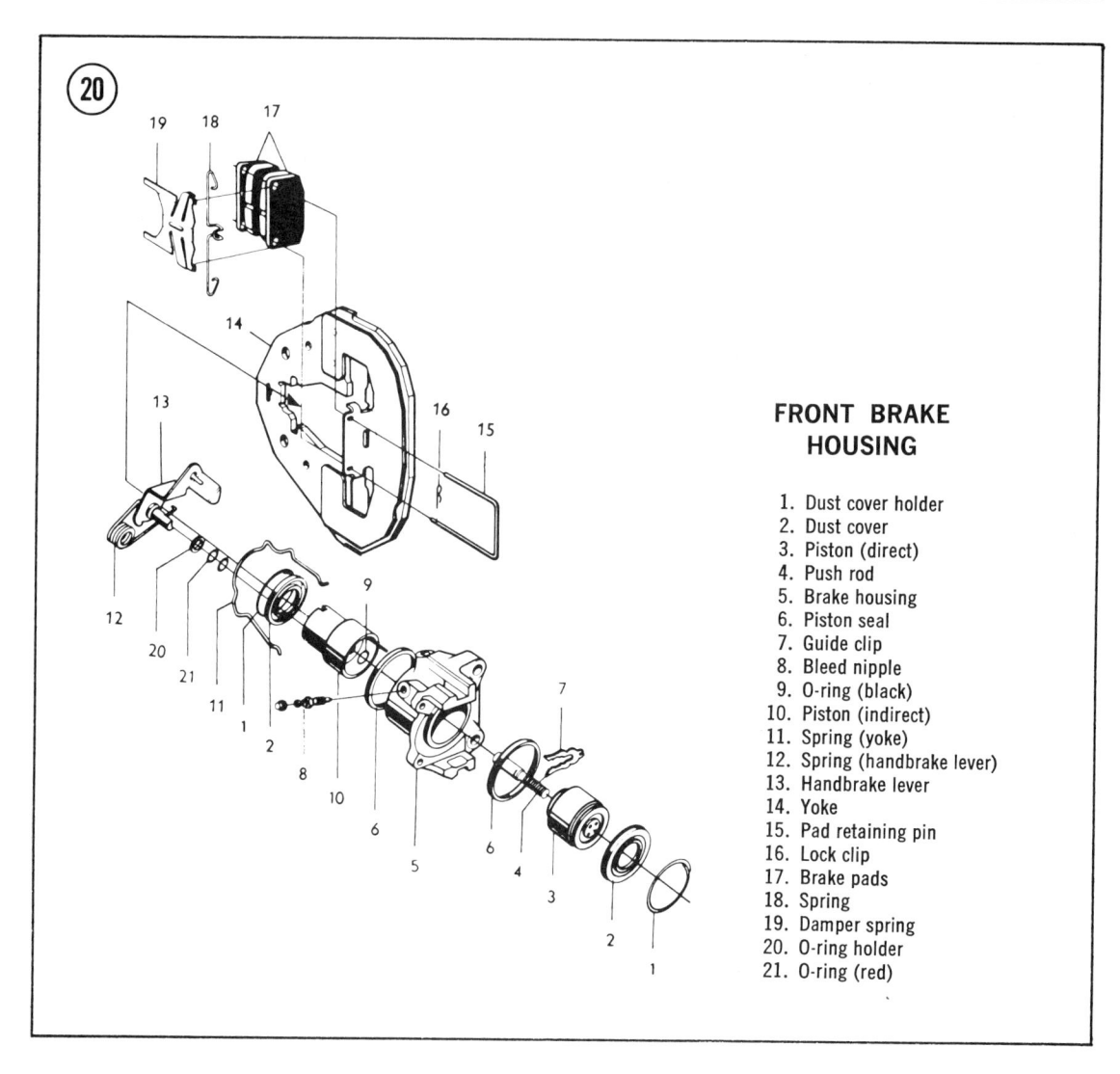

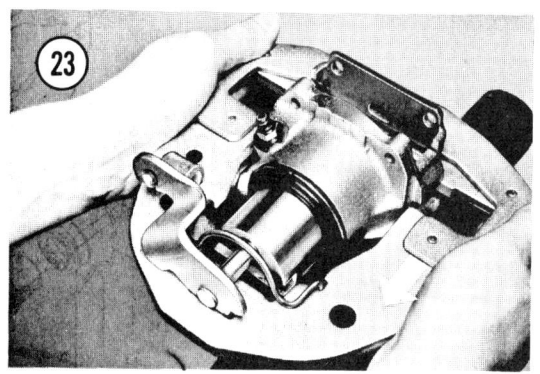

1. Dust cover holder
2. Dust cover
3. Piston (direct)
4. Push rod
5. Brake housing
6. Piston seal
7. Guide clip
8. Bleed nipple
9. O-ring (black)
10. Piston (indirect)
11. Spring (yoke)
12. Spring (handbrake lever)
13. Handbrake lever
14. Yoke
15. Pad retaining pin
16. Lock clip
17. Brake pads
18. Spring
19. Damper spring
20. O-ring holder
21. O-ring (red)

4. Remove the dust cover retaining ring and dust cover.

5. See **Figure 24**. Force out the indirect piston with compressed air.

6. Press the push rod by hand so that the direct piston is separated from the cylinder.

BRAKES

7. Remove the O-rings and seal rings from the piston and cylinder bore. The O-ring retainer in the handbrake lever should only be removed if damaged.

Assembly
(Front Brake Housing)

1. Fit new O-rings to the indirect piston. The red O-ring should fit in the special O-ring retainer in the hole for the handbrake lever. The black O-ring should fit in the groove for the push rod.

2. Mount the brake housing in a vice. Lubricate the cylinder bore with brake fluid. Fit new piston seals.

3. See **Figure 25**. Fit the anchor plate to the push rod. Press the push rod into the hole in the indirect piston. Be certain that the anchor plate recess comes immediately over the spring pin in the piston.

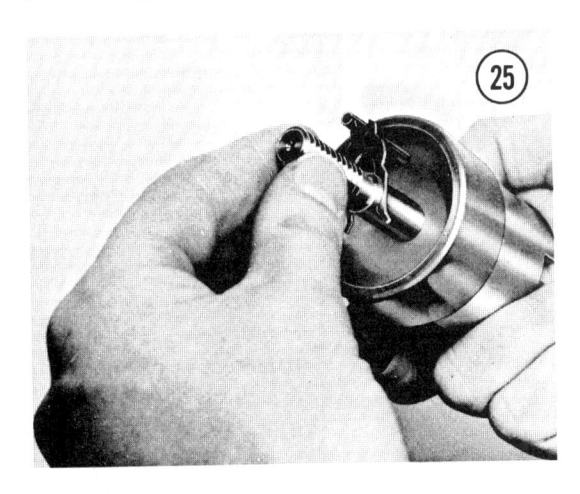

4. See **Figure 26**. Lubricate the indirect piston with brake fluid. Insert it in the brake housing so the yoke recess is directly in line with the cylinder housing groove.

5. Press the direct piston into the cylinder. With Saab tool No. 8996043 or equivalent (**Figure 27**) screw together the piston and push rod. Screw and push in the 2 pistons until the edges of the dust cover grooves are flush with the brake housing.

6. Fit new dust covers and retaining rings.

7. Fit the yoke spring and handbrake lever to the yoke (**Figure 28**).

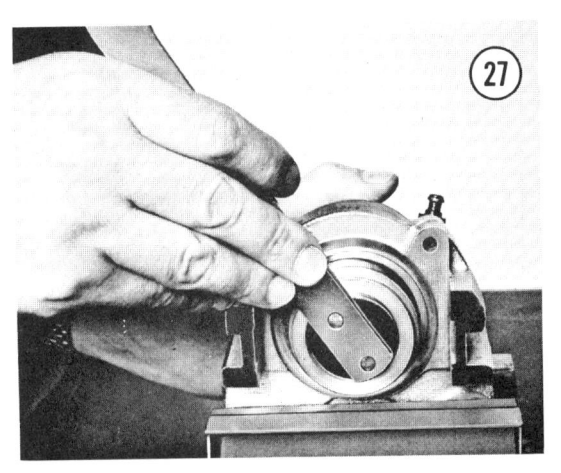

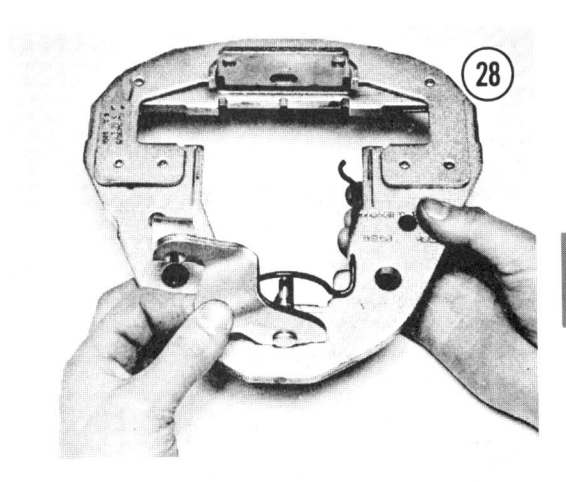

8. Align the edges of the yoke guide with the brake housing grooves. Lift the handbrake lever and fit the end of the axle pin into the hole in the indirect piston. Be sure the yoke fits into the indirect piston recess.

9. Install the handbrake lever return spring.

10. See **Figure 29**. Check the clearance between the sliding surfaces of the brake housing and yokes. Excessive play can cause vibration and noise on braking.

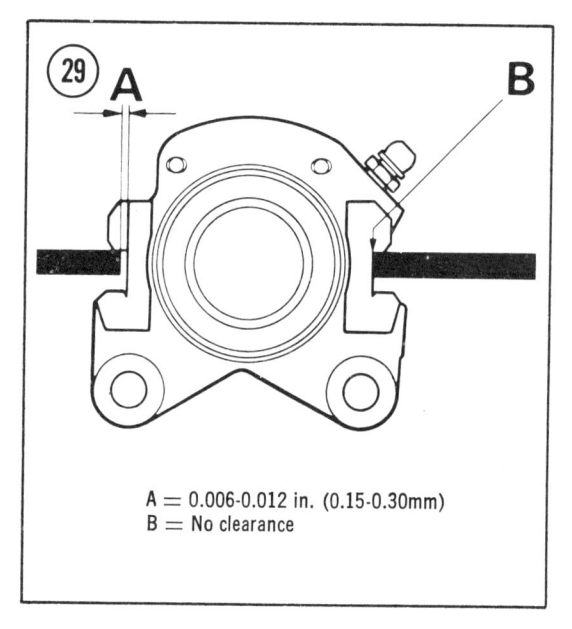

A = 0.006-0.012 in. (0.15-0.30mm)
B = No clearance

Installation
(Front Brake Housing)

1. Be sure that the dust cover has not slipped out of position. Screw the complete brake assembly to the steering knuckle housing (or rear axle). Use a new locking plate.

2. Connect the brake lines.

3. See **Figure 30**. Adjust the handbrake cable so that the distance between the yoke and lever is 0.019±0.003 in. (0.5±0.1mm) when the handbrake lever is in the off position.

> NOTE: *Apply the handbrake lever a few times prior to adjusting to stretch the cable. Adjustment is made at the lever* (**Figure 31**). *The cables are crossed (adjustment of the left handbrake mechanism is made by adjusting the right adjustment nut and vice versa).*

Removal
(Rear Wheel Housing)

1. Remove the brake pads (see *Brake Pad Removal*, this chapter). See **Figure 32**.

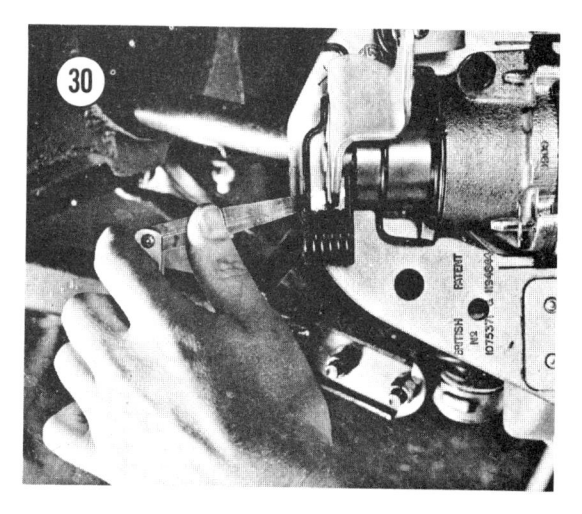

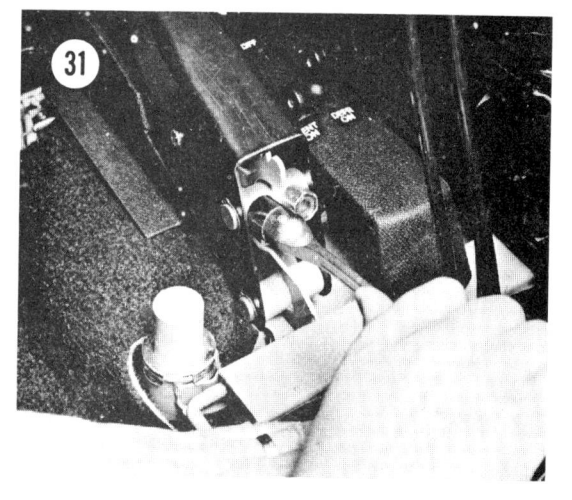

2. Disconnect the brake lines at the brake housing. Plug the connection to avoid brake fluid loss and to prevent contamination of the brake system.

3. Remove the 2 screws holding the brake housing to the rear axle.

Disassembly
(Rear Wheel Housing)

1. Clean the brake housing and mount it in a vise.

2. Remove the brake housing yoke by lifting it toward the bleed screw. Remove the yoke spring.

3. Remove the retaining ring and dust cover.

4. See **Figure 33**. Force out the indirect piston with compressed air.

5. Press out the direct piston with your fingers.

BRAKES

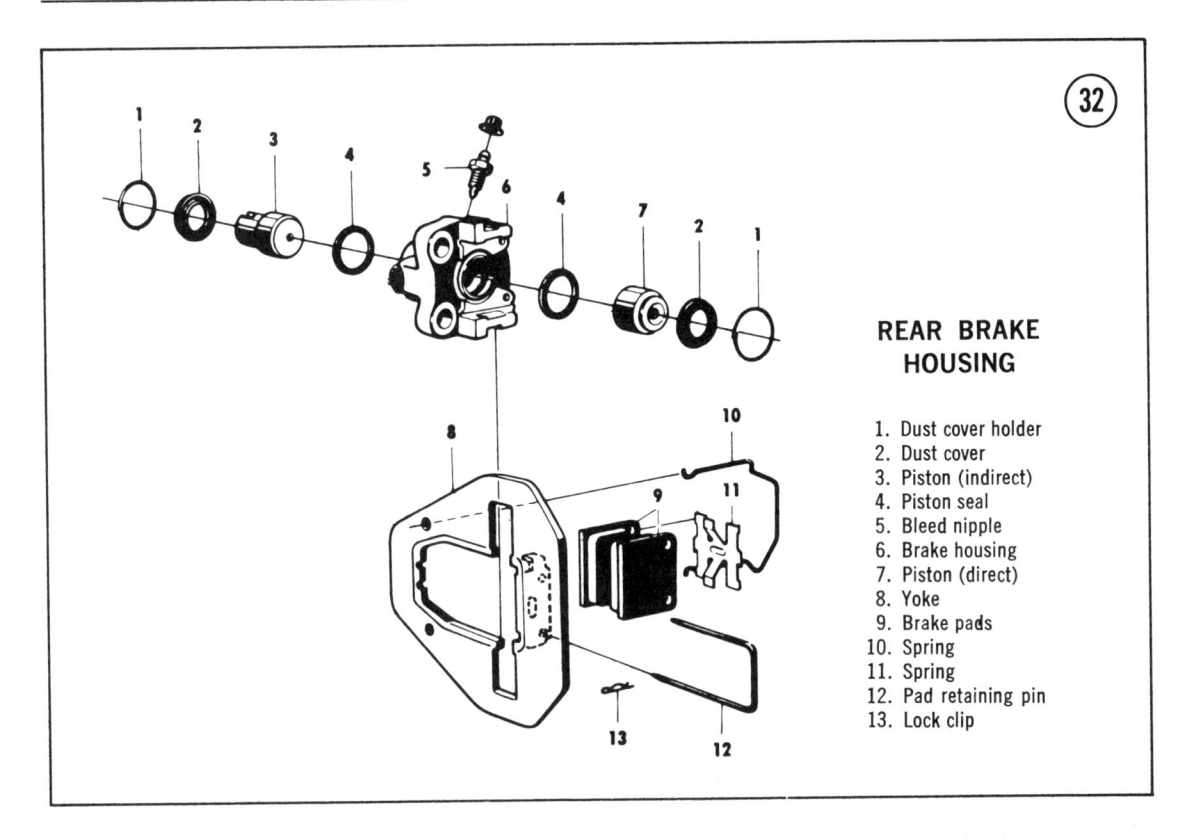

REAR BRAKE HOUSING

1. Dust cover holder
2. Dust cover
3. Piston (indirect)
4. Piston seal
5. Bleed nipple
6. Brake housing
7. Piston (direct)
8. Yoke
9. Brake pads
10. Spring
11. Spring
12. Pad retaining pin
13. Lock clip

6. Remove the brake housing from the vise. Remove the piston seals from the cylinder bore.

Assembly (Rear Wheel Housing)

1. Mount the brake housing in a vise. Use new brake fluid to lubricate the cylinder bore. Fit new piston seals.

2. Push the pistons into the cylinder. Rotate the indirect piston so that the yoke recess is in line with brake housing groove.

3. Fit a new dust cover and retaining ring.

4. Fit the yoke spring to the yoke. Align the yoke so that it fits the brake housing groove and into the indirect piston recess.

5. See **Figure 34**. Check the clearance between the sliding surfaces of the brake housing and yoke. Excessive clearance can result in vibration and noise on braking.

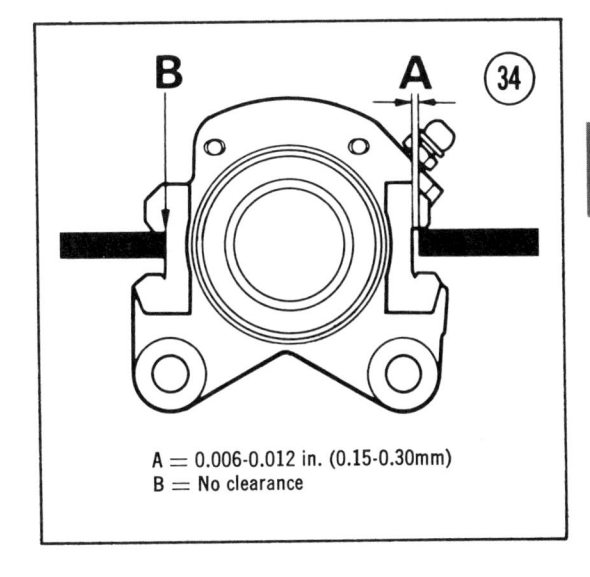

A = 0.006-0.012 in. (0.15-0.30mm)
B = No clearance

Installation
(Rear Wheel Housing)

1. Be sure that the dust cover has not slipped out of position. Screw the complete brake assembly to the steering knuckle housing or rear axle respectively. Use a new locking plate.
2. Connect the brake lines.
3. Install the brake pads (see *Brake Pad Installation*, this chapter).
4. Bleed the brakes (see *Brake Bleeding*, this chapter).

BRAKE DISC

When the brake disc shows sign of heavy wear it should be replaced. Moderate scoring, however, does not necessitate replacement. The disc can be ground a maximum of 0.02 in. (0.5mm) on each side of the brake disc.

Removal/Installation
(95/96 and Sonett)

Refer to **Figure 35**.

1. Remove the hub cap and loosen the shaft nut.
2. Jack up the front of the car. Remove the wheel and shaft nut.
3. Remove the 2 bolts holding the brake housing to the steering knuckle housing. These bolts are accessible from inside of the brake disc. Lift the brake housing clear of the brake disc. Do not disconnect the brake hose. Suspend the brake housing on a piece of wire so no strain is put on the brake hose.
4. Pull the wheel hub (with brake disc attached) using a Saab wheel puller No. 784002 or equivalent.
5. Detach the brake disc from the wheel hub.

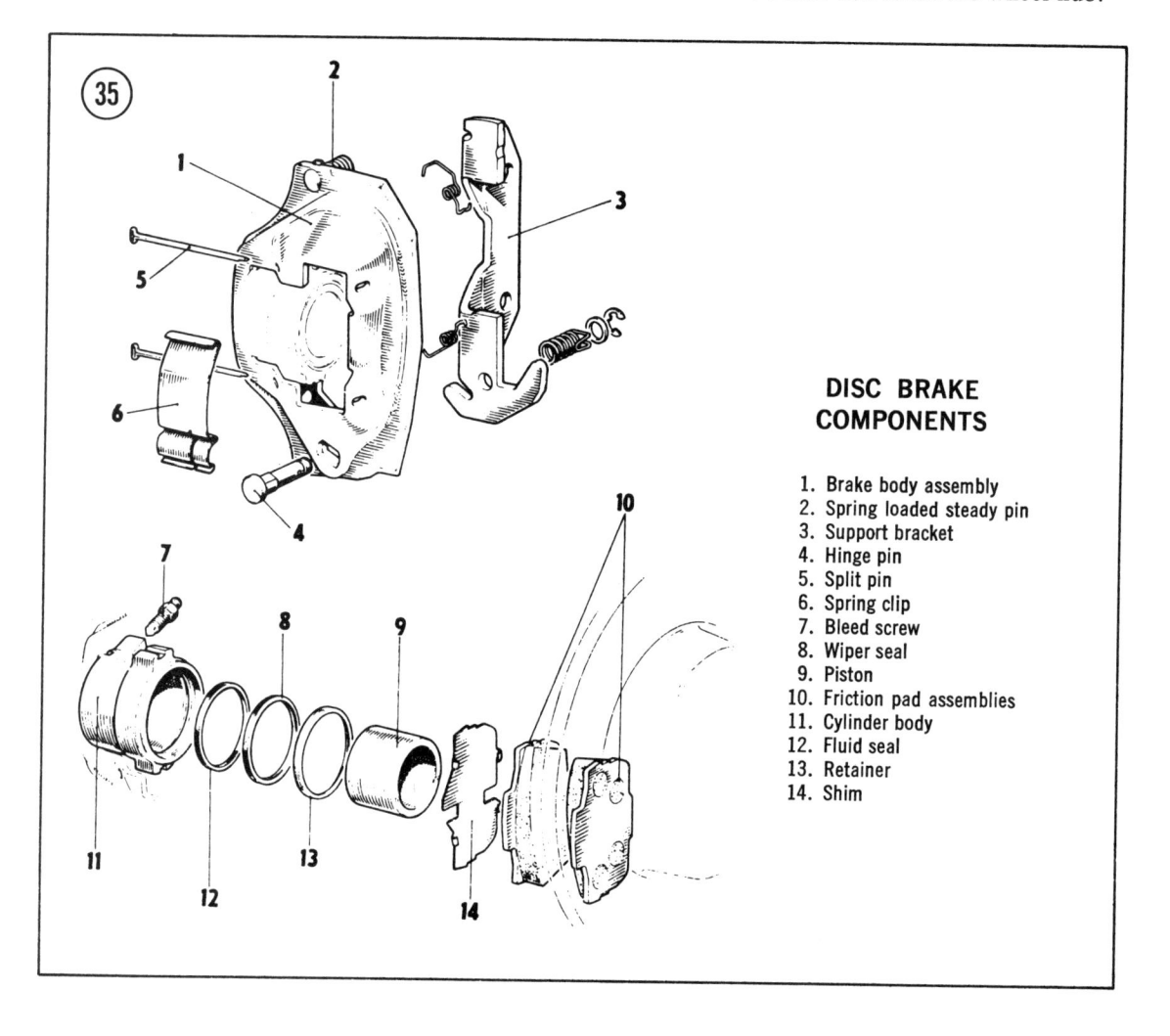

DISC BRAKE COMPONENTS

1. Brake body assembly
2. Spring loaded steady pin
3. Support bracket
4. Hinge pin
5. Split pin
6. Spring clip
7. Bleed screw
8. Wiper seal
9. Piston
10. Friction pad assemblies
11. Cylinder body
12. Fluid seal
13. Retainer
14. Shim

BRAKES

6. Assemble by reversing the removal steps. Pump the brake pedal so that the brake pistons move out toward the disc.

Removal (99 through 1974)

1. Remove the hub cap. Loosen the wheel nuts.
2. Jack up the front end of the car. Remove the wheel nuts and wheel.
3. Remove the 2 screws holding the brake housing to the steering housing. These screws are accessible from inside the steering knuckle housing.
4. Lift the brake housing away from the steering knuckle housing. Do not disconnect brake hose. Be careful not to scratch the brake pistons.
5. See **Figure 36**. Hang the brake housing on a piece of wire to avoid stretching the brake hose. 
6. On a front wheel the parking brake shoes must be released by turning the adjusting screw to clear the drum (**Figure 37**).
7. Back off the 2 disc retaining screws and remove the disc.

Installation
(99 through 1974)

1. Install the disc by reversing the removal steps preceding. When installing the brake housing bolts a new locking plate should be used. 
2. Push the brake pistons well back before the brake housing is mounted on the disc and steering knuckle, because of disc throw compensators.
3. Pump the brake pedal to move the pistons close to the disc.

Removal/Installation
(Front 99, 1975-1976)

1. Apply the handbrake. Remove the nut on the pivot pin.
2. Release the handbrake and remove the 2 screws holding the brake housing to the steering knuckle housing.
3. Rotate the disc so that one of the recesses in the edge of the disc is in line with the brake pads.
4. Lift the handbrake cable or brake hose. Suspend the brake housing on a piece of wire to avoid stretching the brake hose. See **Figure 38**.

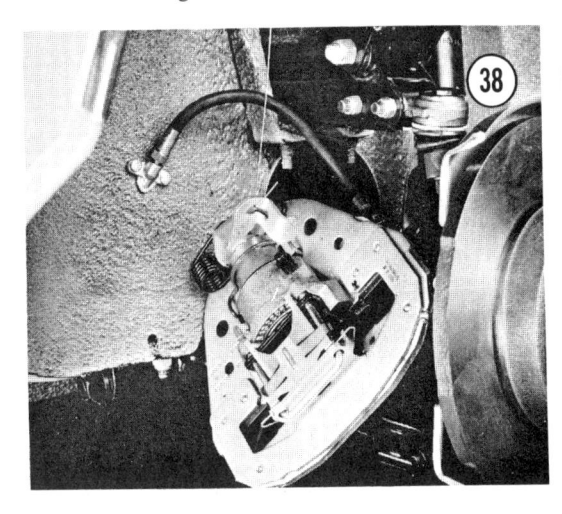

5. See **Figure 39**. Remove the brake disc with the hub from the shaft using Saab puller No. 8995185 and 4 extensions No. 8996050 or Saab puller No. 896084 (later design) or equivalent.

6. Remove the 4 screws holding the brake disc to the hub.

7. Install the brake disc by reversing the removal steps. Use a new lock nut for the driveshaft (if necessary). The nut is locked by peening it into a groove in the shaft. Use a new locking plate for the brake housing screws.

Removal
(Rear 99, 1975-1976)

1. Disconnect the brake hose at the brake housing.

2. Remove the 2 screws holding the brake housing to the rear axle.

3. Remove the 2 disc retaining screws and remove the disc.

4. Install by reversing the removal steps.

BRAKE PADS

Since the disc brakes are self adjusting it is not possible to decide by the length of the pedal stroke if the braking linings are worn. The wheels should be removed every 6,000 miles and the thickness of the brake pads checked. They should be replaced when the thickness of the linings is less than 0.06 in. (1.5mm). It is seldom necessary to bleed the brake system after a simple brake pad replacement.

Removal/Installation
(95/96 and Sonett Models)

1. Jack up the car and remove the wheel.

2. Remove the cotter pins and the spring securing the brake pads. Remove the pads.

3. Clean the uncovered portion of the piston. Be sure there is not rust or dirt on the brake pads' surfaces which contact the bracket and yoke.

4. Drive the piston into the brake housing with the aid of Saab tool No. 786043 or equivalent (**Figure 40**).

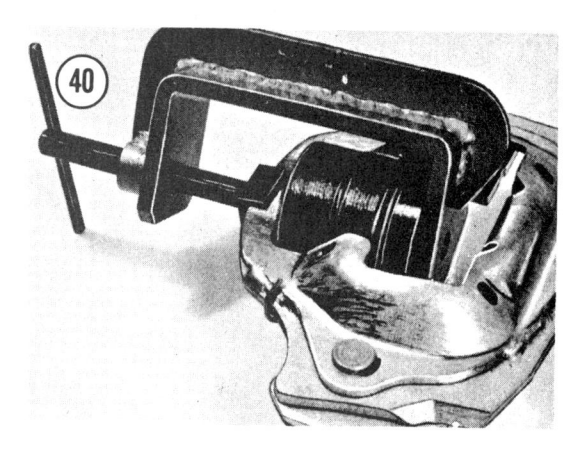

5. Clean the brake disc with trichlorethylene.

6. Turn the movable brake part toward the wheel and fit the outer friction pad. Be sure it moves easily in its position in the yoke. (If used brake pads are refitted they must go back in their original locations.)

7. Turn the moveable brake part backward as far as possible.

8. Fit damping shims to the back of the brake pads. Be sure the shim does not exceed the contours of the pressure plate.

9. Check that the damping shim is fitted with the 2 recesses directly downward in such a way that they are centered on the ends of the piston recess. Install the inner brake pad. The piston recess must be directed downward. (The later model brake piston has a ground contact surface facing the brake pad. The damping shim has been altered so that the piston has the corresponding part facing the friction pad.)

10. Install the spring. The recess in the spring shall lie as close as possible to the outer brake

BRAKES

pad. Fit new cotter pins and lock them. Fit the upper cotter pin first. When fitting the lower cotter pin press the spring upward with the aid of a screwdriver. See **Figure 41**. Fit a new spring if the old one is worn out.

11. Pump the brake pedal in order for the brake pads to be adjusted in toward brake disc.
12. Fill the brake fluid reservoir if necessary.

**Removal/Installation
(99 Through 1974)**

The brake pads must be changed when the thickness of the lining is less than 0.08 in. (2.0mm).

1. Jack up the front or rear end of the car and remove the wheels.
2. See **Figure 42**. When the pads need changing they give warning in the form of stiffer brake pedal resistance and reduced braking effect. This warning comes from the retaining spring, which is about 0.2 in. (5mm) wider than the disc. When the pads are worn the pressure plate of the pad touches the edge of the spring and the braking effect is reduced.
3. See **Figure 43**. Remove the guard plate and locking pins with a drift pin (**Figure 44**).
4. Remove the retaining spring (**Figure 45**). Remove the brake pads.

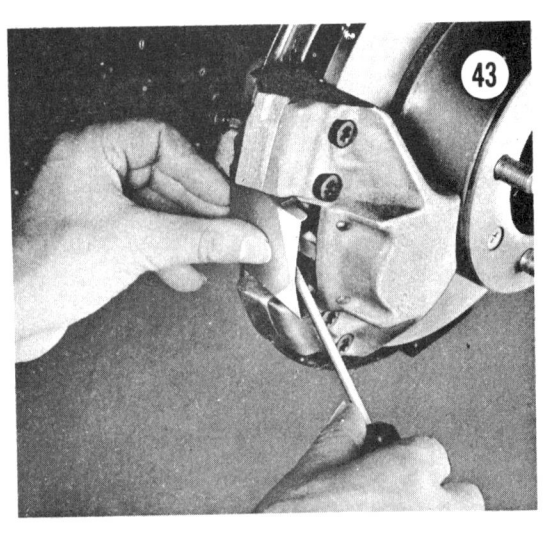

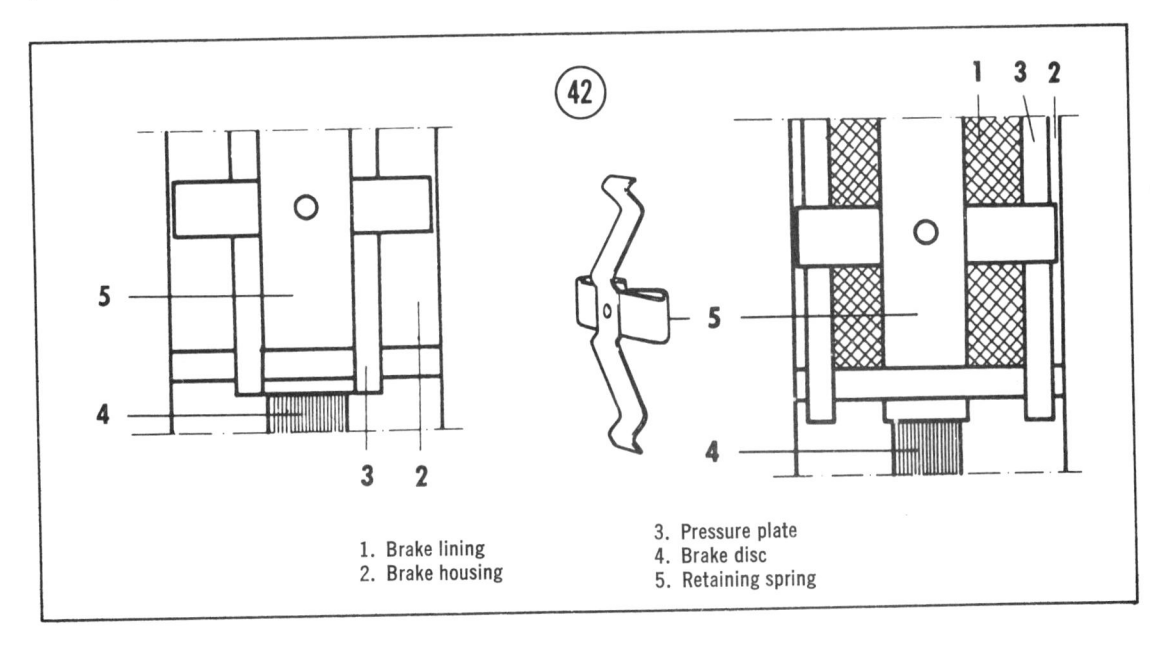

1. Brake lining
2. Brake housing
3. Pressure plate
4. Brake disc
5. Retaining spring

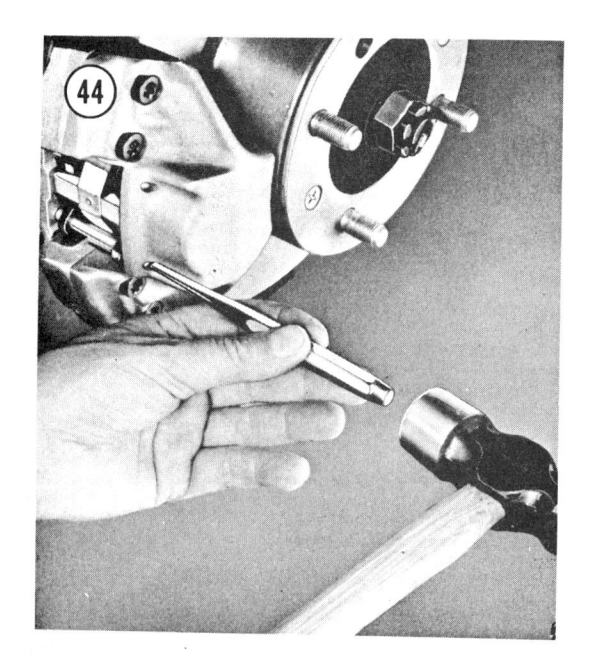

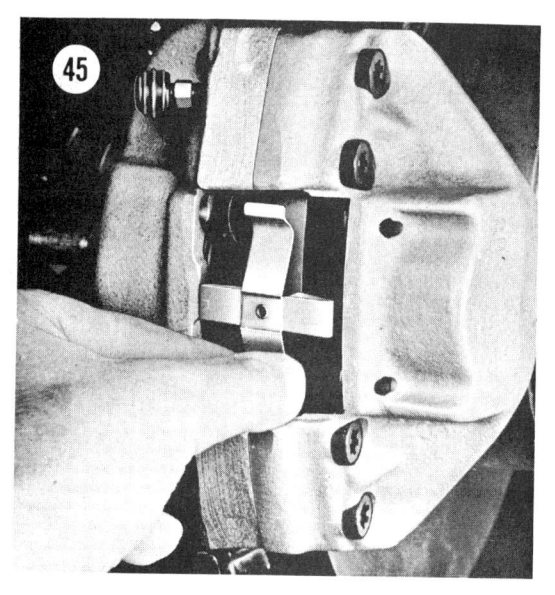

Figure 44

Figure 45

Figure 46

Figure 47

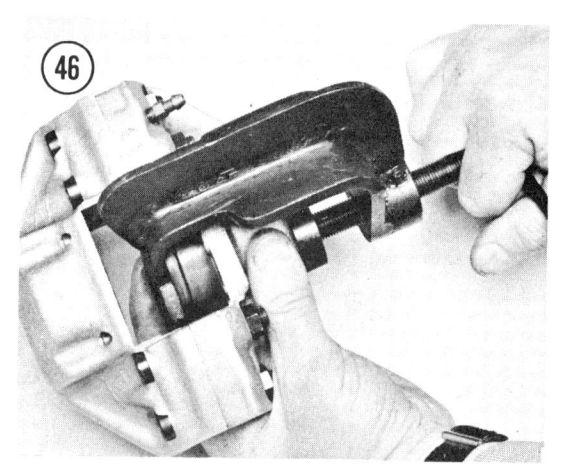

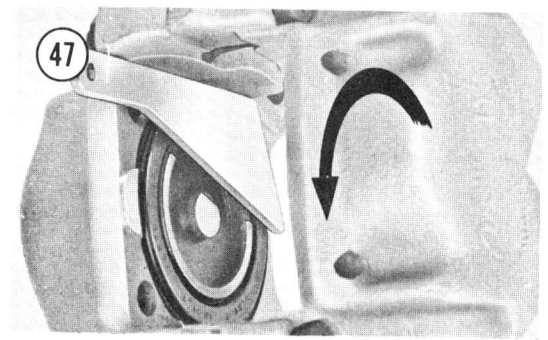

Arrow indicates wheel rotation when driving forward

its back against the direction of rotation. The chamferings of the pistons shall then coincide with the tool. If the position of the pistons is not correct turn them with Saab tool No. 899536 or equivalent.

> NOTE: *On the rear brakes a washer is placed between the brake piston and pad. The washer has a recess and prevents the piston from turning.*

9. Install the brake pads. They should fit easily into the brake housing recess.

10. Install the spring, locking pins, and guard plate.

11. Pump the brake pedal to bring the pads to the brake disc. Top the brake fluid reservoir if necessary.

Removal/Installation (99, 1975-1976)

The brake pads must be replaced when the thickness of the lining is less than 0.080 in. (2.0mm).

5. Replace any damaged dust seals. If dirt has entered, the brake must be reconditioned.

6. Push the pistons back into the cylinder using Saab tool No. 784132 or equivalent (**Figure 46**). The brake fluid level will rise during this operation; it may be necessary to drain off some of the fluid.

7. Wash the brake disc with trichlorethylene.

8. See **Figure 47**. Check the fit of the brake pistons with Saab tool No. 899534 or equivalent. Move the tool into the brake housing with

BRAKES

1. Clean the brake housing thoroughly.
2. Rotate the brake disc so that one of the recesses in the edge of the disc is in line with the brake pads.
3. See **Figure 48**. Remove the damper spring, pin retaining clip, and pad retaining pin.

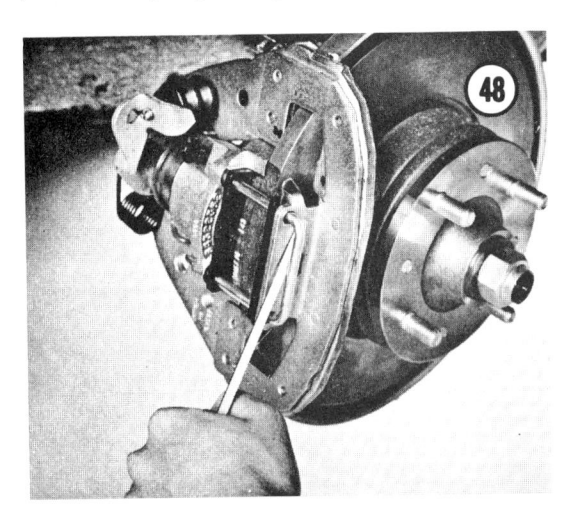

4. Remove the brake pads. If they are seated firmly, use Saab extractor No. 8995771 or equivalent (**Figure 49**).

5. Be sure the dust cover retainer is in place and in good condition. If evidence of dirt having entered or corrosion is found, new pistons and seals should be installed.
6. Connect a hose to the bleeder nipple on the brake housing. Place the other end in a clean glass jar.

7. See **Figure 50**. The brake pistons must be pushed back into the cylinder. On the front wheel disc brake this can be done by rotating the direct piston with Saab tool No. 8996043 at the same time that the piston is pressed into the cylinder. This is achieved on the rear wheel by pushing the direct piston into the cylinder with the handle of tool No. 8996043 or equivalent (**Figure 51**). A small quantity of brake fluid will flow out of the bleeder nipple.

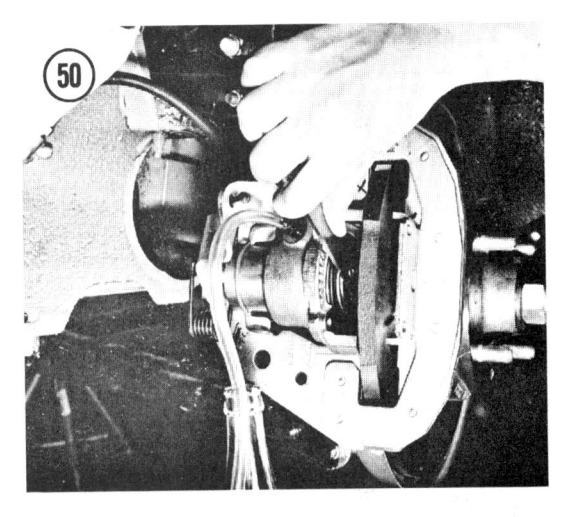

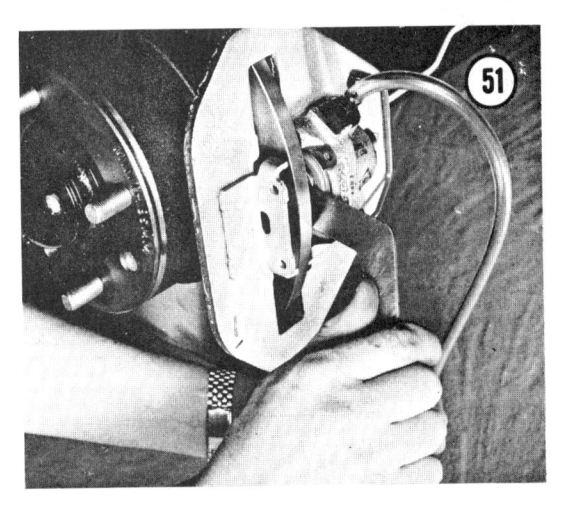

DRUM BRAKES
(95/96 AND SONETT)

The rear wheel brakes have a wheel cylinder mounted in the backplate. The cylinder is fitted with 2 pistons, each one acting on a brake shoe. See **Figure 52**. The linings should be checked at 6,000 mile intervals by looking through the

Figure 52 DRUM BRAKE
1. Adjustment
2. Spring
3. Handbrake link

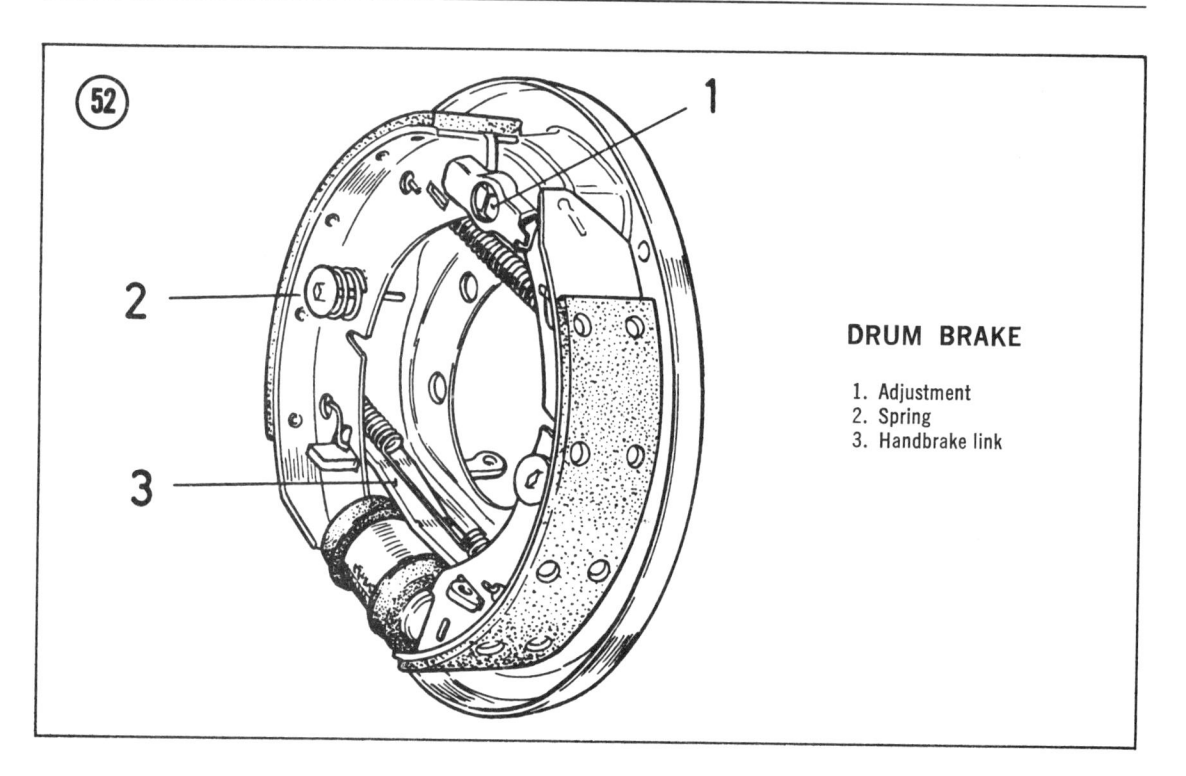

inspection hole in the drum. The linings should be changed at a thickness of 0.1 in. (2.5mm). Replacement shoes are available.

Brake Drum Removal/Installation

1. Remove the cotter pin and shaft nut.
2. Jack up the car and remove the wheel.
3. Release the handbrake. Adjust the rear brake shoes with the adjusting screw (back it off). See **Figure 53**.
4. Remove the brake drum with Saab puller No. 784002 or equivalent.
5. Install the brake drum by reversing the preceding steps. Tighten the shaft nut with a torque wrench to 65 ft.-lb.

> NOTE: *While the drum is removed for a change of brake linings, inspect the brake drums. If they are badly scored they should be replaced. If mild scoring is evident the drums can be machined to a maximum diameter of 8.059 in. (204.7mm).*

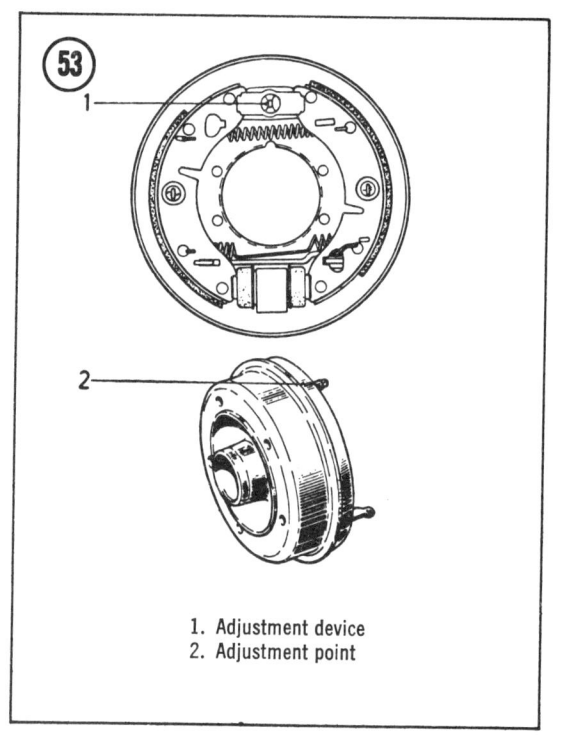

Figure 53
1. Adjustment device
2. Adjustment point

Brake Shoe Removal/Installation

1. With the brake drum removed (see *Brake Drum Removal/Installation*, preceding), remove the springs (Figure 52) by grasping the cupped retainer with a pair of pliers, pushing slightly inward, and turning it 90 degrees to release it.

BRAKES

2. Disengage the top of the brake shoes from the adjuster cam slots by prying the shoes outward against the pressure of the return spring. Pry the bottom shoes out of their wheel cylinder slots next. Disconnect the shoes from the handbrake lever, remove the return springs, handbrake lever, and spring.

CAUTION
Do not depress the brake pedal while the brake shoes are not in place.

3. Position the new shoes so their leading and trailing ends are in the correct position. Place the shoe return springs in position (refer to Figure 52). Pick the shoes up, slightly spreading them apart to maintain spring tension, and place the shoes in position on the backplate, making sure they fit correctly into the adjustment and piston slots. Insert the handbrake lever in the slot in the shoe, and in the hole in the opposite brake shoe. Be certain that the return spring is located properly.

4. Install the brake drum (see *Brake Drum Removal/Installation*, preceding) and adjust the brakes (see *Brake Adjustment*, this chapter).

HANDBRAKE (95/96 AND SONETT)

The mechanical handbrake on the 95/96 and Sonett models acts on the rear wheel brakes only. When the handbrake lever is actuated the movement is transmitted to the rear wheel brakes via cables. These actuate the brake shoes mechanically. See **Figure 54**.

Handbrake Cable Removal

1. Remove one of the front seats and the rear seat cushions. Jack up the car and remove the rear wheels.

2. Back off and remove the adjusting nut under the handbrake lever.

3. Pull the cable sheathing out of the sleeve beneath the rear seat cushion.

4. Remove the clamps holding the cable to the rear axle.

5. Remove the pin holding the clevis on the brake lever.

6. Remove the grommet from the inclined panel in the rear axle tunnel.

7. Pull the entire brake cable out rearward.

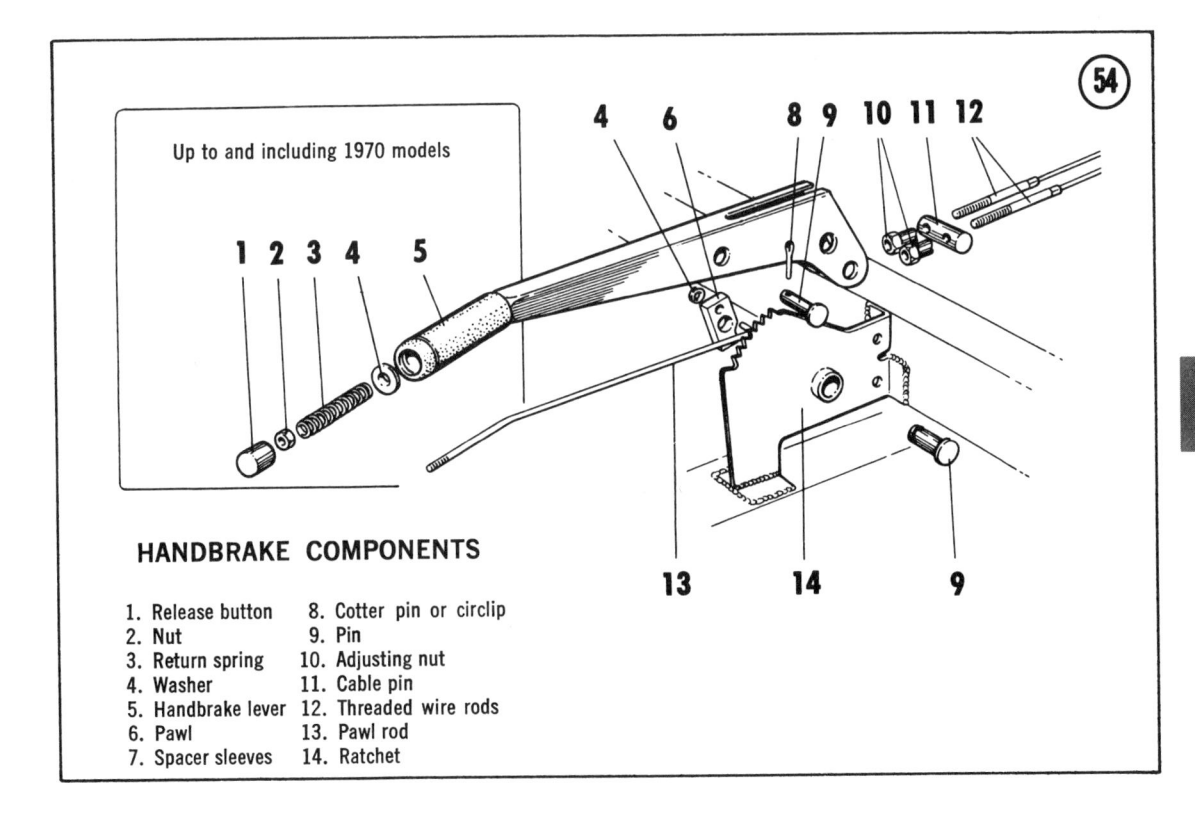

HANDBRAKE COMPONENTS

1. Release button
2. Nut
3. Return spring
4. Washer
5. Handbrake lever
6. Pawl
7. Spacer sleeves
8. Cotter pin or circlip
9. Pin
10. Adjusting nut
11. Cable pin
12. Threaded wire rods
13. Pawl rod
14. Ratchet

Handbrake Cable Installation

1. Replace the grommet onto the cable.

2. Thread the cable (threaded end first) up through the inclined panel in the rear axle tunnel and through the sleeve under the rear seat to the handbrake lever. Be sure the grommet in the front inclined panel has not been dislocated.

3. Refit the adjusting nut.

4. Connect the clevis to the brake lever. Secure the pin.

5. Fit the grommet in the inclined panel in the rear axle tunnel and secure the cable to the rear axle with 2 clamps.

HANDBRAKE
(99 THROUGH 1974)

The handbrake acts on separate front wheel drums. The handbrake is located between the front seats. Its action is transmitted to the brake drums mechanically by cables. See **Figure 55**. The upper ends of the brake shoes are pressed against the support pieces by the upper tension spring. The lower ends connect with the adjusting device and are held against it by a spring. This type of mounting makes the brake shoes self-centering and partly self-applying. The brake shoes should be replaced when the lining is less than 0.02 in. (0.5mm) thick.

Handbrake Cable Removal

1. Remove the front seats and carpet.

2. Remove the front heating system duct and valve housing assembly.

3. Remove the knob from the free-wheel control lever.

4. Place the car in reverse. Remove the ignition key. Unscrew the gear lever cover and lift it off.

5. Remove the handbrake lever cover. Unscrew the adjusting wire screws. Pull the handbrake lever up so the wires can be loosened. Remove the rear duct with the heater control.

6. Remove the wire clamp from the floor tunnel.

7. Remove the front wheel. Loosen the wire retainers from the wheel housings. Loosen the retainer straps on the steering gear.

8. Pull the wire out from the wheel end.

Handbrake Cable Installation

1. To install reverse the removal steps, preceding. Be sure the rubber grommet in the dash

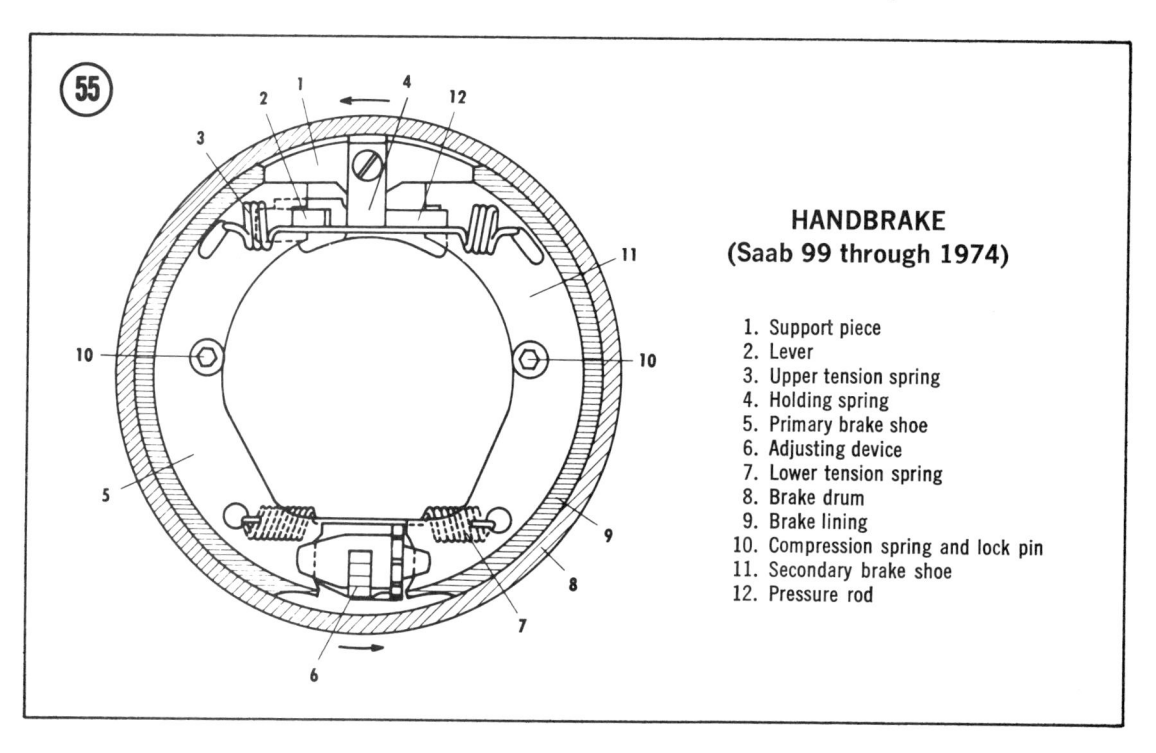

HANDBRAKE
(Saab 99 through 1974)

1. Support piece
2. Lever
3. Upper tension spring
4. Holding spring
5. Primary brake shoe
6. Adjusting device
7. Lower tension spring
8. Brake drum
9. Brake lining
10. Compression spring and lock pin
11. Secondary brake shoe
12. Pressure rod

BRAKES

panel bulkhead is not damaged. Make note of the crossover of the wires and be sure they are installed in the same way.

2. After the handbrake cable is installed adjust the parking brake shoes (see *Brake Adjustment*, this chapter), then the wires.

Handbrake Lever Removal/Installation

1. Remove the left front seat.
2. Remove the handbrake lever cover.
3. Loosen the wire adjusting screws completely and remove them.
4. Pull the shaft lock ring and remove the shaft far enough to clear the ratchet.
5. Remove the lock ring from the lower shaft bolts. Pull the bolt out and lift off the lever.
6. Install by reversing the preceding steps.

Brake Drum/Shoe (Handbrake) Removal

1. Apply the handbrake and remove the front wheel hub caps. Loosen the wheel nuts.
2. Jack up the front end of the car and remove the wheel. Release the handbrake.
3. Unscrew the brake housing from the steering knuckle housing. Lift it off the brake disc.

> NOTE: *The brake housing should be hung from a piece of wire so it does not stretch the brake hose.*

4. Remove the brake drum retaining screws and pull off the drum.

Brake Drum/Shoe (Handbrake) Disassembly

1. Unhook the upper return spring using Saab tool No. 899560 or equivalent (**Figure 56**).
2. Remove the 2 retaining springs and remove the brake shoes by pulling them downward (**Figure 57**).

Brake Drum/Shoe (Handbrake) Assembly

1. Loosen the wire adjustment to avoid straining the wire before installing new linings.
2. Coat the 3 sliding studs on the shield, lever arm joint, and adjusting screw with grease.
3. Install the brake shoes and adjustment (the short sleeve should face forward on the right-

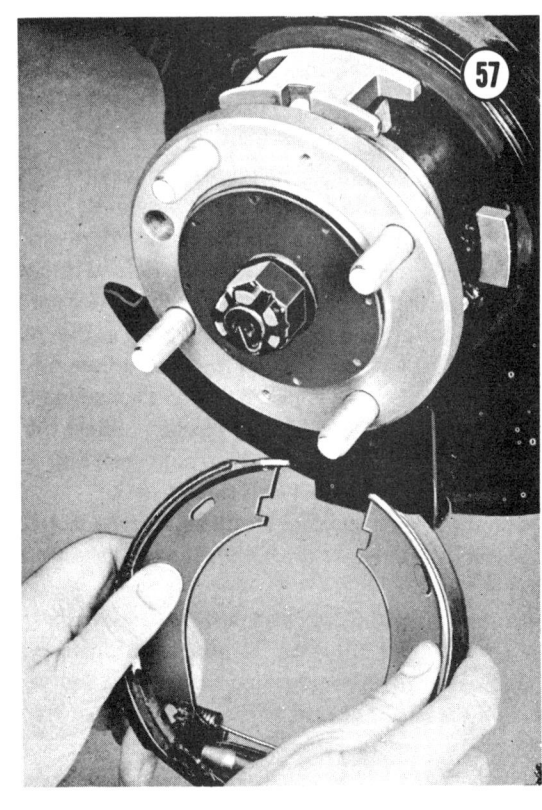

hand side and backward on the left-hand side). Connect the lower tension spring so that it is inside shoes after mounting.

4. Insert the brake shoes from below (between the brake shield and wheel hub) to their location against the support piece. Fit them in the groove on the lever arm and link.

5. Mount the compression springs and upper tension spring.

6. Push on the wire end of the lever arm to check the operation. Be sure that the adjustment device is screwed in.

Brake Drum/Shoe (Handbrake) Assembly

1. Mount the brake drum. If it will not slip easily over the shoes it is probably because the shoes are not correctly centered.

2. Install the retaining screws and brake housing. Be sure that the brake hose is not twisted.

3. Make certain that brake pads clear disc. Adjust the handbrake (see *Brake Adjustment*).

4. Mount the wheel and hub cap.

HANDBRAKE
(99, 1975-1976)

Refer to **Figure 58**. The 1975-1976 Saab 99 models feature an automatic adjustment device on the handbrake mechanism in conjunction with 2 brake pistons. The handbrake lever acts on a thrust plate which mechanically actuates the 2 pistons by means of a push rod. The automatic adjustment device is built into the direct piston. Each time the handbrake is applied and released the handbrake adjusts itself.

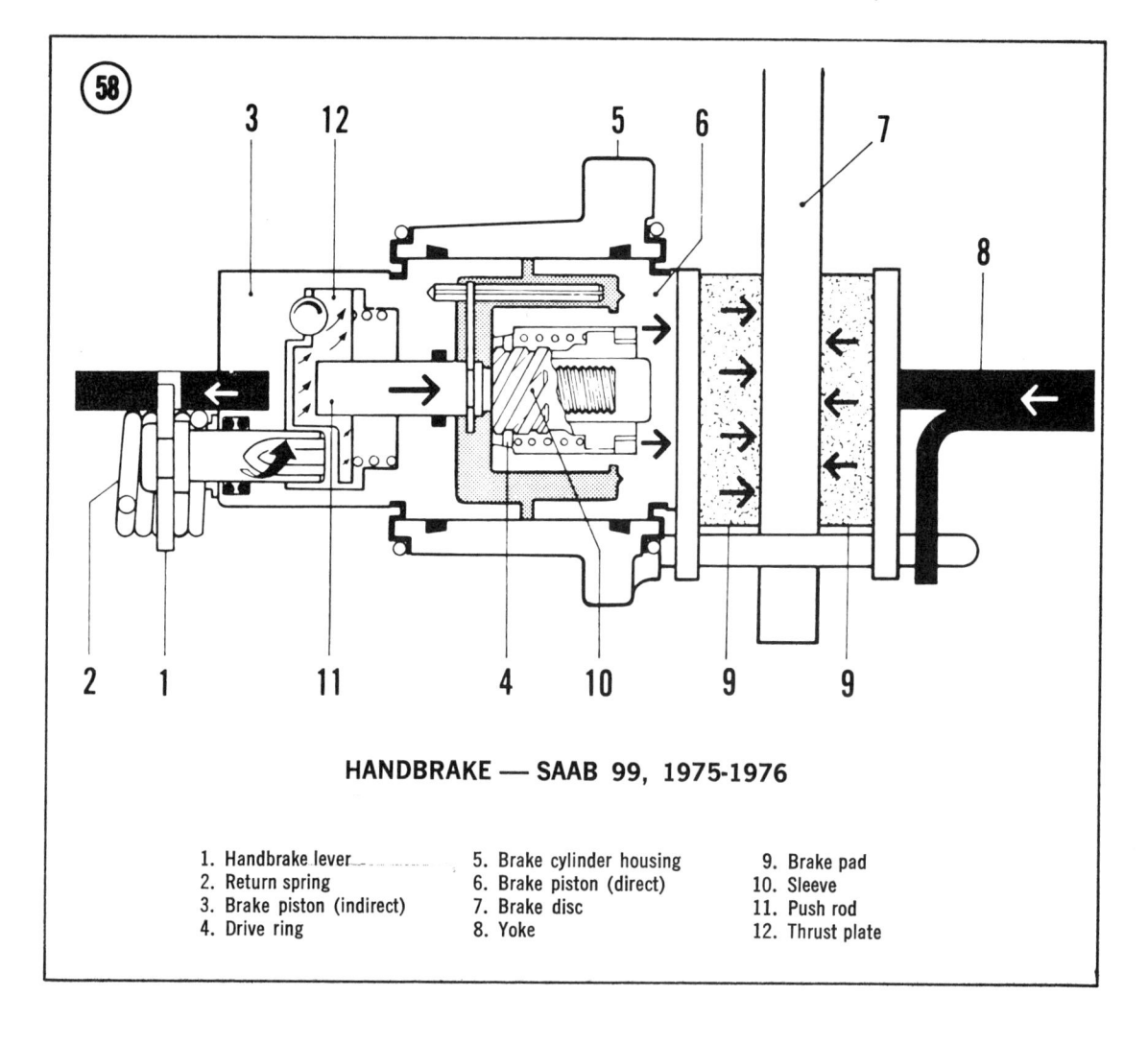

HANDBRAKE — SAAB 99, 1975-1976

1. Handbrake lever
2. Return spring
3. Brake piston (indirect)
4. Drive ring
5. Brake cylinder housing
6. Brake piston (direct)
7. Brake disc
8. Yoke
9. Brake pad
10. Sleeve
11. Push rod
12. Thrust plate

BRAKES

Handbrake Cable Removal

1. Remove the front seat (driver's side) and the carpeting to expose the heating system air ducts.
2. Remove the gear lever cover.
3. Remove the plate covering the air ducts. Remove the air ducts.
4. Disconnect the cable from the adjustment nut on the handbrake lever.
5. Remove the clip holding the 2 cables to the floor.
6. Remove the rubber bushing in the wheel housing and disconnect the cable from the handbrake lever at the brake cylinder housing.
7. Remove the cable.

Handbrake Cable Installation

1. Install by reversing the removal steps, preceding. The cables should cross each other on the floor of the passenger compartment.
2. Apply the handbrake several times after the cables have been installed in order to stretch the cables. Then adjust the cables with the adjustment nut at the handbrake lever and the yoke on the brake housing so that the distance between the yoke and handbrake lever is 0.019 in.± 0.003 in. (0.5mm±0.1mm) when the handbrake is in the off position. See **Figure 59**.

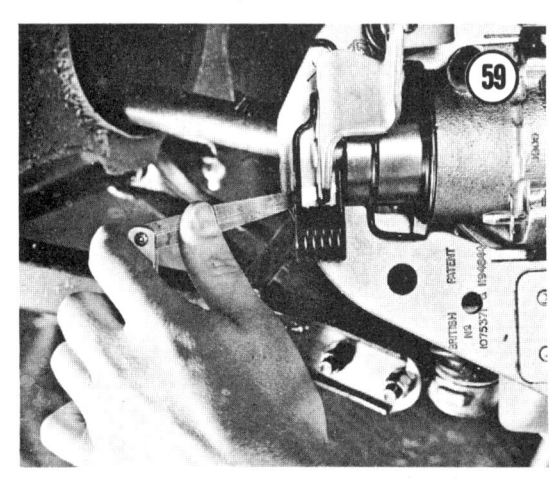

Handbrake Lever Removal

1. Disconnect the 2 cables from the adjustment nuts.
2. Remove the locking pin from the pivot pin and pull out the latter.

Handbrake Lever Installation

Install by reversing the removal steps, preceding. If the pawl button (**Figure 60**), pawl rod, or any other part in the handbrake lever has been removed, the position of the pawl button must be checked. After the lever has been fitted and the brake applied the distance between the top edge of the button and the handbrake lever should be 0.32 in.±0.08 in. (8.0±2.0mm). The pawl button can be adjusted by screwing or unscrewing it on the push rod.

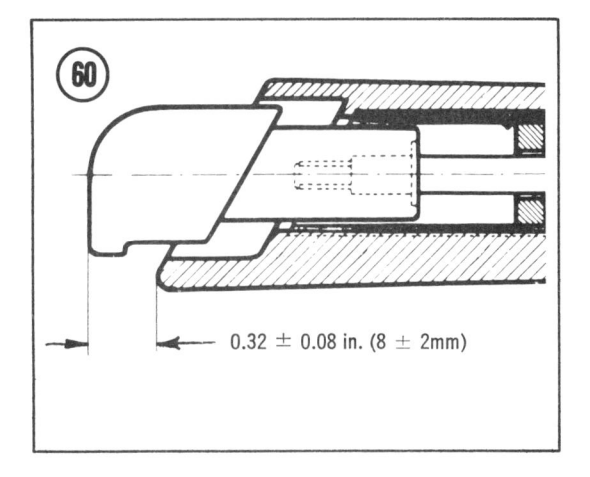

BRAKE BLEEDING

Bleeding of the brake system (which is the removal of any air, leaving only brake fluid) must be carried out when a component in the system has been removed. A bleeder nipple is fitted to each brake housing. The following procedure is used:

1. Block the wheels and release the handbrake.
2. Fill the brake fluid reservoir and check to be sure that the vent holes in the cap are not blocked.
3. Pump the brake pedal several times.
4. Connect a hose to the bleeder nipple at the left rear wheel. Place the other end of the hose in a clean jar partly filled with brake fluid. The end of the hose must be kept below the surface of the brake fluid in the container at all times. Open the bleeder screw on the brake housing half a turn. See **Figure 61**.
5. Have an assistant gently depress the brake pedal completely, then release it. Repeat after a short pause. Do this until the fluid discharged is

free from air bubbles. Tighten the bleeder screw immediately after the final downward stroke of the brake pedal (while the pedal is still down).

6. Repeat Steps 4 and 5 preceding with the right front wheel. Then change to the primary circuit by bleeding first the right rear wheel, then the left front wheel.

7. After bleeding both systems, fill the brake fluid reservoir.

> NOTE: *During brake bleeding the brake warning lamp will light up as a result of uneven pressure in the system. The lamp will go out as soon as the piston in the brake valve of the master cylinder returns to its central position, i.e., as soon as the brakes are used after bleeding has been accomplished.*

> CAUTION
> *Never reuse old brake fluid. Use only fresh brake fluid of the recommended specification.*

BRAKE ADJUSTMENT

The front wheels have self-adjusting disc brakes. Consequently it will be necessary to adjust brake shoes on rear wheel brakes only.

Brake shoe wear shows up as excessive travel in the brake pedal or handbrake lever before the brakes take hold. The distance between the pedal and lower part of the dash panel must not be less than the values shown in the following drawings. **Figure 62** shows the minimum distance permissible between the depressed pedal and toe-board for 95/96 models through 1968. **Figure 63** is for 95/96 models from 1969 onward.

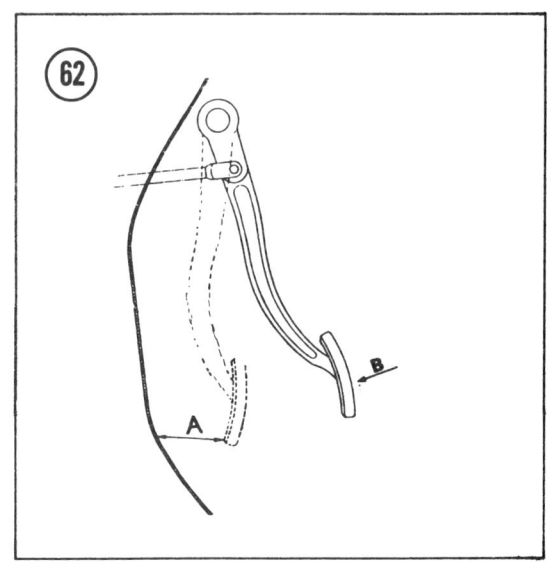

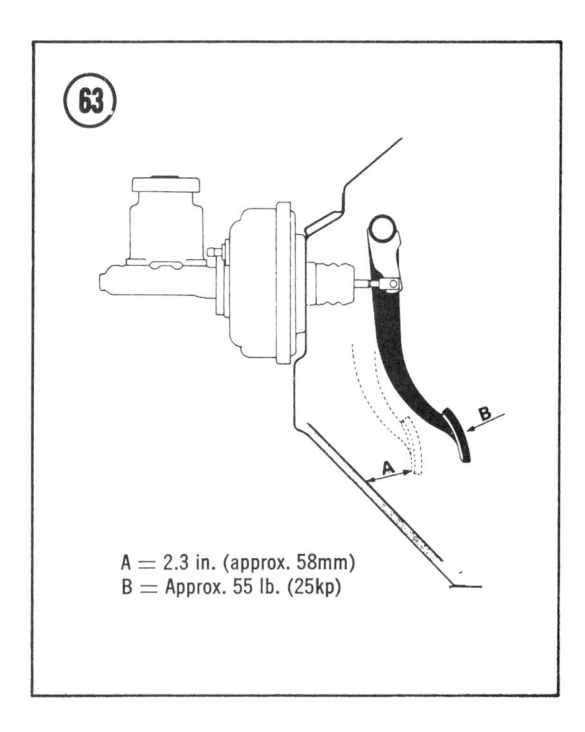

A = 2.3 in. (approx. 58mm)
B = Approx. 55 lb. (25kp)

Adjust the rear brakes as follows:

1. Jack up the rear of the car so the wheels clear the ground. The brakes can be adjusted without removing the wheels.

2. Release the handbrake fully.

BRAKES

3. Depress the brake pedal hard several times in order to center the rear brake shoes.

4. See **Figure 64**. Turn the square adjusting screw located on the rear of the backplate until the wheel is locked. Back off a notch at a time until the rear wheel rotates freely.

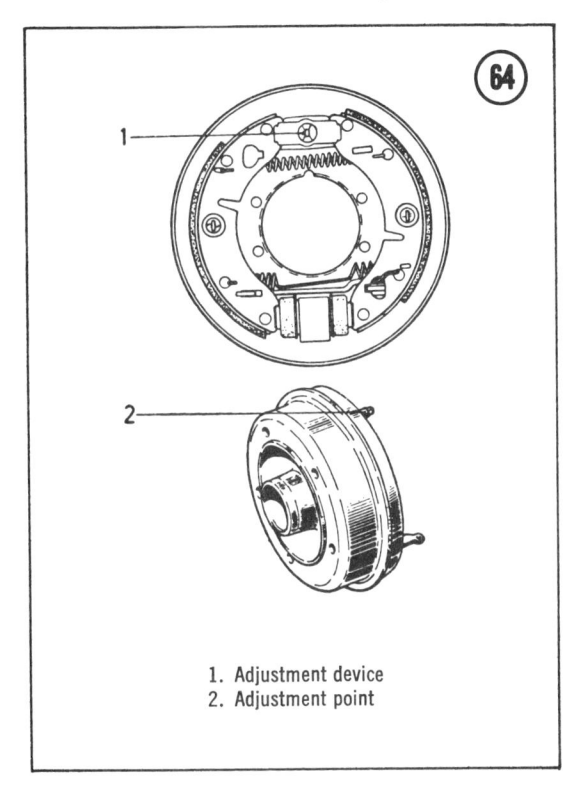

1. Adjustment device
2. Adjustment point

5. After adjusting check the free movement of the pedal (see *Brake Pedal*, this chapter). If the clearance is less than recommended the brake shoes won't return when the brake pedal is released.

6. If the adjusting screw cannot be tightened enough to lock the rear wheel the brake linings are worn too badly and should be replaced.

Handbrake Adjustment (95/96 and Sonett)

The handbrake adjustment is taken care of automatically when the rear brakes are adjusted.

Handbrake Adjustment (99 Through 1974)

1. Apply the handbrake, remove the front wheel hub caps, and loosen the wheel nuts.

2. Jack up the front end of the car and place jackstands under the front suspension arms. Release handbrake and remove the front wheels.

3. Be sure that the brake pads clear the disc and that the lever arm doesn't influence the position of the parking brake shoes on adjustment. Release the wire adjustment at the handbrake lever end.

4. Line up the hole in the drum with the teeth of the adjusting screw (**Figure 65**). Insert a screwdriver into the hole and place its point between the teeth of the screw. Turn the screw until the drum can only just be turned by hand. Back off the screw by 1 or 2 teeth. Apply and release the handbrake lever in order to center the shoes.

5. Turn brake drum. Light contact is acceptable, but if the drum cannot be turned fairly easily back the screw off still another notch or two.

6. Repeat the adjustment on the other wheel.

7. Pull handbrake on. On 99 models through 1970 the brake should begin to take hold at the 2nd notch and be fully applied at the 3rd notch. From 1971 onward the brake should begin to take hold at the 4th notch and lock the wheels fully at the 6th or 7th notch.

8. Mount the wheels after cleaning all contact surfaces. Tighten the nuts until the wheel is firmly seated. Then lower the car to the ground and tighten the wheel nuts to a torque of 65-80 ft.-lb. Fit the hub caps.

Handbrake Adjustment
(99, 1975-1976)

The handbrake adjustment is taken care of automatically each time the handbrake is applied and released.

BRAKE PEDAL
(95/96 THROUGH 1968)

The brake pedal is carried on the same shaft as the clutch pedal and fitted with self lubricating bearings. See **Figure 66**.

66
1. Stoplight switch
2. Brake warning contact

Removal/Installation

1. Remove the steering column and gear shift shaft.

2. Detach the clutch cylinder fork from the clutch pedal.

3. Remove the cotter pins from both ends of the shaft.

4. Remove the clutch pedal and return spring from the shaft.

5. Unscrew the master cylinder push rod at the adjusting nut. Pull out the shaft and remove the brake pedal.

6. Check the bearing for wear. Fit new bushings if necessary.

7. Install by reversing the preceding steps. Adjust the brake pedal free movement as outlined in *Brake Pedal Free Movement*, following.

Brake Pedal Free Movement

There must always be proper clearance between the master cylinder piston and the brake pedal push rod when the pedal is at rest in order to ensure that the master cylinder piston will return fully every time the brake pedal is released. See **Figure 67**. The clearance, measured at the tip of the pedal, should be 0.12-0.24 in. (3.0-6.0mm). Measured between the push rod and piston the clearance should be 0.024-0.047 in. (0.6-1.2mm). Adjust as follows:

1. Back off the locknut.

2. Turn the hex part of the push rod until the correct clearance is obtained at the tip of the pedal.

3. Tighten the locknut.

BRAKE PEDAL
(95/96 1969 ON)

Removal/Installation

1. Remove the protective cover of the steering wheel shaft.

2. Remove the brake light and brake warning contacts bracket. See **Figure 68**.

68

BRAKES

**BRAKE PEDAL AND MASTER CYLINDER
(95/96 through 1968)**

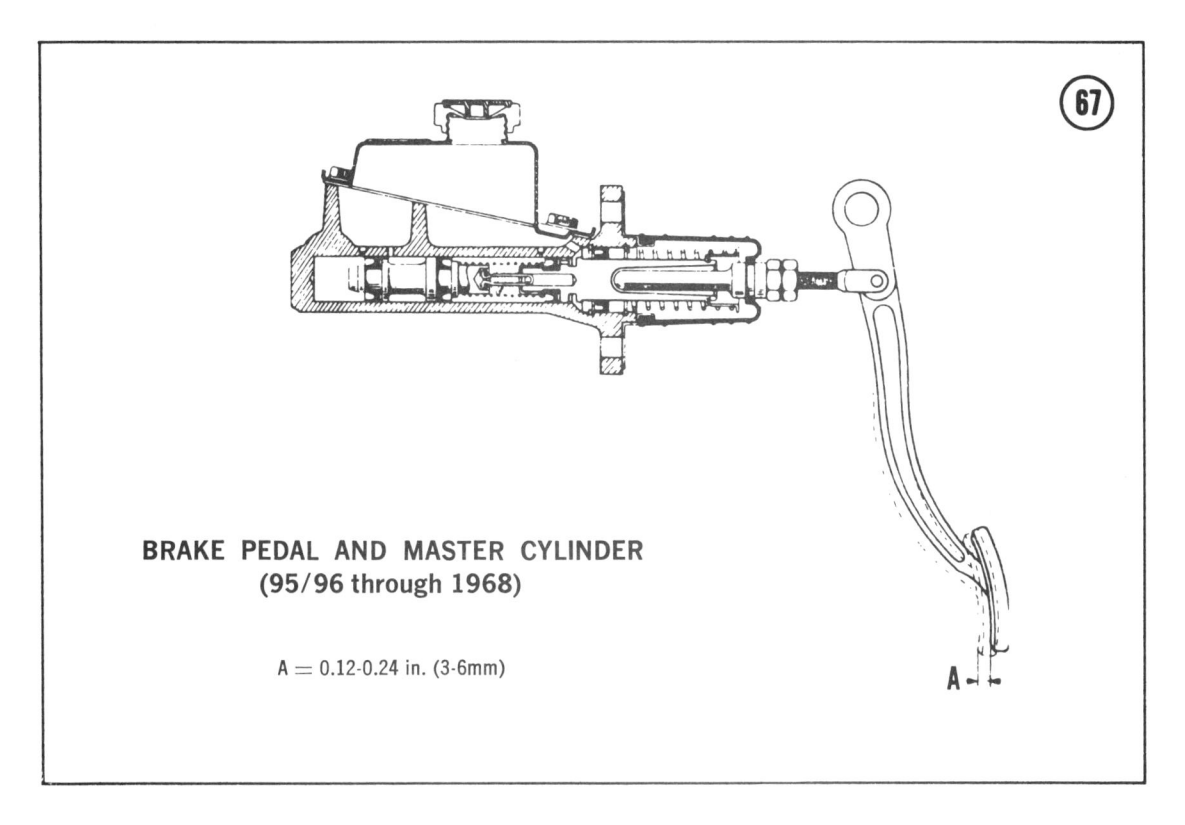

A = 0.12-0.24 in. (3-6mm)

3. Loosen the brake cylinder push rod by removing cotter pin (**Figure 69**) and shaft bolt.

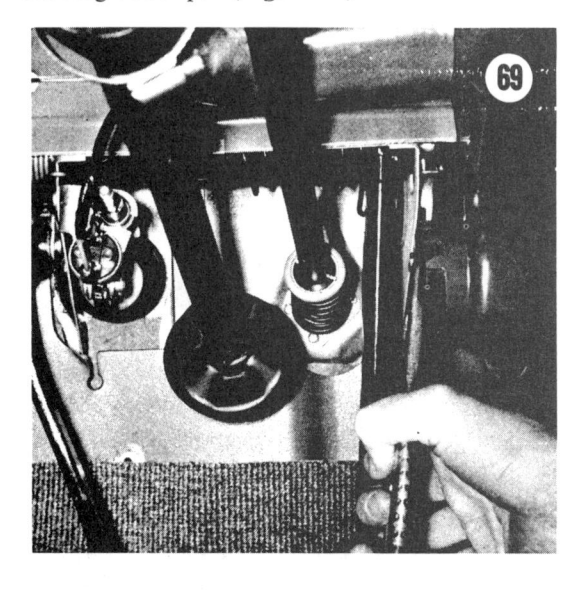

4. Loosen the clutch pedal spring.

5. Remove the cotter pin from the right hand end of the pedal shaft.

6. Pull the shaft out to the left and remove the brake pedal.

7. Check the bearing for wear. Renew bushings as necessary.

8. Install by reversing the preceding steps.

BRAKE PEDAL (SONETT)

The brake pedal and clutch pedal are carried on a common shaft, which in turn is carried in 2 brackets welded to the dash panel and floor. The master cylinder is attached to the dash panel. Brake pedal movement is transmitted to the master cylinder via a push rod of adjustable length.

Removal/Installation

Each pedal can be removed separately if the pedal shaft is removed.

1. Remove the floor mat and wallboard panels. Remove the gear lever knob and rubber boot. Remove the gearbox cover (4 screws).

2. Remove the screws holding the pedal plate. Lift out both parts.

3. Release the clutch pedal push rod by removing the cotter pin and shaft bolt.

4. Release the brake pedal and clutch pedal return springs.

5. Tap out the slotted pins and pull out the pedal shaft.

6. Detach the push rod from the rubber boot. Lift the brake pedal away from the master cylinder (it will be accompanied by the push rod).

7. Install by reversing the preceding steps.

Brake Pedal Free Movement

The clearance between the master cylinder piston and brake pedal push rod (with brake pedal at rest) should be 0.12-0.24 in. (0.6-1.2mm). Adjust as follows:

1. Back the locking nut off.

2. Turn the hex part of the push rod until the correct clearance is obtained at the tip of the pedal.

3. Tighten the locking nut.

BRAKE PEDAL (99 THROUGH 1974)

Removal/Installation

1. Disconnect the electric wiring and remove the brake light and brake warning contact holder. (The holder is fixed to the pedal shaft with 2 screws.)

2. Remove the eccentric shaft where the pedal is connected to vacuum power assist push rod.

3. Pull the split pin from the right hand end of the pedal shaft. Push the shaft out.

4. Remove the brake pedal.

5. Install by reversing the preceding steps.

Brake Pedal Adjustment

The position of the brake pedal (in relationship to the clutch pedal) can be adjusted by means of an eccentric pin where the brake pedal connects to the vacuum power assist push rod.

BRAKE PEDAL (99, 1975-1976)

Removal/Installation

1. See **Figure 70**. Remove pedal return spring.

2. Remove the lower circlip on the brake pedal pull rod.

3. Remove the pedal pin locknut and push out the pedal pin.

4. Replace worn bushings by pressing them out and inserting new ones. New bushings must be greased with ball bearing grease prior to installation.

5. Install by reversing the preceding steps.

Brake Pedal Adjustment

Adjustment of the brake pedal (in relation to the clutch pedal) is accomplished by adjusting the length of the pull rod from the brake pedal. Adjust as follows:

1. Remove the lower circlip on the pull rod and the return spring on the pedal.

2. Pull up the rubber bellows in the dash panel. Remove the push rod locknut. (The rubber bellows and locknut can be reached from the engine compartment.)

3. Rotate the lower pull rod fork to obtain the correct length.

4. Tighten the locknut after adjustment and reassemble the pull rod, circlip, and return spring.

BRAKES

BRAKE PEDAL AND MASTER CYLINDER
(Saab 99, 1975-1976)

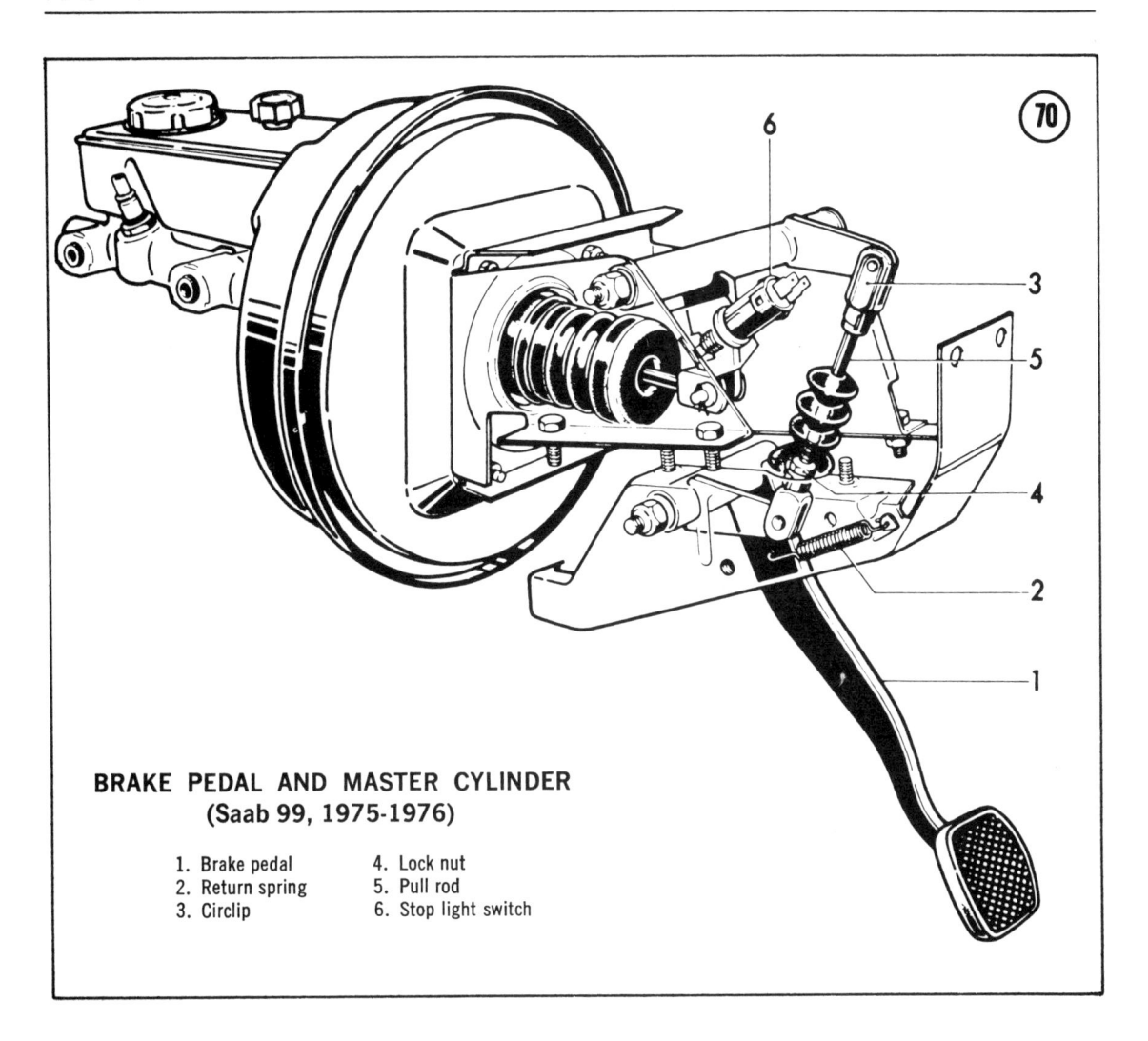

1. Brake pedal
2. Return spring
3. Circlip
4. Lock nut
5. Pull rod
6. Stop light switch

CHAPTER THIRTEEN

PERFORMANCE IMPROVEMENT

This chapter talks about performance — what it consists of, and how to improve it. It explains what various high-performance parts will and won't do, and discusses the ways parts and systems affect each other. For the inexperienced or unwary, it points out common mistakes.

While there is a wide variety of high-performance equipment available, few of you will ever actually enter your car in competition. Therefore, this chapter has been prepared with street-oriented modifications in mind.

Most of the accessories in this chapter are of the "bolt-on" variety. Bolt-on equipment materials and designs change frequently. We cannot control how the equipment will be installed, or how the car will be used. Good judgment and common sense will help you avoid disappointment. "Bolt-on," as used here, means accessories which you can add to your car with ordinary hand tools and a reasonable degree of mechanical expertise. Generally speaking, if you can carry out the service procedures outlined in this manual, you can also install the bolt-on, high-performance accessories illustrated in this chapter.

It is impossible for us to show you how to install all of the items discussed in this chapter — it would take an entire book — but we will show you what is available, and we'll supply you with the addresses and other vital information to get you going.

> **CAUTION**
> *Clymer Publications cannot guarantee or be responsible for performance, possible damage to the car, or personal injury resulting from the performance modification procedures given in this manual.*

WHAT DO YOU WANT?

You may be able to answer the question better after reading this chapter, but at some point, it's going to need serious thought. Every modification has its tradeoffs. Quicker cornering may come at the expense of a rougher ride. Increased horsepower can mean reduced gas mileage and shorter engine life. And of course, performance can be expensive, in both money and time. The best way to guarantee getting what you want is to modify the car one step at a time, in a logical order.

Chassis Modifications

Without question, the chassis should be modified first. It is foolish (and dangerous) to modify an engine for more horsepower than the chassis is capable of handling.

Chassis modifications are generally less expensive (and easier to make) than engine modifications, and you can add various bits and pieces (heavy-duty shocks, stiffer sway bars, etc.) as you get the money. Therefore, if for no other reason than economy, the chassis-first approach makes sense.

Quite possibly, in view of today's 55 mph speed limit, you may decide to modify the chassis only, and leave the stock engine alone. Chassis improvements will allow you to travel from one point on the map to another in less time, and with less dramatics (body lean, wheel hop, etc.), even without an increase in horsepower.

Engine Modifications

As mentioned previously, you should not even consider modifying the engine until you have modified the chassis. Of course, this does not apply to the addition of such items as an electronic ignition system, or a more efficient exhaust system. These will improve performance and gas mileage without adding too much horsepower for the suspension and brakes to cope with.

> NOTE: *The stock engine should always be checked for soundness, then tuned perfectly before attempting any modifications. Raising the horsepower is a sure way to destroy a tired engine.*

It is possible to modify your engine to almost any horsepower stage that you wish. Conventional engine modification components are available (high-lift cams, lightweight pistons, exhaust systems, etc.), as well as turbocharger kits, so you are free to pick and choose, using your own mechanical (and financial) capabilities as a guide.

Body Modifications

Body modifications are the last step in the modification process. When your chassis has been properly set up (stiffer springs, heavier sway bars, modified shock absorbers, etc.) and your engine has been modified and tuned to the proper degree, the only area of modification left to explore is the body.

Air-flow devices, such as spoilers and air dams (which provide more downforce on the chassis at high speed), are more effective at high speed than when used at the legal speed limit, although they are worthwhile even then. At high speed they add tremendously to the overall stability of the car.

Fender flares, which are attached to the body by bolts or rivets, can be used to cover extra-wide wheels and tires. The flares can be molded in and painted to match the car, or left as is for a serious, functional appearance.

Replacing heavy stock body panels (fenders, hood, doors, trunk lid, etc.) with lightweight fiberglass components makes a great deal of sense, as reducing overall weight is more effective than adding horsepower. With less weight, your car will accelerate faster without additional horsepower; it will corner better, as there is less inertia that forces it to continue in a straight line when the front wheels are turned to negotiate a curve; and it will stop faster, since there is less momentum to force it to continue going forward when the power is cut off and the brakes are applied.

Fiberglass body components are also an ideal replacement for damaged or rusted steel body panels.

ACCESSORY SOURCES

Table 1 at the end of this chapter lists manufacturers and/or suppliers who offer a complete range of accessories (everything from the smallest add-on part to complete engines).

THE BASICS

These are the details that need attention before you get to the fun stuff. The main rule is start with a healthy car. Performance modification usually means brisk driving. A brief technical inspection will ensure that the car is up to it.

All bolts in the front and rear suspensions should be checked for looseness. This includes wheel lug nuts.

Front wheel bearings should be adjusted. If the maintenance schedule says it's near time to repack them, go ahead and do it.

Unless the car is nearly new, the front suspension should be checked for wear.

Table 2　CHASSIS HANDLING GUIDE*

Adjustment	To Increase Understeer	To Increase Oversteer
Front tire pressure	Lower	Higher
Rear tire pressure	Higher	Lower
Front tire section	Smaller	Larger
Rear tire section	Larger	Smaller
Front wheel camber	More positive	More negative
Rear wheel camber	More negative	More positive
Front springs	Stiffer	Softer
Rear springs	Softer	Stiffer
Front anti-sway bar	Thicker (stiffer)	Thinner (weaker)
Rear anti-sway bar	Thinner (weaker)	Thicker (stiffer)
Weight distribution	More forward	More rearward

*Courtesy Quickor Engineering, Beaverton, Ore.

Brakes should be carefully inspected. Check pad and lining wear, and look for damaged discs or drums. Make sure the brake pedal is firm. If in doubt, bleed the brakes or repair the hydraulic system.

CHASSIS MODIFICATIONS

The following chassis modifications will result in a noticeable improvement in handling. For the most part, items such as heavy-duty shock absorbers, sway bars, etc., are installed the same way as their stock counterparts (refer to the appropriate chapters in the main body of this manual for procedures).

Refer to **Table 2** for a chassis handling guide.

Wheels and Tires

This should be the first area you look at. Tires affect cornering, braking, rolling resistance, ride quality, and noise level. The right selection can make solid improvements in all these areas, at reasonable cost and with little effort. Inadequate tires will neutralize any improvement to suspension or brakes.

First, size up what you have. A set of good quality 70-series radials on 5 in. wheels is fine for most street applications. You can modify the suspension, then come back to the tires later if necessary.

If you decide to shop for tires, you'll need to know what the letters and numbers mean. On a tire designated "165SR-15," for example, the 165 is the width of the tire (cross section, not tread width) in millimeters. The S indicates the tire's ability to sustain a given high speed. No letter is lowest, S is higher, H is higher still, and V is highest. The R stands for radial. The 15 is the wheel diameter in inches.

Two of the most important characteristics of a tire are its coefficient of friction and slip angles. Coefficient of friction describes the ability of a tire to resist sliding when subjected to a force. The maximum force that a tire can sustain without sliding may be described as the "limit of adhesion" for that tire.

In order for a tire to be steered, i.e., maintain a desired course, it must be *rolling,* not sliding. A sliding tire has absolutely no directional discretion. It will slide sideways just as willingly as forward.

Friction is only important at the "limit of adhesion." Obviously, at that point it assumes overwhelming importance as the tire "breaks loose." But tire friction does not explain any of the handling characteristics of an automobile *below* the limit of adhesion of the tires.

To explain handling behavior such as understeer and oversteer, you must understand another important tire characteristic — slip angle.

A rolling tire normally follows a path in line with the direction of the tread. But if the tire is subjected to a side force, e.g., during cornering, the tire deflects and its patch diverges from the path in line with the tread. The tire actually

Figure 1

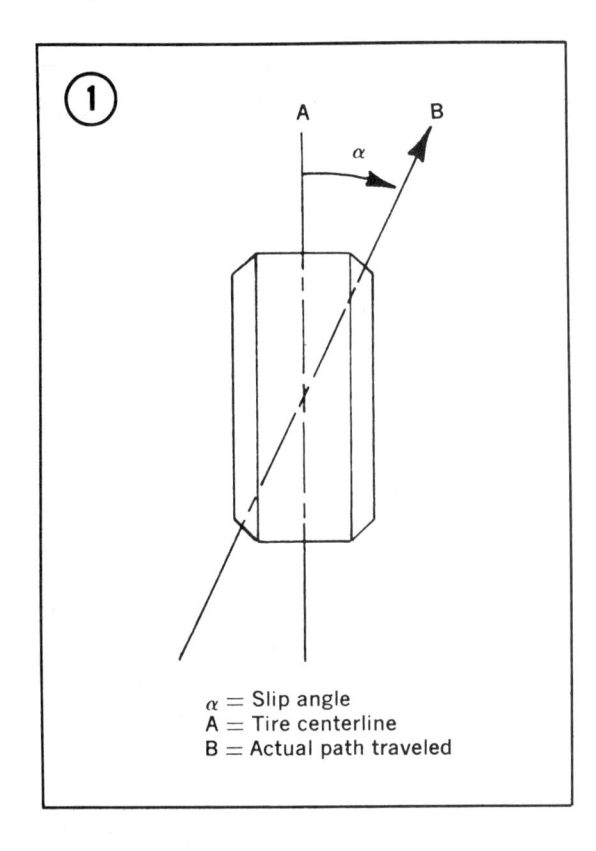

α = Slip angle
A = Tire centerline
B = Actual path traveled

travels in a direction at an angle to the direction that the tire points. This angle is called a "slip angle." See **Figure 1**.

Slip angle is one of those unfortunate, misleading terms that we are stuck with. It does not mean that the tire is sliding. The tire does not have to be anywhere near its limit of adhesion to operate at a slip angle. Slip angle causes the familiar effects of understeer, oversteer, and neutral steering.

Oversteer occurs when the slip angle at the rear tires changes more than at the front tires. This steers the car into a smaller circle than intended and increases centrifugal force. Increased centrifugal force in turn causes the tires to operate at even higher slip angles, making the car steer into an even smaller circle, and so on. It is truly a "vicious circle," which if allowed to continue will result in a spin-out, even in the hands of a skilled driver.

Understeer occurs when the slip angle at the front tires changes more than at the rear. The car steers into a larger circle than intended, reducing centrifugal force. This decreases the tire slip angle and further increases the circle, thereby decreasing centrifugal force, and so on. The car automatically seeks a turning circle which balances tire forces with no correction from the driver.

Understeer may seem more desirable than oversteer, but if the equilibrium turning circle is larger than the curvature of the road, the driver may helplessly watch his car head for the bushes.

Neutral steer means that slip angles change at the front and rear at the same rate. The vehicle path tends to follow the curvature of the road without a tendency to increase or decrease the turning circle.

Slip angle is not fixed for any tire. Factors that change it are centrifugal force, wind gusts, road plane (level, banked), wheel plane (camber, toe, deflection), and vertical forces (acceleration, braking, lateral weight transfers).

Since the slip angle at which a tire operates is constantly changing, there is no such thing as a "state of understeer," for example. A car which understeers under one set of circumstances may oversteer under another set. Neutral steer is simply the transition between oversteer and understeer; it is not a condition which can be set up and maintained by chassis tuning.

Several manufacturers produce excellent radial tires: Semperit, Veith, Michelin, Goodyear, Pirelli, and Goodrich. All offer good road holding (some better in the wet than others), reasonable ride comfort, and long tread life (a characteristic of all radial tires).

> NOTE: *Racing tires shouldn't be used on the street. They have very thin, easily damaged sidewalls. Racing tires meant for dry pavement are dangerously slippery on wet pavement. Those meant for wet pavement use super-soft rubber compounds which wear very quickly, and may overheat on dry pavement.*

With wider tires, you'll need wider wheels. Widened steel wheels are available, or you can have your own steel wheels widened by a specialty shop. The most popular accessory wheels are cast aluminum or magnesium "mags." Those shown in **Figure 2** are typical.

Three things must be considered when buying wheels: compatibility with tubeless tires, wheel width, and wheel offset.

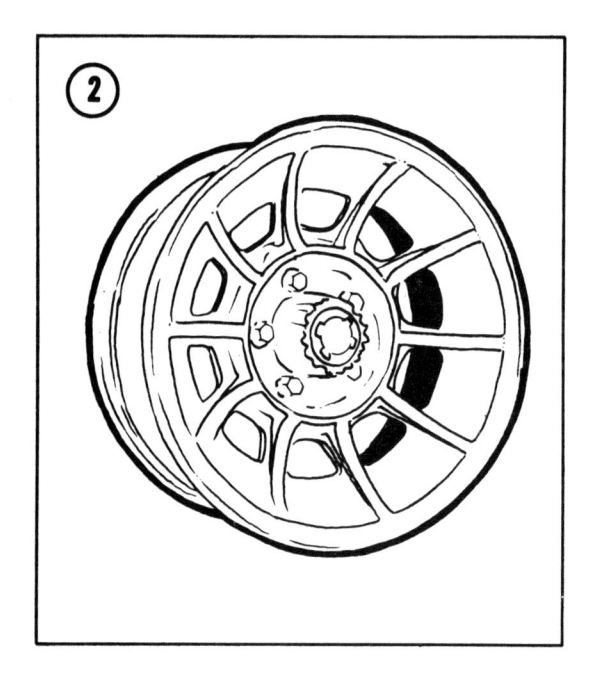

Some "mag" wheels require tube-type tires. If you're going to use tube-type tires anyway, this doesn't matter. Check before buying, though, to make sure your tires and wheels are compatible.

Wheel width should be proportional to the tire. As a rule of thumb, the wheel should be approximately two inches narrower than the tire's cross-section width. Once you've selected a specific brand of tire, the tire dealer can give you exact size recommendations.

Wheel offset (**Figure 3**) is the relationship of the wheel center to the wheel rim. Positive offset moves the wheel rim outward (the car's track is wider). Negative offset moves the wheel rim inward (the car's track is narrower). Too much negative offset can cause clearance problems between the tires and wheel wells. In front, the wheels may rub on the brake calipers or tie rod ends. Too much positive offset may cause the tires to rub on the fenders. Also, positive offset increases the strain on wheel bearings and hubs. If you use wheels with much positive offset, the wheel bearings should be checked frequently for wear.

The number of wheel manufacturers makes it impossible for us to list them all here, so you will have to do some of the detective work yourself and check through automotive magazines such as *Road & Track, Car & Driver,*

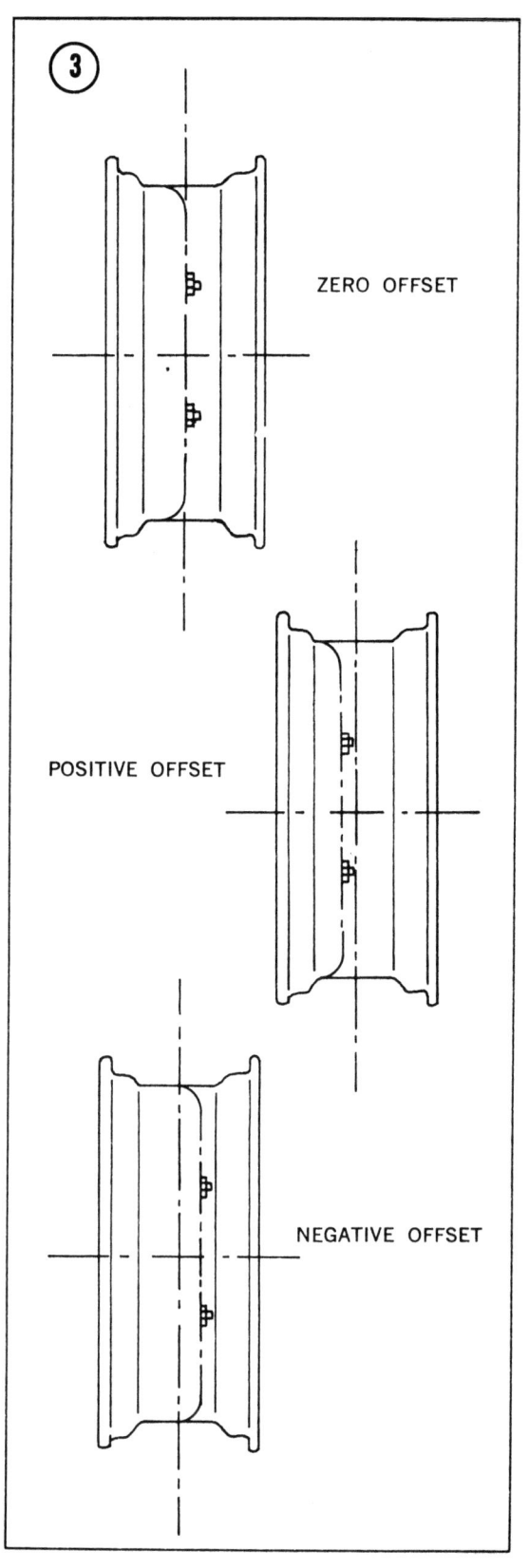

PERFORMANCE IMPROVEMENT

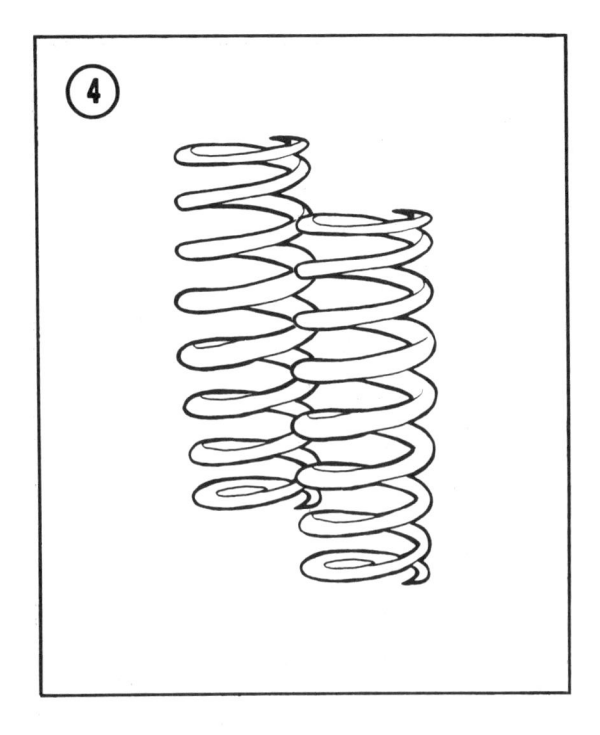

Autoweek, etc., and send for some of the catalogs from these wheel manufacturers.

> NOTE: *In addition to obtaining the catalogs offered by the various wheel manufacturers, you will find a wealth of information concerning tires and wheels in Auto World's Motorsports Catalog (refer to **Table 1** for their address).*

Once you've picked out a combination of wheels and tires, have a pair of them mounted and installed, one on the front and one on the rear. Check clearance with the suspension bottomed out, and with the front wheels at full left and full right lock.

If the tire dealer doesn't want to let you try a set before buying (and you don't feel like looking for another tire dealer), offer to pay the mounting charge if the tires don't fit. When you're spending hundreds of dollars to last thousands of miles, it's worth $10 or so to avoid a bad purchase.

CAUTION
Alloy wheels can easily be chipped or gouged during tire mounting, and some are more difficult to balance than steel wheels. Have mounting and balancing done by a shop experienced with alloy wheels.

Sway (Anti-roll) Bars

These bars reduce body roll during hard cornering, resulting in a flatter cornering attitude and better control and tire adhesion.

It is necessary to "balance" the car by carefully coordinating the diameter of the rear sway bar with that of the front one. A rear sway bar should definitely not be installed without using a front sway bar which has a larger than stock diameter.

Installation of sway bars is a simple nuts-and-bolts operation requiring a couple of hours of work. Kits generally come with installation instructions.

Front and Rear Springs

Heavy-duty springs are available for street, autocross, or race conditions (refer to **Figure 4**), and installation is straightforward. Refer to the procedures outlined in the proper chapter of the main body of this manual.

The addition of stiffer springs reduces "body wallow" in corners and generally keeps the car more stable on winding or undulating roads.

> NOTE: *Heavy-duty shocks must be used in conjunction with stiffer springs, as conventional shock absorbers cannot control the movements set up by stiffer springs.*

The installation of some high-performance coil springs will reduce the height of your car by an inch or more, so take this into consideration when buying wheels and tires.

Your local Saab dealer normally stocks these stiffer front and rear springs (front spring part No. 00 14 639; rear spring part No. 00 14 647).

Shock Absorbers

The installation of high-performance shock absorbers is an absolute necessity if you choose to install heavy-duty springs. Even if you keep the stock springs, it is a good idea to install high-performance shock absorbers, which control the road wheels much better than stock shock absorbers, due to their special valving and construction.

There are a number of popular shock absorbers available for high-performance cars:

Koni, Mulholland, Bilstein, KYB, and Boge seem to be the front-runners. All are excellent; the choice is simply a personal one which you must make. Refer to **Figures 5 and 6**.

Bilstein and Koni shock absorbers are routinely stocked by most of the accessory suppliers listed in **Table 1**. Your local Saab dealer carries them too (Bilstein front shock absorbers, part No. 00 14 530; rear shock absorbers, part No. 00 14 548; Koni front shock absorbers, part No. 02 20 061, rear shock absorbers, part No. 02 20 079).

If you have never driven a car equipped with high-performance shock absorbers of this quality, you will immediately appreciate the difference in handling.

Suspension Bushings

Stock suspension bushings are fairly soft, to give a smooth, quiet ride. However, their softness allows the suspension to flex, making control less precise. Harder bushings increase control, but may also roughen the ride and increase road noise.

Wheel Spacers

Wheel track can easily be widened by adding wheel spacers. Installation is easy: simply remove the wheels, slip the spacers over the wheel studs, and install the wheels again. Refer to **Figure 7**. Increasing the track makes the car more stable in corners, as it widens the car's stance.

Another use for wheel spacers is to gain additional brake caliper clearance when installing special alloy wheels.

> CAUTION
> *Spacers may keep the wheel nuts from threading all the way onto the studs. In this case, longer studs must be installed.*

Brake Linings

Several manufacturers offer excellent high-performance brake pads which can be installed in place of the stock brake pads. Repco pads seem to be the most popular, and they are widely available in auto parts stores. These pads offer more consistent control and less

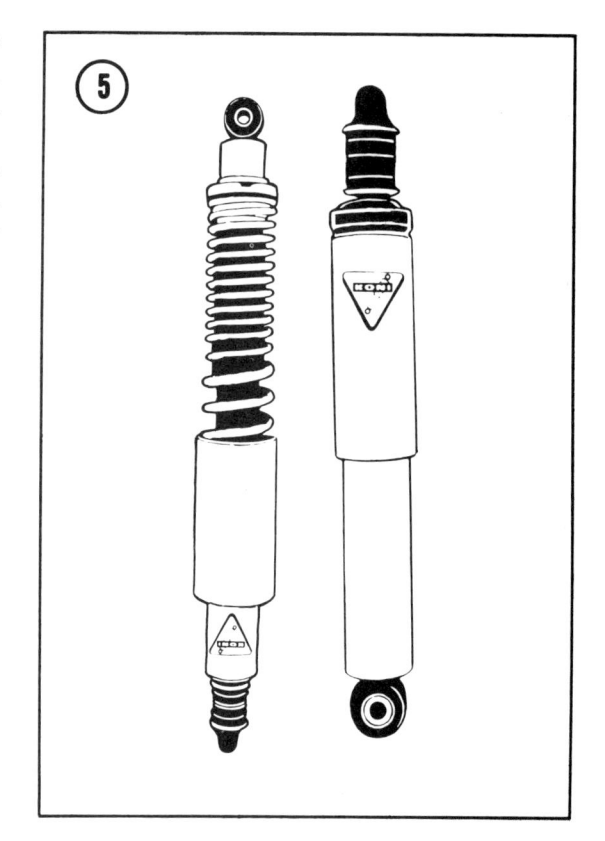

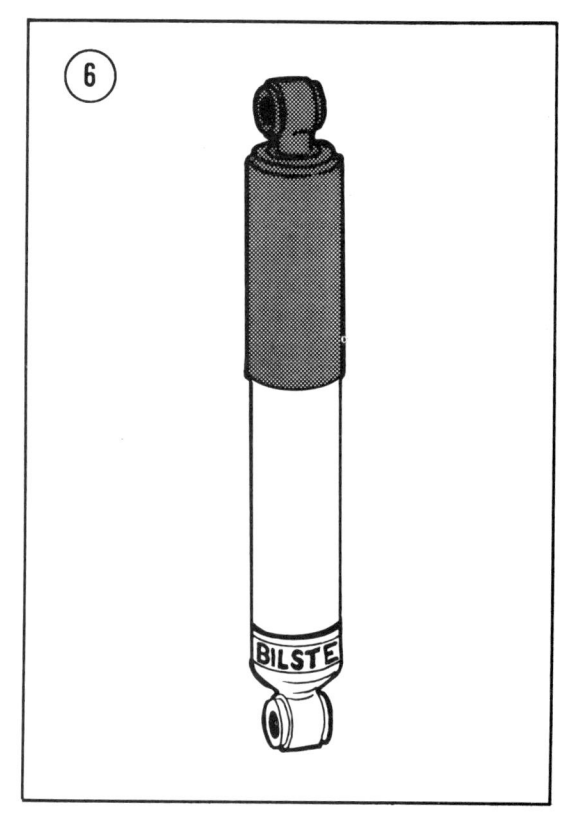

PERFORMANCE IMPROVEMENT

ENGINE MODIFICATIONS

Engine modifications should be carried out in logical sequence in order to extract the most benefit from each component. The recommended modifications are given in stages, starting with components which will increase efficiency and performance, as well as laying the groundwork for more extensive modifications.

STAGE I

Many stock engines suffer from a mediocre ignition system, restricted exhaust system, and a fuel system which "breathes" through a less-than-ideal air filtering system. The simple addition of an efficient header/exhaust system, a high-performance ignition coil, an electronic ignition system, and a more efficient air filter will bring a surprising increase in horsepower and make the engine start more easily, deliver better gas mileage, and (in the case of the ignition) need less maintenance than its stock counterpart.

Ignition Coil

Many manufacturers offer "hotter" ignition coils which are supposed to provide more voltage to your distributor (and therefore to your spark plugs). Some do, and some don't. Most of the reputable manufacturers (Accel, Mallory, Bosch, etc.) offer high-quality ignition coils that meet their claims. They are a simple nuts-and-bolts replacement item for your stock coil. Refer to **Figure 8**.

Your Saab dealer stocks (or can order) Saab Sport & Rally ignition coil and cable sets.

Electronic Ignition

There are also many manufacturers who offer electronic ignition systems such as Mallory, Permatune, Allison, Jacobs, Tiger, Piranha, etc. These units are easy to install and reasonably priced. High-performance coils are mandatory or recommended with some; others replace the coil altogether.

There are two basic types of electronic ignition. One type retains the points, but uses them only to carry a low-voltage trigger signal. This prolongs point life. The other type replaces the points with a photo-optical or magnetic trigger.

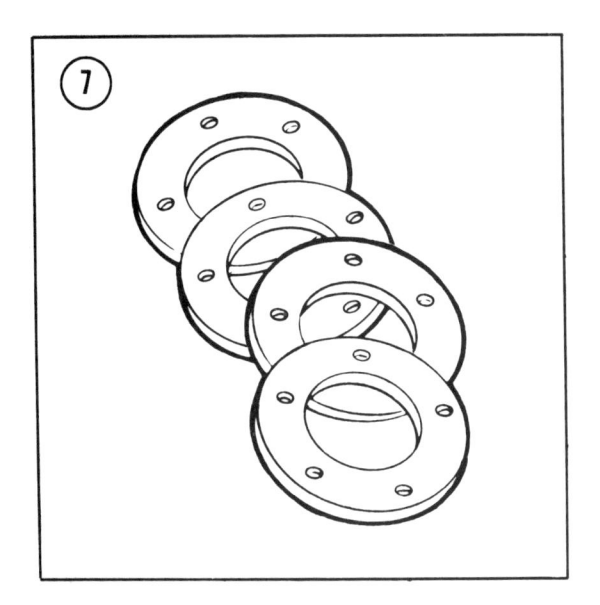

fading during heavy braking, less brake dust, and they do not squeal.

Your Saab dealer stocks competition brake pad kits, too. Ask for Front Brake Pad Kit No. 00 14 563, or Rear Brake Pad Kit No. 00 14 571.

WARNING
It is not recommended that competition brake pads be used for street use. These pads require considerable warming up before they become really efficient. When cold, they are actually less effective than stock brakes and require enormous pedal pressure to bring the car to a halt.

These highly accurate triggering systems provide stable ignition timing, and eliminate point bounce at high rpm.

All of the systems provide a longer lasting, higher voltage spark. This allows easier starting and may increase horsepower and gas mileage. It also ensures that the spark plugs will fire at high rpm. See **Figure 9**.

In addition to the many accessory manufacturers, your Saab dealer stocks (or can order) a Saab Sport & Rally electronic ignition (part No. 02 20 123).

Spark Plugs and Spark Plug Wires

A modified engine usually requires plugs just slightly colder than stock.

Spark plugs are designed to work within a specific heat range. Below 1,000°F (550°C), carbon deposits do not burn off the tip and may form a conducting track which short circuits the plug. Above 1,550°F (850°C), the plug tip gets so hot it can pre-ignite the mixture like a glow plug. The spark plug operates best when center electrode is 1,300-1,400°F (700-750°C).

Modified engines usually run hotter and require a "cold" plug that can dissipate heat rapidly. This prevents the center electrode from running hotter than desired. The center electrode and insulating core are made short so that there is a short heat conduction path to the metal body and the comparatively cool cylinder head. Refer to **Figure 10**.

A cold-running engine requires a hot plug that does not quickly dissipate the heat. Thus, the central electrode stays hotter. Otherwise, the central electrode temperature would drop below the desired range. The central electrode is made long so that the heat conduction path is long. Refer to **Figure 10**.

Most plug manufacturers use a number to indicate heat range. Champion uses higher numbers to indicate a higher heat range. For example, an N9 plug is hotter than an N5. Bosch and NGK use lower numbers for higher heat ranges. For example, a Bosch W95T2 plug is hotter than a W125T2. An NGK BP6ES is hotter than a BP7ES.

It is a good idea to replace your stock spark plug wires with high-energy capacity, high-performance spark plug wires such as the Thunder-

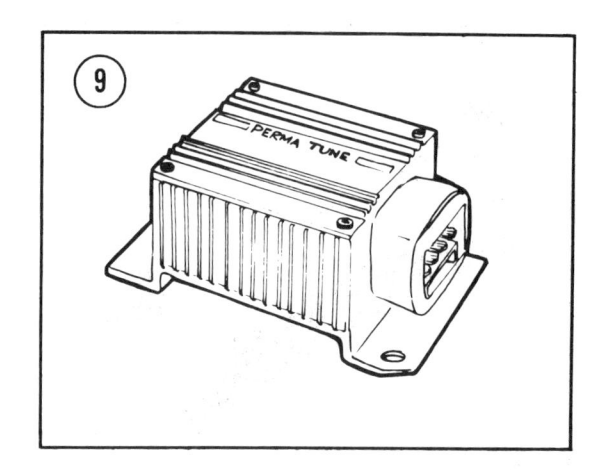

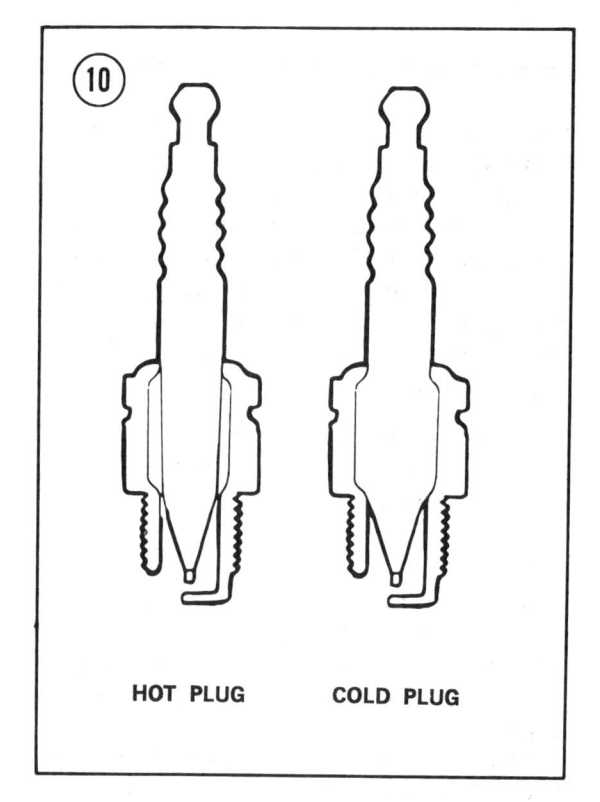

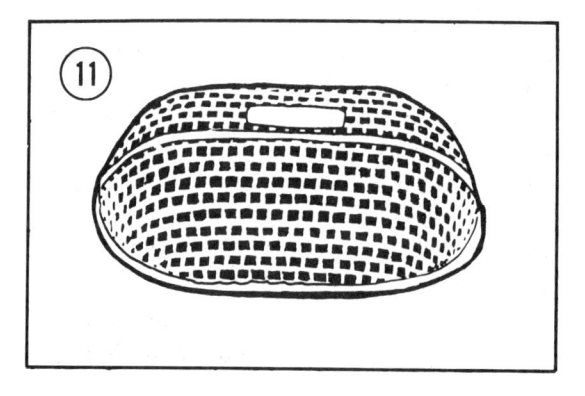

PERFORMANCE IMPROVEMENT

⑫

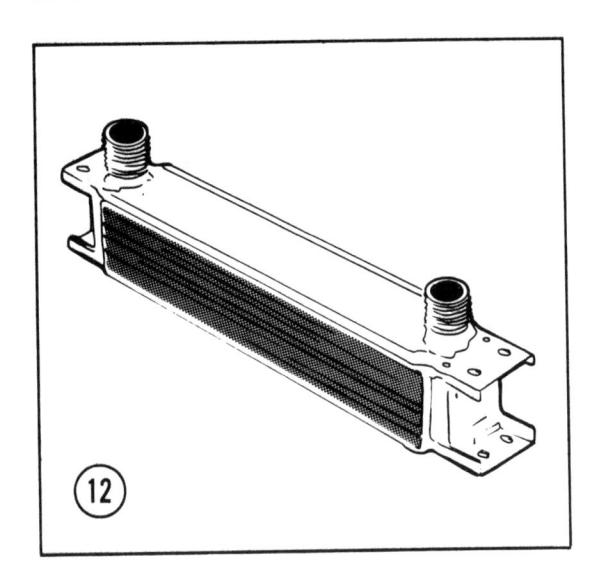

volt "Fire Wire" offered by Auto World (see **Table 1**). This metallic wire is made up of 19 strands of silver-plated copper (finished size is 16 ga., 7mm in diameter), and covered with special silicone rubber that is immune to ozone, corona, moisture, corrosion, cracking, and hardening. The rubber is self-extinguishing and resists extreme heat and cold (+600°F to −100°F) with a temperature rating of 550°F.

> NOTE: *Metallic plug wires create radio interference, so you may have to use noise suppressors with them.*

Exhaust System

Replacing the stock exhaust system with an efficient header and complete free-flow exhaust system can improve the performance of a stock engine, and is necessary for a highly modified engine.

"Back pressure" (the accumulation of exhaust gas in the exhaust system which has not found its way out of the engine from the previous exhaust stroke at the time that the intake stroke takes place) can rob an engine of 15-20% of its horsepower. By simply providing a smooth, uninterrupted path for this exhaust gas to be expelled from the engine, the maximum fresh charge of air and fuel can be drawn into the cylinders, providing all of the horsepower that your engine was designed for.

> NOTE: *The addition of a more efficient exhaust system is occasionally against the law, due to Federal smog regulations. Check the laws in your state to see if they apply.*

Header quality can vary widely from one manufacturer to another. Before buying, note whether the mounting surface is flat and smooth. If not, it must be surface ground to prevent exhaust leaks. Make sure welds are strong, even, and gas-tight. Poor fit is a common problem, so some drilling and filing may be necessary.

A Saab Sport & Rally exhaust system is available from your Saab dealer (on special order from Sweden), which gives a 6-8 hp increase on a 2-liter carburetted engine; 8-10 hp on a 2-liter fuel injected engine. Check with him regarding price, availability, and waiting time.

Air Cleaners

Replacing the standard air cleaner with a more efficient unit is a simple operation. It improves the appearance of the engine compartment, and permits the engine to breathe better. Approximately 2-3 horsepower can be gained from the installation of this simple accessory, and it is virtually "free" horsepower, as it is obtained without adding any strain to your engine. Refer to **Figure 11**.

STAGE II

Stage II modifications include all Stage I modifications, plus the addition of an oil cooler; baffled, high-capacity oil sump; lightweight flywheel; and heavy-duty clutch.

Oil Cooler

In the interests of making your engine live as long as possible while putting out all of the horsepower you require, it is a good idea to install an engine oil cooler.

Accessory oil coolers built especially for your car are available from some of the manufacturers listed in **Table 1**, or you can install one of the universal accessory oil coolers, as illustrated in **Figure 12**. These bolt-on, multi-finned alloy coolers keep the oil from reaching extreme temperatures which can eventually destroy an engine. There are many sizes and configurations to choose from.

Oil Sump

The installation of a baffled, high-capacity oil sump only takes a few minutes (it is installed the same way as a stock one), and it is a worthwhile addition to your engine because of the extra margin of safety it provides. The baffles and extra oil capacity prevent oil starvation during hard cornering or acceleration. (Oil starvation can occur even when negotiating a freeway on-ramp; it is a result of oil sloshing to one side of the oil sump, away from the oil pump pickup.) This extra safety is vital for any car driven "enthusiastically" as oil starvation can destroy an engine very quickly.

Contrary to what many say, added oil capacity will not reduce oil temperatures. It may take longer to heat the larger quantity of oil, but eventually it will get just as hot.

Finned oil sumps do not significantly reduce oil temperatures. The oil at the bottom of the sump is cooled, but this increases its viscosity and it remains there instead of circulating through the engine. In addition, the cooler oil in the bottom insulates the oil above it so that no further cooling occurs.

Finned oil sumps are even less effective in lowering oil temperatures if they are polished or chromed. Sandblasting, black anodizing, or painting with flat black paint will improve their heat radiating capability.

Flywheel

Replacing the stock, heavy flywheel with a lightweight one will result in an immediate gain in acceleration. The engine reaches its maximum rpm much faster due to the reduction of flywheel mass. Also, the engine returns to idle very quickly when you let up on the gas, as there is no heavy flywheel that wants to keep on rotating.

These high-performance flywheels are also dynamically balanced to reduce vibration at high speed.

Competition flywheels are not suited for street use. In addition to smoothing out the engine's power pulses, a flywheel's weight provides momentum to keep the engine turning when the clutch is engaged. With a super-light racing flywheel, very high engine speeds are necessary to move away from a stop. In many cases, it is necessary to rev the engine to several thousand rpm and pop the clutch.

Clutch

Most stock clutches are not capable of handling increased horsepower without slipping. Before you really dig into the engine's internal parts (as in Stage III), it is wise to replace the stock clutch with a heavy-duty, balanced one. If you have also installed an aftermarket flywheel, make sure the flywheel and clutch are compatible.

STAGE III

The modifications which you have performed in Stages I and II provide a healthy, quicker-than-stock engine which is still very much understressed. Quite likely you can stop at this point, unless you really have a need for additional horsepower, since an engine modified to Stage II specifications, used with the suspension modifications outlined earlier, will get your car over the road with admirable quickness and ease.

Stage III involves the engine's internal parts, and this is where you start paying a lot to get a lot. There is a whole range of possibilities in this stage, from a simple camshaft change to an all-out performance rebuild. This involves replacing the camshaft, cylinder head, pistons, connecting rods, crankshaft, bearings, and carburetion setup with high-performance parts.

> NOTE: *Engine modifications, as mentioned earlier, are sometimes in conflict with Federal and/or State emission laws. Check with your local authorities before performing any of these modifications.*

Camshafts

A camshaft modified for street or autocross use opens the valves earlier and farther than a stock camshaft, and closes them later. This allows more fuel and air to enter the cylinder, and allows more exhaust gas to clear the cylinder.

Mild-performance camshafts improve power and throttle response over a broad rpm range.

PERFORMANCE IMPROVEMENT

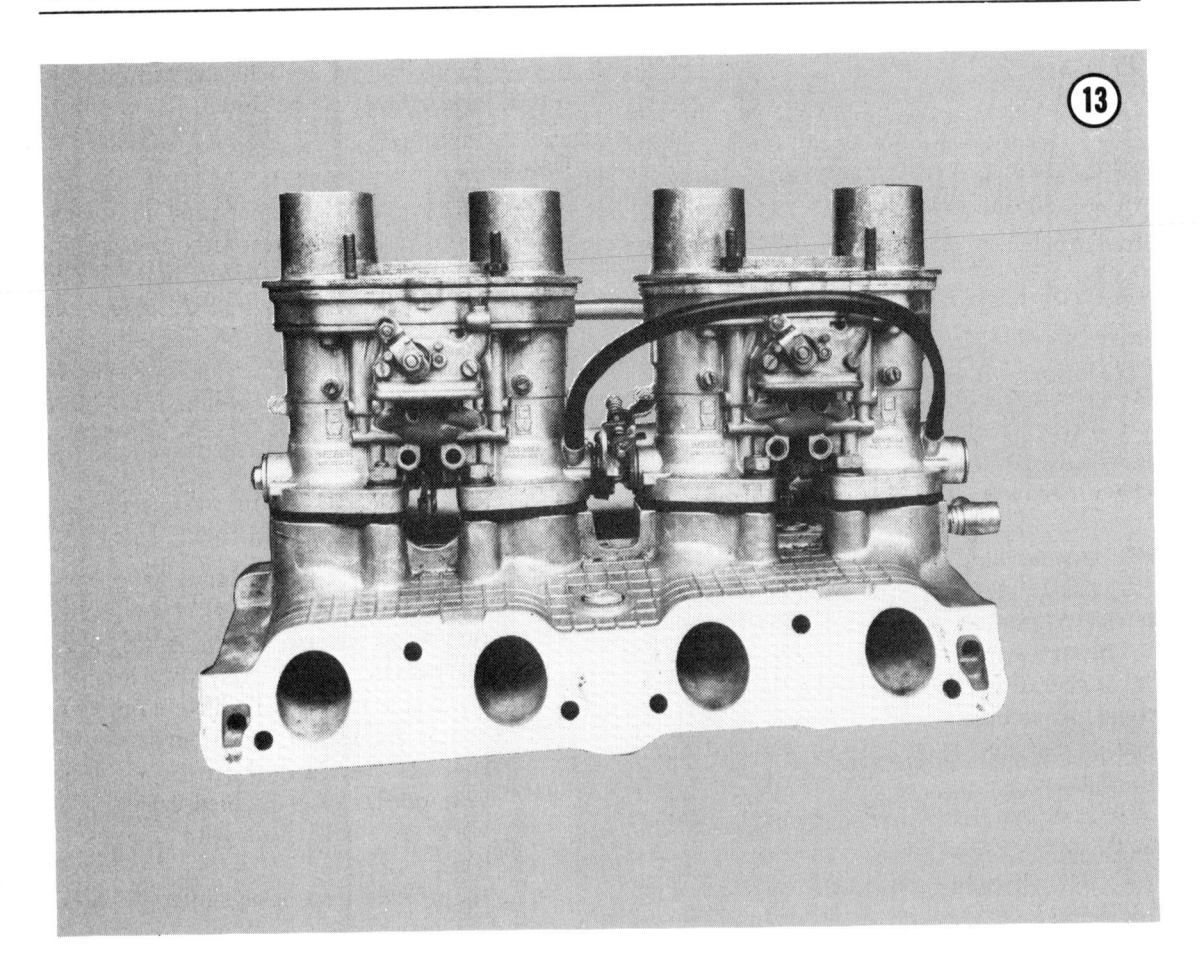

As the grind becomes more radical, the power band narrows and the idle becomes rough.

With a mild grind, heavy valve springs are usually the only modification required. With more radical grinds, improved carburetion and increased compression may be necessary to get the most out of the camshaft.

Steel camshafts offer the greatest resistance to wear. If you buy a cast iron camshaft, make sure it has been hardened.

Carburetion

Weber carburetors are the overwhelming choice of most engine modifiers. These Webers are usually mounted on the individual manufacturer's polished and ported alloy intake manifold and come complete with all linkage and instructions. Refer to **Figure 13**.

The purpose of installing one or more larger carburetors on an efficient intake manifold is to let the engine "breathe" deeper (take in a denser fuel/air mixture) than the stock carburetion system allows.

With their removable jets and venturis, Webers can be set up for any engine, from stock to full race. Each manufacturer or supplier of these carburetion systems has his own pet camshaft/carburetion combinations for street or autocross use. Follow their recommendations (racing setups seldom work satisfactorily on the street).

Cylinder Head

Special cylinder heads increase horsepower due to their larger intake and exhaust valves, polished and ported intake and exhaust ports, and "cc'ed" and polished combustion chambers. They may also be milled for higher compression.

> NOTE: *"Cc'ed" means that the combustion chambers have been contoured so that each one has exactly the same*

capacity. This is done so that the shape of each combustion chamber is as close to identical as possible, which will result in increased horsepower.

"Porting and polishing" means that the intake and exhaust ports have been carefully enlarged, followed by careful matching and polishing of the junction points where the intake and exhaust manifolds meet the cylinder head. This is done so that there are as few restrictions to the incoming fuel charge and outgoing exhaust gas as possible. This operation should be done by a professional.

"Milling the head" means metal has been ground from the head's block mating surface. This makes the combustion chambers smaller and increases compression. It also brings the valves closer to the block and pistons, so these parts may have to be notched to keep the valves from hitting them.

You can buy heads already modified, or have your own head reworked by a specialty shop.

Valves tend to "float" off their seats at high engine rpm, because stock valve springs are not strong enough to snap the valves back down onto their valve seats completely before the rotating camshaft lobes start to push them back up to open them again on the next cycle. This steals horsepower, as the cylinder is not completely sealed during its power stroke. Replace the stock valve springs with heavy-duty valve springs. These stiffer springs seat the valves immediately, even at high rpm.

The use of oversize valves in any cylinder head (even a stock one reworked to accept these valves), will result in more horsepower.

Pistons

Replace the stock pistons with lightweight, balanced, forged aluminum pistons to reduce rotating weight. This will increase engine rpm and result in more horsepower. In addition, these pistons are stronger than stock ones.

Performance pistons often raise the compression ratio. This is a good way to gain horsepower, but it shouldn't be carried to extremes. With a ratio higher than about 10:1, it may be difficult to find gas with a high enough octane rating to prevent detonation (pinging). Detonation creates extreme heat that can burn valves and melt holes right through piston crowns.

Oversize pistons must be used when the cylinders are bored to a larger diameter than stock. This is done when the cylinders are worn to a point where engine performance is affected. It is also done to increase the cubic displacement of the engine to produce more horsepower.

Your Saab dealer carries (or can order) 91mm cast aluminum piston/connecting rod assemblies (part No. 00 15 099).

Connecting Rods

It helps to replace the stock connecting rods with lightweight, polished, and balanced connecting rods at the same time that you install the high-performance pistons mentioned previously. The weight reduction and precise balancing increase engine rpm and lengthen engine life.

Your Saab dealer carries (or can order) Sport & Rally 91mm cast aluminum piston/connecting rod assemblies (part No. 00 15 099).

Crankshaft

Replace the stock crankshaft with a precision ground, polished, lightened, and balanced high-performance crankshaft. As with the connecting rods and pistons mentioned previously, higher engine rpm and extra strength will result.

> NOTE: *The stock crankshaft assembly (crank, bearings, connecting rods, and pistons) can be polished, shot peened (for additional strength), and balanced if you cannot afford to purchase the more expensive high-performance components mentioned earlier. Check the Yellow Pages of your telephone directory for a shop near you which specializes in engine balancing. Be sure to inspect and measure all dimensions with a micrometer and make any repairs necessary prior to balancing.*

Bearings

Heavy-duty main and connecting rod bearings should be used whenever the engine is

PERFORMANCE IMPROVEMENT

modified for more performance. Vandervell bearings are widely used in high-performance engines, and are available in most auto parts stores, or from the mail order outlets listed in **Table 1**.

TURBOCHARGING

The easiest way to obtain a significant increase in horsepower is by turbocharging your engine. Turbocharging can be used as an alternative to Stage III, as outlined in the previous section, or in conjunction with Stage III modifications, providing that the compression ratio is kept down to that recommended by the individual turbocharger manufacturers for their kits. (High-compression ratios are not compatible with turbocharging for street use.)

> NOTE: *It is advisable to discuss any engine modifications which you have already made (or would like to make) with the turbocharger manufacturer prior to purchasing and installing the turbocharger kit.*

Turbocharging Theory

Special high-lift cams, multiple carburetors such as the big Webers outlined in Stage III, high-compression heads, and tuned exhaust systems can't compare to simply forcing more air/fuel mixture into the cylinders with a properly designed turbocharger system. Furthermore, if properly maintained, a turbocharged engine seems to live approximately as long as a normally aspirated one.

Anyone reading this chapter is probably familiar with the basic operation of a naturally-aspirated, 4-cycle, spark-ignition engine. On the intake stroke, the descending piston draws an air/fuel charge through the intake valve. Theoretically, the volume of the incoming air/fuel charge should equal the volume of the cylinder at full throttle. In fact, this is impossible to achieve. The incoming charge volume is less than the cylinder volume. The reasons are:

a. Small, but unavoidable pressure drop through the fuel induction system
b. Restrictions in intake manifold ports and valves
c. Incomplete exhaust of burned gases from previous cycle
d. Exhaust valve and exhaust manifold port restrictions

The ratio between induced air/fuel volume (at 60°F and 14.7 psi) and calculated cylinder volume (piston area x stroke) is usually expressed as a percentage and is called "volumetric efficiency." If the induced charge equals the cylinder volume, the volumetric efficiency is 100%; most engines have a volumetric efficiency of about 80%.

In order to increase power from an engine, all we have to do is get more air/fuel charge into the cylinder. One method is to design very low restriction intake and exhaust systems. This explains how some exotic racing engines with tuned intake and exhaust systems achieve nearly 100% volumetric efficiency over a very narrow speed range. However, they are not nearly flexible enough for everyday street driving.

Another method is to force the air/fuel charge into the combustion chamber under pressure, using a compressor. This will force more charge into an engine than is possible with low restriction and tuned intake/exhaust systems, and it will do it over a much broader speed range. This is how a turbocharger works. See **Figure 14**.

A turbocharger consists of a turbine wheel and a compressor wheel. See **Figure 15**. Exhaust gases from the engine drive the turbine wheel at speeds of up to 120,000 rpm. The compressor wheel, in turn, pumps a tremendous volume of air to the engine, under pressure. The turbocharger sucks through the standard fuel intake system, although some turbocharger kit manufacturers offer a Weber carburetor as an option, which increases the efficiency still more. The compressor is sealed to ensure that the oil is not drawn into the intake system from the turbocharger lubrication system.

Turbocharger Installation

Most turbocharger kits come with complete instructions. Installation time depends upon your own mechanical skill, but an average time is approximately 12 hours, depending on your

CHAPTER THIRTEEN

⑭

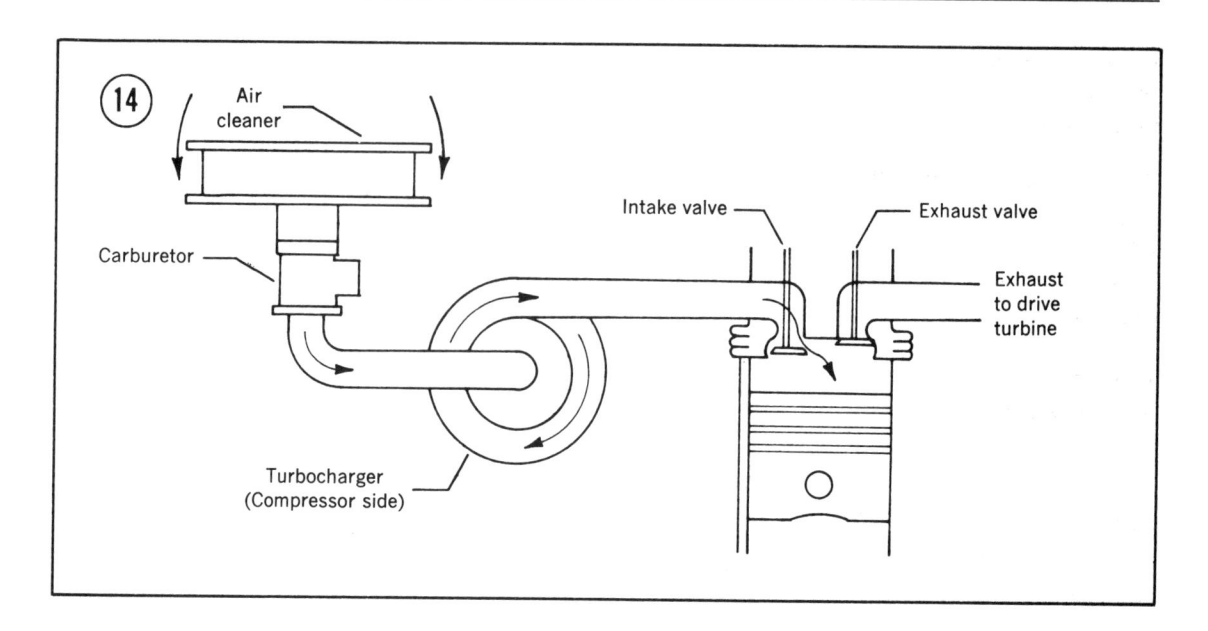

Air cleaner

Carburetor

Turbocharger (Compressor side)

Intake valve

Exhaust valve

Exhaust to drive turbine

⑮

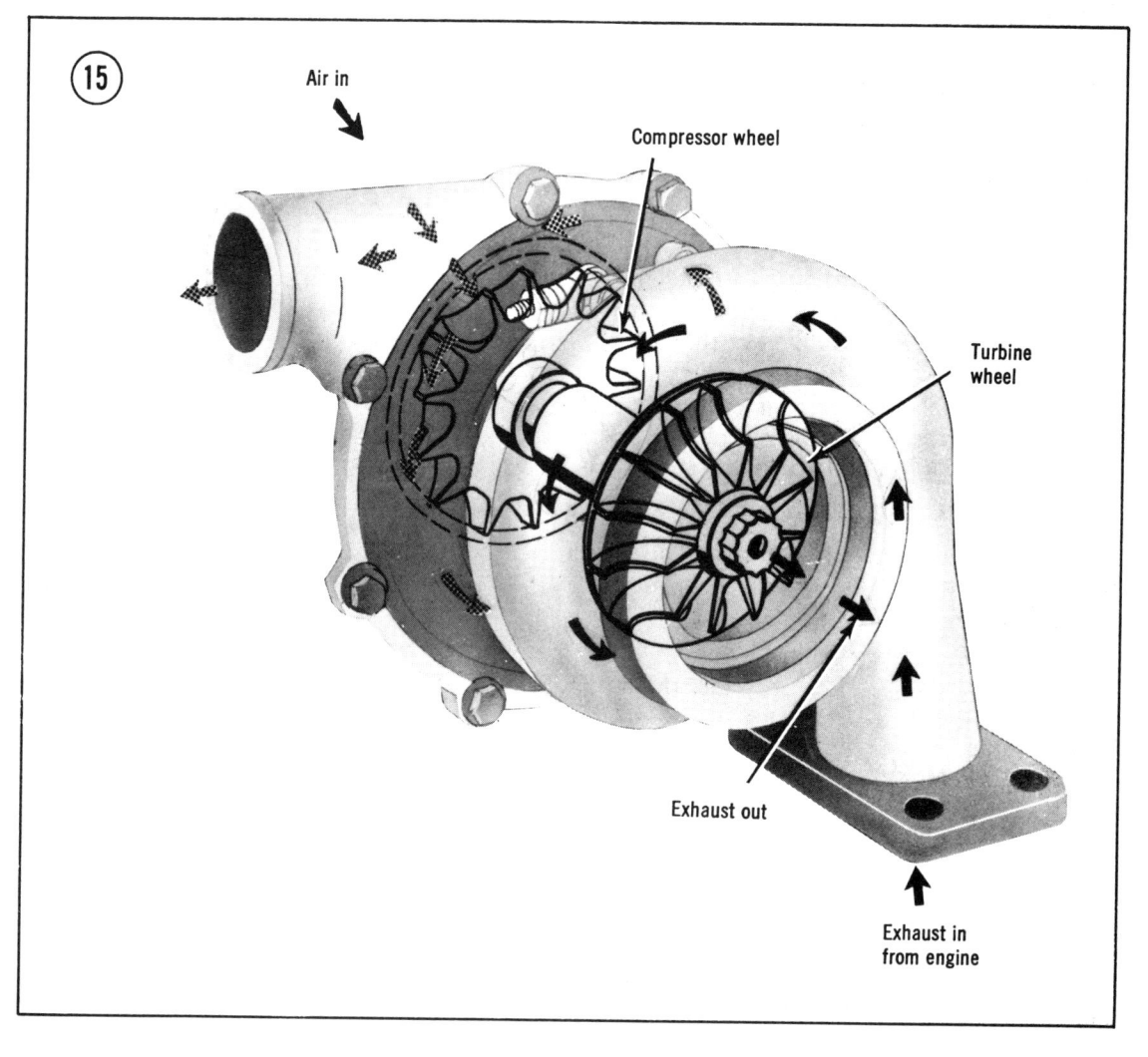

Air in

Compressor wheel

Turbine wheel

Exhaust out

Exhaust in from engine

PERFORMANCE IMPROVEMENT

working conditions and tool collection (although no special tools are required other than normal mechanic's tools).

Turbocharger Maintenance

The main maintenance item consists simply of changing the oil every 3,000 miles, in order to provide the turbocharger with a clean supply of lubricant.

Fuels Recommended For Turbocharger Operation

Catalytic converter-equipped cars must use unleaded gasoline; non-catalytic converter-equipped cars must use premium fuel.

> NOTE: *Always use the highest octane fuel that you can buy.*

Turbocharger Performance

At low rpm, the turbocharger is hardly a factor in engine performance — this is one of the main advantages of this efficient, power-producing unit; when you don't need it, it literally "loafs"; when you do need it, stand on the throttle and watch what happens. The turbo boost comes on at medium rpm and steadily increases to its maximum boost. The power is delivered smoothly, since the turbo just starts pumping air in increased volume as the exhaust gases flow faster. The "turbo-lag" that you hear so much about has been reduced to a minimum and presents very little problem.

DRIVE TRAIN

With the suspension system firmed up and the engine putting out an abundance of horsepower, the object now is to deliver all of this horsepower to the ground in an efficient manner.

Transmission

Careful matching of transmission gears and final drive ratio with your engine's power curve will result in a car that is smooth and powerful. Refer to **Table 1** for availability, and check with supplier for their gear ratio recommendations.

Close ratio gear sets are available from your Saab dealer (on special order from Sweden). The complete set is part No. 00 15 354.

Ring and Pinion Gears

The final drive ratio determines the top speed and acceleration times. A lower gear ratio (higher numerically) provides faster acceleration and a lower top speed (and also results in the engine turning more rpm's at any given road speed than a higher final drive gear ratio). A higher gear ratio (lower numerically) provides a bit less acceleration, but higher top speed, and at 55 mph, for instance, the engine will be turning over several hundred rpm less than a car equipped with a lower final drive gear ratio.

A 6:31 final drive ratio set is available from your Saab dealer (on special order from Sweden). Ask for part No. 00 15 362. This set is constructed of high quality steel alloy.

Limited Slip Differential

A limited slip differential allows both front wheels to apply power to the ground evenly under all conditions. When one wheel spins on wet pavement on a car not equipped with a limited slip differential, the remaining wheel receives no torque from the engine at all, as all power is diverted to the wheel that is spinning uselessly.

A limited slip differential is an absolute necessity, especially when the driven wheels have the job of trying to transfer to the ground the considerable power that your modified engine is transmitting to them.

Your Saab dealer can order a Saab limited slip differential for you from Sweden (part No. 00 15 552).

BODY MODIFICATIONS

The final step in modifying your car is the replacement of the standard, heavy body panels with lightweight fiberglass units; and the addition of aerodynamic devices called spoilers and air dams.

Spoilers

The prime objective of a front spoiler is to keep air from flowing under the car, which has a tendency to lift the car at high speeds. The spoiler directs the air up over the hood, creating a high pressure area at that point which actually

CHAPTER THIRTEEN

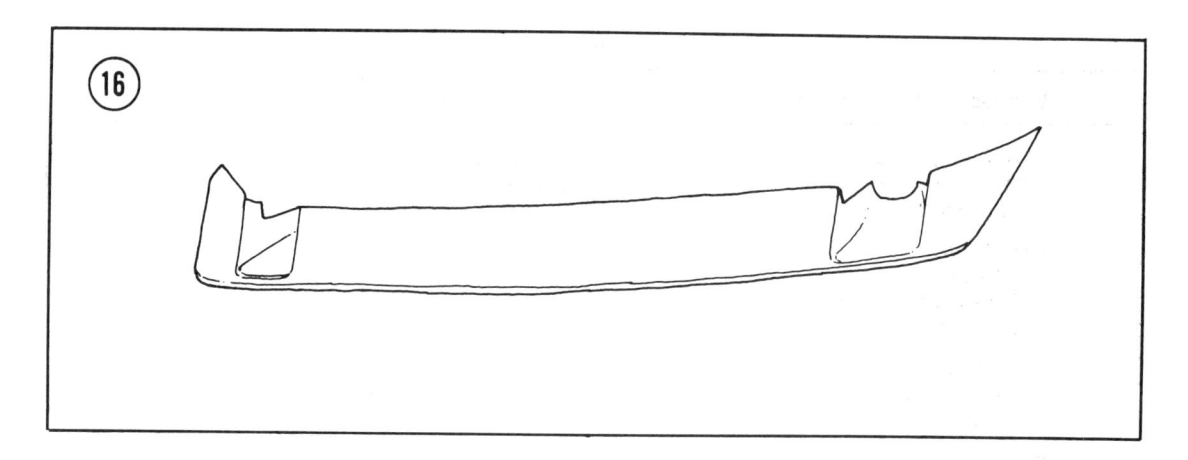

(16)

creates downforce on the front wheels. This device works very well at higher speeds; at low speeds the effect is somewhat lessened, but still worthwhile. Some spoilers are equipped with ducts that route cooling air to the front brakes. See **Figure 16**.

An air dam's purpose is also to keep air from flowing under the car, thus creating a low pressure area beneath the car, which in turn increases greater downforce on the car due to the normal air pressure on top of the car. The air dam is more effective than a conventional spoiler at low speeds, because its effectiveness is not dependent on its ability to push air up and over the hood to create a downforce (which only occurs at fairly high speeds).

Strangely enough, even though the air dam adds to the car's frontal area, the overall drag is actually reduced due to the fact that the car's irregularly-shaped chassis no longer catches the wind as it did prior to installing the air dam. Therefore, air drag under the chassis is greatly reduced.

A rear spoiler's job is to smooth out the turbulent air which follows in the wake of the car. This improves the air flow and lessens drag.

A front spoiler is available from your Saab dealer. Ask for part No. 00 16 444 (Saab 99 models) or 00 21 196 (Saab 95 and 96 models). A rear spoiler is also available (Saab part No. 00 16 451, for 3- and 5-door models).

IN CONCLUSION

The components illustrated in this chapter, if properly selected and installed, will result in a far safer, more enjoyable, better handling, and far quicker car than the one you purchased in stock form.

As indicated previously, due to the very large variety of components available, it has been impossible to list, in detail, all of the variations and specifications for each item. Rather, we have tried to show you generally what is available, what the accessory is designed to do, and when it should be used.

PERFORMANCE IMPROVEMENT

Table 1   ACCESSORY SOURCES

Manufacturer/Supplier	Accessories Offered
ADDCO Industries 701 Watertower Rd. Lake Park, Fla. 33403	Sway bar kits (Catalog free)
ANSA Mufflers Corp. P.O. Box 1288 Fitzgerald, Ga. 31750 (912) 423-9302	Ansa exhaust systems
Auto World, Inc. 701 N. Keyser Ave. Scranton, Pa. 18508	Full range of accessories (Turbocharger catalog, $1.00; Motorsports catalog, $1.00)
BAE 3032 Kashiwa St. Torrance, Calif. 90505 (213) 530-4743	Turbocharger kits (Catalog, $2.00)
Bilstein Corp. of American 11760 Sorrento Valley Rd. San Diego, Calif. 92121	Bilstein shock absorbers (Catalog, $2.00)
The Book 3400 E. 42nd St. Minneapolis, Min. 55406 (612) 729-7779	Full range of accessories (Catalog, $2.00)
Cannon Induction Systems 2741 Toledo St. Torrance, Calif. 90503 (213) 328-3060	Weber carburetion systems (Catalog, $1.00)
CCL Enterprises 24 Ledin Dr. Avon, Mass. 02322	Supersprint exhaust systems (Catalog free)
Crown Mfg. Co., Inc. 858 Production Pl. Newport Beach, Calif. 92663	Turbocharger kits (Catalog, $1.00)
Earl's Supply Co. P.O. Box 265 Lawndale, Calif. 90260 (213) 679-1438	High-performance hardware and fittings (Catalog, $2.00)
KAMEI U.S.A., Inc. 5213 W. Broadway Minneapolis, Minn. 55429 (612) 535-5600	Spoilers, air dams, etc. (Catalog free)
Kensington Products Corp. 150 Green St. Hackensack, N.J. 07601	Koni shock absorbers
KYB Corporation of American 207 Eisenhower Lane South Lombard, Ill. 60148	KYB shock absorbers
PAECO Catalog 213 S. 21st St. Birmingham, Ala. 35233	Full range of accessories (Catalog free)

(continued)

Table 1   ACCESSORY SOURCES (continued)

Manufacturer/Supplier	Accessories Offered
Parts & Polish 12952 W. Washington Pl. Los Angeles, Calif. 90066 (213) 391-8206	Full range of accessories (Catalog, $1.00)
Quickor Engineering 6710 S.W. 111th Beaverton, Ore. 97005 (503) 646-9696	Sway bars and springs (Catalog, free)
Race Quip 4760 Hayden Run Rd. Amlin, Ohio 43002 (614) 889-9527	Full range of accessories (Catalog, $1.00)
Saab Dealers (Nationwide)	Bilstein and Koni shock absorbers; front and rear spoilers; transistor ignition, ignition coil and cable set; 91mm cast pistons; brake differential; swinging arms; light alloy 5 in. wheels; modified rear engine support; engine and fuel tank guard plates; roll bar; modified gear ratio sets; modified final drive gears; heavy front and rear coil springs; heavy duty brake pads; limited slip differentials; free-flow exhaust system. (Some of these items must be special ordered from Sweden through your local Saab dealer; some are stocked in the U.S.)
Stebro 10 Leach St. Massena, N.Y. 13662	Stebro exhaust systems
Time Machines, Inc. 13 Neptune Ave. Brooklyn, N.Y. 11235 (212) 743-8874	Full range of accessories (Catalog free)
Turbo Systems 12954 Washington Blvd. Los Angeles, Calif. 90066 (213) 391-8701	Turbocharger kits (Catalog, $1.00)
WREP Industries, Ltd. 2965 Landwehr Rd. Northbrook, Ill. 60062 (312) 498-0670	Full range of accessories (Catalog, $2.00)

SUPPLEMENT

1977 AND LATER SERVICE INFORMATION

> The Saab 99 has changed little during the period of time covered by this supplement. Saab continues its tradition of evolution, rather than revolution, a tradition which contributes to this car's excellent reputation for reliability, economy, and high resale value.
>
> Except for the pertinent information given in this supplement, all information given in the various chapters in the front of this book apply to 1977-1979 models as well.

CHAPTER TWO

LUBRICATION, MAINTENANCE, AND TUNE-UP

To ensure good performance, dependability, and safety, regular preventive maintenance and periodic lubrication is necessary. This plus a thorough tune-up at the recommended intervals will keep your Saab in top operating condition.

PREVENTIVE MAINTENANCE

Scheduled checks and maintenance keep a car running smoothly. Refer to Chapter Two in the front of this book and carry out the maintenance procedures in the same sequence for best results, referring to **Table 1** in this supplemental chapter for the appropriate lubricant and time interval recommendations.

ENGINE TUNE-UP

The purpose of an engine tune-up is to restore power and performance lost over a gradual period of time due to normal wear.

Because of Federal laws limiting the exhaust emissions, it is important that the engine tune-up be done accurately, using the specifications listed in **Table 2** in this supplemental chapter.

Economical, trouble-free operation can be assured if a complete tune-up is performed every 15,000 miles.

Tune-ups consist of three general categories: compression, ignition, and carburetion. Carburetion adjustments should not be attempted until the compression and ignition phases have been completed.

Refer to Chapter Two in the front of this book and carry out the tune-up in the same sequence for best results, referring to **Table 2** in this supplemental chapter for the appropriate late-model specifications.

Ignition Timing

Effective with the 1978 Saab models, a breakerless ignition is standard equipment. No maintenance is required on this unit. Ignition timing is accomplished by following the same procedure outlined in Chapter Two, *Engine Tune-up* section under *Ignition Timing (Saab 99)* procedure. Set timing to specifications given in **Table 2** in this supplemental chapter.

Table 1   MAINTENANCE INFORMATION

Maintenance intervals	
Engine oil change	Every 5,000 miles
Manual transmission oil change	Every 15,000 miles
Automatic oil change	Every 20,000 miles (check every 5,000 miles)
Recommended lubricants and capacities	
Engine oil	4 qt. SE 10W-30 or 10W-40 (with filter)
Automatic transmission	FLM Spec. M2C 33F
Automatic final drive	1.3 qt. SAE 80 GL4 or GL5
Manual transmission	3 qt. SAE 75 (1977 models); SE 10W-30 (1978-1979 models)
Power steering	ATF-FLM Spec. M2C 33F
Cooling system	
Capacity	8.5 U.S. qt. (50% ethylene glycol)
Pressure cap	13-17 psi

Table 2 TUNE-UP SPECIFICATIONS

Firing order	1-3-4-2
Spark plugs	NGK BP6ES or Bosch W175T30
Spark plug gap	0.024-0.028 in. (0.6-0.7mm)
Idle speed	875 ± 50 rpm (engine warm, fan off)
Contact breaker gap	
1977 models	0.016 in. (0.4mm)
1978-1979 models	Breakerless
Dwell angle	
1977 models	50° ± 3°
1978-1979 models	Breakerless
Valve clearance	
Intake	Checking clearance, 0.006-0.0012 in. (0.15-0.30mm); setting clearance, 0.008-0.010 in. (0.20-0.25mm), engine cold
Exhaust	Checking clearance, 0.014-0.020 in. (0.35-0.50mm); setting clearance, 0.016-0.018 in. (0.040-0.045mm), engine cold
Ignition timing	20° BTDC @ 2,000 rpm, vacuum advance disconnected
Cylinder head torque	69 ft.-lb.
Emissions controls	
49-state models	EGR and Pulse Air
Calif. models	Lambda and catalyst
CO % @ idle	
1977, 49-state	1% ± 0.5% (plug air injection)
1977, Calif. models	0.75% + 0.25%, − 0.50% (disconnect oxygen sensor lead)
1978-1979 49-state models	0.75% ± 0.25% (plug air injection)
1978-1979 Calif. models	0.75% + 0.25%, − 0.50% (disconnect oxygen sensor lead)
Decel time, 3,000 rpm to idle	5 ± 1 seconds (set to 3 ± 1 seconds above 4,000 ft. altitude)

CHAPTER FOUR

ENGINE

Refer to **Table 3** for torque specifications for critical engine fasteners.

Table 3 ENGINE FASTENER TORQUE RECOMMENDATIONS

Component	Torque (in Ft.-lb.) 1.75/1.85 Liter	2.0 Liter	Component	Torque (in Ft.-lb.) 1.75/1.85 Liter	2.0 Liter
Main bearing bolts	58	79	Water pump		
Connecting rod bolts	40	40	Bolt	18	18
Crankshaft belt pulley bolt	62	137	Nut	–	11
Flywheel bolts	44	43	Oil pump to block bolts	18	13
Gable plate bolts	7	14	Valve cover bolts	1.5	1.4
Idle shaft plate bolts	18	14	Spark plugs	15	20
Idler shaft sprocket bolt	18	18	Oil filter center bolt	18	–
Camshaft bearing cap bolts	17	13	Intake manifold	18	13
Camshaft sprocket bolts	10	14	Exhaust manifold	27	18
Cylinder head bolts	54	69	Thermostat housing	18	13
Cylinder head nuts	54	–	Throttle valve housing	–	13

CHAPTER EIGHT

ELECTRICAL SYSTEMS

Effective with the 1978 Saab, a breakerless ignition is standard. Ignition timing for this unit is covered in the preceding section under *Ignition Timing*. Removal and installation procedures are given in the following procedure.

Removal/Installation

1. Disconnect ignition cables.

2. Release spring clips and remove distributor cap.

3. Disconnect low voltage wire from ignition coil.

4. Remove vacuum hose.

5. Crank engine over until the flywheel marking is at ignition position for the No. 1 cylinder.

6. Remove bolts holding distributor to engine block, then remove distributor.

7. To install, be sure that the flywheel position is as indicated in Step 5, preceding.

8. Rotate distributor shaft until rotor points approximately 50 degrees clockwise from the mark on the edge of the distributor housing, which indicates the firing position for the No. 1 cylinder.

9. Install distributor in engine block with vacuum control unit facing flywheel. As you insert the distributor into the engine, the rotor will turn counterclockwise approximately 50 degrees. Be sure that gears mesh properly.

> NOTE: *When distributor is fully inserted in the engine, the marks on the distributor housing and rotor should be aligned.*

10. Install distributor retaining bolts (but do not tighten completely).

11. Set ignition timing (refer to preceding supplemental chapter under *Ignition Timing* procedure), then tighten distributor retaining bolts.

CHAPTER NINE

CLUTCH, TRANSMISSION, AND DIFFERENTIAL

Refer to **Table 4** for torque specifications for manual and automatic transmission fasteners.

Table 4 FASTENER TORQUE RECOMMENDATIONS

Component	Ft.-lb.	Component	Ft.-lb.
AUTOMATIC TRANSMISSION		**AUTOMATIC** (con't)	
Converter-to-flywheel bolts	20-30	Oil pump-to-converter housing	13-18
Chain cover-to-converter housing	10-15	Governor cover bolts	5-8
Converter housing-to-transmission case	10-15	Counter weight-to-governor bolts	4-6
		Governor valve side plate	1.7-4
Oil pressure tap plug	4-5	Valve body screws	20-30 in.-lb.
Start inhibitor locknut	4-6	Kickdown cam bracket screws	20-40 in.-lb.
Turbine shaft sprocket bolt	20-25	Valve body mounting bolts	4.5-9
Input shaft sprocket nut	25-30	Front band with ¼ in. spacer	10 in.-lb.
Center support bolts	10-18	Rear band (back off ¾ turn)	10
Side cover bolts	6-9		
Front and rear oil pan bolts	6-9		
Oil pan drain plug	4-6	**MANUAL TRANSMISSION**	
Throttle cable-to-transmission case	8-10	All 5/16 in. bolts	15-21
Pinion nut	180-200	All 8mm bolts	15-18
Pinion housing-to-case bolts	20-25	Speedometer drive	21-36
Seal housing-to-pinion housing bolts	6-9	Release bearing sleeve	4-10
Oil pump cover screw	2-3	Clutch shaft plastic bolt	.75-1.5
Oil pump cover bolts	17-22	Pinion nut (needle bearing end)	21-36

INDEX

A

Air cleaner 101-102, 191
Air filter maintenance. 27
Air injection system 111-112
Alternator 113-115
Axle, rear 140-141

B

Ball-joint replacement 129-133
Battery 12, 113
Bearings 194-195
Bleeding, brake 175-176
Body. 17, 183, 197-198
Brakes
   Adjustment 176-178
   Bleeding. 175-176
   Disc brake housing (Saab 99) 157-164
   Disc removal and installation 164-166
   Drum (95/96 and Sonett) 169-171
   Handbrake. 171-175, 176-178
   Housings (95/96 and Sonett) 155-156
   Lines and hoses 153-154
   Linings, high performance 188-189
   Maintenance 15-16
   Master cylinder 149-153
   Pad removal and installation 166-169
   Pedal 178-181
   Pistons and seals, front
      (95/96 and Sonett) 156-157
   Troubleshooting 35-36
   Wheel cylinders (Saab 99). 157-164
   Wheel cylinder (95/96 and Sonett) 154-156
Breakerless ignition 202, 204

C

Camshafts. 192-193
Carburetor. 77-81, 101, 193
Chassis 182-183, 184-189
Clutch
   Adjustment. 124
   Bleeding 125
   Maintenance. 13
   Master cylinder 124-125
   Pedal 124
   Performance improvement 192
   Pressure plate 123
   Release bearing 123
   Removal and installation (Saab 99) 121-122
   Removal and installation
      (95/96 and Sonett) 122-123

Slave cylinder 125
Troubleshooting 34
Compression test. 19-20
Connecting rods 194
Contact point maintenance 24-27
Cooling system
   Coolant changing 97-98
   Expansion tank. 89
   Fan motor. 98
   Radiator 89-95
   Radiator coolant 11
   System diagram 90-95
   Thermostat 96-97
   Troubleshooting 36
   Water hoses and pipe 96
   Water pump 96
Crankcase ventilation 103-106
Crankshaft. 194
Cylinder head 193-194

D

Deceleration valve. 99-101
Differential 35, 127-128, 197
Disc brake 164-166
Disc brake housing (Saab 99) 157-164
Distributor 23-24, 116-118
Drive belts 11
Drive train 197
Drum brakes (95/96 and Sonett) 169-171

E

EGR maintenance 108-111
Electrical system
   Alternator 113-115
   Battery. 12, 113
   Breakerless ignition. 204
   Distributor 23-24, 116-118
   Distributor cap 119
   Ignition coil 116
   Ignition system. 116-119
   Impulse contact point. 118-119
   Performance improvement. 189-191
   Starter 30-31, 115-116
   Starter solenoid. 116
   Voltage regulator 115
Electronic ignition 189-190
Emission control systems
   Air cleaner 101-102
   Air injection system 111-112
   Carburetor 101
   Crankcase ventilation. 103-106

INDEX

Deceleration valve 99-101
EGR maintenance 108-111
Evaporative loss system 102-103
Engine
   Assembly (Saab 99) 61-67
   Assembly (95/96 and Sonett) 49-56
   Disassembly (Saab 99) 56-61
   Disassembly (95/96 and Sonett) 46-49
   Engine/transmission separation 46
   Installation 45
   Performance improvement 183, 189-197
   Removal 39-45
   Specifications 68-76
   Specifications (torque recommendations,
      1977 and later) 204
   Troubleshooting 31-33
Evaporative loss system 102-103
Exhaust system
   Emission control system 106-112
   Maintenance 14-15
   Muffler 85-88
   Performance improvement 191
Expansion tank 89

F

Fan motor 98
Flywheel 192
Free wheel 126-127
Fuel system
   Carburetor 77-81, 101
   Fuel injection system 81-82
   Fuel pump, electric 83-84
   Fuel pump, mechanical 82-83
   Fuel tank 84-85
   Maintenance 27
   Troubleshooting 33-34

G

Gear ratio 197

H

Handbrake
   Adjustment 176-178
   95/96 and Sonett 171-172
   99 through 1974 172-174
   99, 1975-1976 174-175
Heating system diagram 90-95
Hubs 144-148

I

Identification numbers 1-5
Ignition system
   Breakerless ignition 202, 204
   Coil 116, 189

Distributor 23-24, 116-118
Distributor cap 119
Electronic ignition 189-190
Timing (95, 96 and Sonett V4) 26
Timing (99) 27
Troubleshooting 33
Vacuum regulator 118
Impulse contact point 118-119

L

Links, side 142
Lubrication (see Maintenance
   and lubrication)

M

Maintenance and lubrication
(also see Tune-up)
   Battery 12
   Brakes 15-16
   Checks, routine 10-11
   Clutch 13
   Differential 13-14
   Drive belts 11
   Engine compartment 11
   Exhaust system 14-15
   Final drive 14
   Oil, engine 12-13
   Oil filter, engine 13
   Power steering 13
   Radiator coolant 11
   Shock absorbers 17
   Steering 16-17
   Suspension 16-17
   Transmission, automatic 14
   Transmission, manual 13-14
   Wheel and tire inspection 16
   1977 and later maintenance
      information 202
Manual organization 1
Master cylinder, brake 149-153
Master cylinder, clutch 124-125
Muffler 85-88

O

Oil change, engine 12, 13
Oil cooler 191
Oil filter, engine 13
Oil sump 192

P

Performance improvement
   Accessory sources 199-200
   Body 183, 197-198
   Chassis 182-183, 184-189

INDEX

Drive train 197
Engine 183, 189-195
  General information 182-184
  Turbocharging................... 195-197
Pistons 194
Pressure plate 123

R

Radiator 89
Radiator coolant 11, 97-98
Rotor maintenance 24-26

S

Service hints 7-9
Shock absorbers 17, 134, 143-144, 187-188
Slave cylinder 125
Spark plugs 20-23, 190-191
Specifications, engine 68-76
Specifications, tune-up 29
Spoilers 197-198
Springs, high performance 187
Springs, rear 138-140
Starter 115-116
Starter solenoid 116
Starter troubleshooting 30-31
Steering (see Suspension and
  steering, front)
Suspension and steering, front
  Alignment 36-38
  Ball-joint replacement 129-133
  Maintenance 16-17
  Power steering maintenance 13
  Shock absorbers 17, 134
  Steering gear 133-134
  Tie rod ends 133-134
  Troubleshooting 36-38
Suspension, rear
  Axle 140-141
  Camshaft removal 57
  Center bearing 142
  Hub/wheel bearings 144-148
  Links, side 142
  Shock absorbers 143-144
Suspension bushings 188
Sway bars 187

T

Thermostat 96-97
Tires 16, 184-187
Tools, recommended 5-7
Transmission
  Description 125-126
  Engine/transmission separation 46
  Final drive, automatic 14
  Free wheel 126-127
  Maintenance 13-14
  Performance improvement 197
  Torque specifications (1977 and later) 205
  Troubleshooting 34-35
Troubleshooting
  Brakes 35-36
  Charging system 31
  Clutch 34
  Cooling system 36
  Differential 35
  Engine 31-33
  Exhaust emission control 34
  Fuel system 33-34
  Ignition system 33
  Starter 30-31
  Steering and suspension 36-38
  Transmission 34-35
Tune-up
  Air filters 27
  Breakerless ignition 202, 204
  Carburetor oil damper 27
  Contact points 24-25, 26-27
  Compression test 19-20
  Distributor 23-24
  Dwell angle adjustment 25, 27
  Equipment hook-up 18
  Fuel filter 27-28
  Fuel system 27
  Ignition timing 26, 27
  Rotor replacement 24-25, 26
  Spark plug inspection 20-23
  Specifications (1967-1976) 29
  Specifications (1977 and later) 202, 203
  Throttle control 27
  Valve clearance adjustment 18-19
Turbochargers 195-197

V

Vacuum regulator 118
Valve clearance adjustment 18-19
Voltage regulator 115

W

Water hoses and pipes 96
Water pump 96
Wheels
  Alignment 36-38
  Bearings 144-147
  Maintenance 16, 134-135
  Performance improvement 184-187
Wheel cylinder, brake (Saab 99) 157-164
Wheel cylinder, brake
  (95/96 and Sonett) 154-156
Wheel spacers 188

MAINTENANCE LOG

DATE	TYPE OF SERVICE	COST	REMARKS

NOTES

NOTES